Re:ZERO -Starting Life in Another World-

THE ROSWAAL MANOR GIRLS' MEET (CHANGING ROOM EDITION)

Tappei Nagatsuki
Illustration: Shinichirou Otsuka

Re:ZERO -Starting Life in Another World- Chapter 2: A Week at the Mansion ③
Short Story Extra

The Roswaal Manor Girls' Meet (Changing Room Edition)

1

"Hwaaaaah~."

Yawning from the morning sleepiness, the girl wiped the moisture from her eyelashes with the back of her hand.

She had long, silver hair and beautiful violet eyes. She possessed a fairylike loveliness, although her slightly sleep-disheveled nightgown was a charming indication that she was a little different.

Just before that nightgown was about to slip off her pale, slender, quivering shoulders altogether...

"You mustn't, Lady Emilia. If you rub your eyes like that, they shall become red."

The girl directly behind her reached out to put a stop to the eye rubbing, as well as to hold up her slipping nightgown. Emilia made a sleepy noise in reply to the admonition and turned around.

"Mm... Yes, I understand...but I think that's making too big a deal of it."

"Small considerations are important. One must keep her hair tidy, no matter how troublesome it may be. The Great Spirit must tell you so as well."

"Muu, meanie..."

Emilia puffed her cheeks in dissatisfaction as she sat in a chair. Standing behind her was a blue-haired girl—Rem—was meticulously combing Emilia's long silver hair.

It was early in the day, and she had just woken up. They were in the mansion's changing room.

—For Emilia, mornings always began with another person taking care of her hair.

Leaving her hair in someone else's hands wasn't a sign of Emilia's laziness. Rather, those around her couldn't stand to leave her to her own devices. They couldn't let Emilia be seen as someone who was indifferent to her appearance... Though in that sense, perhaps Emilia's slacking did lead to their intervention.

Rem gently continued her work as she spoke.

"If you do not care to do it yourself, then please allow me or the Great Spirit to assist you."

"...Haaaagh."

Emilia grudgingly nodded before sighing deeply.

Rem, who excelled at all domestic duties, not only handled myriad odd jobs inside the mansion but was also highly skilled at personal grooming. Mysteriously, Rem's touch on her hair was enough to make Emilia happy and content. She felt sorely tempted to fall back asleep.

"Lady Emilia, you've managed to get up already. You can't go back to sleep now. I'm tired, too, you know..."

"Hafh... Ah, yes, I'm sorry, Ram. You're right. I'm getting reaaally sleepy, though."

"I understand how you feel. Rem's fingers lead you straight to the heavens."

The girl Emilia spoke with thrust out her chest as she offered praise. It was Rem's older sister, Ram, who looked like a mirror image of her twin except for the pink hair and pink eyes.

Unlike Rem, Ram simply watched and did nothing to help, but Emilia saw nothing odd about this. The two sisters always divvied up work this way.

Ram's praise brought a faint redness to Rem's cheeks as she finally gave Emilia a pat on the shoulder.

"Having Sister praise me so will make me blush... All right, Lady Emilia, I have finished."

During the conversation, Rem had finished weaving the silver strands into a beautiful braid.

"Wow, thank you... Yeah, I'm sure Puck will be very satisfied. You've been a big help," Emilia said.

"This is merely part of my expected duties. However, it is rare for the Great Spirit to speak of Lady Emilia's appearance, is it not?"

The Great Spirit Rem referred to was Puck, the little cat spirit with whom Emilia had formed a pact. As Emilia's self-declared father figure, the meddlesome kitty was always vocal about her grooming. For that reason, he was with her in the mornings to see to her hair and her selection of clothes without fail, but—

"Seems he was up late last night. Apparently he was playing with Subaru until really late, so he's sleeping in this morning. Goodness, he's incorrigible..."

"With Barusu, you say? Quite some nerve, staying up late when he has work this morning..." Ram replied, scowling as Emilia cracked a smile despite her chagrin.

Emilia, seeing Rem nod at her sister's words, formed an increasingly strained smile. Ram continued:

"So the Great Spirit has taken time off because of playing with Barusu late at night... Meaning, his unreliability affects not only himself but spreads to those around him."

"But, Sister, thanks to Subaru, the two of us are able to select Lady Emilia's clothing for this morning."

"True. That's an achievement for Barusu."

"That counts as one of his achievements? Why?"

Emilia tilted her head in response to the sisters' conversation. Rem's response began with "Well..."

"It is always the Great Spirit's job to pick what clothes you wear. There's usually no room for Sister or me to argue. But today is different."

"Lady Emilia, you don't have any opinion on how you should dress, right? In that case, we have unchallenged authority here. I'm brimming with excitement..."

Emilia felt rather confused seeing exactly how excited the twins were about the current situation. Usually, neither showed much expression, but while discussing what clothes they would have Emilia try on were serious and rich with amusement.

As Ram had pointed out, Emilia was clueless about how to dress herself. It made sense to sit back and let the two of them prepare her outfit for the day if they were enjoying it so much. At least, that's what Emilia had thought at first, but—

"I might be feeling just a bit lonely, being left out like this... Wait, I know!"

"Lady Emilia?"

Earlier she had been unable to join the sisters' conversation and had been left with nothing to do, but now there was a twinkle in Emilia's eyes. Seeing this, Ram's eyes narrowed for a moment. Emilia puffed up with pride. Noticing that she was practically saying *I have a great plan!* out loud, Rem and Ram exchanged glances.

"Tee-hee, I have a reaaally good idea. Hear me out!"

"...I'm afraid to ask, but what have you come up with?"

"I'm happy you're both so earnest about picking out my outfit for the day, but you two always wear maid uniforms, right? I think that's a bit of a waste."

Emilia paid no heed to Ram's roundabout reply and confidently raised a finger before she continued.

"Since we have the opportunity, I thought maybe I'd like to see you both in some different clothes for a change."

2

"To think that it is not Subaru but Lady Emilia saying such a thing..."

Hearing Rem's comment, Emilia replied.

"Ah, did Subaru say the same thing before? But right now I can understand how he feels. I'm happy I get to see the two of you in cute outfits. It'll be fun."

"In Barusu's case, his ulterior motives were obvious, so we declined, but..."

Ram quickly trailed off. It was clear as day that they could not refuse Emilia's proposal or her beaming smile.

As Ram and Rem stood side by side, Emilia excitedly brought her hands together in front of her chest. After all, they were dressed completely differently from normal. In the three or four months Emilia had known them, she had never once seen them in any clothes other than maid outfits. She was extremely grateful for the change of pace.

"Thanksee, thanksee!"

"Lady Emilia, that reaction seems heavily influenced by Barusu..."

"Mm-hmm, I just tried copying Subaru a little. But I'm still reeeally happy!"

Seeing Emilia clasp her hands with a satisfied sigh, Ram responded by twirling in place. The hem of her skirt floated up in a cute, girly fashion.

Ram's current outfit was not as provocatively exposing at the shoulders and back as her usual maid outfit. However, the soft, white-motif, feminine garment was far more charming than the usual black servant's attire. The charm was further accentuated by the large ribbon on her head in place of her usual maid's headdress.

Ram stroked her hair back in a perfectly lovely pose, leaving Emilia deeply satisfied.

"My goodness, how humiliating. I am wearing this with great reluctance."

Ram stroked her hair back in a perfectly lovely pose, leaving Emilia deeply satisfied. She was discovering the joy of dressing others up.

"As expected of Sister, no matter what Sister wears, it only makes her beauty shine all the more...!"

"Thanks. But you look marvelous, too, Rem. I'm glad my little sister is so adorable."

Ram had a faint, subtle smile on her face as she accompanied her praise with a teasing stroke of Rem's forehead.

Compared to the gentle elegance of Ram's outfit, the clothes Rem wore were far frillier, with a sweetness reminiscent of another mansion resident, Beatrice. Rem now had short, twin ponytails on the sides of her head, nicely complementing the sugary look of her dress.

"Yes, my eyes didn't deceive me. I was completely right that having nothing but maid outfits all the time is a waste. Right?"

"Our uniforms are according to Master Roswaal's preferences, so I must agree with them. However, I will say that...thanks to Lady Emilia, I got a chance to see Rem looking very pretty."

"You reaaally don't like being upfront with your feelings, Ram. Don't you think so, Rem?"

"I believe Sister dresses according to every day's needs more than sufficiently: for work, for errands, for shopping, for combat, for attending, for time off... It's more than

adequate."

"But those are all maid uniforms..."

Rem was counting the types on her fingers, but the maid clothes had no difference in appearance. Emilia was somewhat concerned that Rem wasn't interested in hearing such a reply, but for once, Rem's expression softened as she gave a response.

"I jest, Lady Emilia. I, too, am happy to see Sister in pretty clothing."

"...Oh, are you? I'm glad, then. But you're reaaally cute, too, Rem."

"Thank you very much. However, we should finally bring this fun to an end."

Rem's gaze shifted to above the changing room door as she spoke. The magic time crystal there was becoming a deeper green, indicating that they had entered the morning hours. Ram and Rem had their duties at the mansion, and Emilia had her daily communing with minor spirits to attend to.

"What a shame. But we can't fool around here forever..."

Then Ram followed up on Emilia's comment.

"Yes, that is correct. And if we do not change soon, Barusu, who can't read the atmosphere, might come barging right in. If he were to see me like this, I would deeply regret it."

"Tee-hee, poor you. Ah, but don't you want to show that off to Roswaal?"

Though there was a moment's hesitation, Ram shook her head to rid herself of lingering regret.

"...I can imagine precisely what Master Roswaal would say, so I shall refrain."

It was a bit of a shame, and it made her feel a little lonely, but it couldn't be helped—and that very moment...

The green crystal swaying between Emilia's breasts began to glow. The next instant, the light manifested in the world as a little cat spirit.

"—Sorry about that, Lia. I was sleeping in. Did you get up from bed properly?"

"Oh, Puck."

Then, the little cat looked around the changing room as he rubbed his round eyes. He blinked in surprise as he murmured, in no way disapproving,

"Ohh? Today it's not just Lia, but you two in pretty outfits, huh?"

As he spoke, the sisters, in the middle of changing clothes, glanced at each other's faces, then back at Emilia. Ram spoke first, before Rem added her comment.

"Somehow, I regret being seen like this by the Great Spirit as well."

"How strange. I feel the same way as you do, Sister. What should we do?"

As the sisters knit their brows, Emilia fell into thought a little.

"Err, when you put it like that, I'm not sure what I should do... Ah, I know!"

She clapped her hands, then opened them back up, letting Puck land on her palms.

"What is it, Lia? Somehow...you have a mischievous look on your face."

"Here's the thing, Puck. I understand, just a little bit, how you feel. So, I think you should understand a little bit of how I feel, too, Puck."

"Mutual understanding is very important. But I have a bad feeling about this somehow... Ah, wait, wait a second!"

The sight of the deep, wry smile on Emilia's face made Puck look unnerved for once. However, Emilia was not one for waiting. Nor were Ram or Rem.

3

—That day, an unusual atmosphere hovered over the dining hall of Roswaal Manor.

Each morning, all residents of the manor gathered there for breakfast. Neither the lord of the manor, nor Beatrice, nor the young male servant, were exceptions to this rule. However—

Among those assembled, Beatrice was even more excited than usual as she stroked Puck's forehead.

"Puckie, you look marvelous. It may be different from your normal look, but it has set my heart aflutter..."

"Ha-ha-ha, thank you, Betty. But if this outfit hadn't impressed you, I miiight have managed to save my pride, small as it is."

Beatrice was cradling Puck in her arms, as she often did, but his appearance was nothing like usual: He wore a pretty dress made out of a handkerchief mixed with some lace and adorned with multiple ribbons. The little gray cat never wore more than fur, but now he was decked in pompous fashion.

Subaru stared at Puck's outfit, lacking any knowledge of the circumstances behind it. He leaned close to Emilia, who sat right beside him, and put a hand over his mouth, as if holding a sensitive, private conversation.

"Er, what's with that? I mean, I get that there's a culture of dressing up pets and all, but what? Is this is your doing, Emilia-tan?"

"Er, well, you see..."

Emilia strained to smile in reply to Subaru's question, gently shifting her eyes toward the seat of honor. Roswaal contentedly watched Beatrice and Puck, with both maids standing behind him, side by side. The two sensed Emilia's gaze, so they raised one hand each.

Both of them made the gesture that Subaru recognized as meaning "fox," leaving him even more mystified than before.

"Emilia-tan?"

Emilia only stuck out her tongue.

What had happened between Emilia and the sisters in the changing room that morning was private. And so, Emilia replied with an adorable wink—

"It's a secret."

<END>

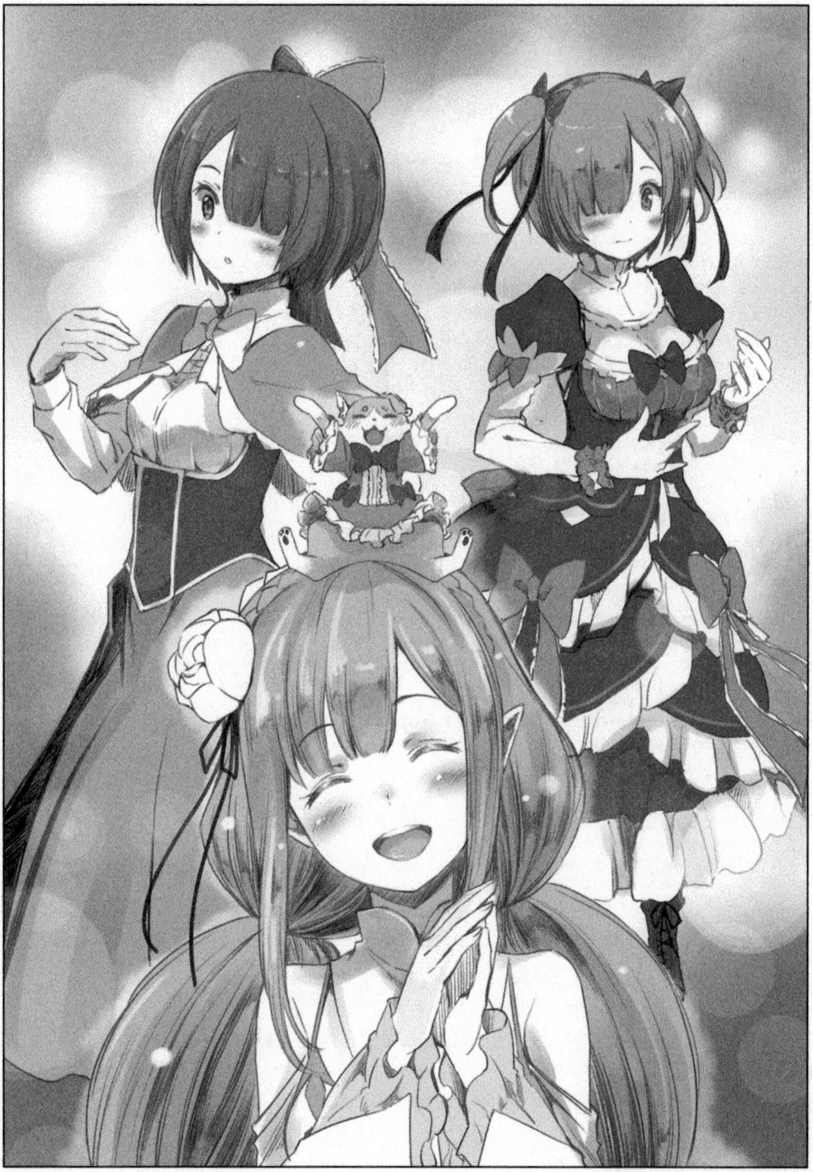

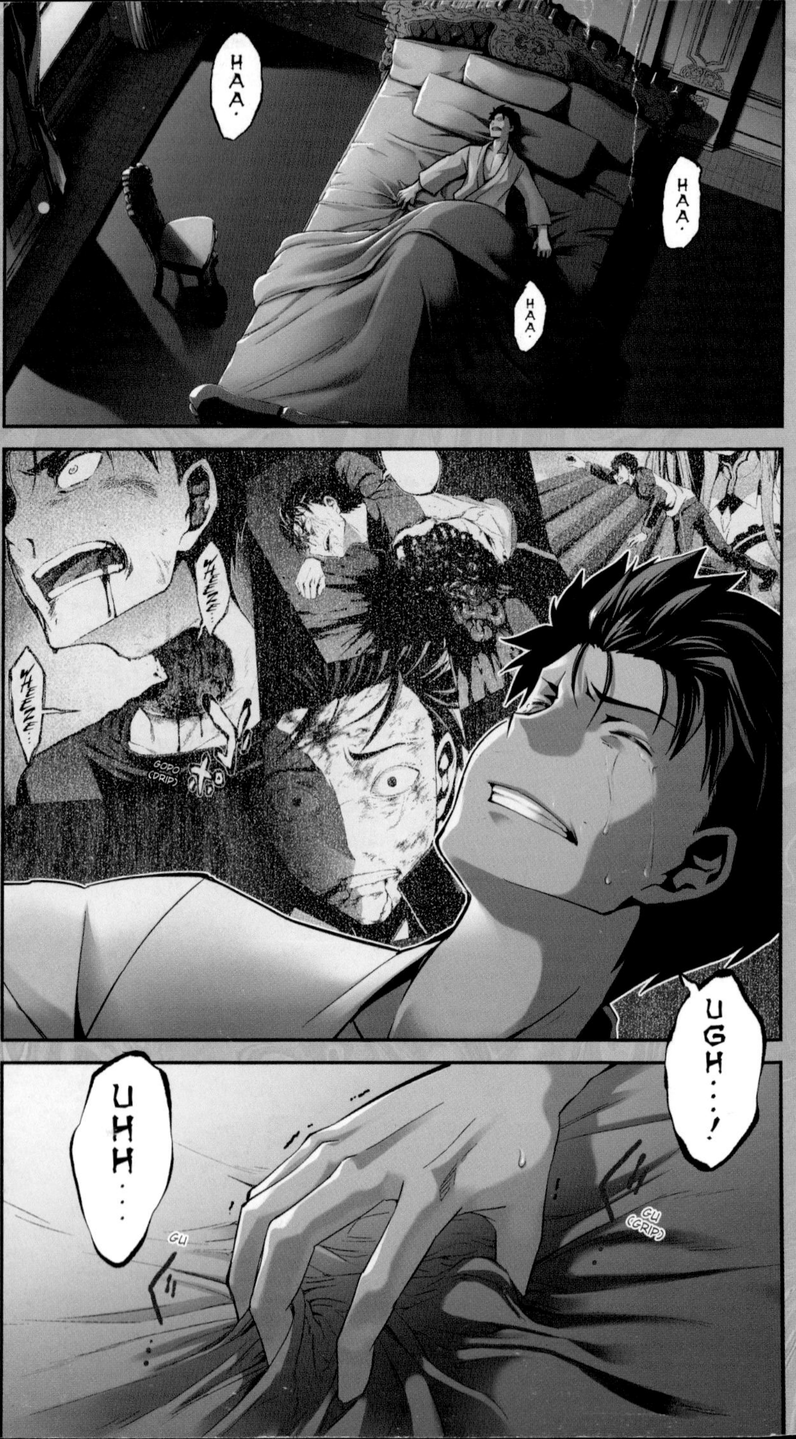
HAA.
HAA.
HAA.
WHEEZE...
GOPO (DRIP)
WHEEZE...
UGH...!
GU (GRIP)
UHH...
GU

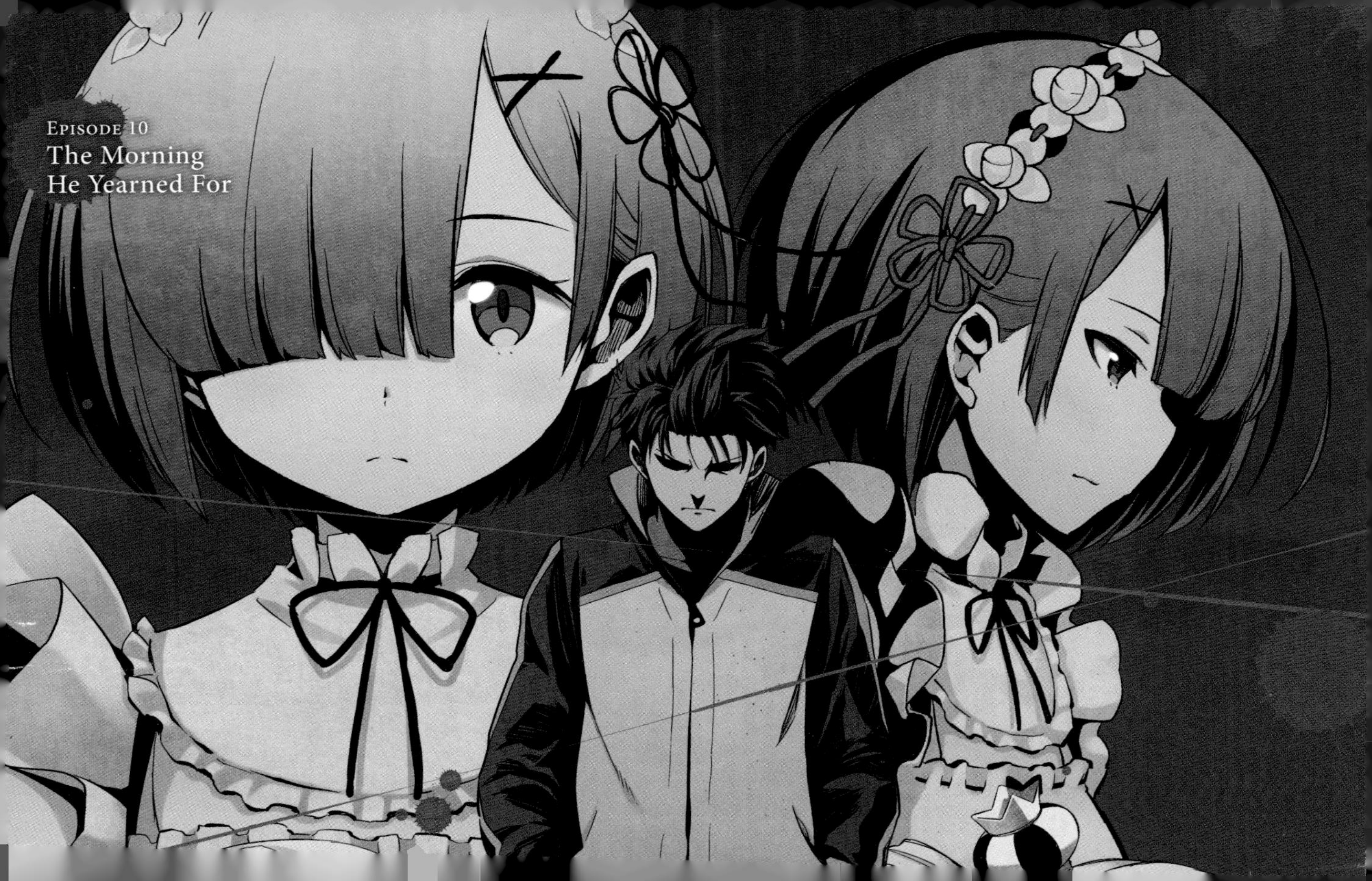
Episode 10
The Morning
He Yearned For

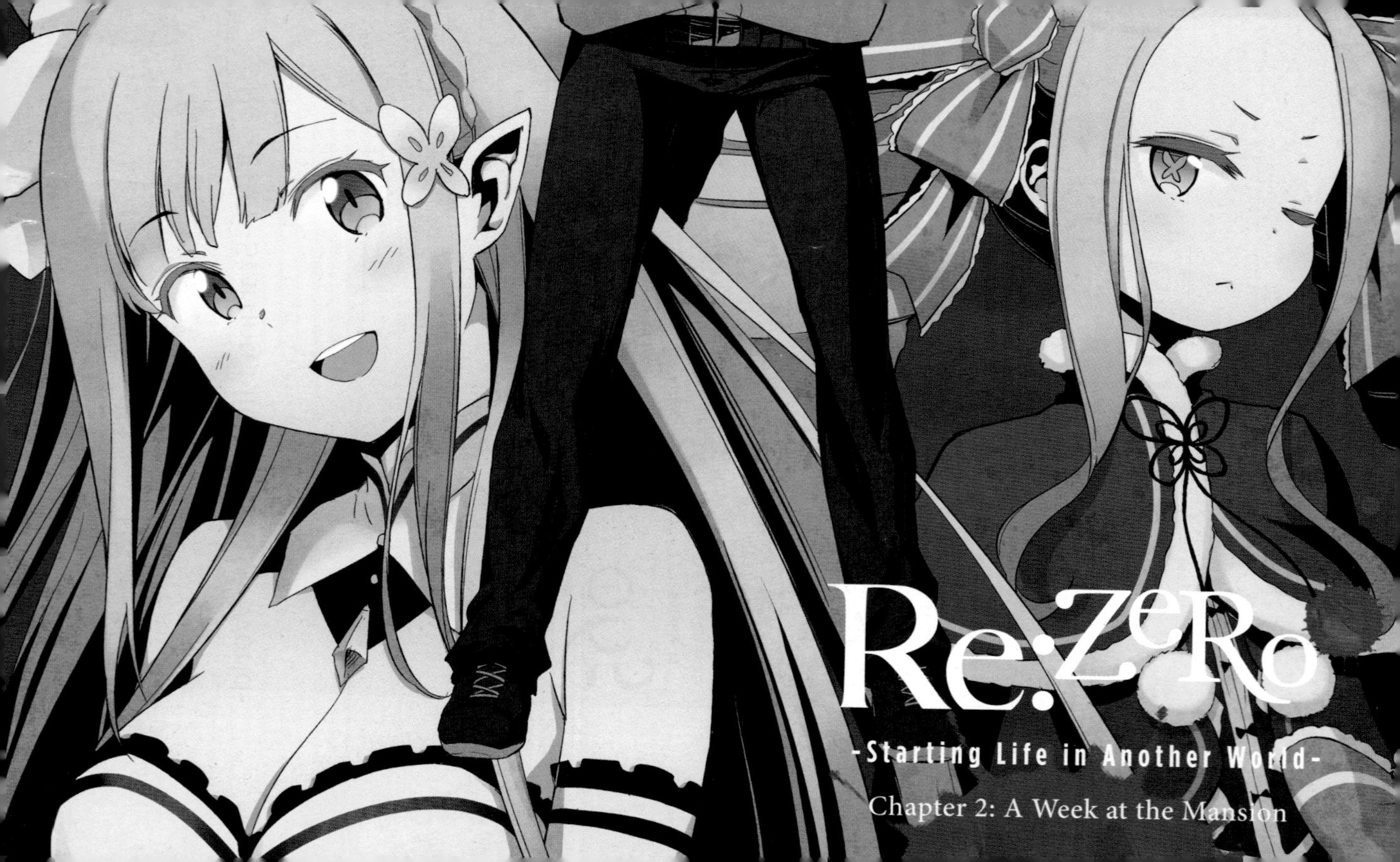
Re:ZeRo
-Starting Life in Another World-
Chapter 2: A Week at the Mansion

Re:ZERO -Starting Life in Another World-

Chapter 2: A Week at the Mansion

The only ability Subaru Natsuki gets when he's summoned to
another world is time travel via his own death. But to save her,
he'll die as many times as it takes.

Contents

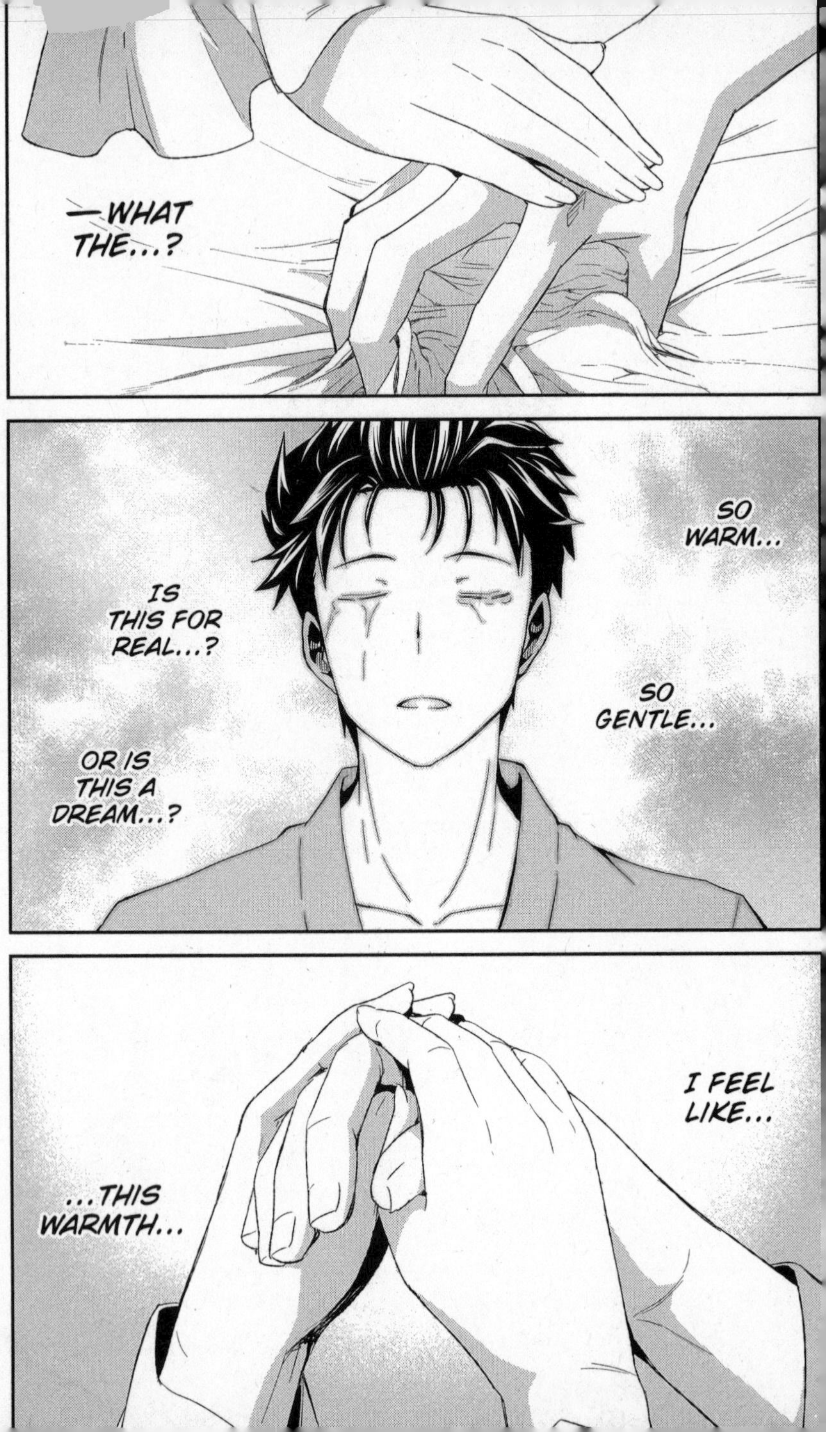
—WHAT THE...?
SO WARM...
SO GENTLE...
IS THIS FOR REAL...?
OR IS THIS A DREAM...?
I FEEL LIKE...
...THIS WARMTH...

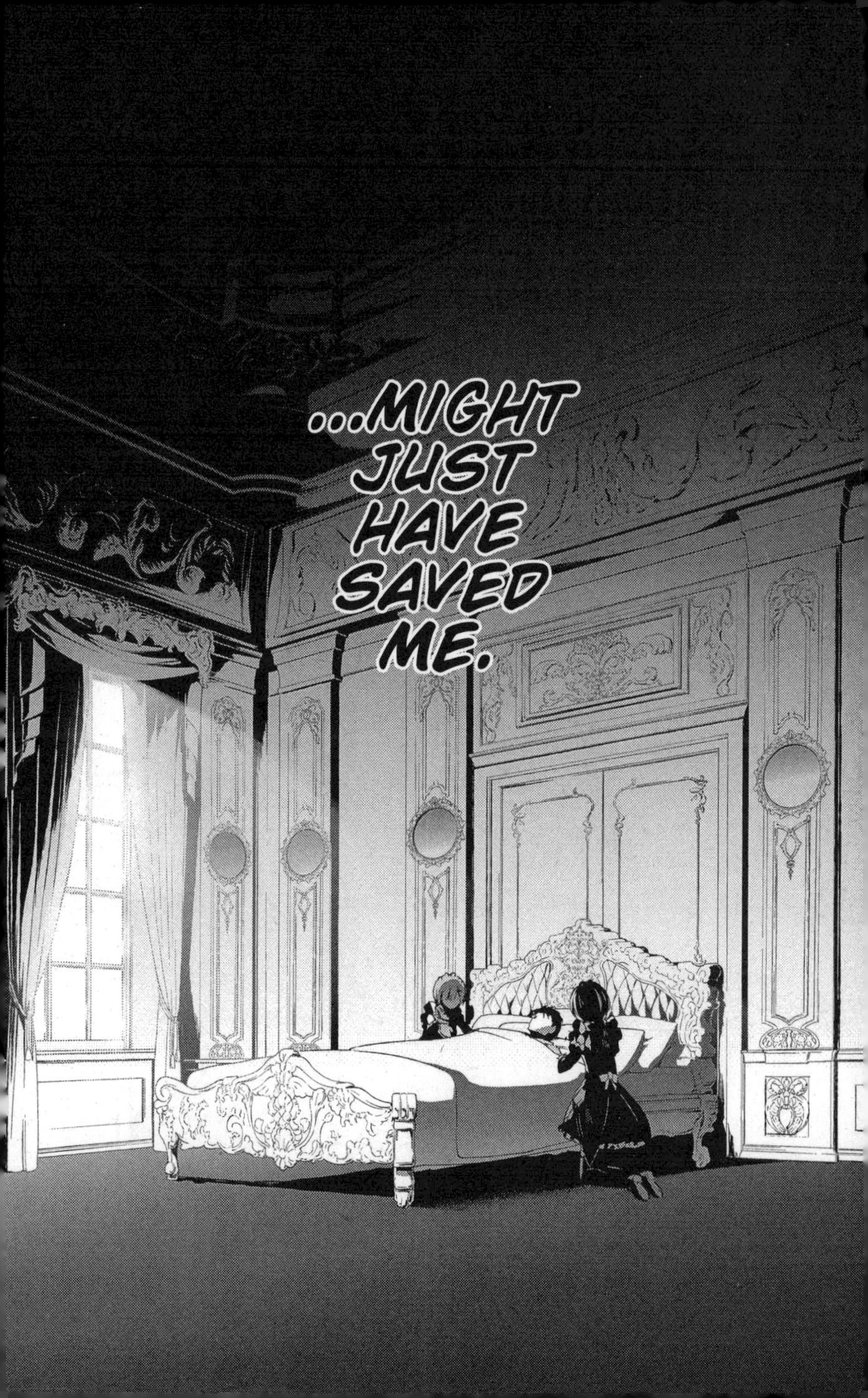
...MIGHT JUST HAVE SAVED ME.

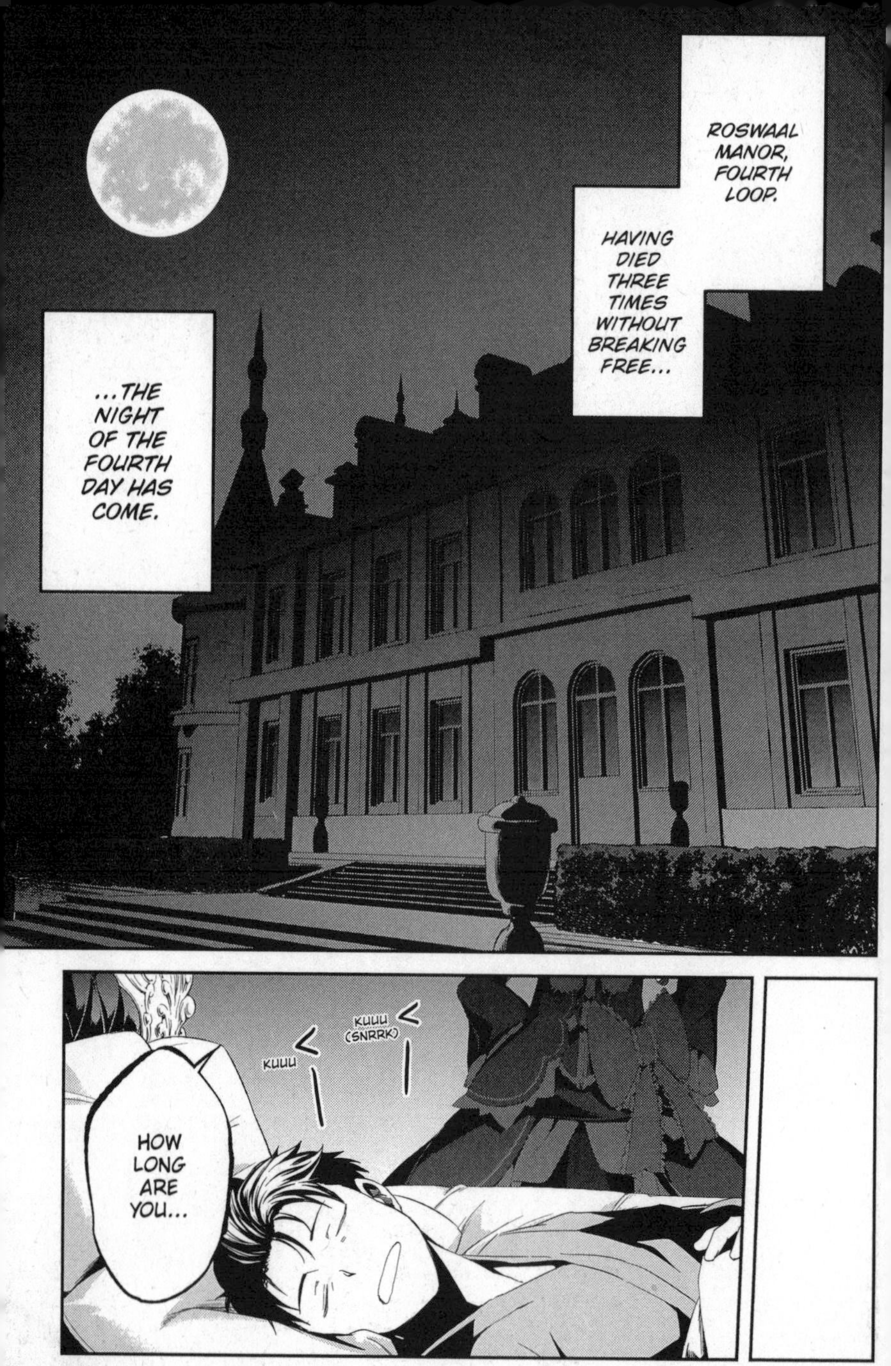
ROSWAAL MANOR, FOURTH LOOP.
HAVING DIED THREE TIMES WITHOUT BREAKING FREE...
...THE NIGHT OF THE FOURTH DAY HAS COME.
KUUU (SNRRK)
KUUU
HOW LONG ARE YOU...

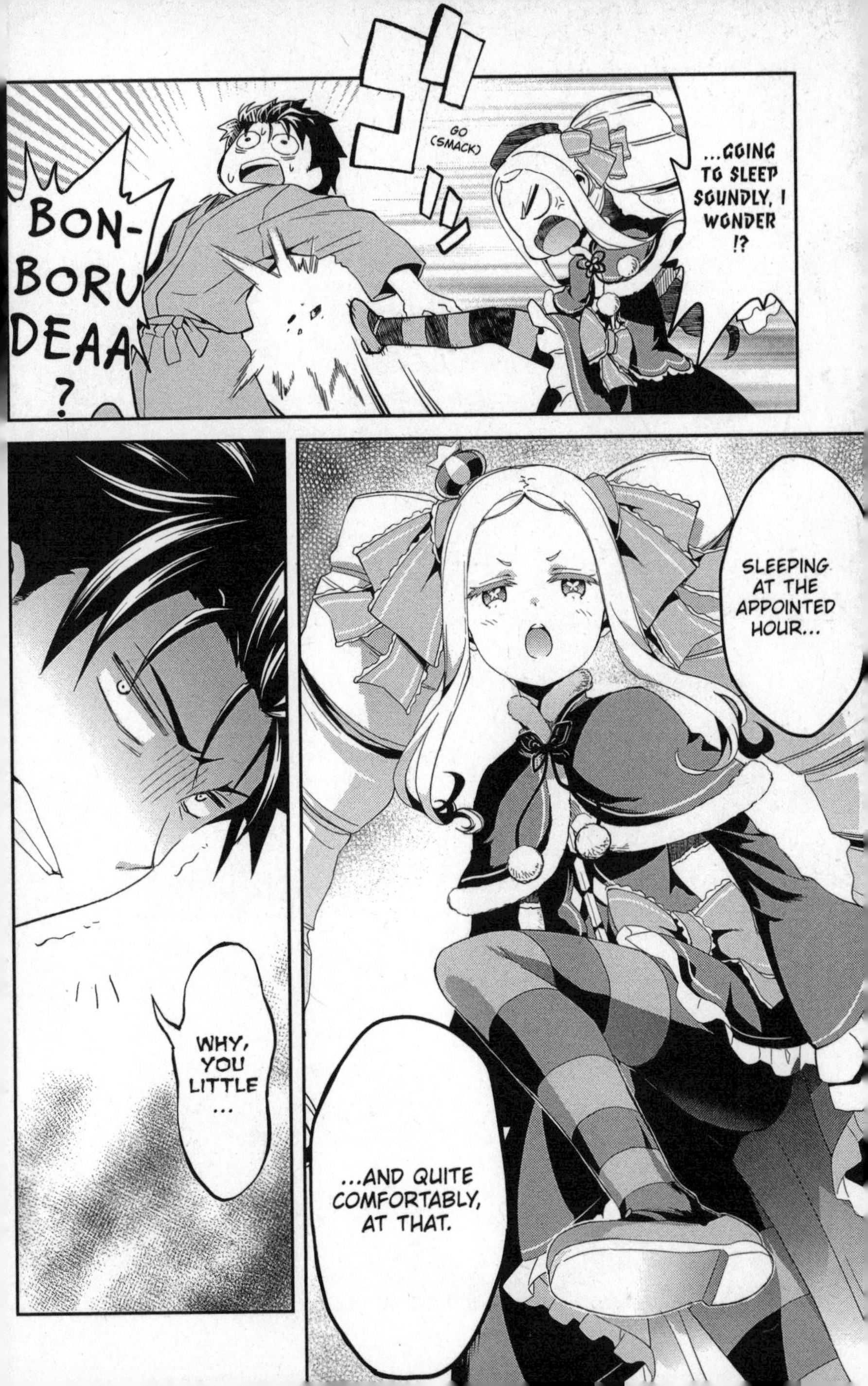
...GOING TO SLEEP SOUNDLY, I WONDER!?
GO (SMACK)
BON-BORU DEAA?
SLEEPING AT THE APPOINTED HOUR...
...AND QUITE COMFORTABLY, AT THAT.
WHY, YOU LITTLE...

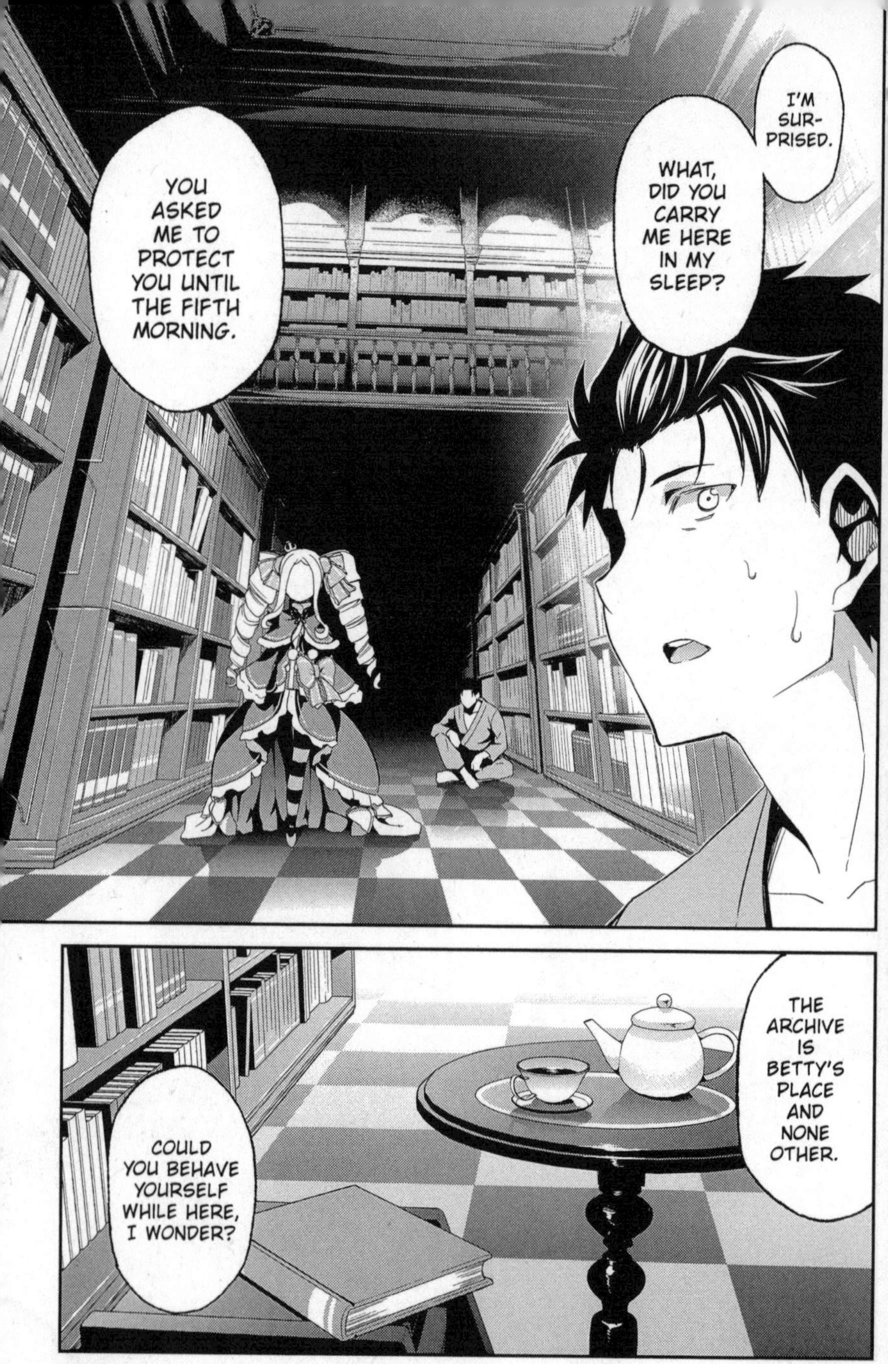
I'M SURPRISED.
WHAT, DID YOU CARRY ME HERE IN MY SLEEP?
YOU ASKED ME TO PROTECT YOU UNTIL THE FIFTH MORNING.
THE ARCHIVE IS BETTY'S PLACE AND NONE OTHER.
COULD YOU BEHAVE YOURSELF WHILE HERE, I WONDER?

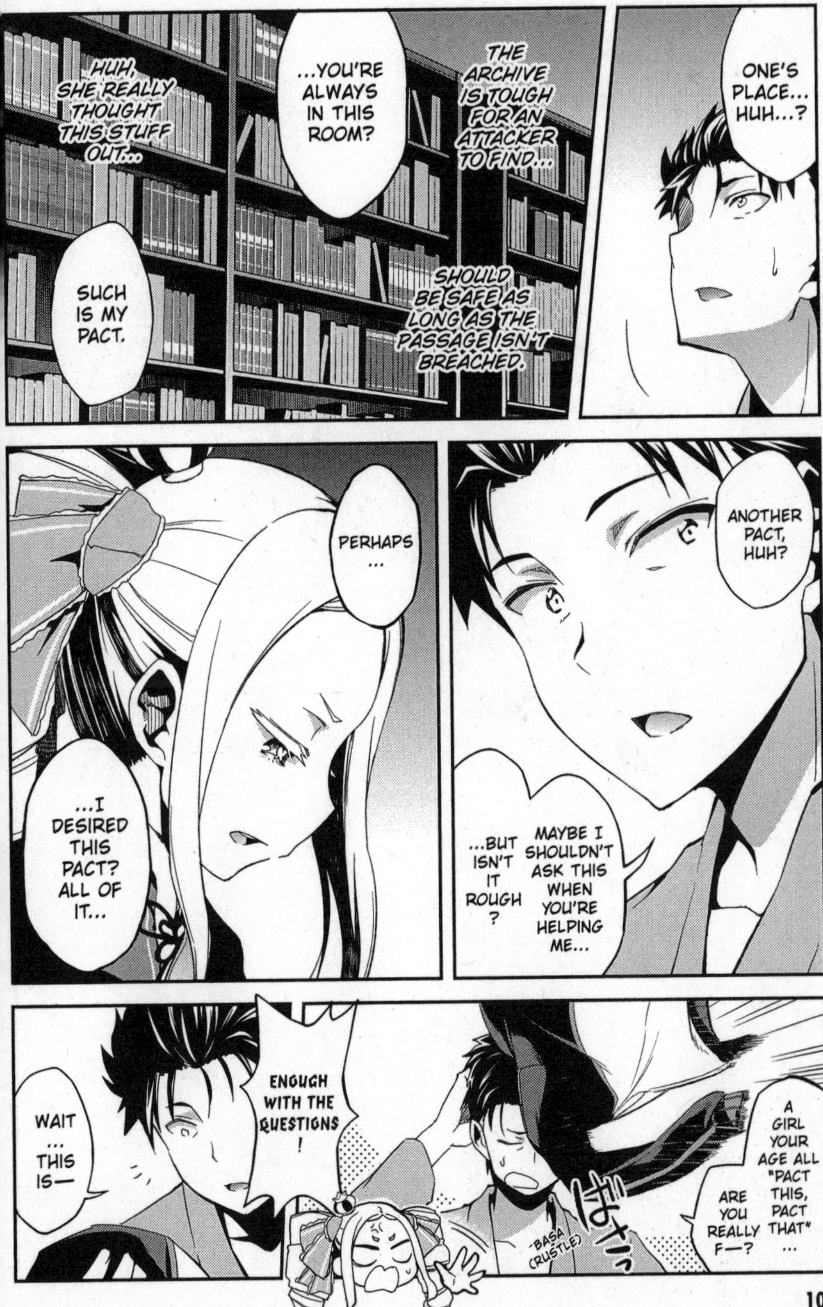
ONE'S PLACE... HUH...?
THE ARCHIVE IS TOUGH FOR AN ATTACKER TO FIND...
...YOU'RE ALWAYS IN THIS ROOM?
HUH, SHE REALLY THOUGHT THIS STUFF OUT...
SHOULD BE SAFE AS LONG AS THE PASSAGE ISN'T BREACHED.
SUCH IS MY PACT.
ANOTHER PACT, HUH?
MAYBE I SHOULDN'T ASK THIS WHEN YOU'RE HELPING ME...
...BUT ISN'T IT ROUGH?
PERHAPS...
...I DESIRED THIS PACT? ALL OF IT...
A GIRL YOUR AGE ALL "PACT THIS, PACT THAT"...
ARE YOU REALLY F—?
ばさっ
BASA (RUSTLE)
ENOUGH WITH THE QUESTIONS!
WAIT... THIS IS—

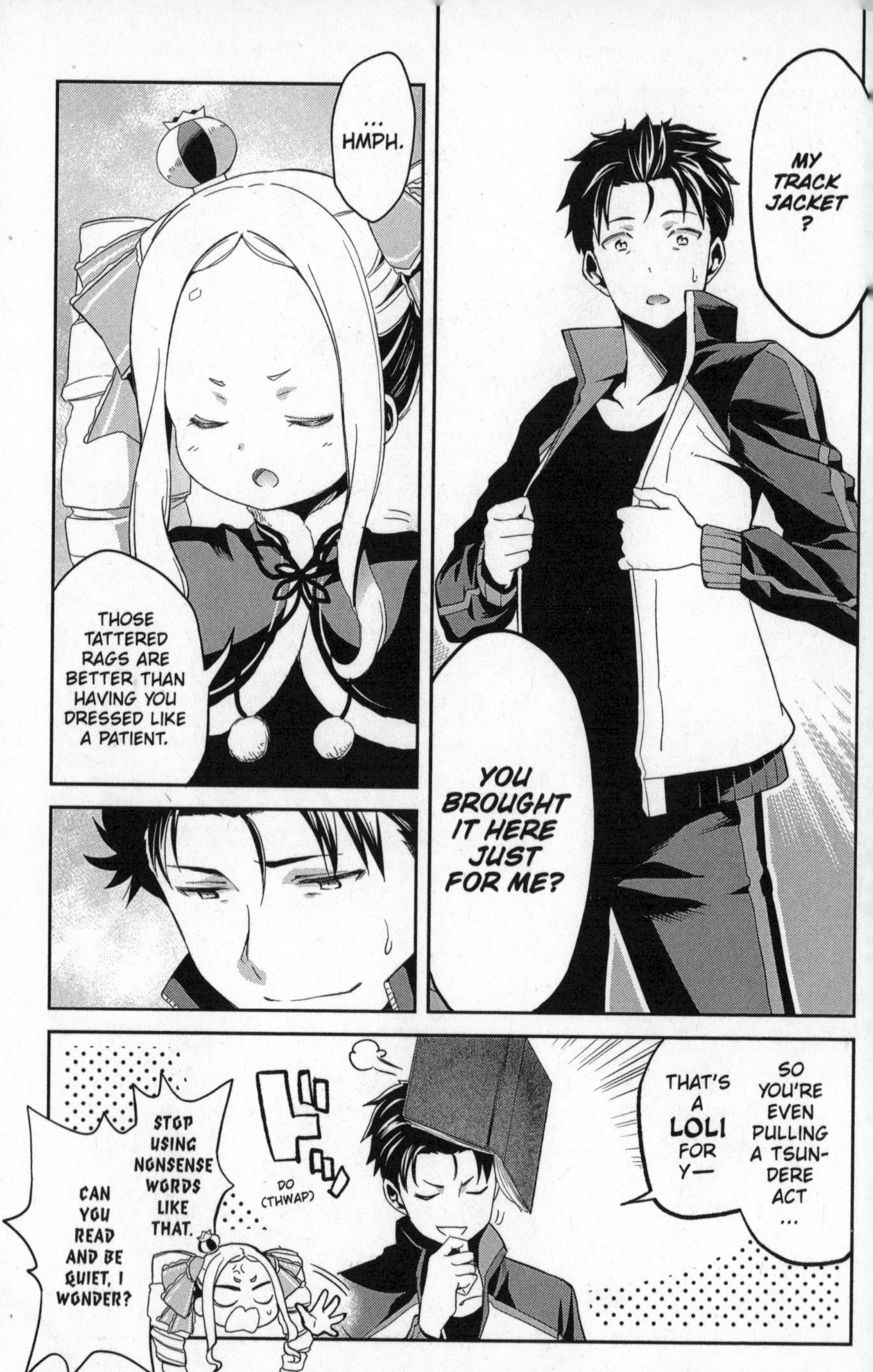
MY TRACK JACKET?
YOU BROUGHT IT HERE JUST FOR ME?
... HMPH.
THOSE TATTERED RAGS ARE BETTER THAN HAVING YOU DRESSED LIKE A PATIENT.
SO YOU'RE EVEN PULLING A TSUNDERE ACT...
THAT'S A LOLI FOR Y—
DO (THWAP)
STOP USING NONSENSE WORDS LIKE THAT.
CAN YOU READ AND BE QUIET, I WONDER?

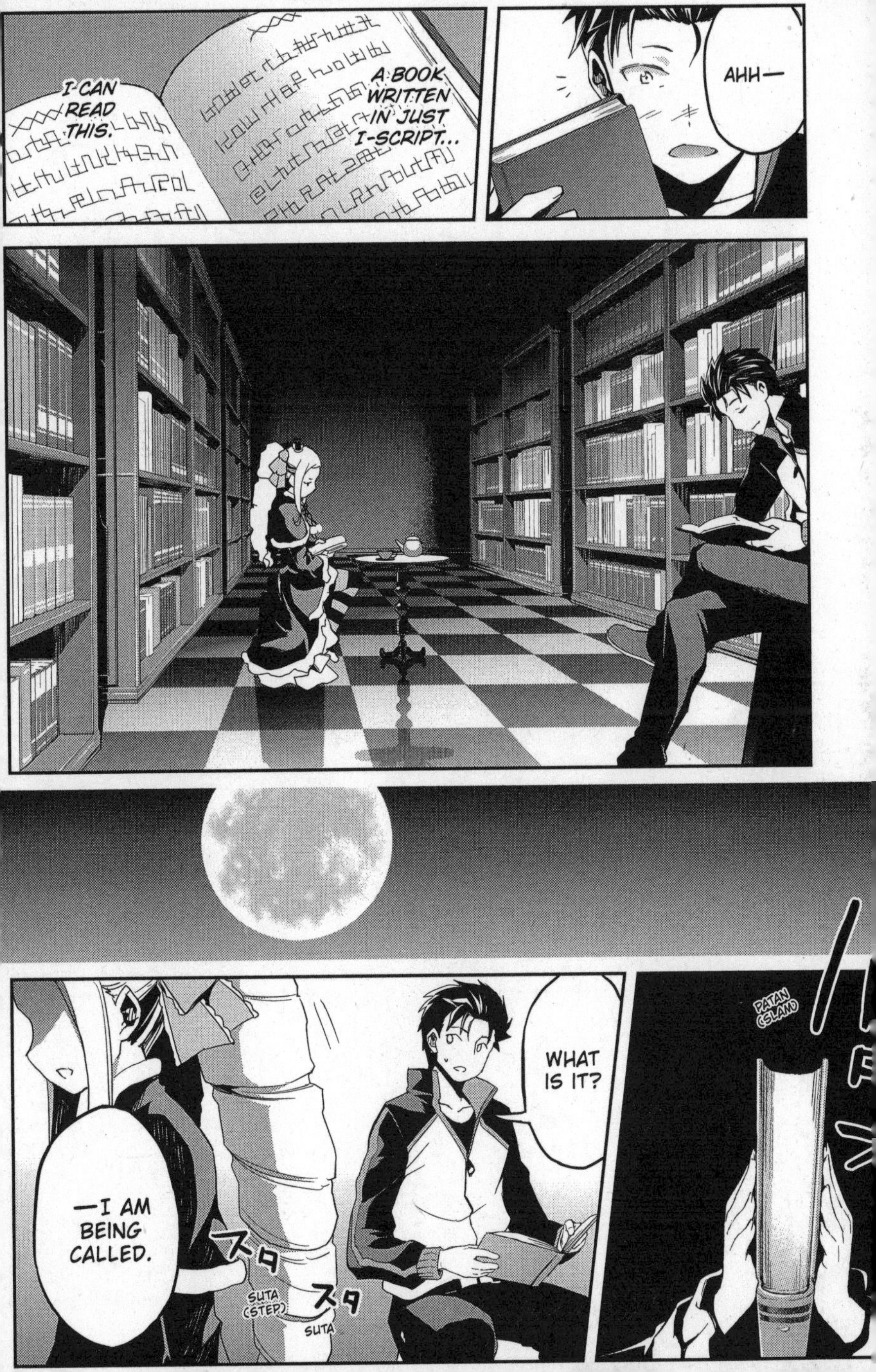
AHH—
A BOOK WRITTEN IN JUST I-SCRIPT...
I CAN READ THIS.
PATAN (SLAM)
WHAT IS IT?
—I AM BEING CALLED.
SUTA (STEP)
SUTA

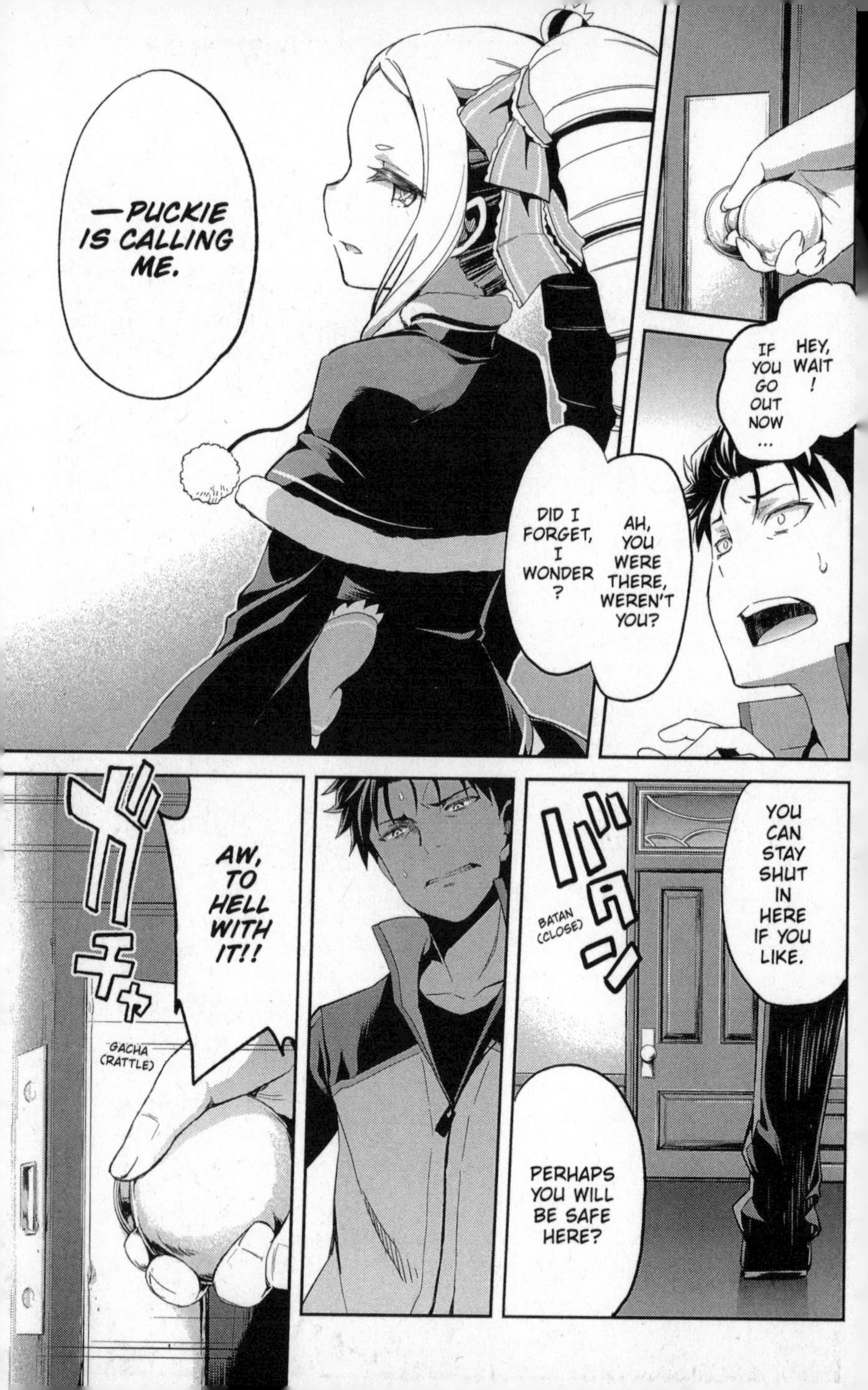
HEY, WAIT! IF YOU GO OUT NOW...
AH, YOU WERE THERE, WEREN'T YOU?
DID I FORGET, I WONDER?
—PUCKIE IS CALLING ME.
YOU CAN STAY SHUT IN HERE IF YOU LIKE.
バタン
BATAN (CLOSE)
PERHAPS YOU WILL BE SAFE HERE?
AW, TO HELL WITH IT!!
ガチャ
GACHA (RATTLE)

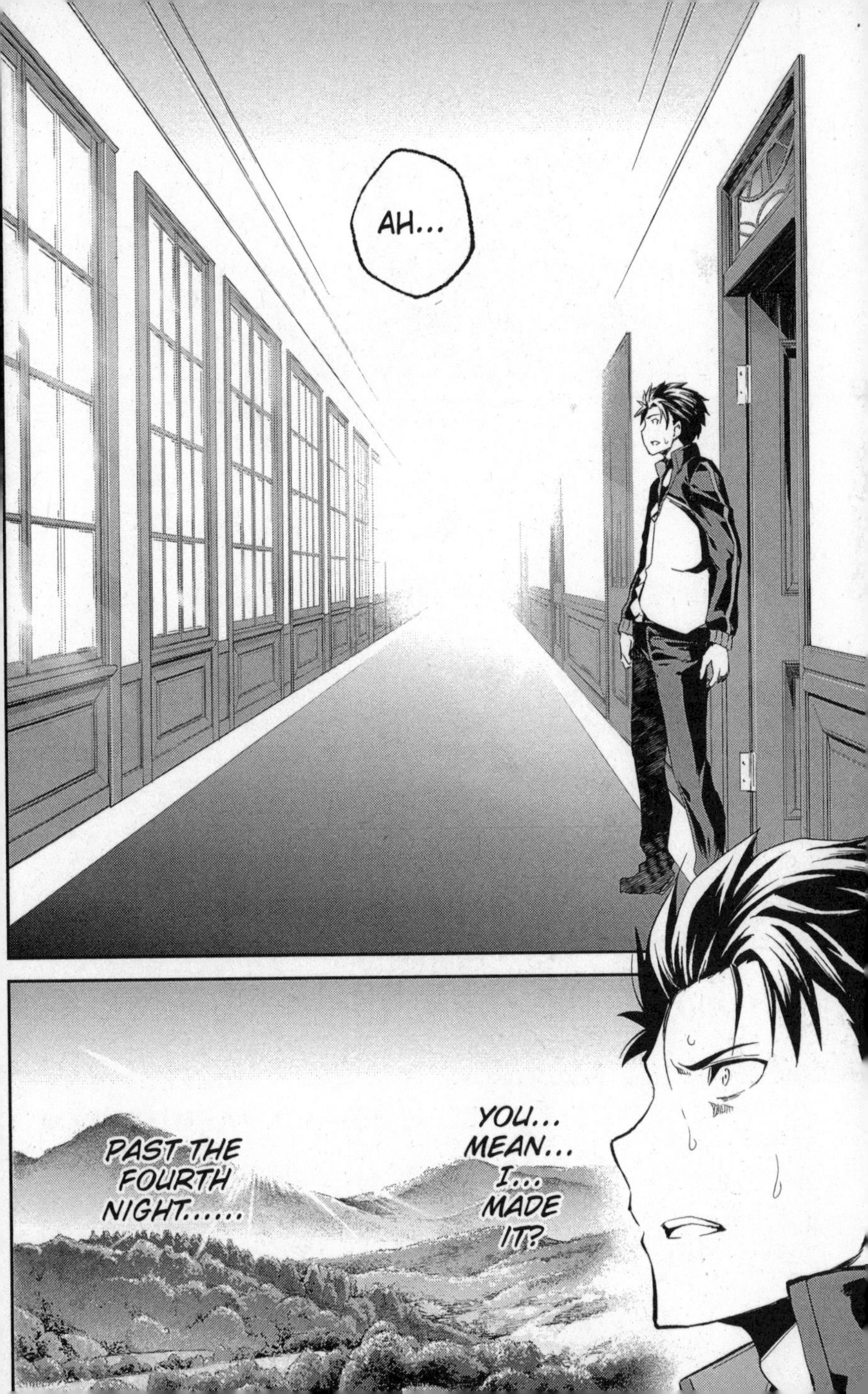
AH...
YOU... MEAN... I... MADE IT?
PAST THE FOURTH NIGHT......

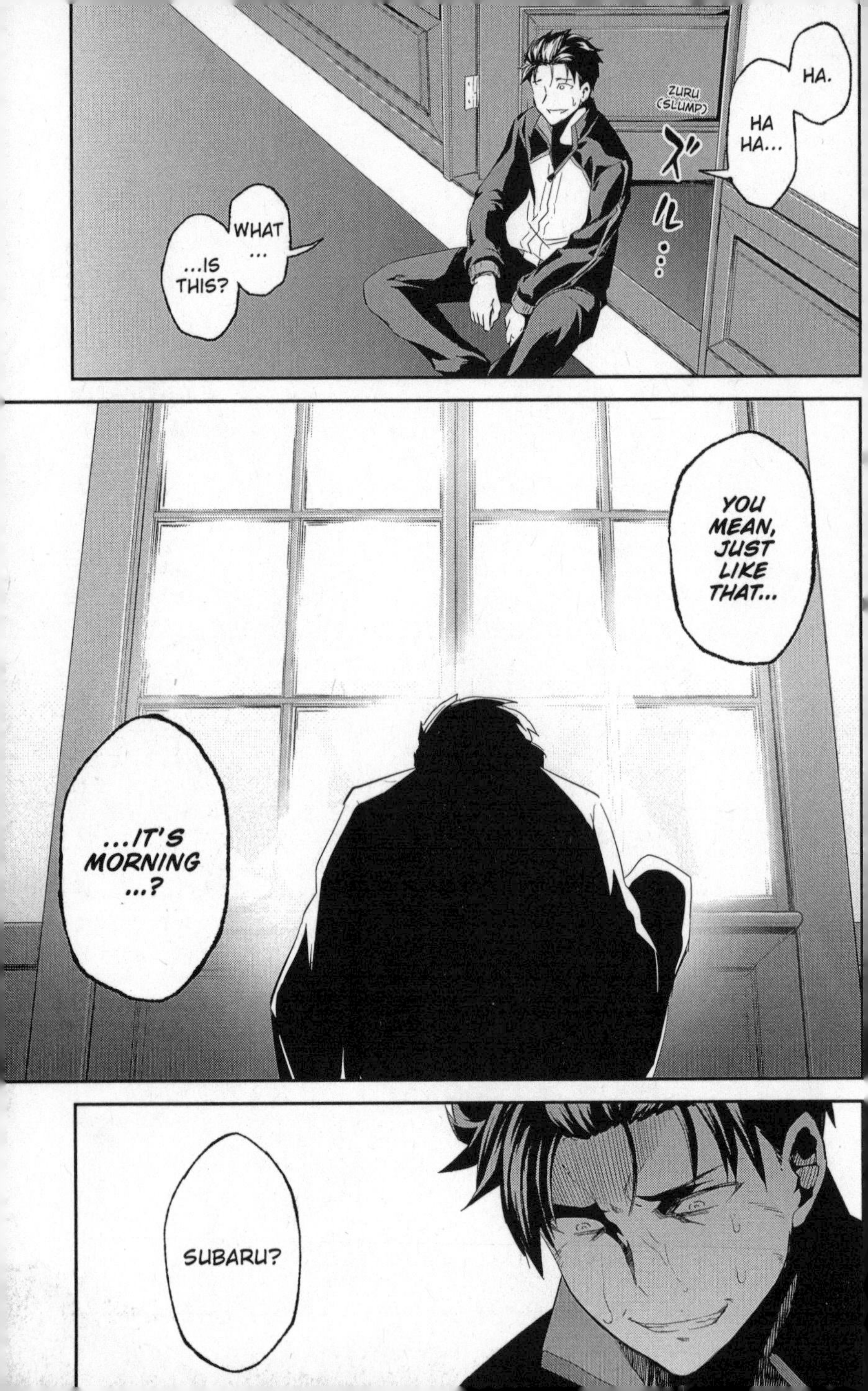
HA. HA HA...
ZURU (SLUMP)
WHAT... ...IS THIS?
YOU MEAN, JUST LIKE THAT...
...IT'S MORNING ...?
SUBARU?

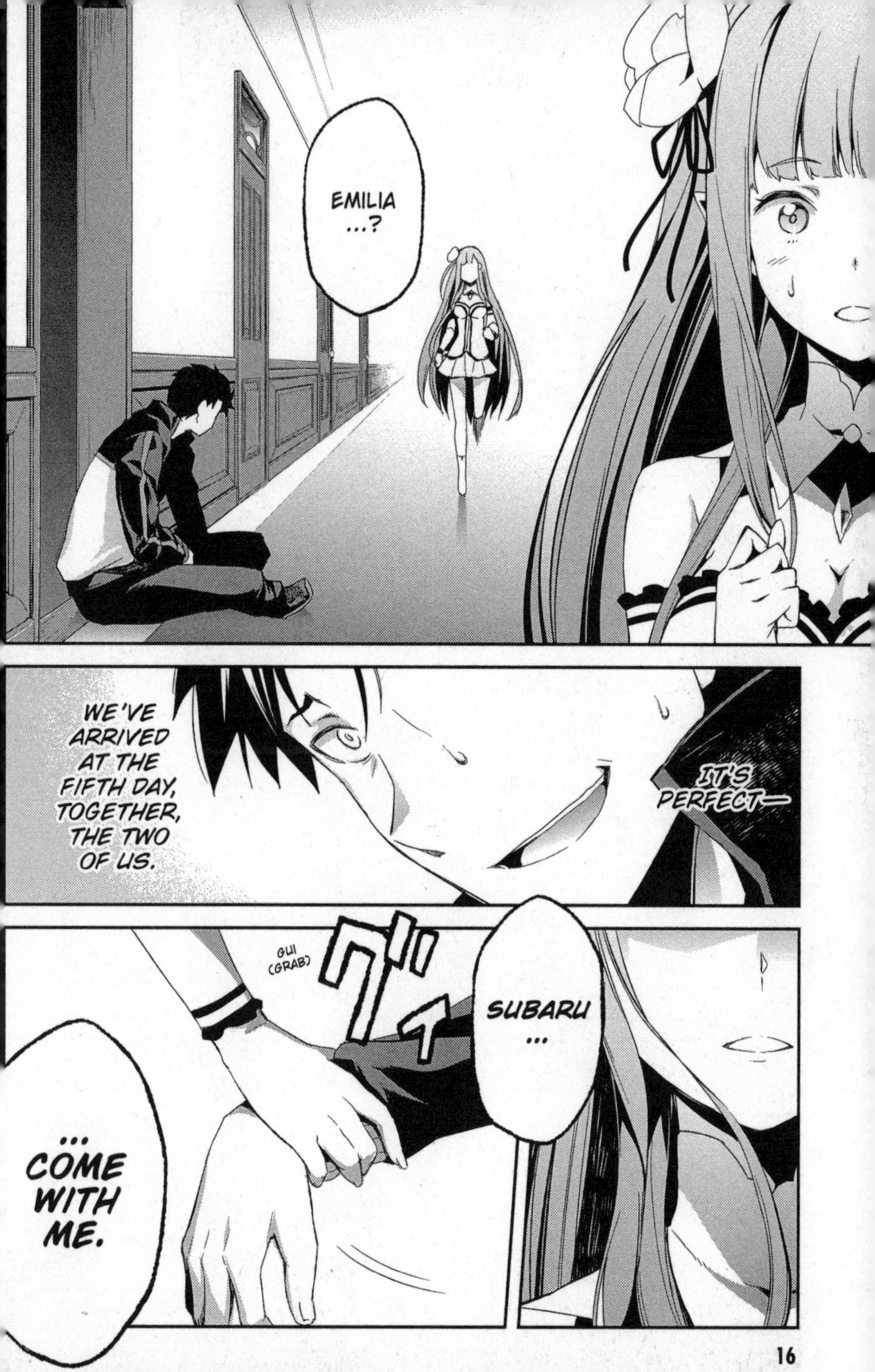
EMILIA ...?
IT'S PERFECT—
WE'VE ARRIVED AT THE FIFTH DAY, TOGETHER, THE TWO OF US.
SUBARU ...
GUI (GRAB)
... COME WITH ME.

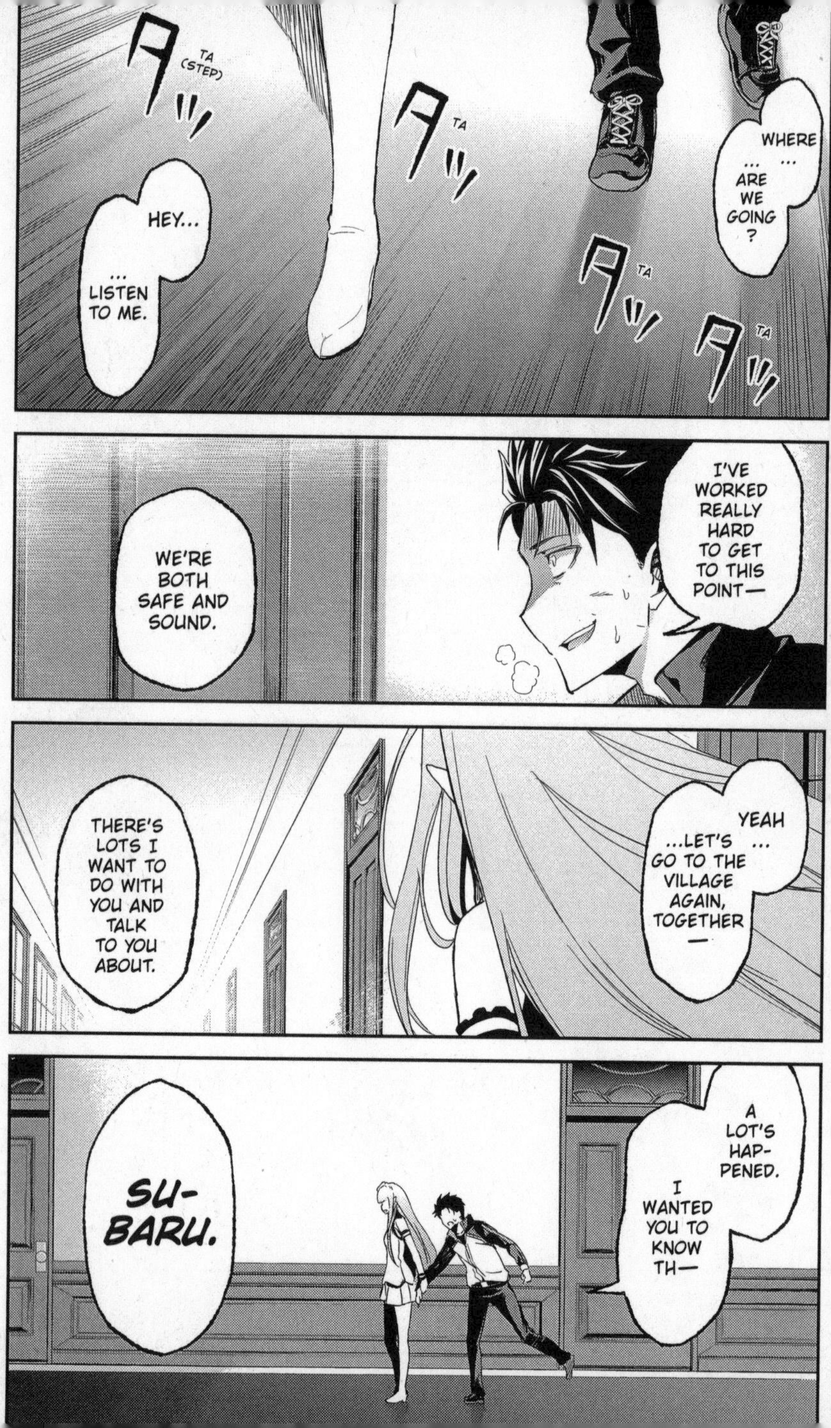
WHERE... ...ARE WE GOING?
TA
TA
TA
TA (STEP)
HEY... ...LISTEN TO ME.
I'VE WORKED REALLY HARD TO GET TO THIS POINT—
WE'RE BOTH SAFE AND SOUND.
YEAH... ...LET'S... GO TO THE VILLAGE AGAIN, TOGETHER—
THERE'S LOTS I WANT TO DO WITH YOU AND TALK TO YOU ABOUT.
A LOT'S HAPPENED. I WANTED YOU TO KNOW TH—
SUBARU.

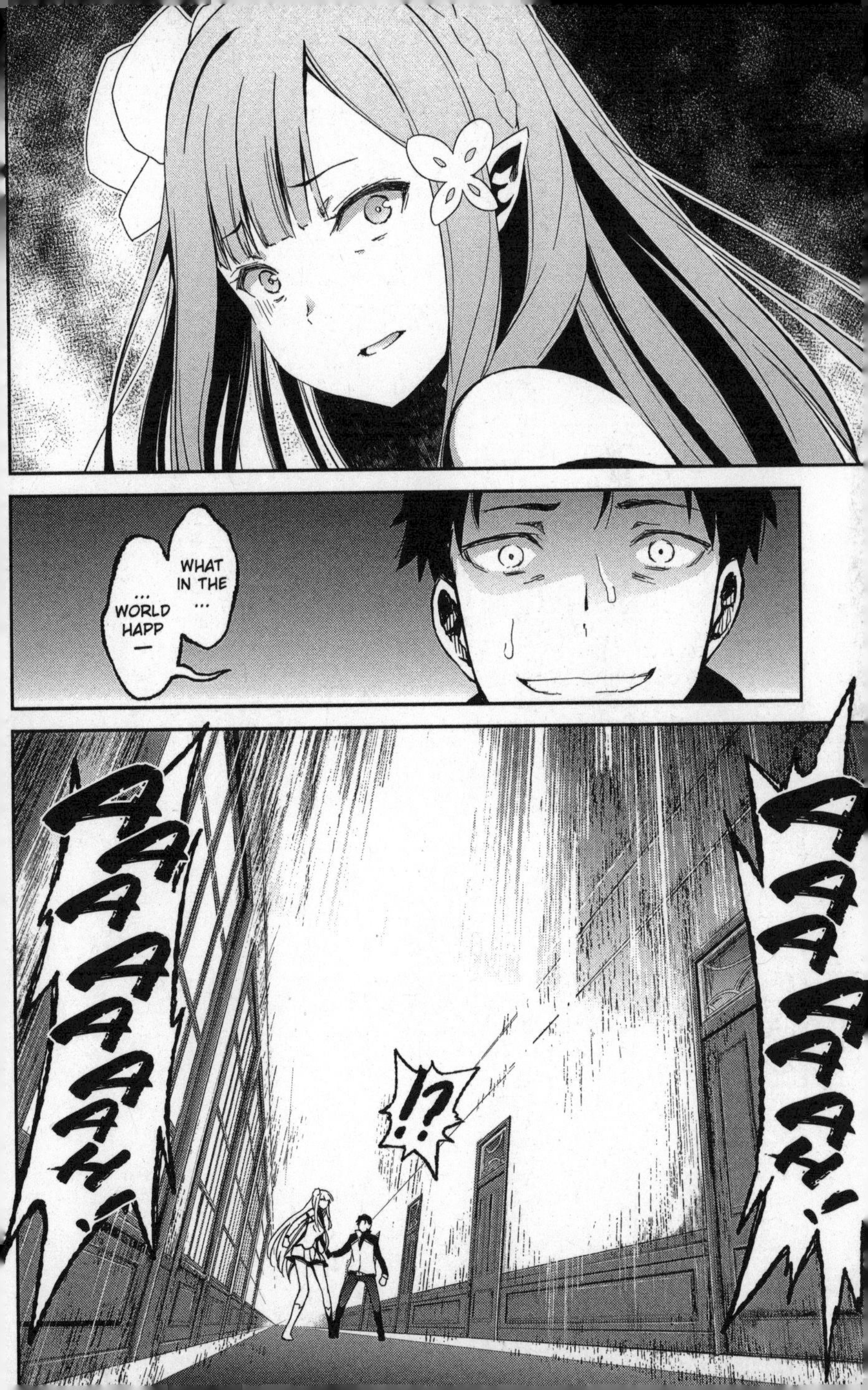
WHAT IN THE ... ... WORLD HAPP—
AAAAAAAH!!
AAAAAAAH!!
!?

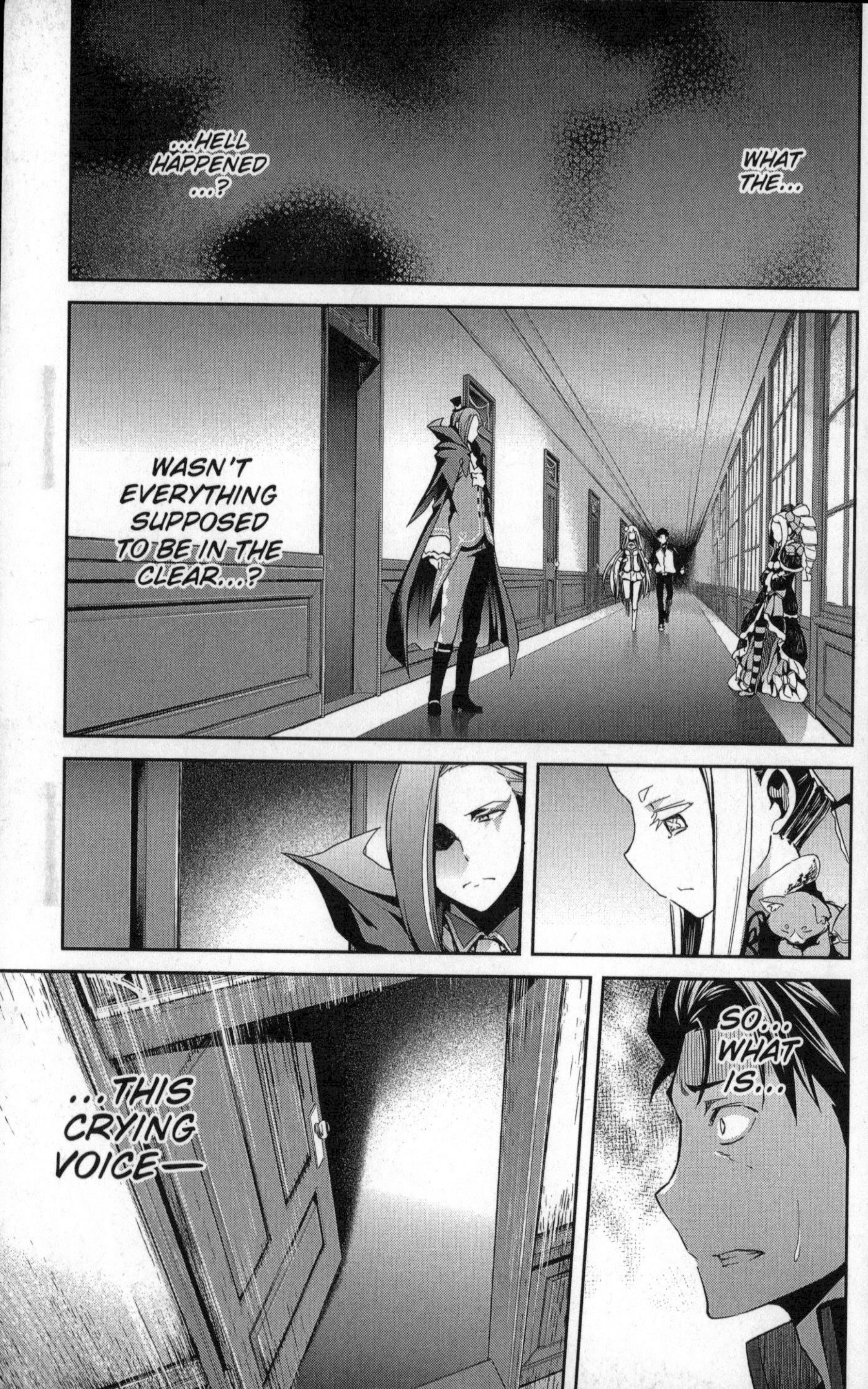
WHAT THE...
...HELL HAPPENED ...?
WASN'T EVERYTHING SUPPOSED TO BE IN THE CLEAR...?
SO... WHAT IS...
...THIS CRYING VOICE—

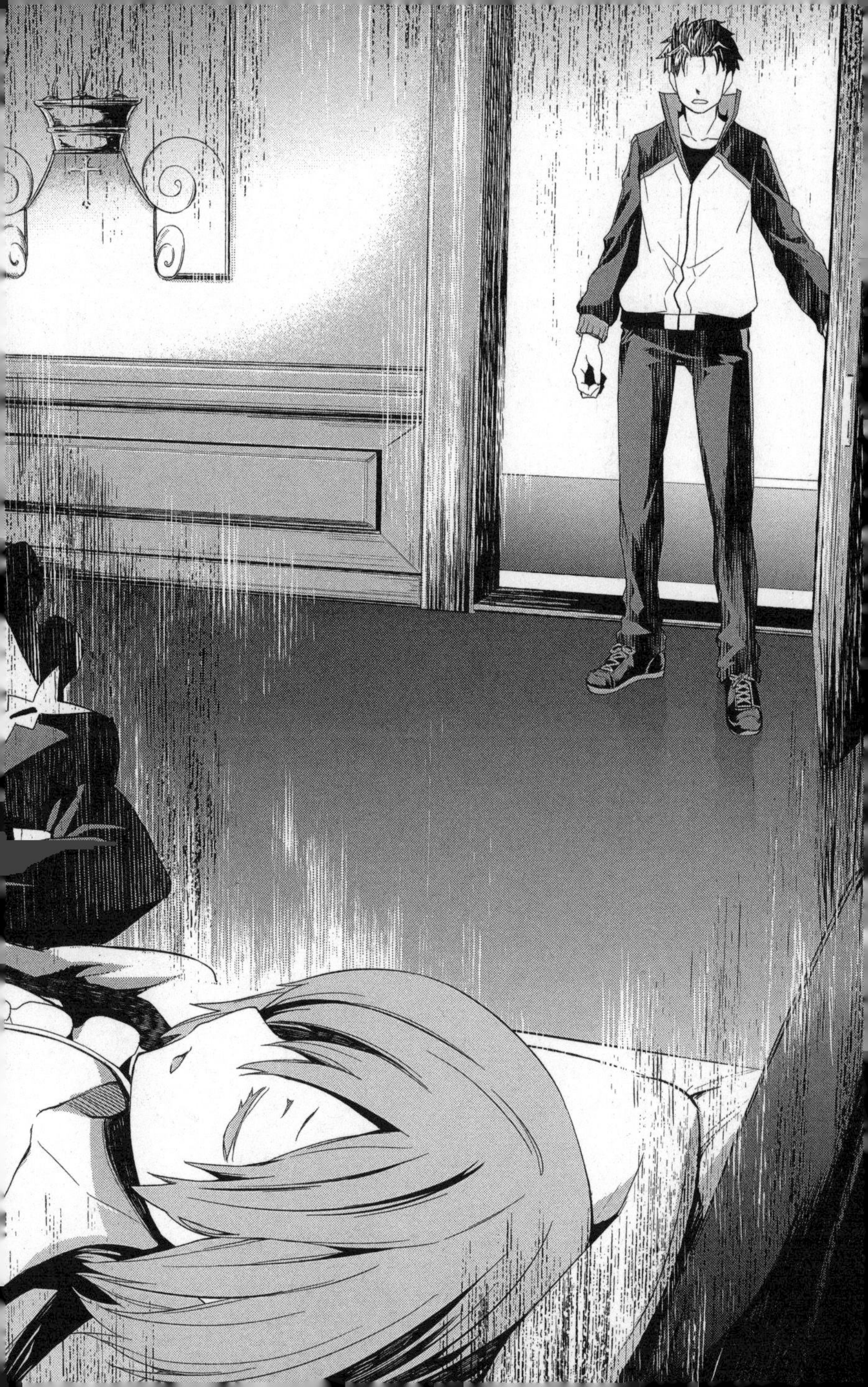

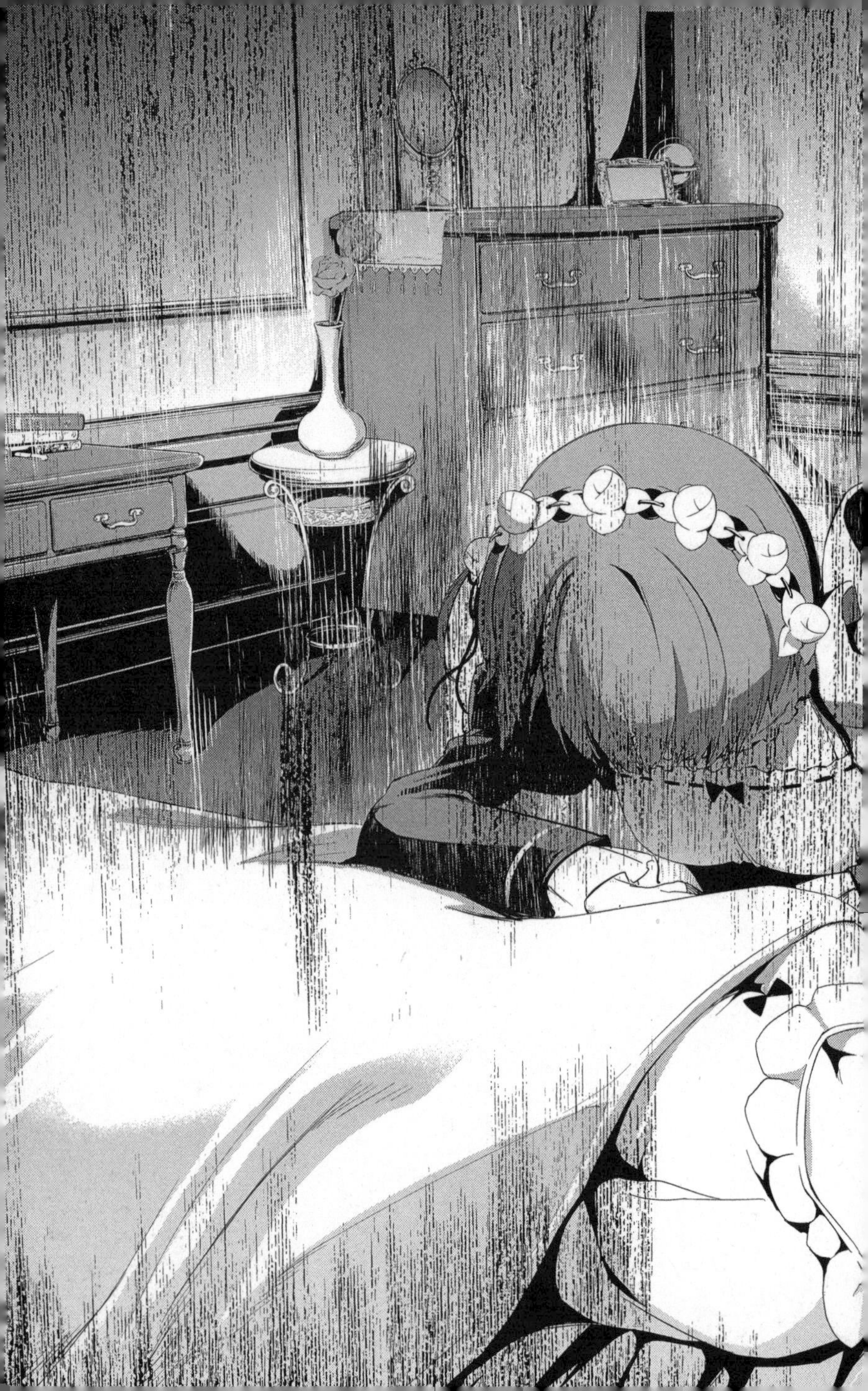

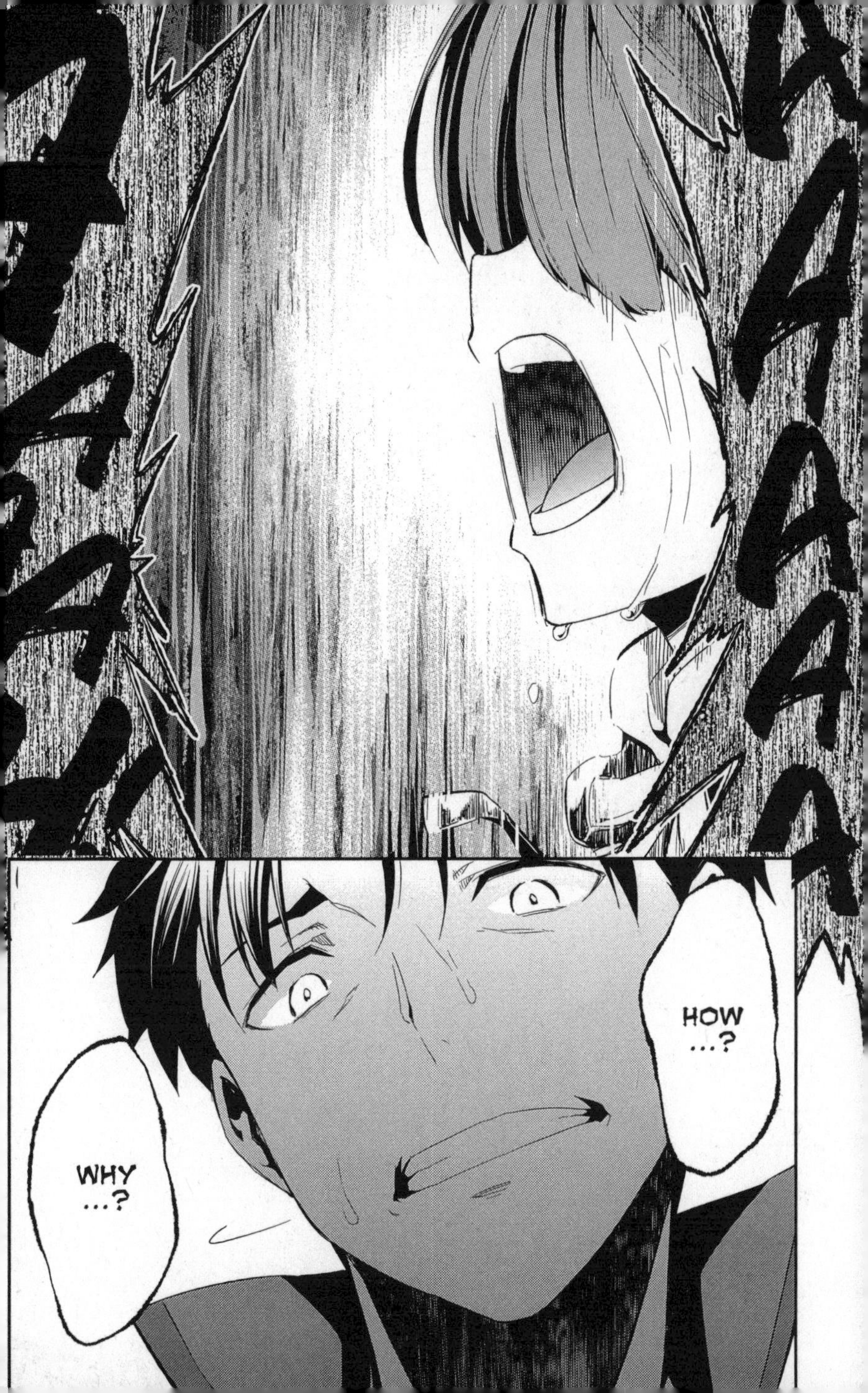
HOW ...?
WHY ...?

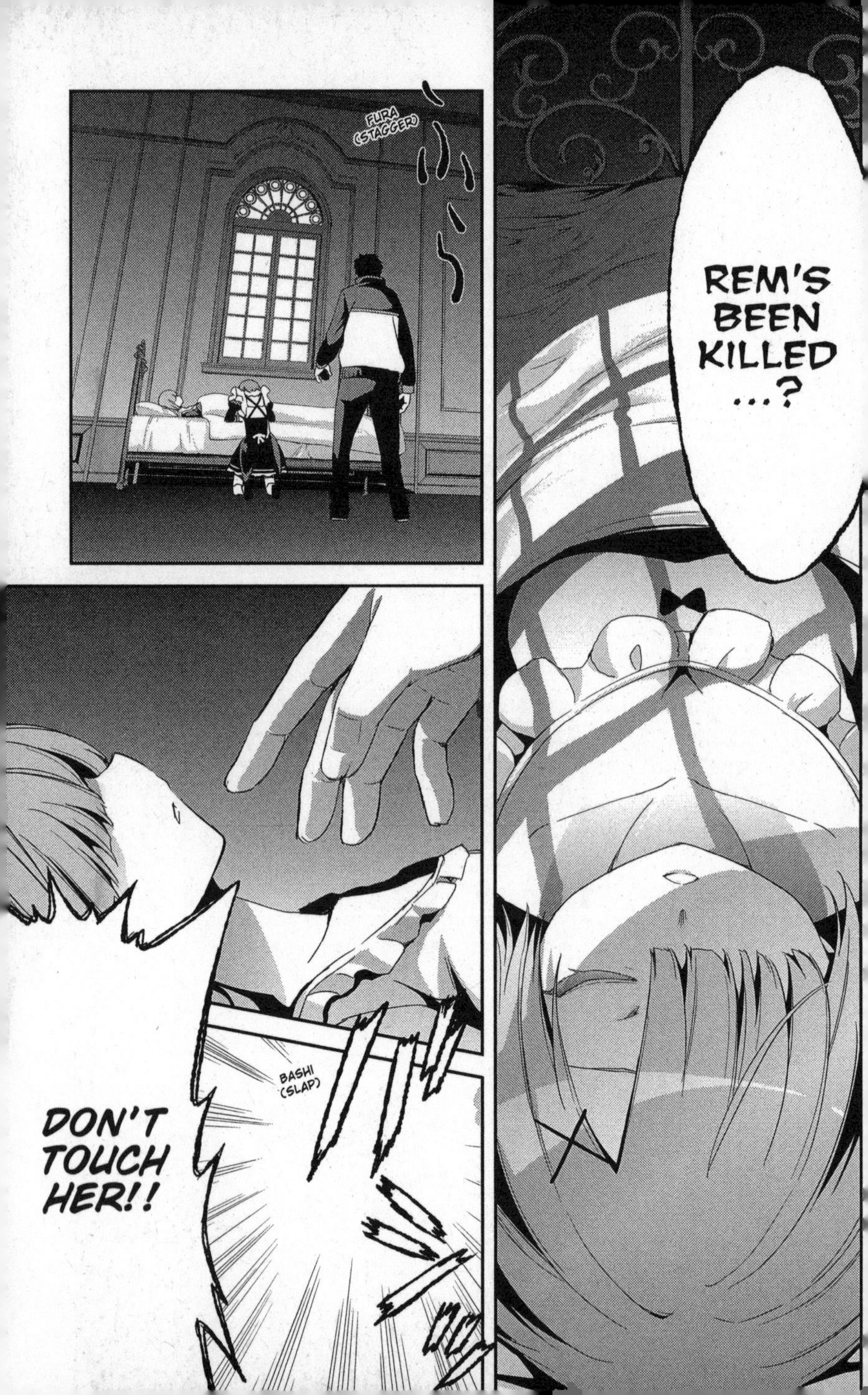
REM'S BEEN KILLED ...?
FURA (STAGGER)
DON'T TOUCH HER!!
BASHI (SLAP)

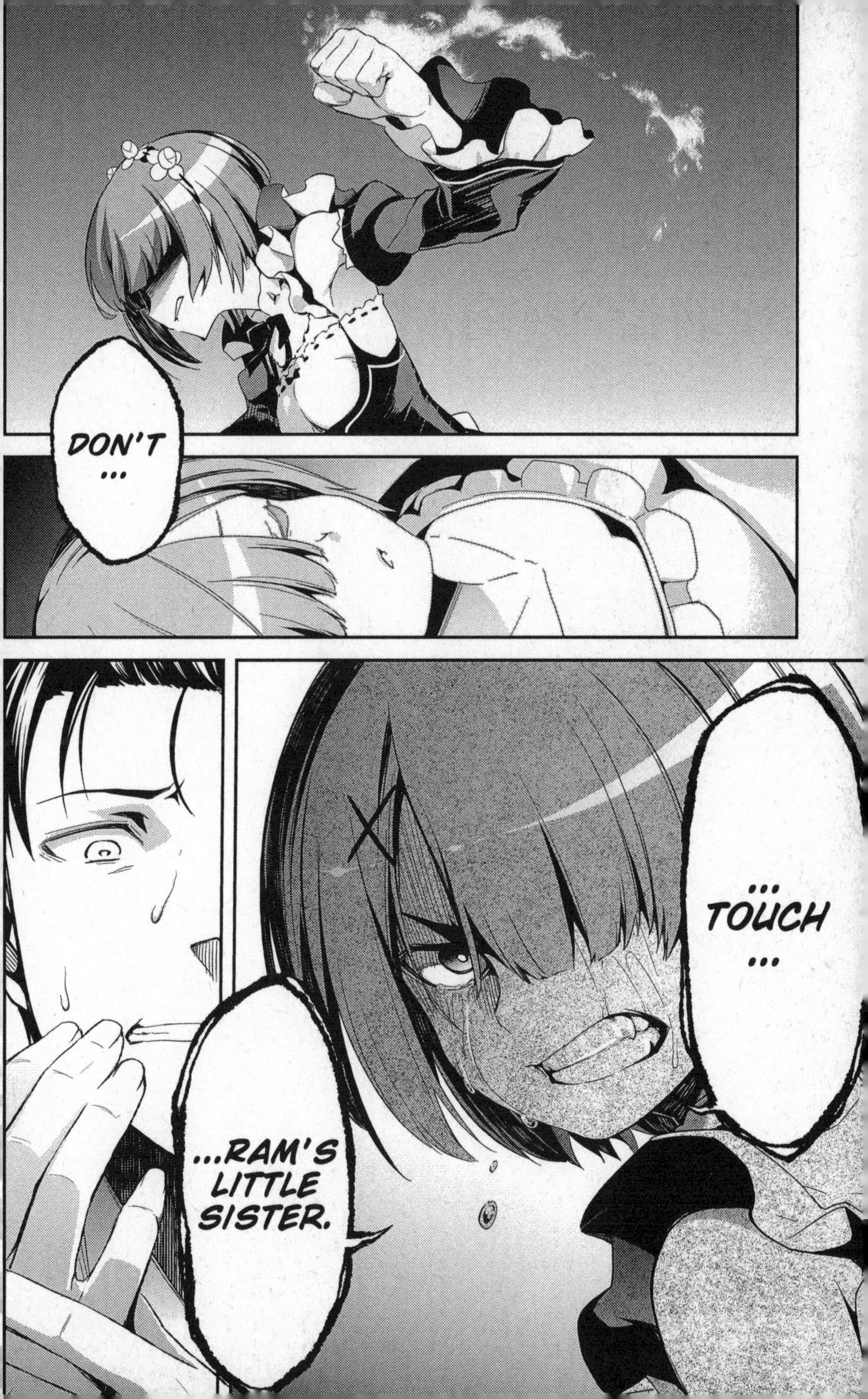
DON'T ...
... TOUCH ...
...RAM'S LITTLE SISTER.

Finally, he reaches the fifth day—
but victory over Mr. Fate will not come so easily.

Rem's death was very impactful but so, too, was Ram's anger.

In this second chapter, it's also the scene where Ram is
depicted at her most human.

The feelings of the older sister for the younger…
and the desire to save her…

Re:ZeRo

-Starting Life in Another World-

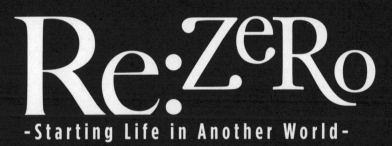

Episode 11 A Happy Nightmare

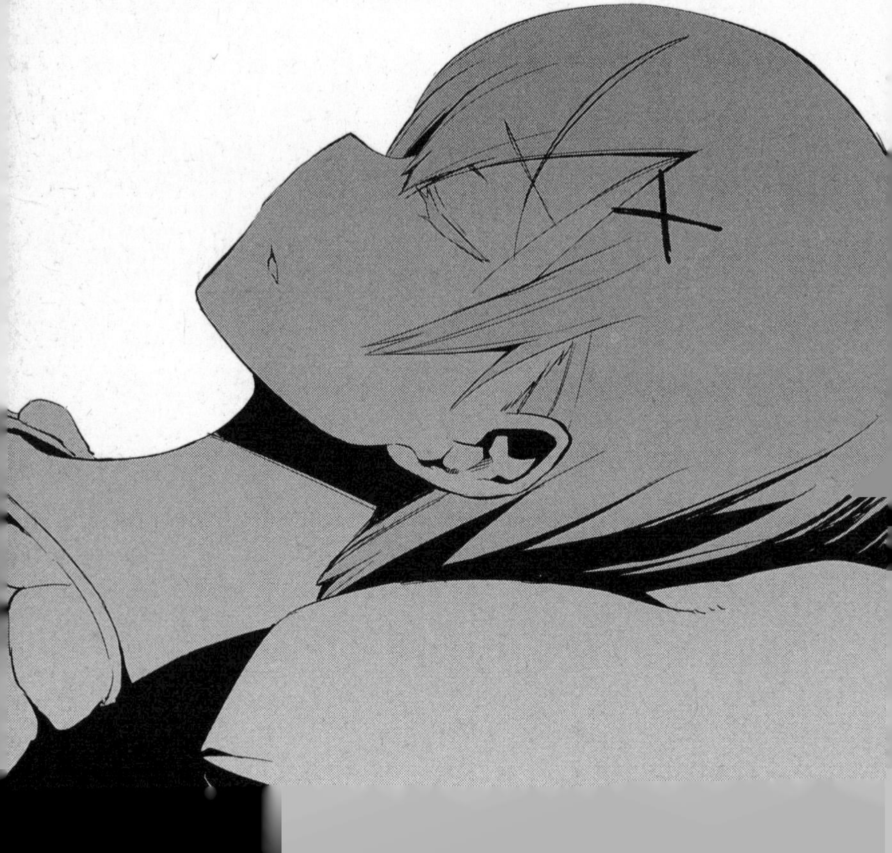

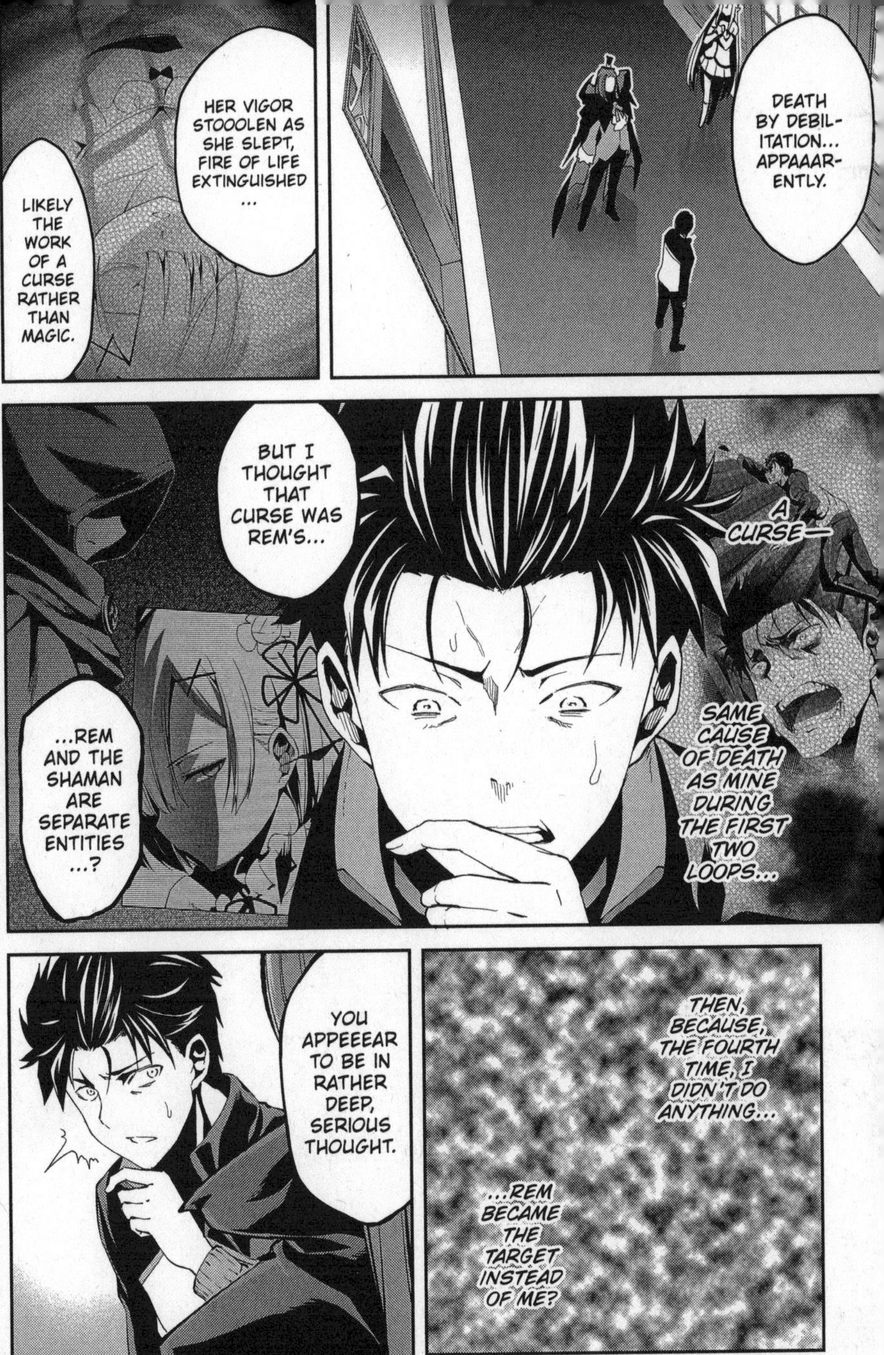
DEATH BY DEBIL-ITATION... APPAAAR-ENTLY.
HER VIGOR STOOOLEN AS SHE SLEPT, FIRE OF LIFE EXTINGUISHED ...
LIKELY THE WORK OF A CURSE RATHER THAN MAGIC.
A CURSE—
SAME CAUSE OF DEATH AS MINE DURING THE FIRST TWO LOOPS...
BUT I THOUGHT THAT CURSE WAS REM'S...
...REM AND THE SHAMAN ARE SEPARATE ENTITIES ...?
THEN, BECAUSE, THE FOURTH TIME, I DIDN'T DO ANYTHING...
...REM BECAME THE TARGET INSTEAD OF ME?
YOU APPEEEAR TO BE IN RATHER DEEP, SERIOUS THOUGHT.

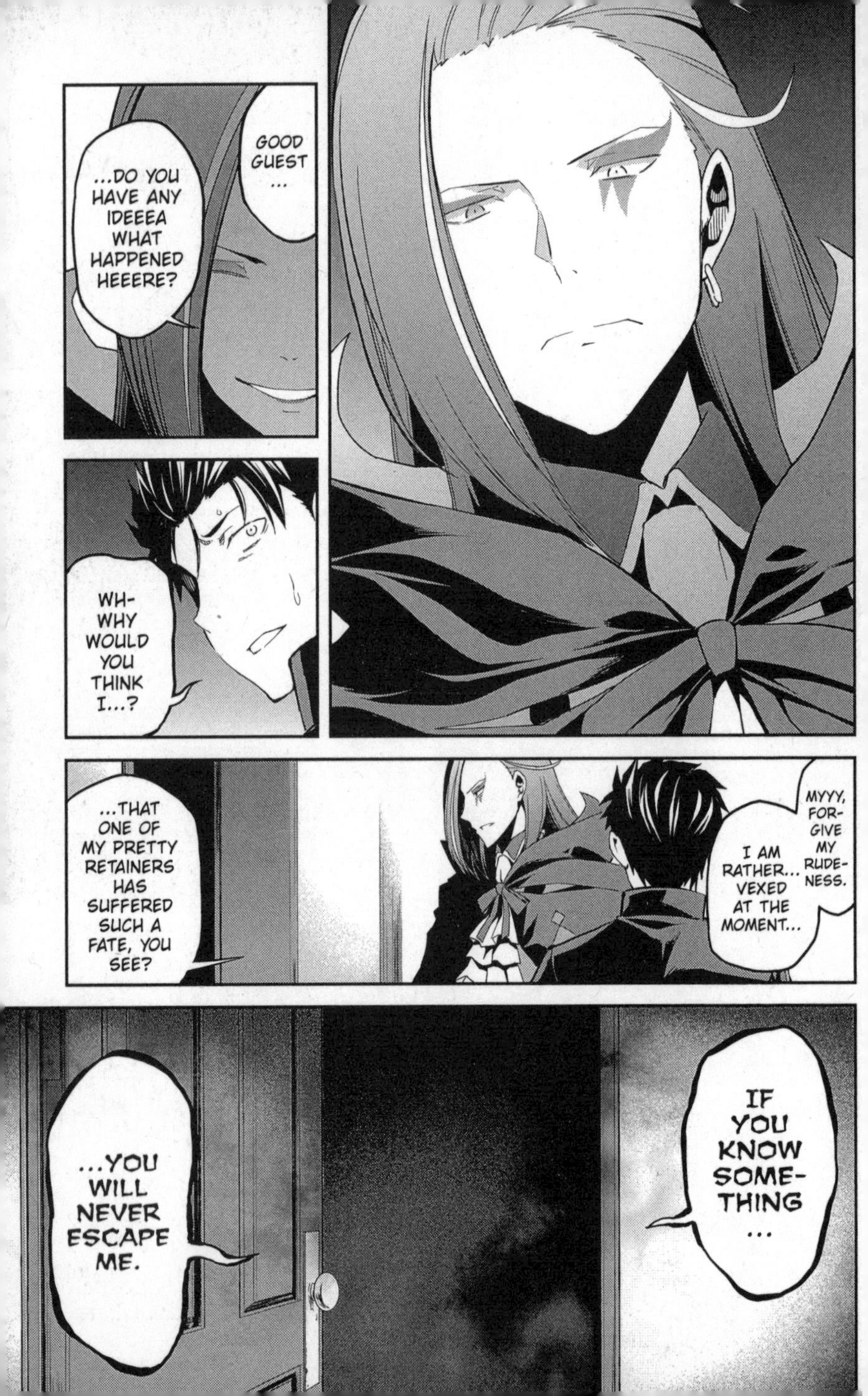
GOOD GUEST...
...DO YOU HAVE ANY IDEEEA WHAT HAPPENED HEEERE?
WH-WHY WOULD YOU THINK I...?
MYYY, FORGIVE MY RUDENESS.
I AM RATHER... VEXED AT THE MOMENT...
...THAT ONE OF MY PRETTY RETAINERS HAS SUFFERED SUCH A FATE, YOU SEE?
IF YOU KNOW SOMETHING...
...YOU WILL NEVER ESCAPE ME.

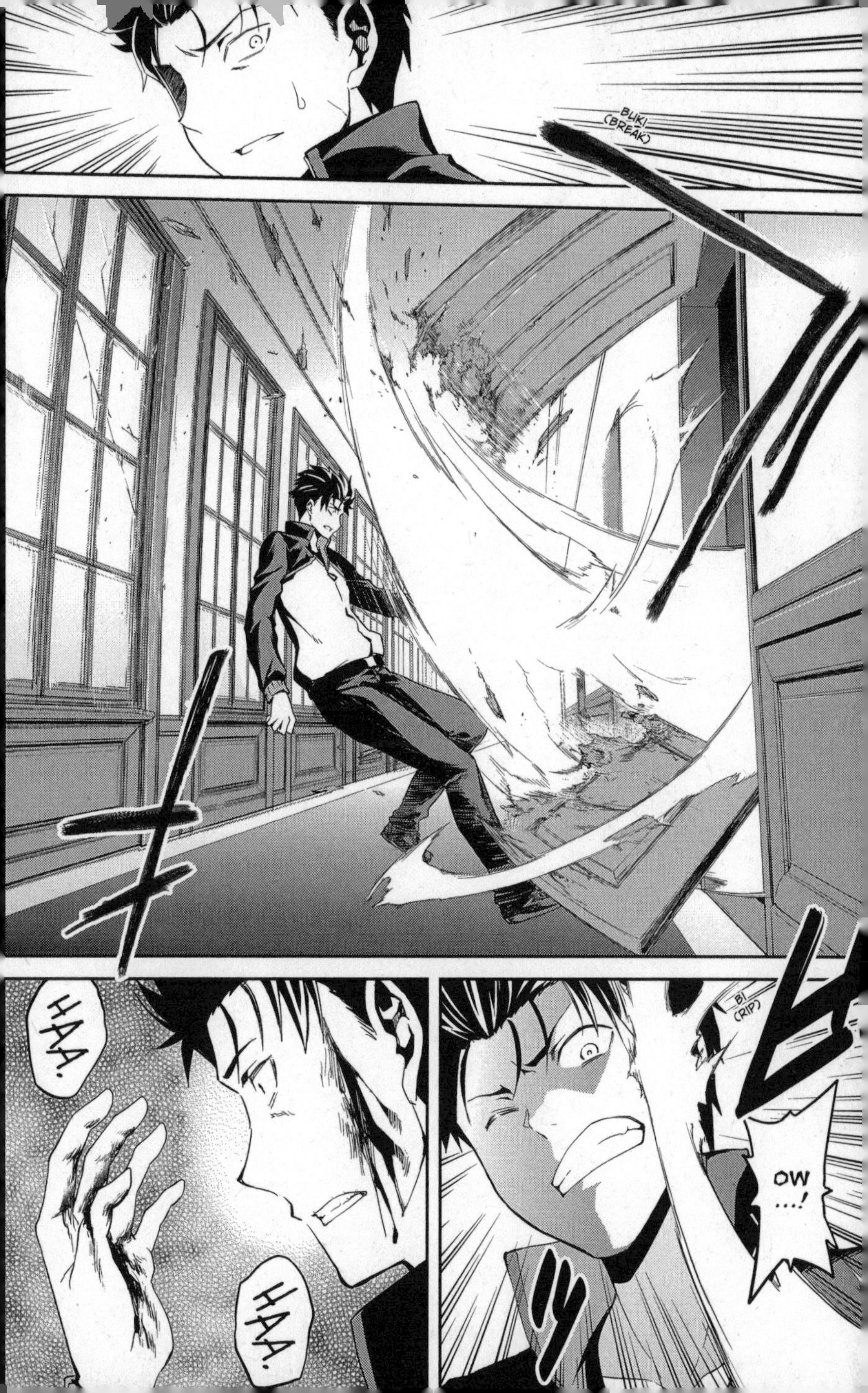
BUKI
(BREAK)
BI
(RIP)
OW
...!
HAA.
HAA.

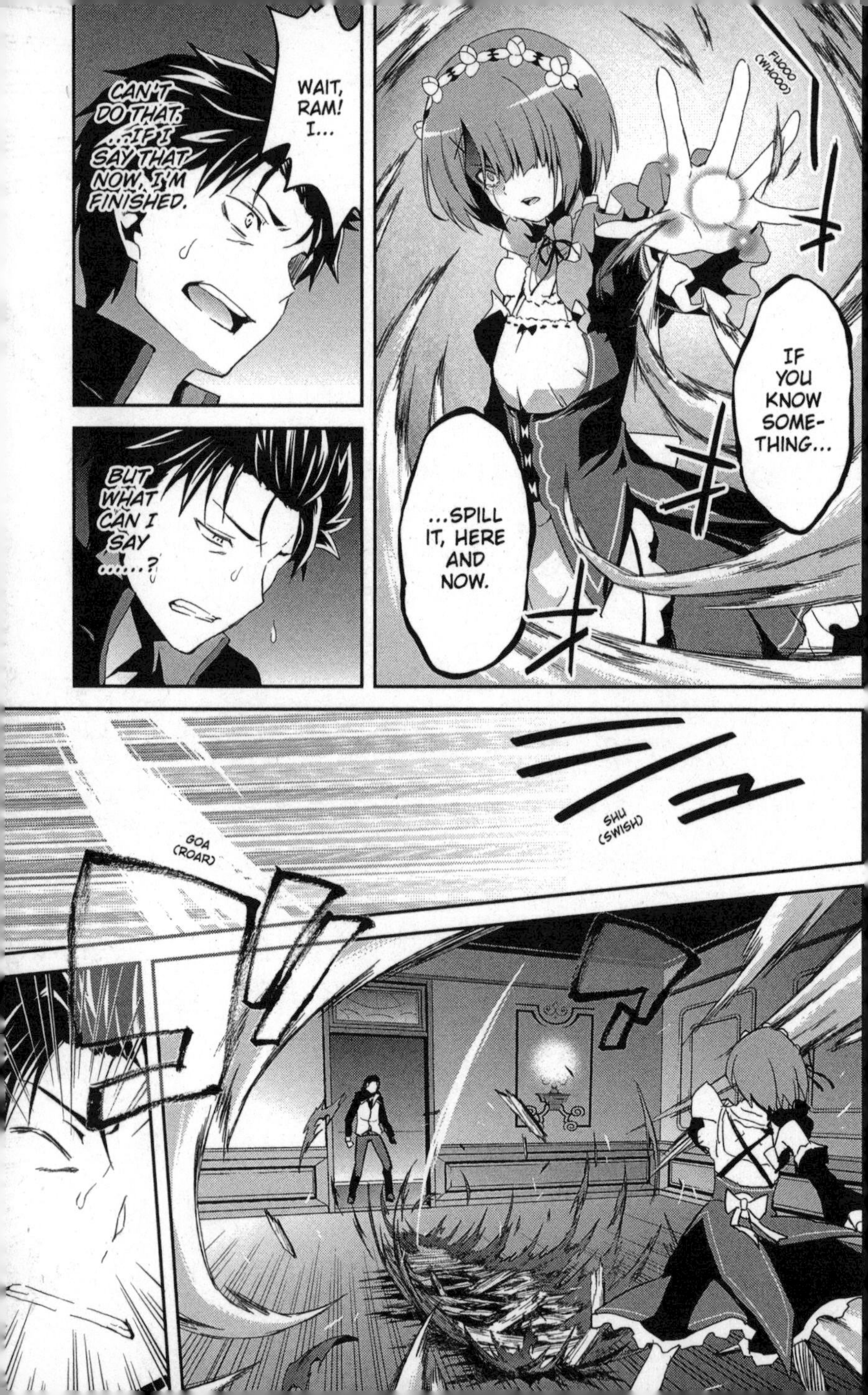
FUOOO (WHOOO)
IF YOU KNOW SOMETHING...
...SPILL IT, HERE AND NOW.
WAIT, RAM! I...
CAN'T DO THAT. ...IF I SAY THAT NOW, I'M FINISHED.
BUT WHAT CAN I SAY ......?
SHU (SWISH)
GOA (ROAR)

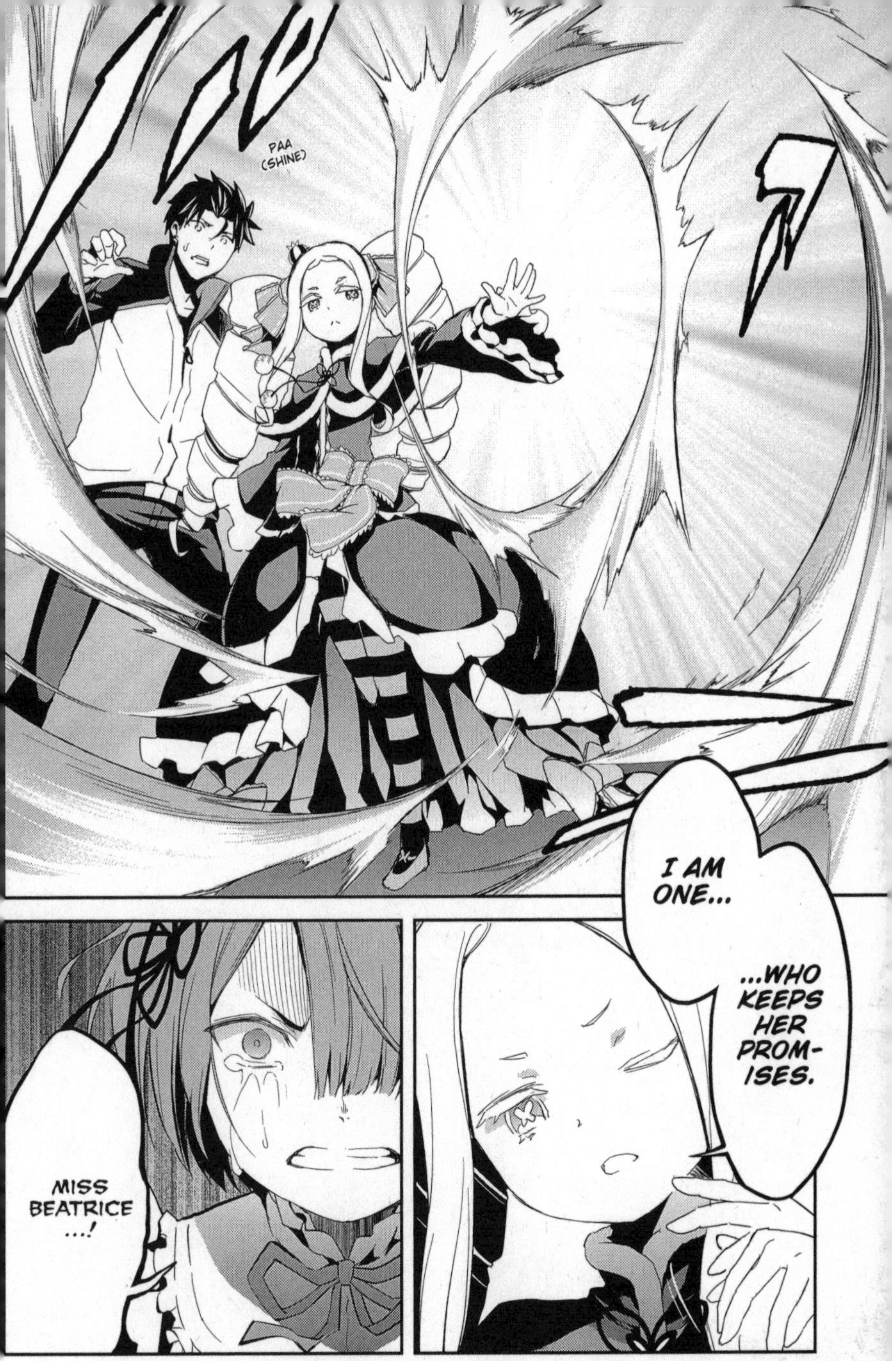
PAA (SHINE)
I AM ONE...
...WHO KEEPS HER PROM-ISES.
MISS BEATRICE ...!

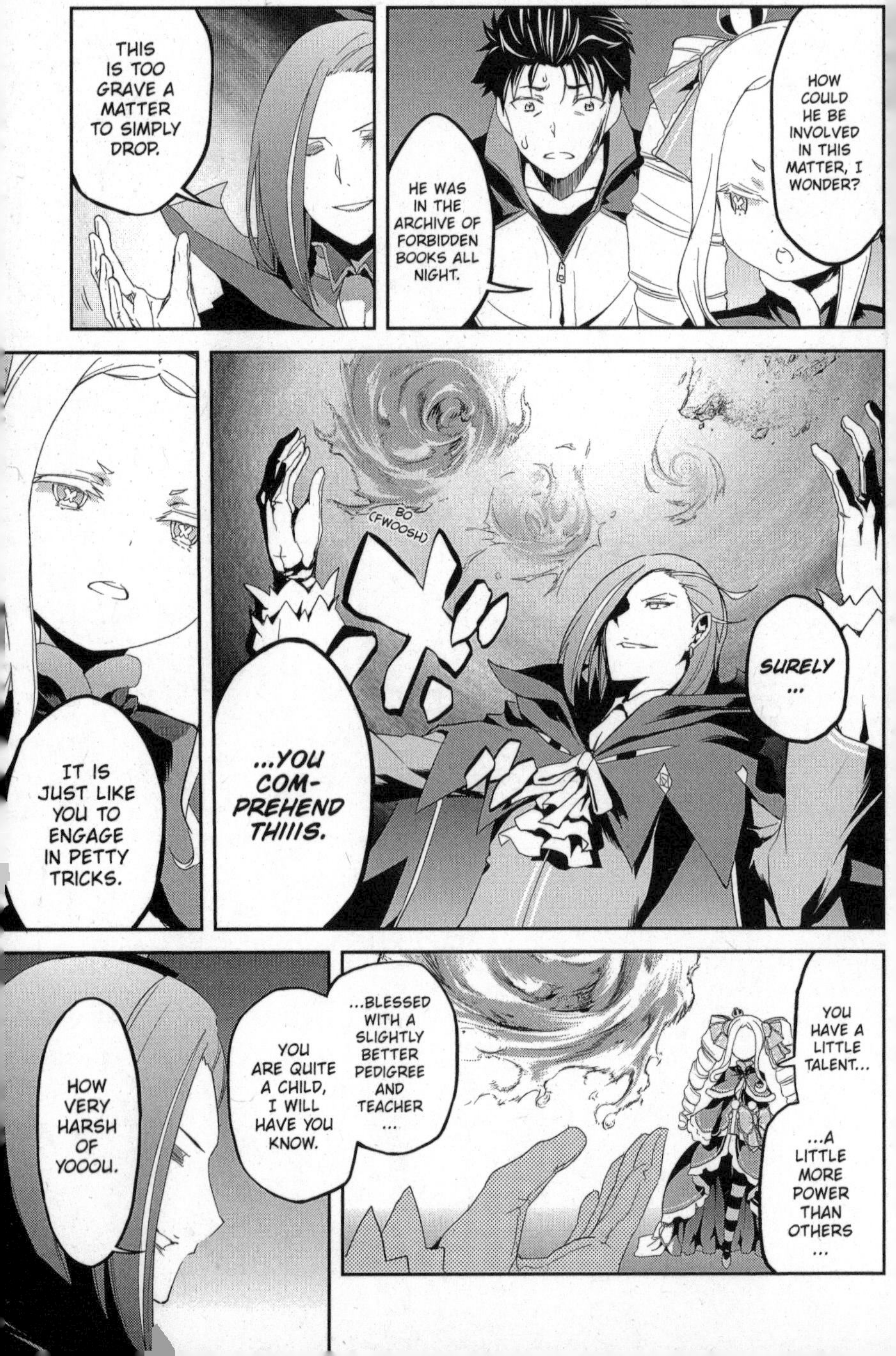
HOW COULD HE BE INVOLVED IN THIS MATTER, I WONDER?
HE WAS IN THE ARCHIVE OF FORBIDDEN BOOKS ALL NIGHT.
THIS IS TOO GRAVE A MATTER TO SIMPLY DROP.
SURELY ...
BO (FWOOSH)
...YOU COMPREHEND THIIIS.
IT IS JUST LIKE YOU TO ENGAGE IN PETTY TRICKS.
YOU HAVE A LITTLE TALENT...
...A LITTLE MORE POWER THAN OTHERS ...
...BLESSED WITH A SLIGHTLY BETTER PEDIGREE AND TEACHER ...
YOU ARE QUITE A CHILD, I WILL HAVE YOU KNOW.
HOW VERY HARSH OF YOOOU.

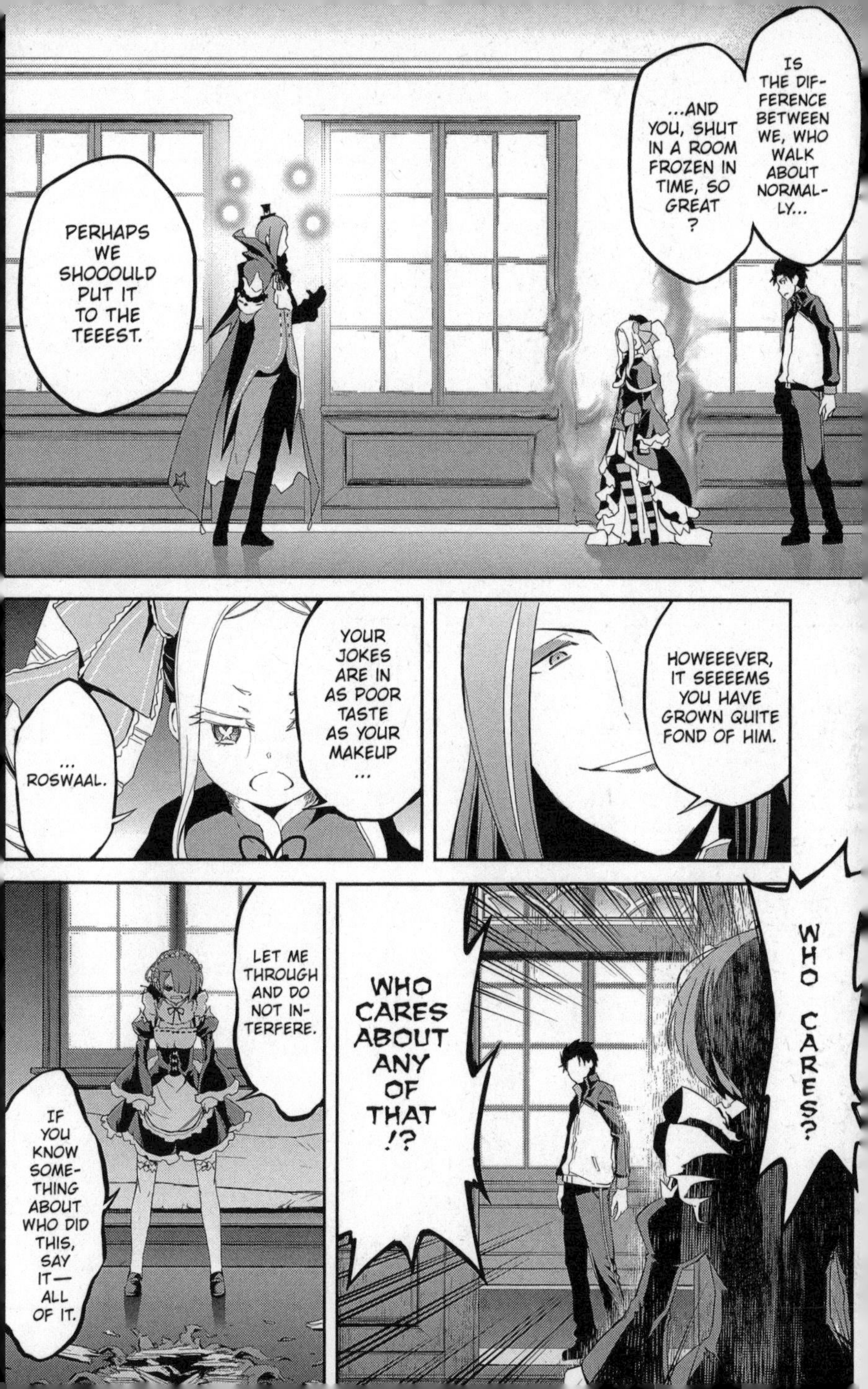
IS THE DIFFERENCE BETWEEN WE, WHO WALK ABOUT NORMALLY...
...AND YOU, SHUT IN A ROOM FROZEN IN TIME, SO GREAT?
PERHAPS WE SHOOOULD PUT IT TO THE TEEEST.
HOWEEEVER, IT SEEEEMS YOU HAVE GROWN QUITE FOND OF HIM.
YOUR JOKES ARE IN AS POOR TASTE AS YOUR MAKEUP...
...ROSWAAL.
WHO CARES?
WHO CARES ABOUT ANY OF THAT!?
LET ME THROUGH AND DO NOT INTERFERE.
IF YOU KNOW SOMETHING ABOUT WHO DID THIS, SAY IT—ALL OF IT.

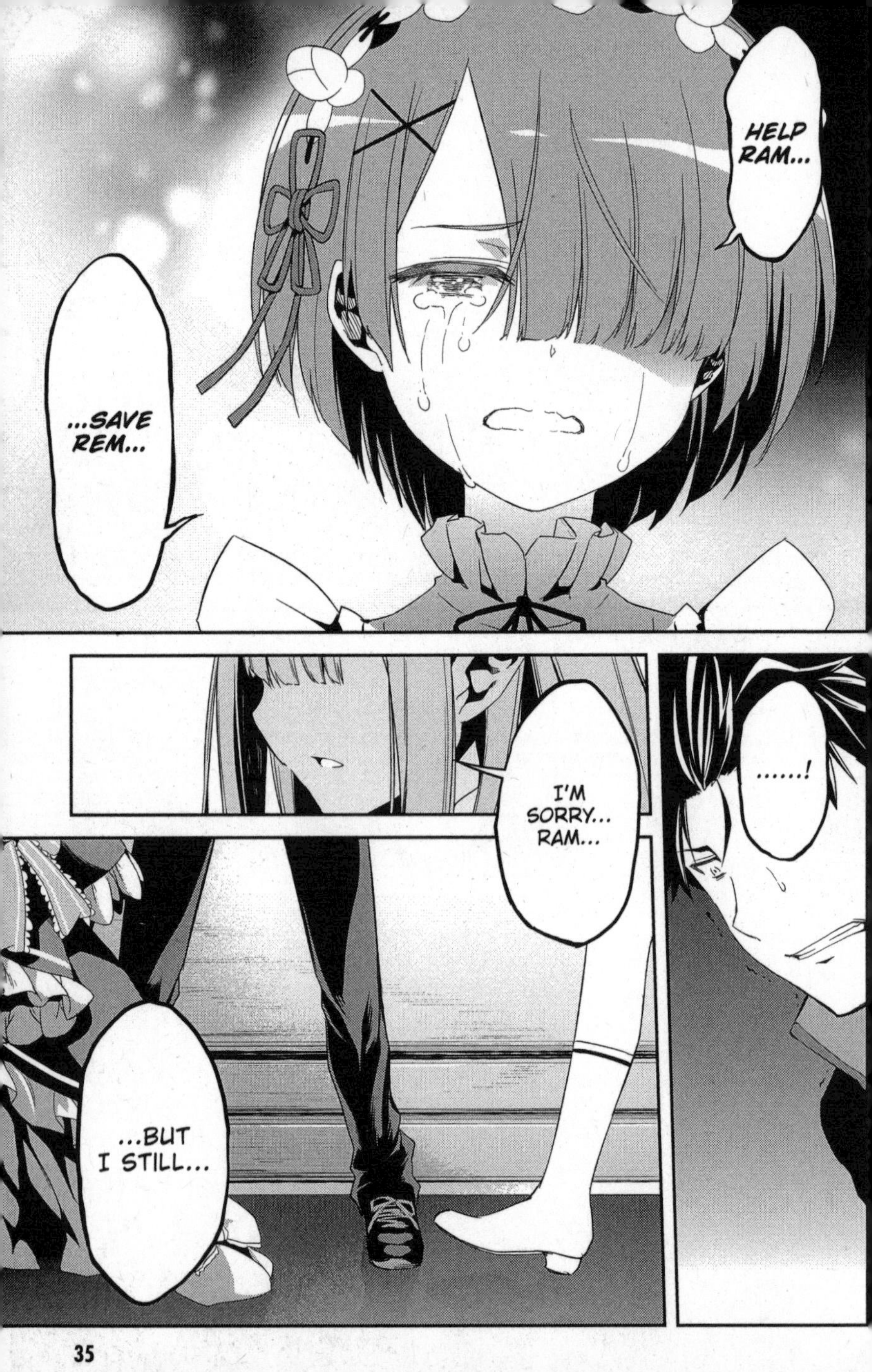
HELP RAM...
...SAVE REM...
......!
I'M SORRY... RAM...
...BUT I STILL...

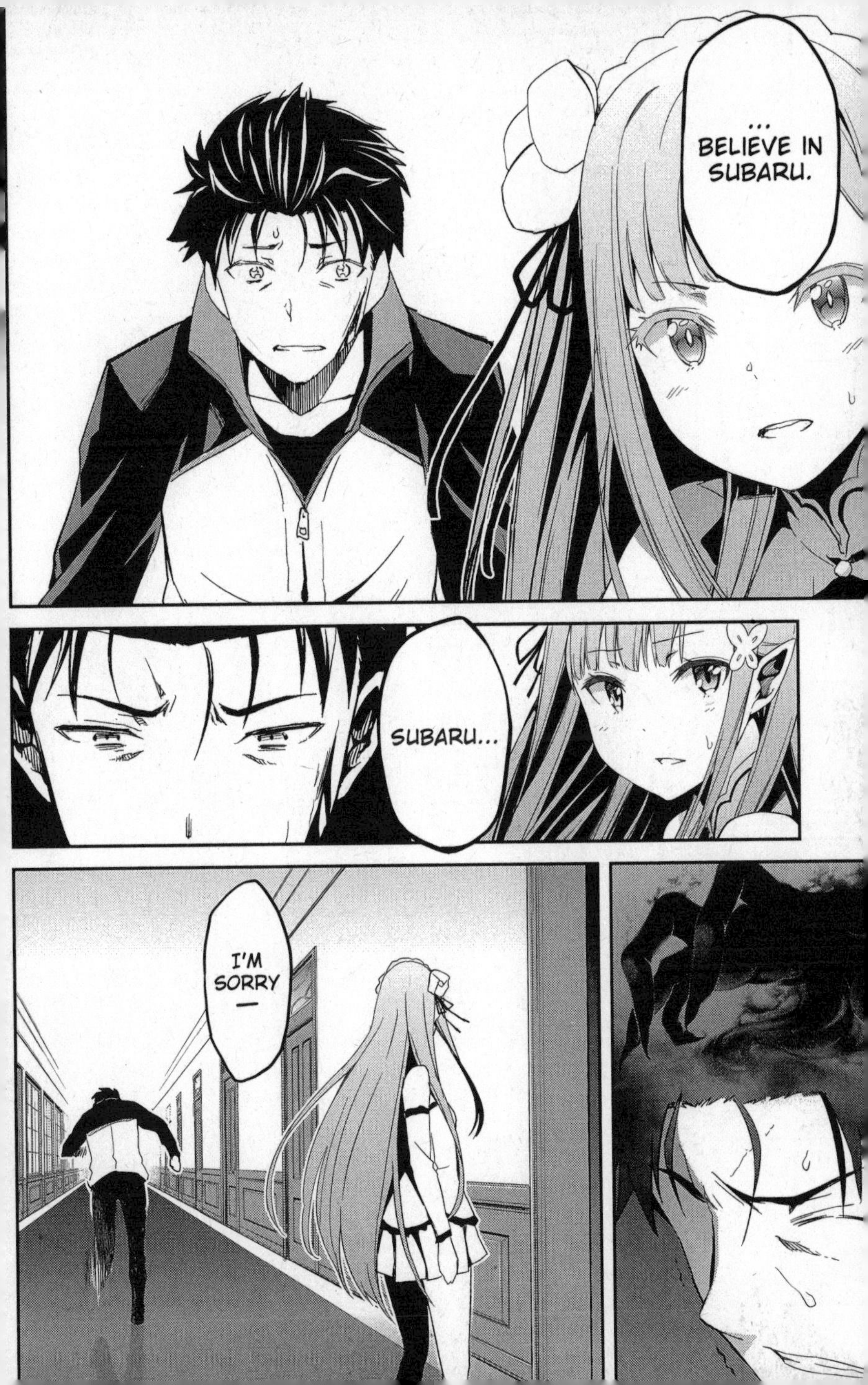

... BELIEVE IN SUBARU.
SUBARU...
I'M SORRY —

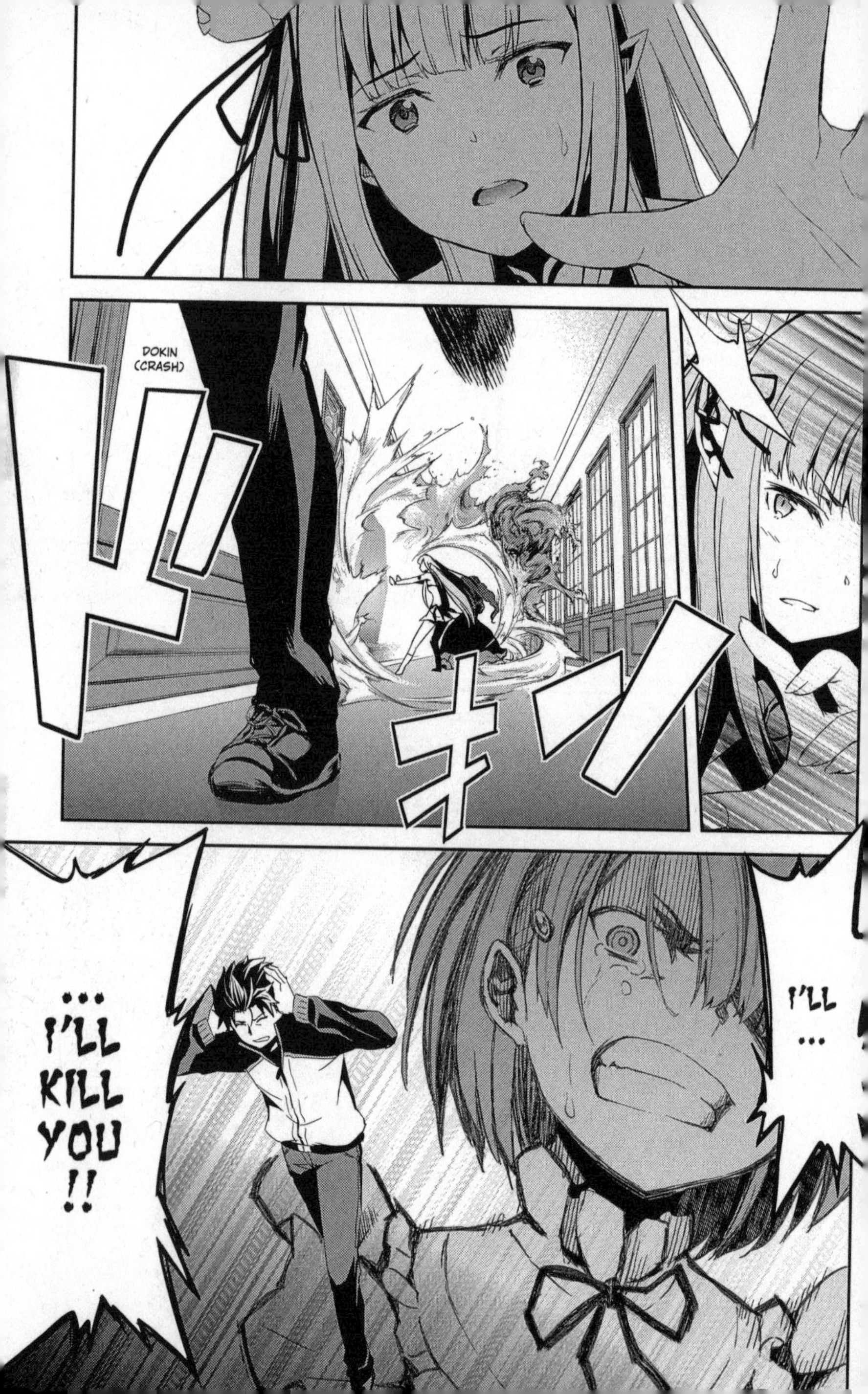
ドッキン
DOKIN (CRASH)
I'LL ...
... I'LL KILL YOU!!

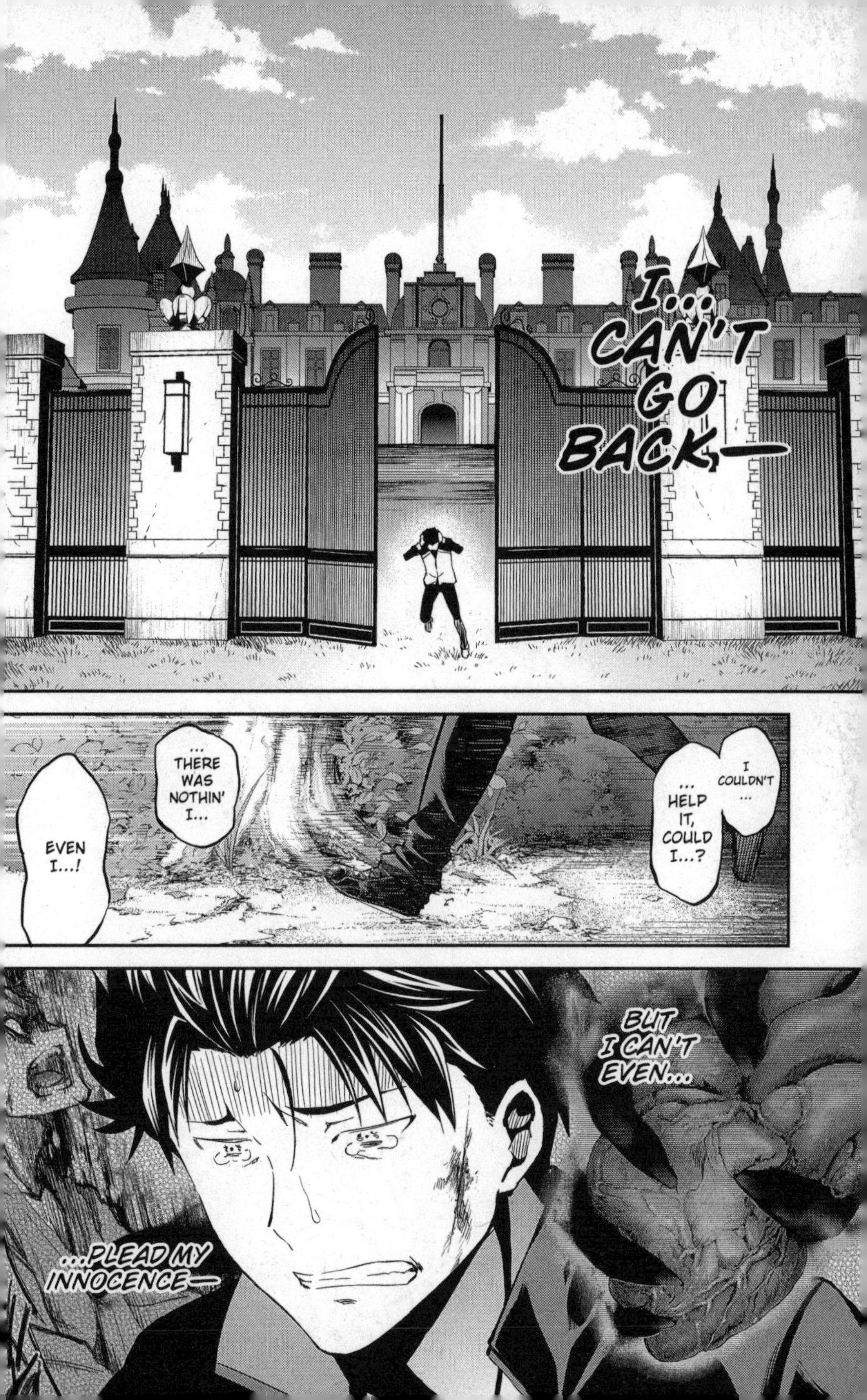
I... CAN'T GO BACK—
I COULDN'T ...
... HELP IT, COULD I...?
... THERE WAS NOTHIN' I...
EVEN I...!
BUT I CAN'T EVEN...
...PLEAD MY INNOCENCE—

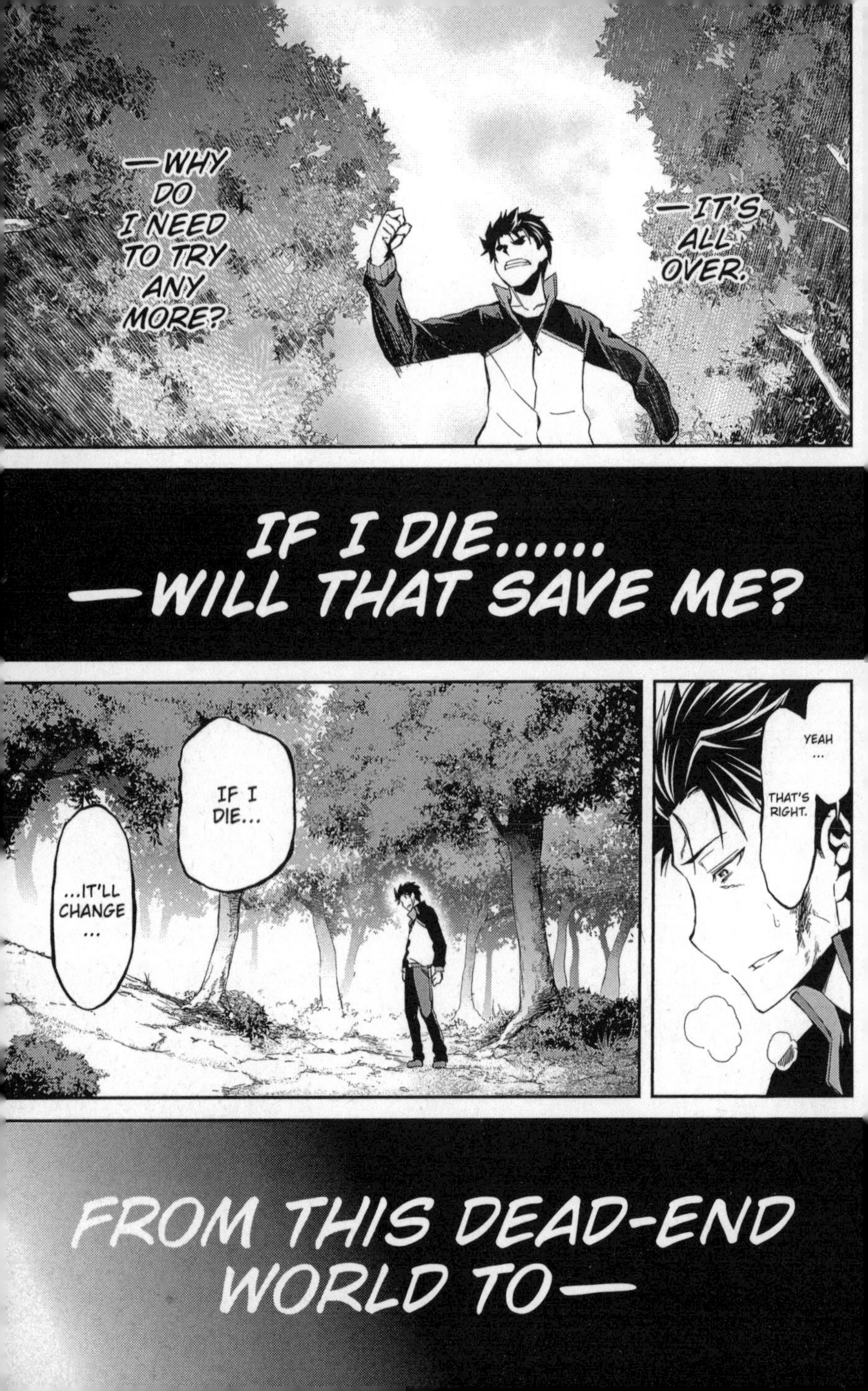
—IT'S ALL OVER.
—WHY DO I NEED TO TRY ANY MORE?
IF I DIE......
—WILL THAT SAVE ME?
YEAH ...
THAT'S RIGHT.
IF I DIE...
...IT'LL CHANGE ...
FROM THIS DEAD-END WORLD TO—

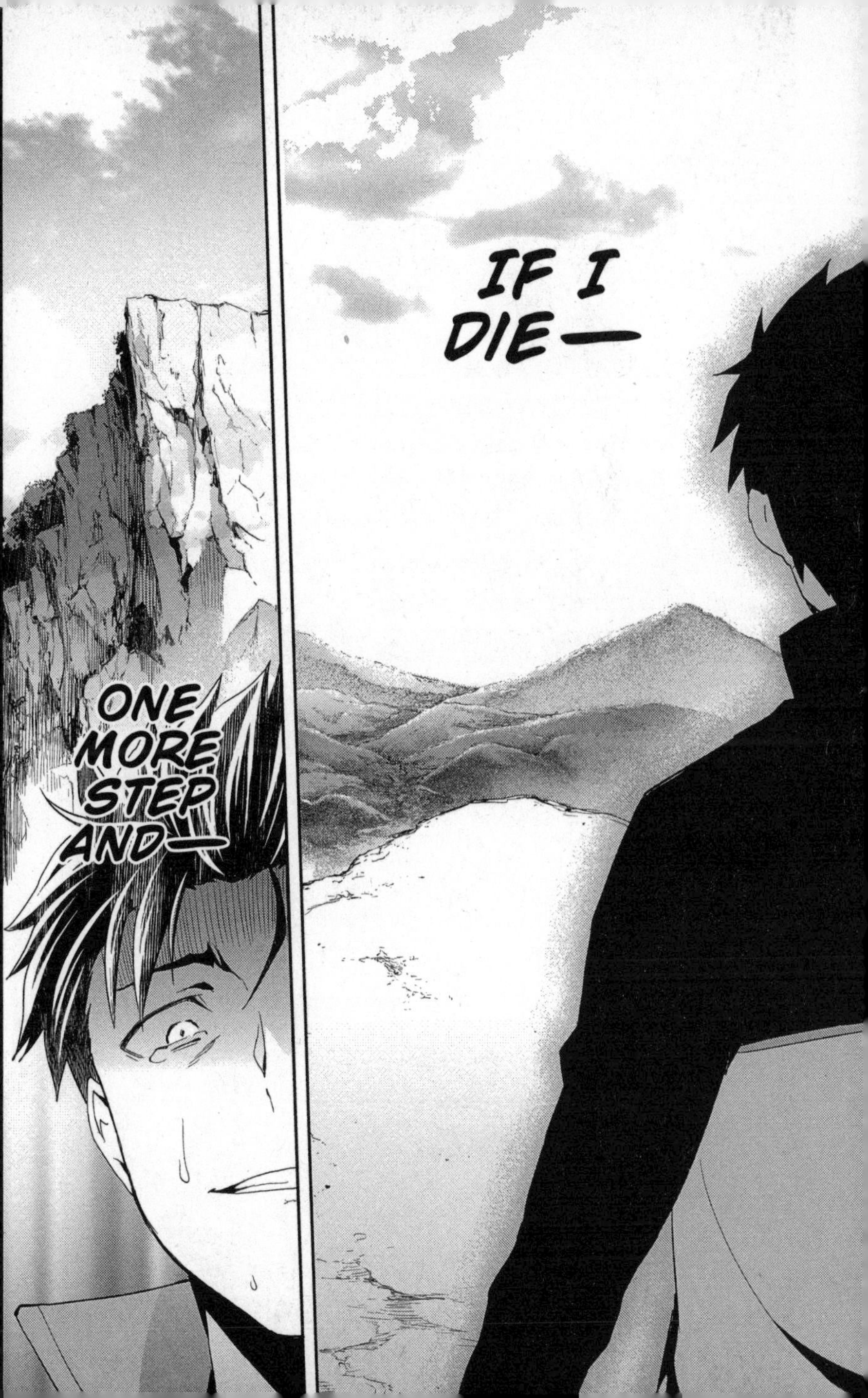
IF I DIE—
ONE MORE STEP AND—

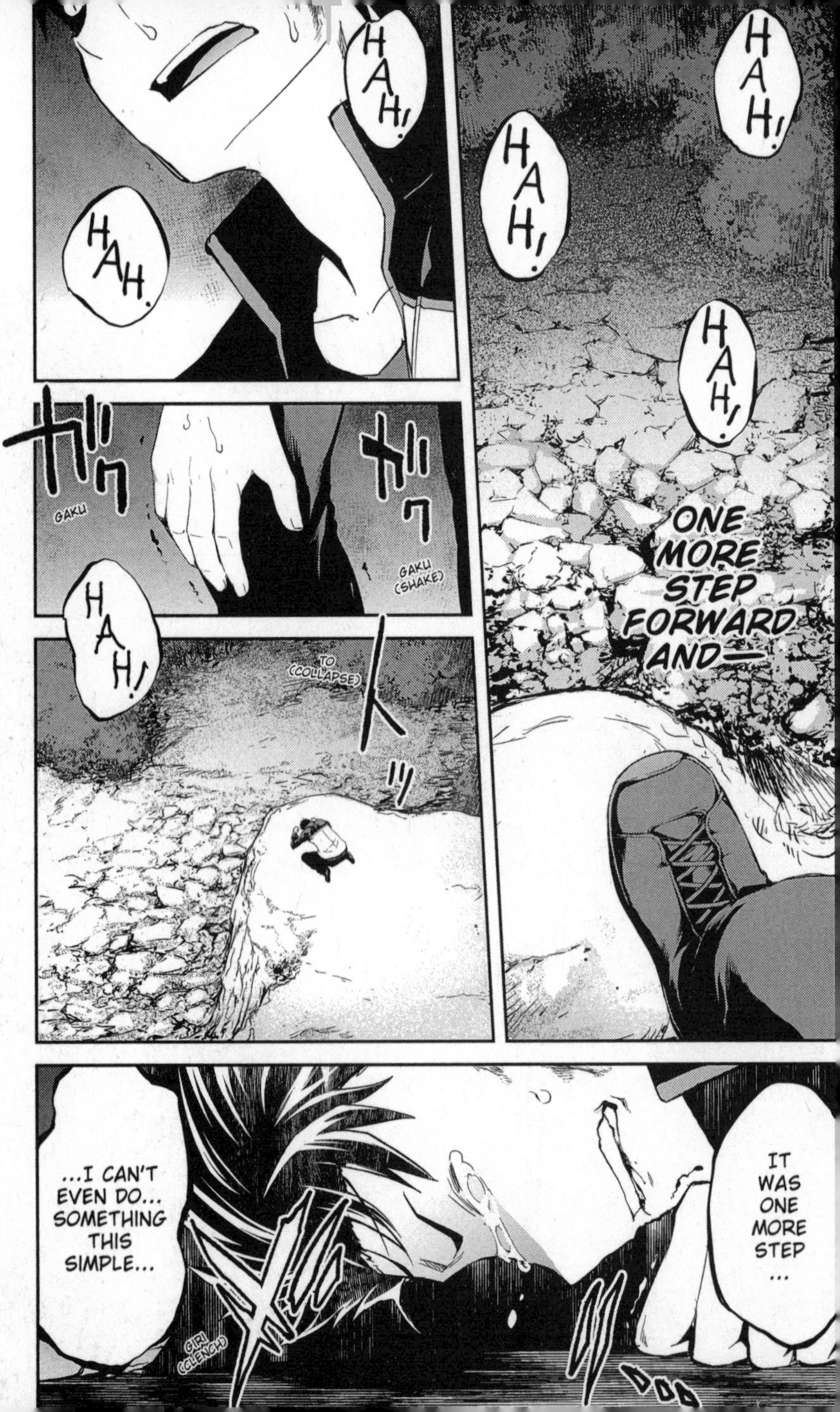
HAH!
HAH!
HAH!
ONE MORE STEP FORWARD AND—
HAH!
HAH.
ガク
GAKU (SHAKE)
ガク
GAKU
HAH!
トッ
TO (COLLAPSE)
IT WAS ONE MORE STEP...
...I CAN'T EVEN DO... SOMETHING THIS SIMPLE...
GIRI (CLENCH)

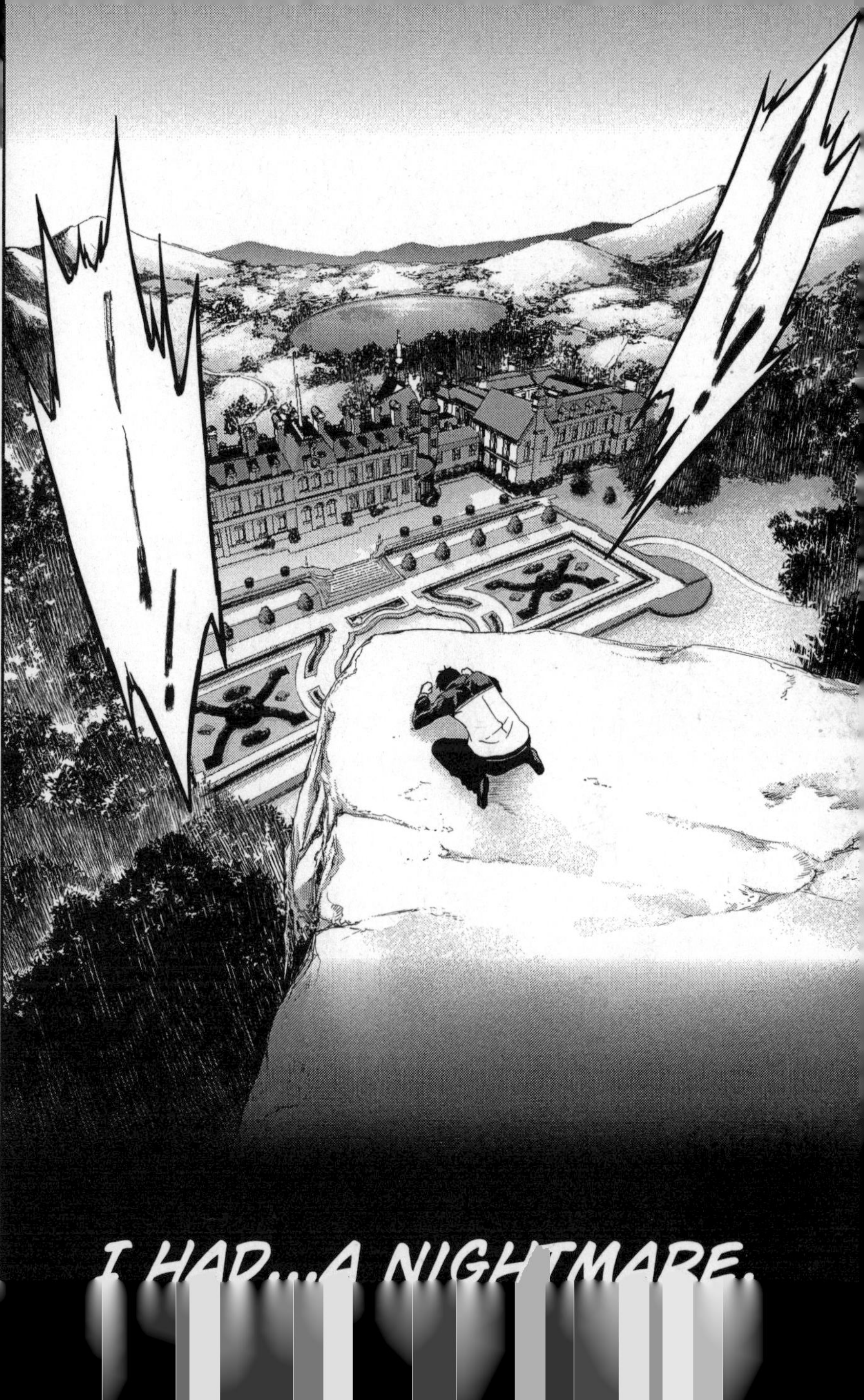
I HAD...A NIGHTMARE.

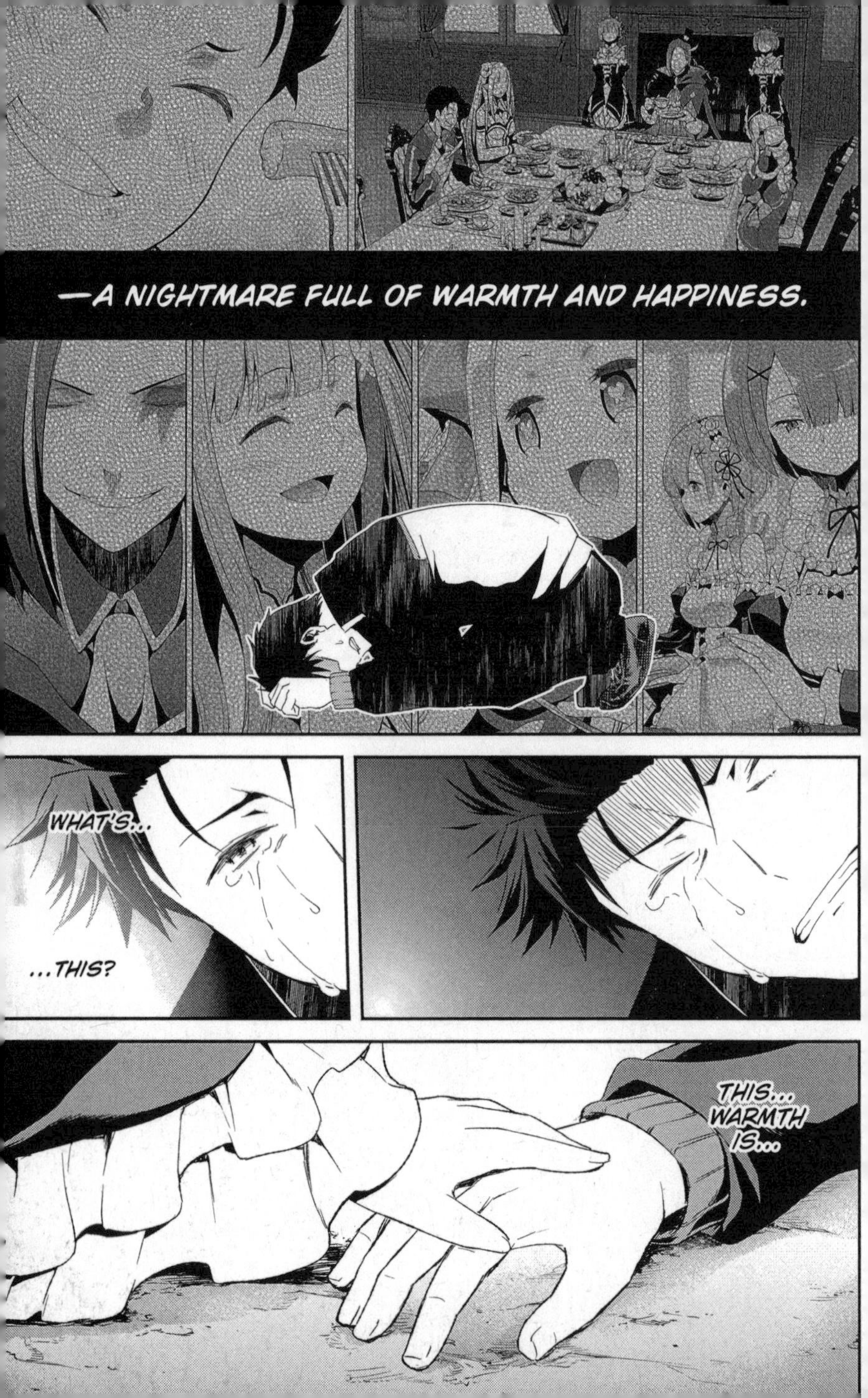
—A NIGHTMARE FULL OF WARMTH AND HAPPINESS.
WHAT'S...
...THIS?
THIS... WARMTH IS...

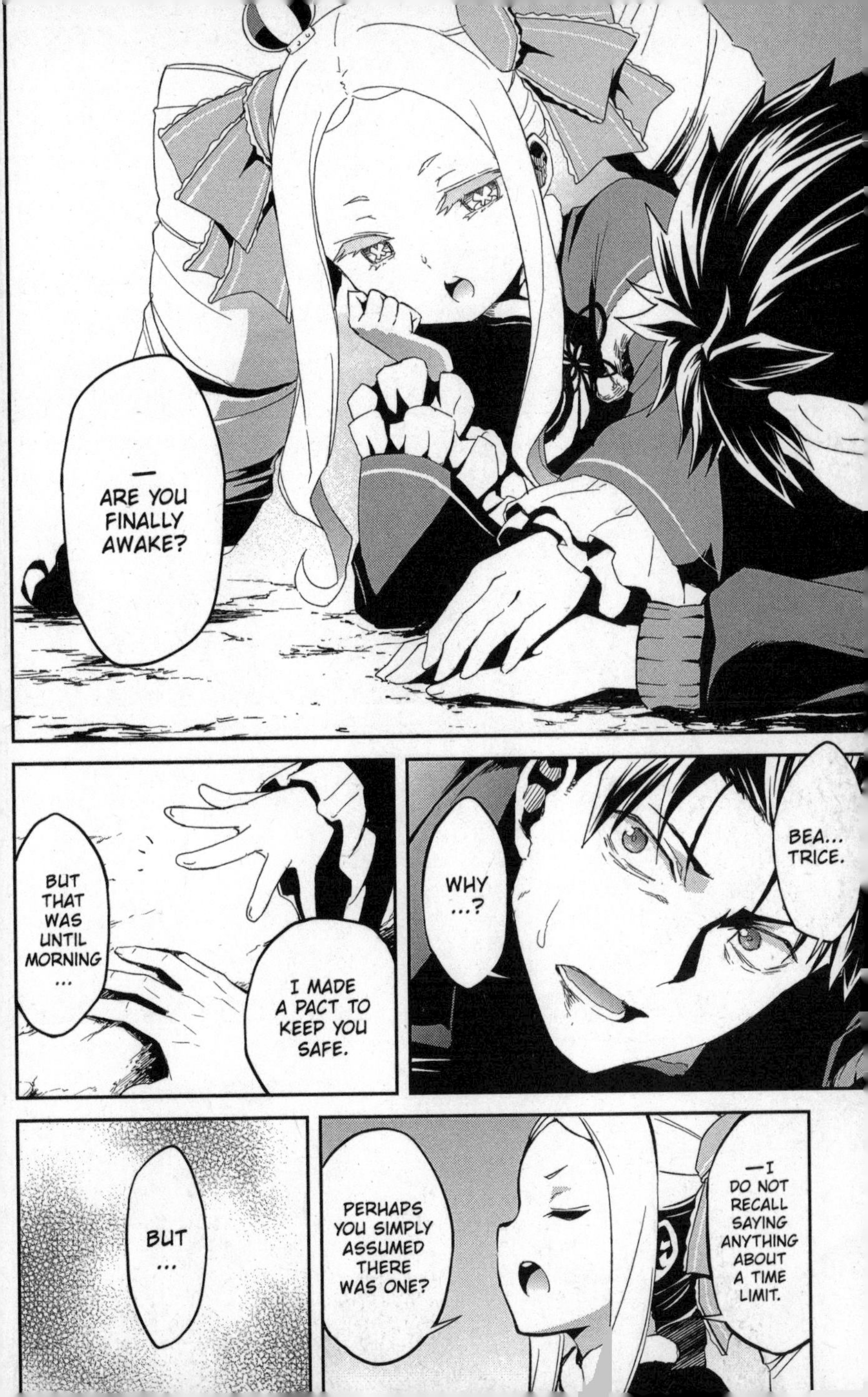
— ARE YOU FINALLY AWAKE?
BEA... TRICE.
WHY ...?
I MADE A PACT TO KEEP YOU SAFE.
BUT THAT WAS UNTIL MORNING ...
—I DO NOT RECALL SAYING ANYTHING ABOUT A TIME LIMIT.
PERHAPS YOU SIMPLY ASSUMED THERE WAS ONE?
BUT ...

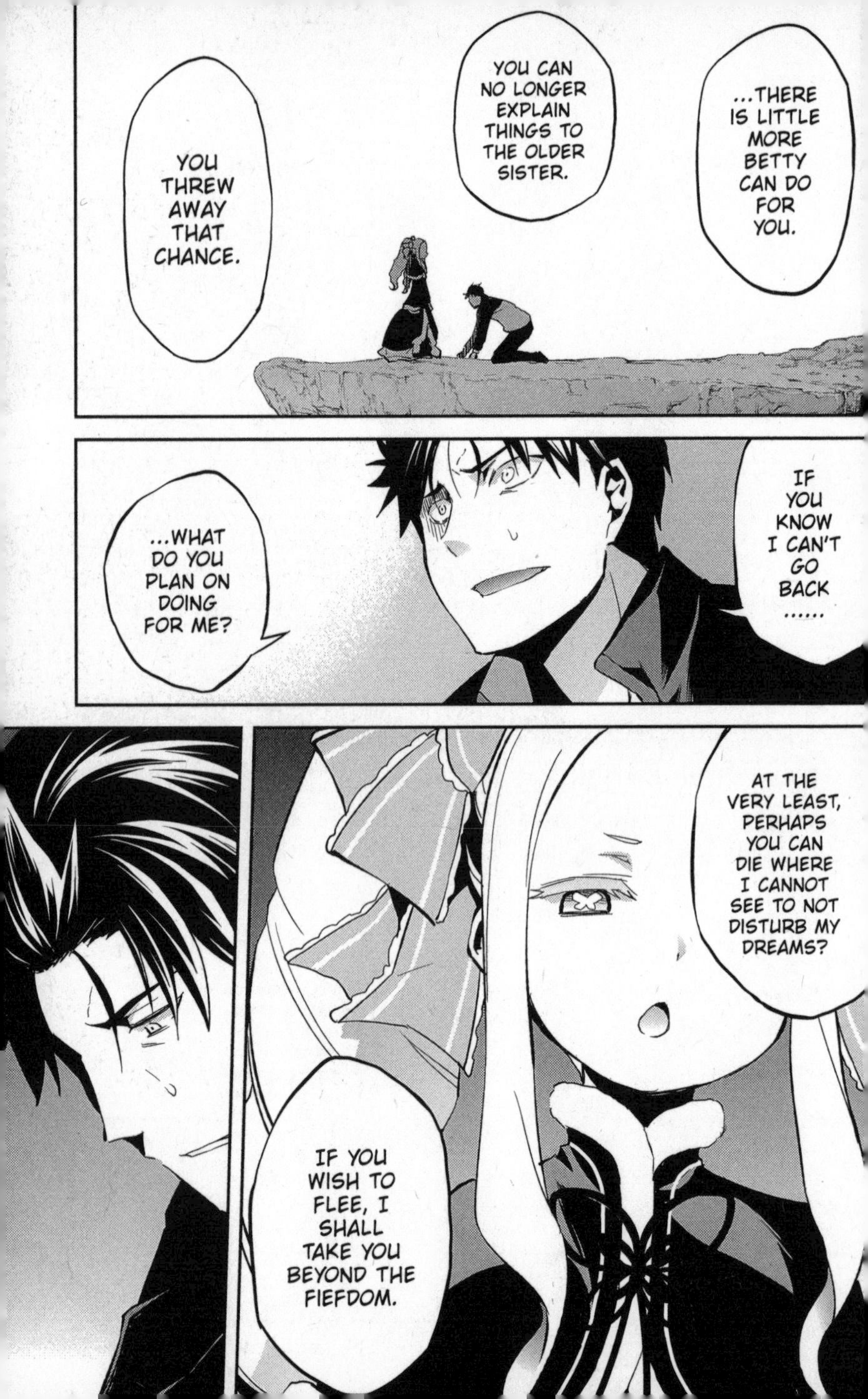
...THERE IS LITTLE MORE BETTY CAN DO FOR YOU.
YOU CAN NO LONGER EXPLAIN THINGS TO THE OLDER SISTER.
YOU THREW AWAY THAT CHANCE.
IF YOU KNOW I CAN'T GO BACK ......
...WHAT DO YOU PLAN ON DOING FOR ME?
AT THE VERY LEAST, PERHAPS YOU CAN DIE WHERE I CANNOT SEE TO NOT DISTURB MY DREAMS?
IF YOU WISH TO FLEE, I SHALL TAKE YOU BEYOND THE FIEFDOM.

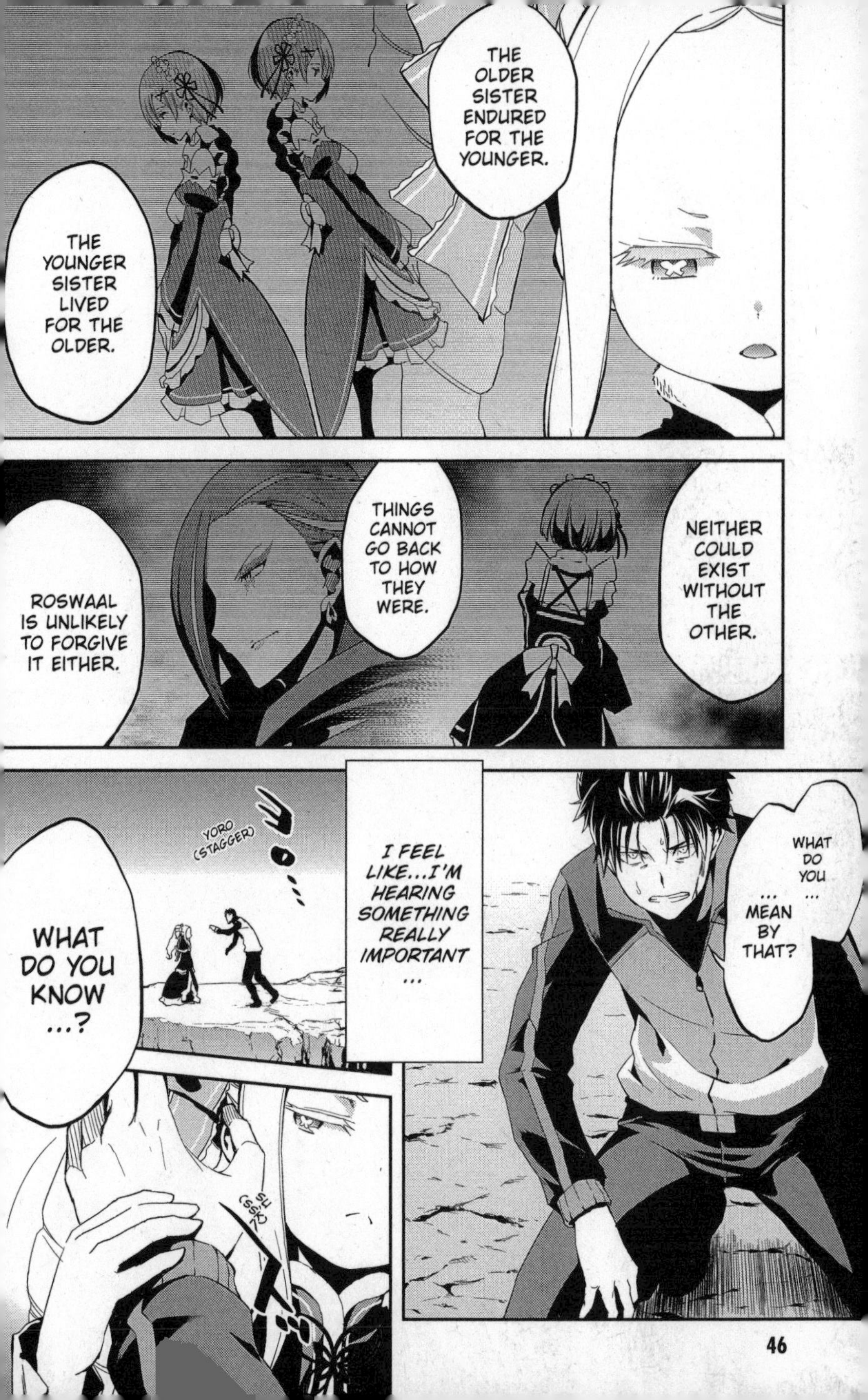
THE OLDER SISTER ENDURED FOR THE YOUNGER.
THE YOUNGER SISTER LIVED FOR THE OLDER.
NEITHER COULD EXIST WITHOUT THE OTHER.
THINGS CANNOT GO BACK TO HOW THEY WERE.
ROSWAAL IS UNLIKELY TO FORGIVE IT EITHER.
WHAT DO YOU ... ... MEAN BY THAT?
I FEEL LIKE...I'M HEARING SOMETHING REALLY IMPORTANT...
YORO (STAGGER)
WHAT DO YOU KNOW ...?
SU (SSK)

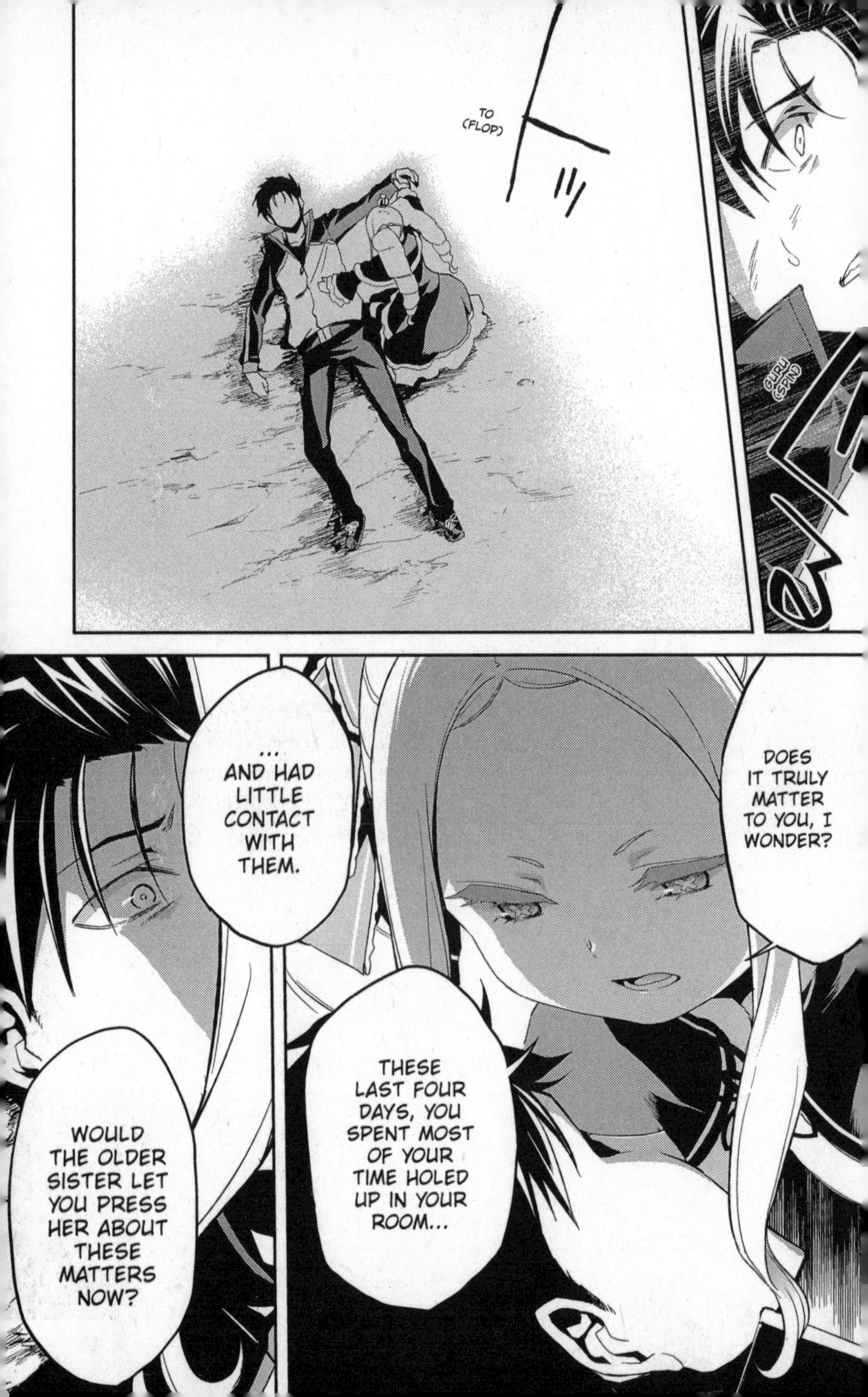

GURU (SPIN)
TO (FLOP)
DOES IT TRULY MATTER TO YOU, I WONDER?
THESE LAST FOUR DAYS, YOU SPENT MOST OF YOUR TIME HOLED UP IN YOUR ROOM...
... AND HAD LITTLE CONTACT WITH THEM.
WOULD THE OLDER SISTER LET YOU PRESS HER ABOUT THESE MATTERS NOW?

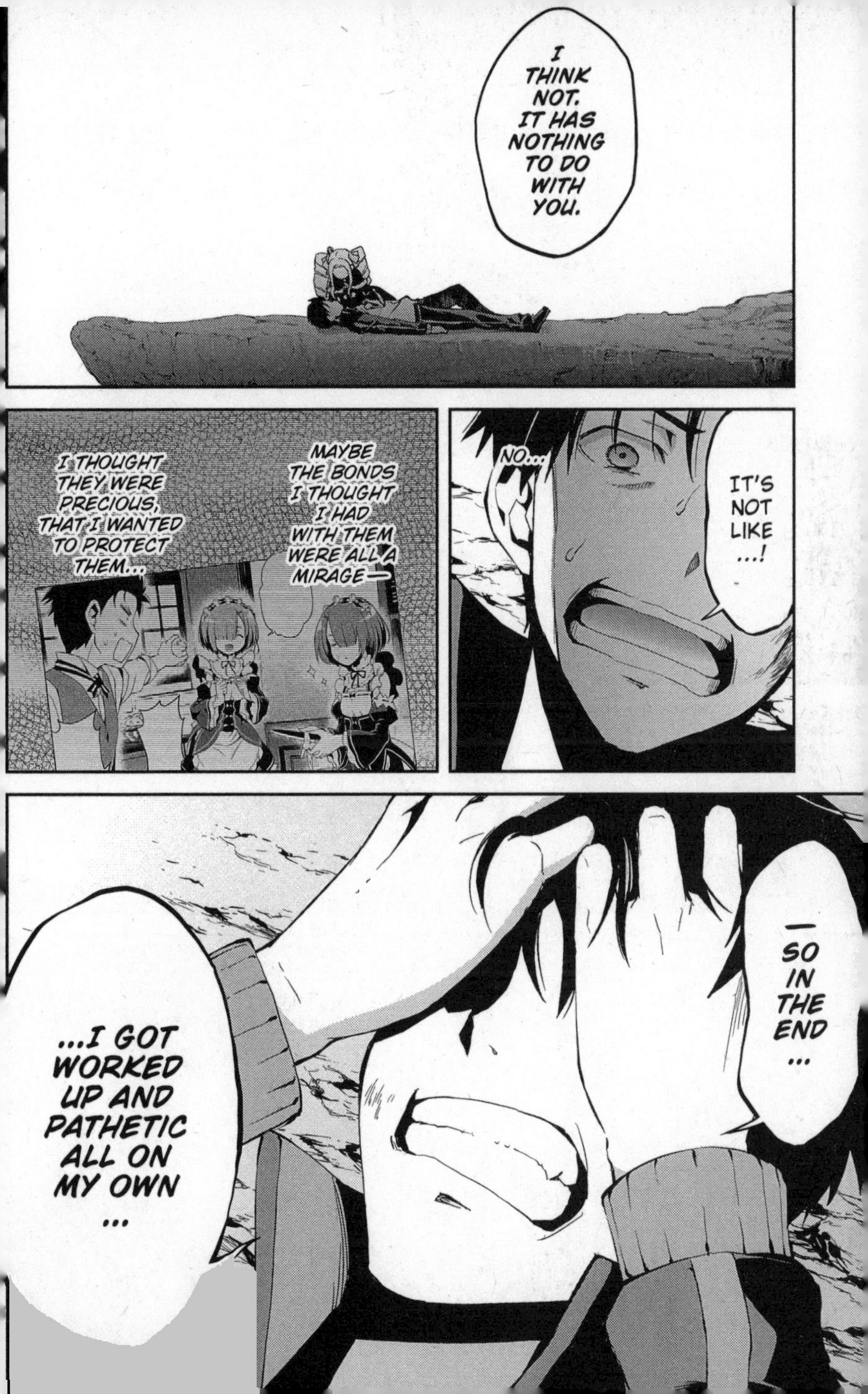
I THINK NOT. IT HAS NOTHING TO DO WITH YOU.
NO...
IT'S NOT LIKE ...!
MAYBE THE BONDS I THOUGHT I HAD WITH THEM WERE ALL A MIRAGE—
I THOUGHT THEY WERE PRECIOUS, THAT I WANTED TO PROTECT THEM...
—SO IN THE END ...
...I GOT WORKED UP AND PATHETIC ALL ON MY OWN ...

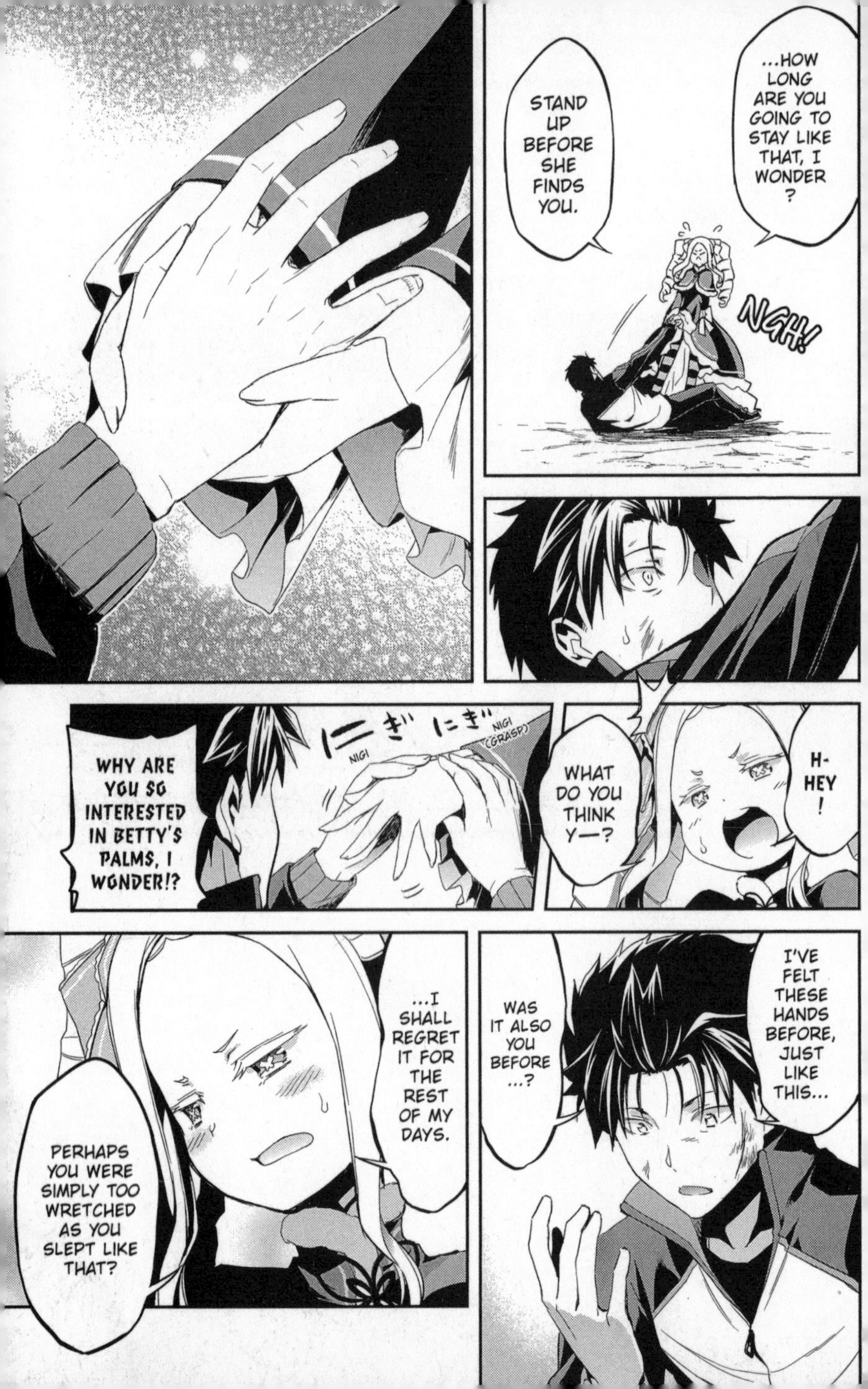
...HOW LONG ARE YOU GOING TO STAY LIKE THAT, I WONDER?
STAND UP BEFORE SHE FINDS YOU.
NGH!
H-HEY!
WHAT DO YOU THINK Y—?
にぎ にぎ
NIGI
NIGI (GRASP)
WHY ARE YOU SO INTERESTED IN BETTY'S PALMS, I WONDER!?
I'VE FELT THESE HANDS BEFORE, JUST LIKE THIS...
WAS IT ALSO YOU BEFORE...?
...I SHALL REGRET IT FOR THE REST OF MY DAYS.
PERHAPS YOU WERE SIMPLY TOO WRETCHED AS YOU SLEPT LIKE THAT?

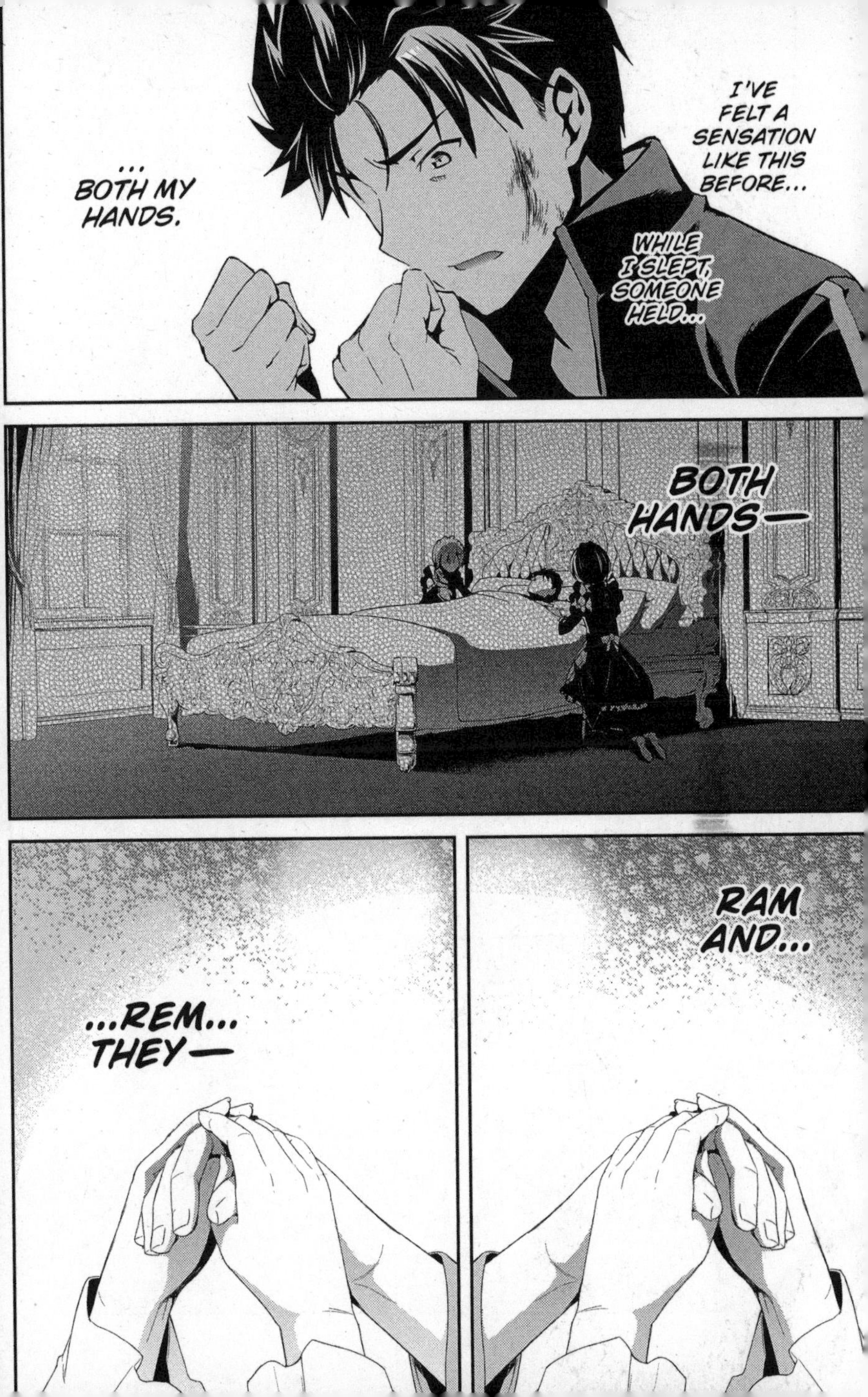
I'VE FELT A SENSATION LIKE THIS BEFORE...
WHILE I SLEPT, SOMEONE HELD...
...BOTH MY HANDS.
BOTH HANDS—
RAM AND...
...REM... THEY—

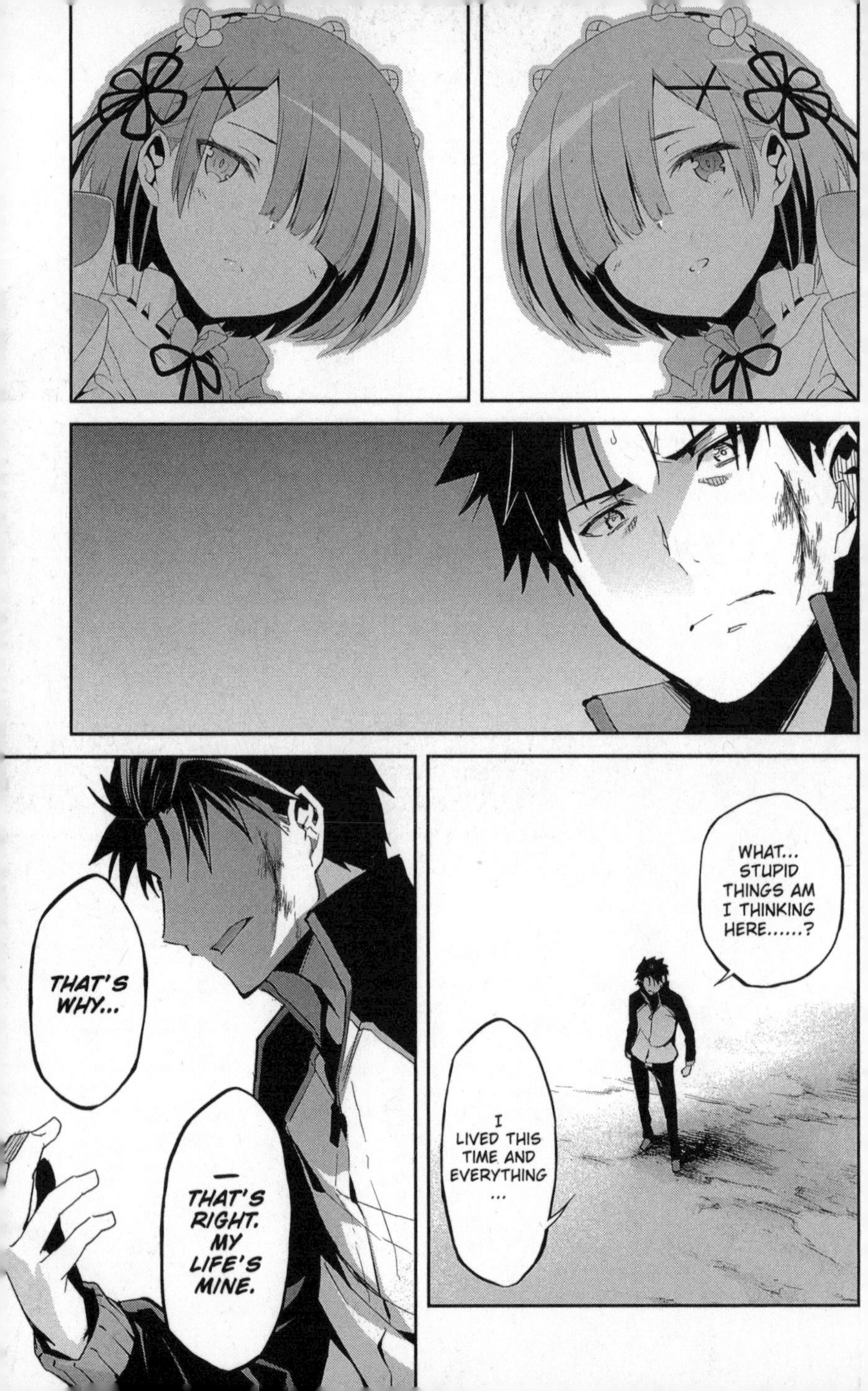
WHAT... STUPID THINGS AM I THINKING HERE......?
I LIVED THIS TIME AND EVERYTHING ...
THAT'S WHY...
— THAT'S RIGHT. MY LIFE'S MINE.

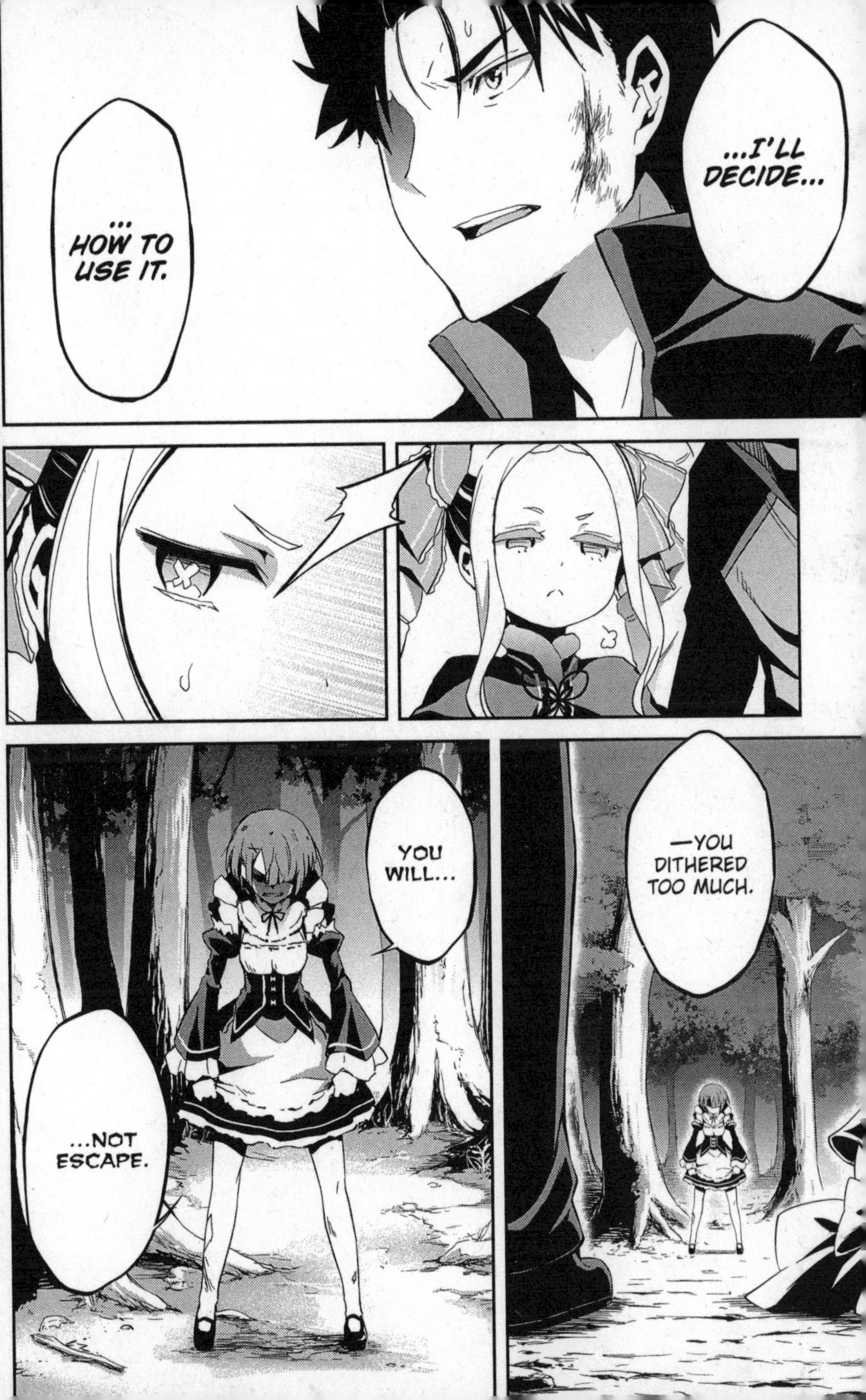
...I'LL DECIDE...
... HOW TO USE IT.
—YOU DITHERED TOO MUCH.
YOU WILL...
...NOT ESCAPE.

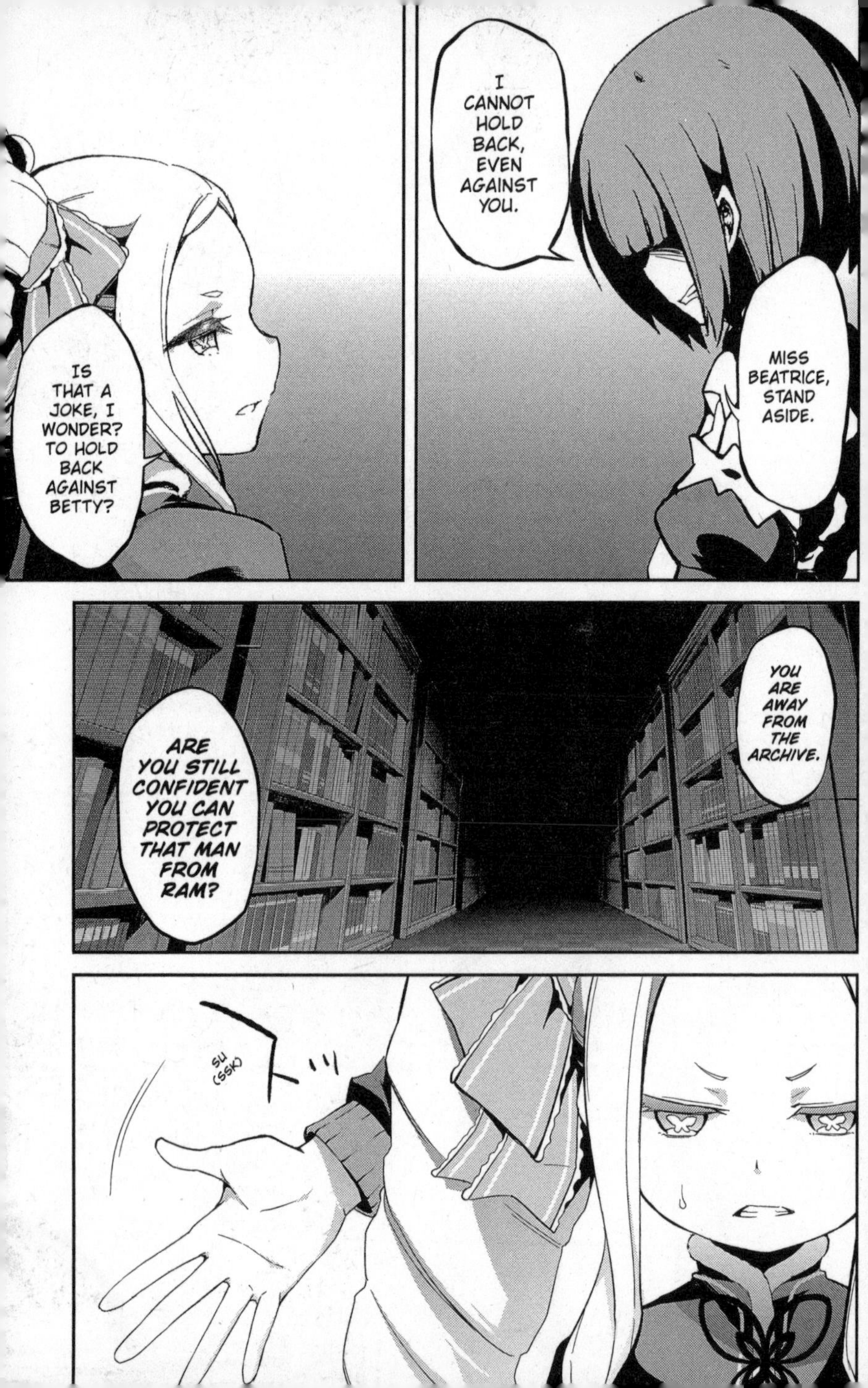
MISS BEATRICE, STAND ASIDE.
I CANNOT HOLD BACK, EVEN AGAINST YOU.
IS THAT A JOKE, I WONDER? TO HOLD BACK AGAINST BETTY?
YOU ARE AWAY FROM THE ARCHIVE.
ARE YOU STILL CONFIDENT YOU CAN PROTECT THAT MAN FROM RAM?
SU (SSK)

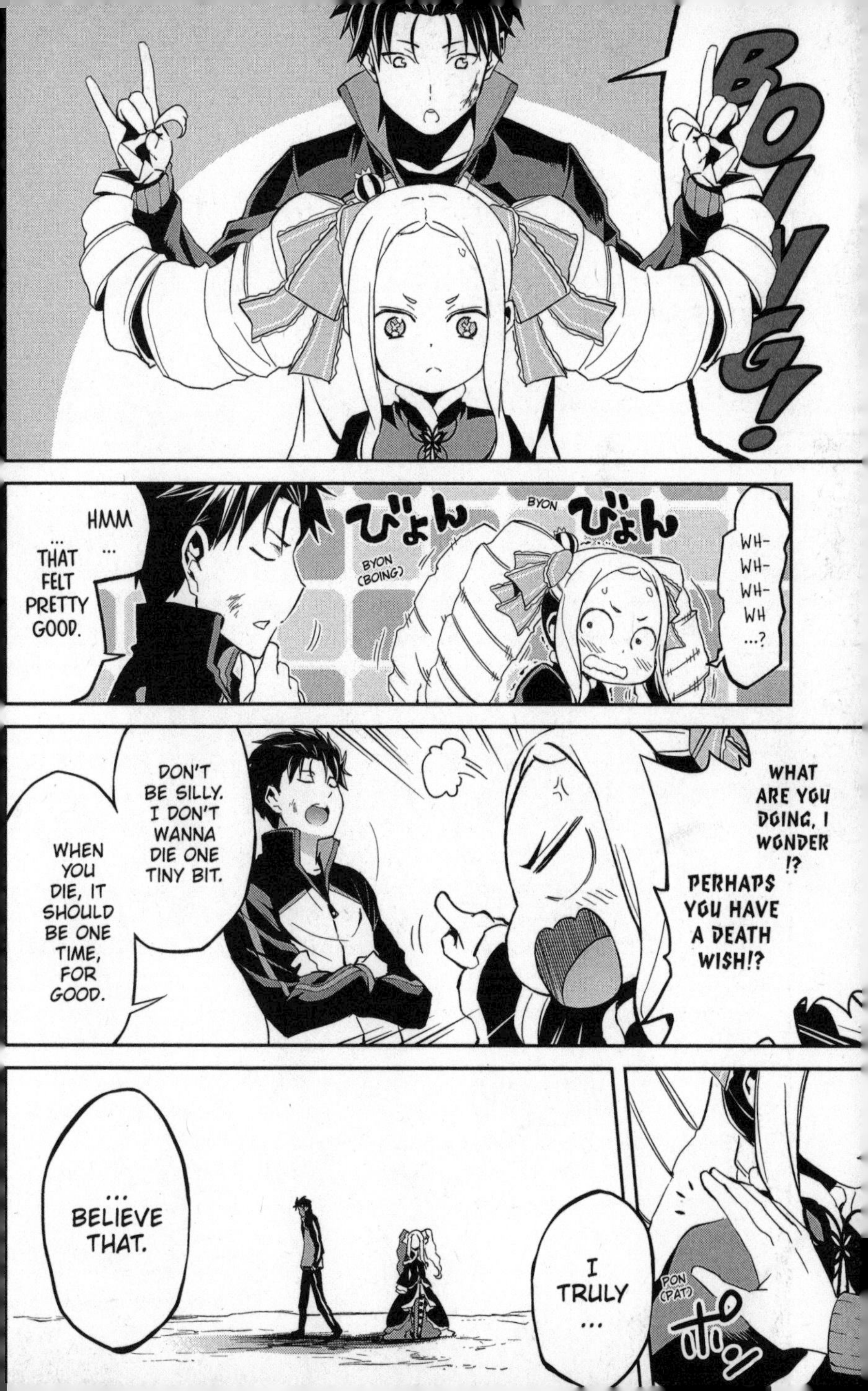
BOING!
WH- WH- WH- WH ...?
びょん
BYON
びょん
BYON (BOING)
HMM ... THAT FELT PRETTY GOOD.
WHAT ARE YOU DOING, I WONDER!?
PERHAPS YOU HAVE A DEATH WISH!?
DON'T BE SILLY. I DON'T WANNA DIE ONE TINY BIT.
WHEN YOU DIE, IT SHOULD BE ONE TIME, FOR GOOD.
ぽん
PON (PAT)
I TRULY ...
... BELIEVE THAT.

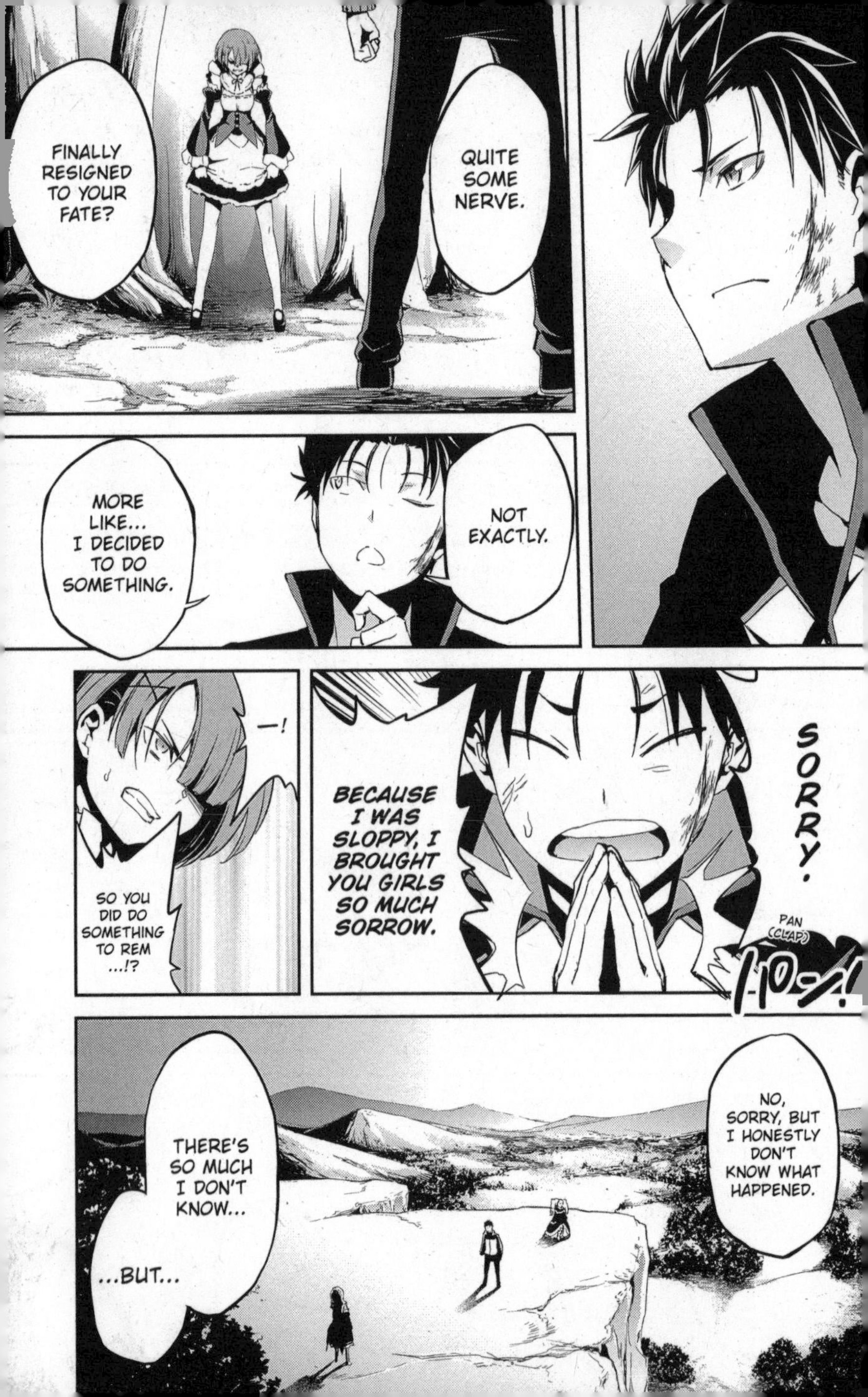
QUITE SOME NERVE.
FINALLY RESIGNED TO YOUR FATE?
NOT EXACTLY.
MORE LIKE... I DECIDED TO DO SOMETHING.
SORRY.
PAN (CLAP)
BECAUSE I WAS SLOPPY, I BROUGHT YOU GIRLS SO MUCH SORROW.
—!
SO YOU DID DO SOMETHING TO REM ...!?
NO, SORRY, BUT I HONESTLY DON'T KNOW WHAT HAPPENED.
THERE'S SO MUCH I DON'T KNOW...
...BUT...

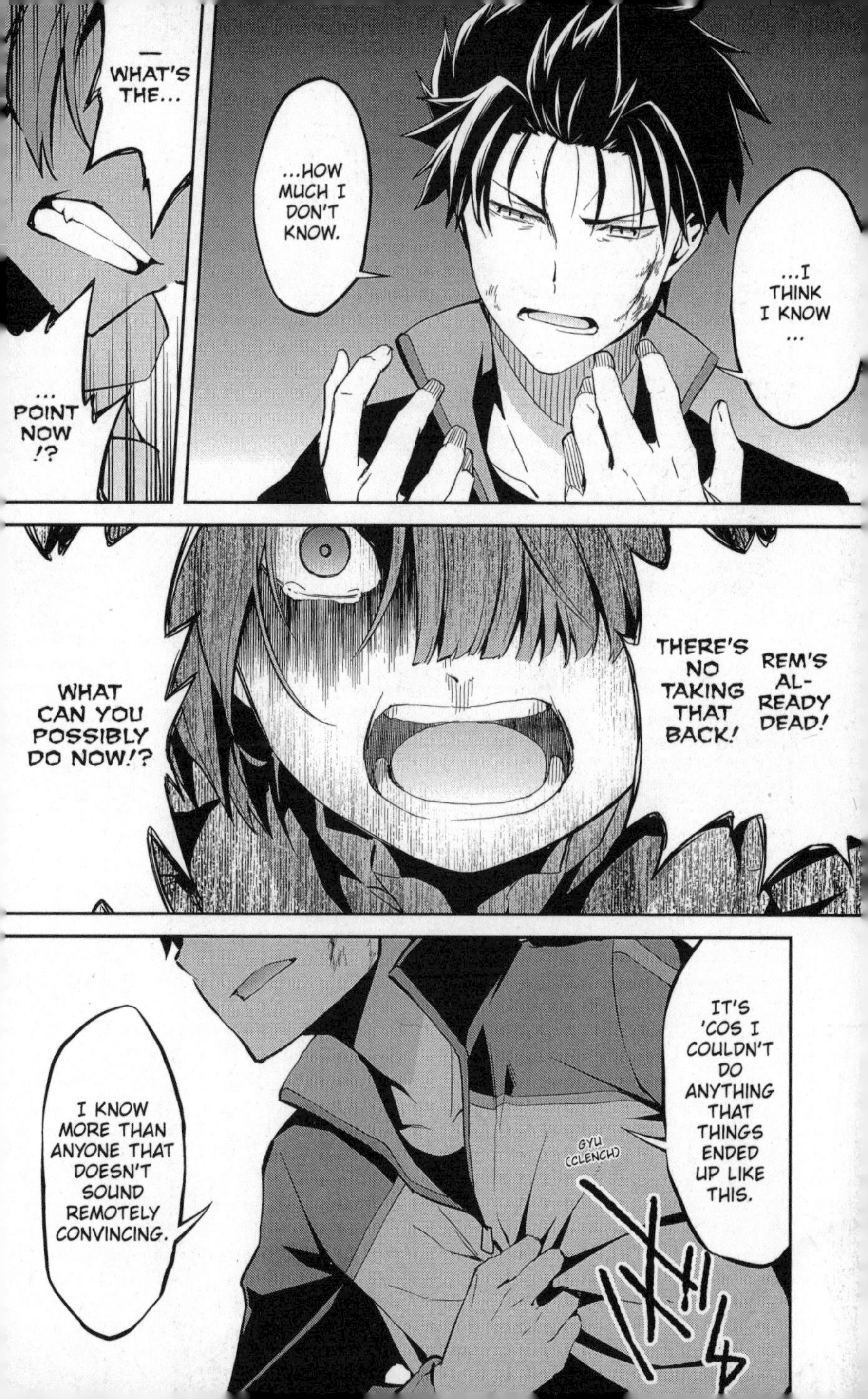
...I THINK I KNOW ...
...HOW MUCH I DON'T KNOW.
—WHAT'S THE...
...POINT NOW!?
REM'S AL-READY DEAD!
THERE'S NO TAKING THAT BACK!
WHAT CAN YOU POSSIBLY DO NOW!?
IT'S 'COS I COULDN'T DO ANYTHING THAT THINGS ENDED UP LIKE THIS.
GYU (CLENCH)
I KNOW MORE THAN ANYONE THAT DOESN'T SOUND REMOTELY CONVINCING.

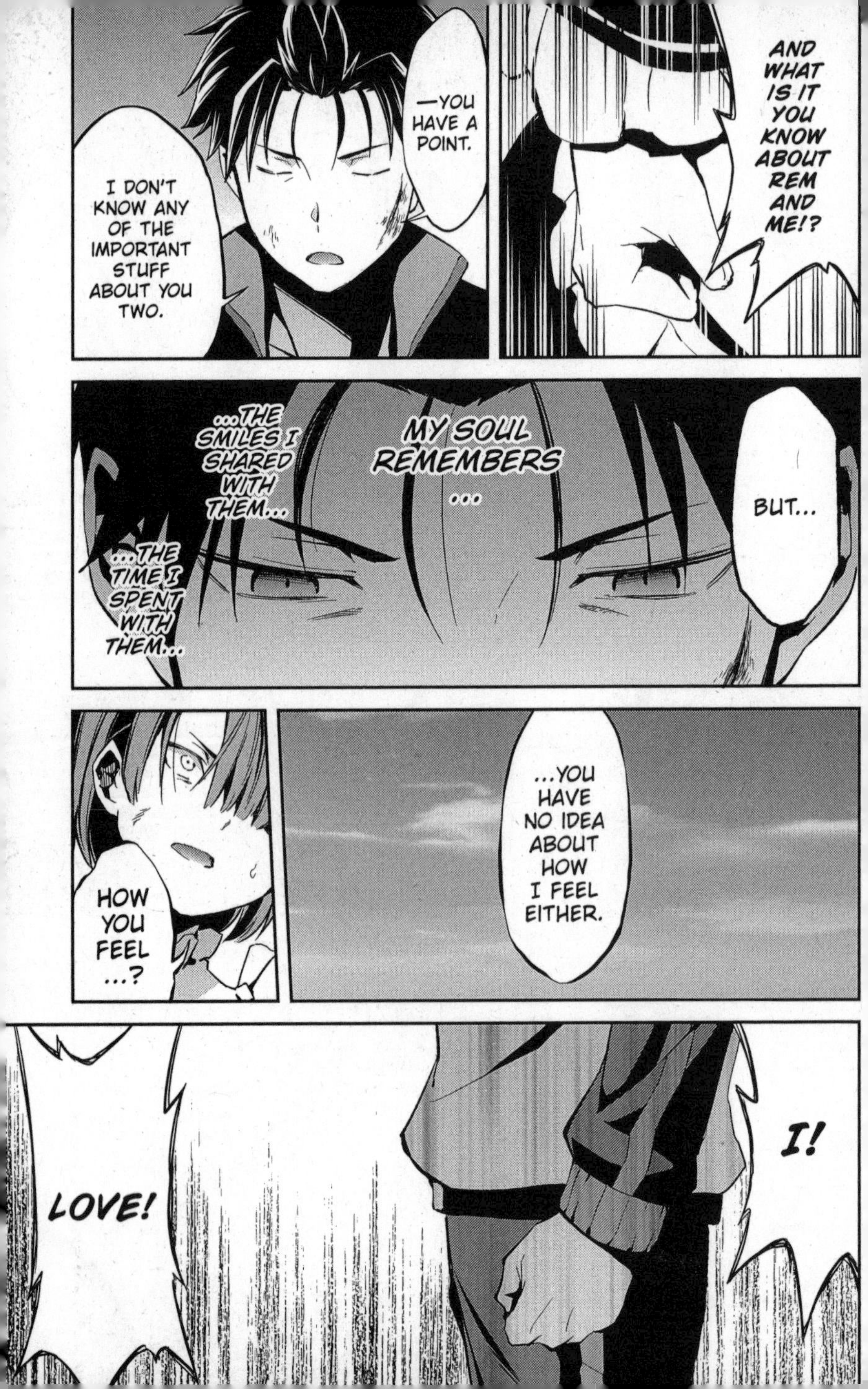
AND WHAT IS IT YOU KNOW ABOUT REM AND ME!?
—YOU HAVE A POINT.
I DON'T KNOW ANY OF THE IMPORTANT STUFF ABOUT YOU TWO.
BUT...
MY SOUL REMEMBERS...
...THE SMILES I SHARED WITH THEM...
...THE TIME I SPENT WITH THEM...
...YOU HAVE NO IDEA ABOUT HOW I FEEL EITHER.
HOW YOU FEEL...?
I!
LOVE!

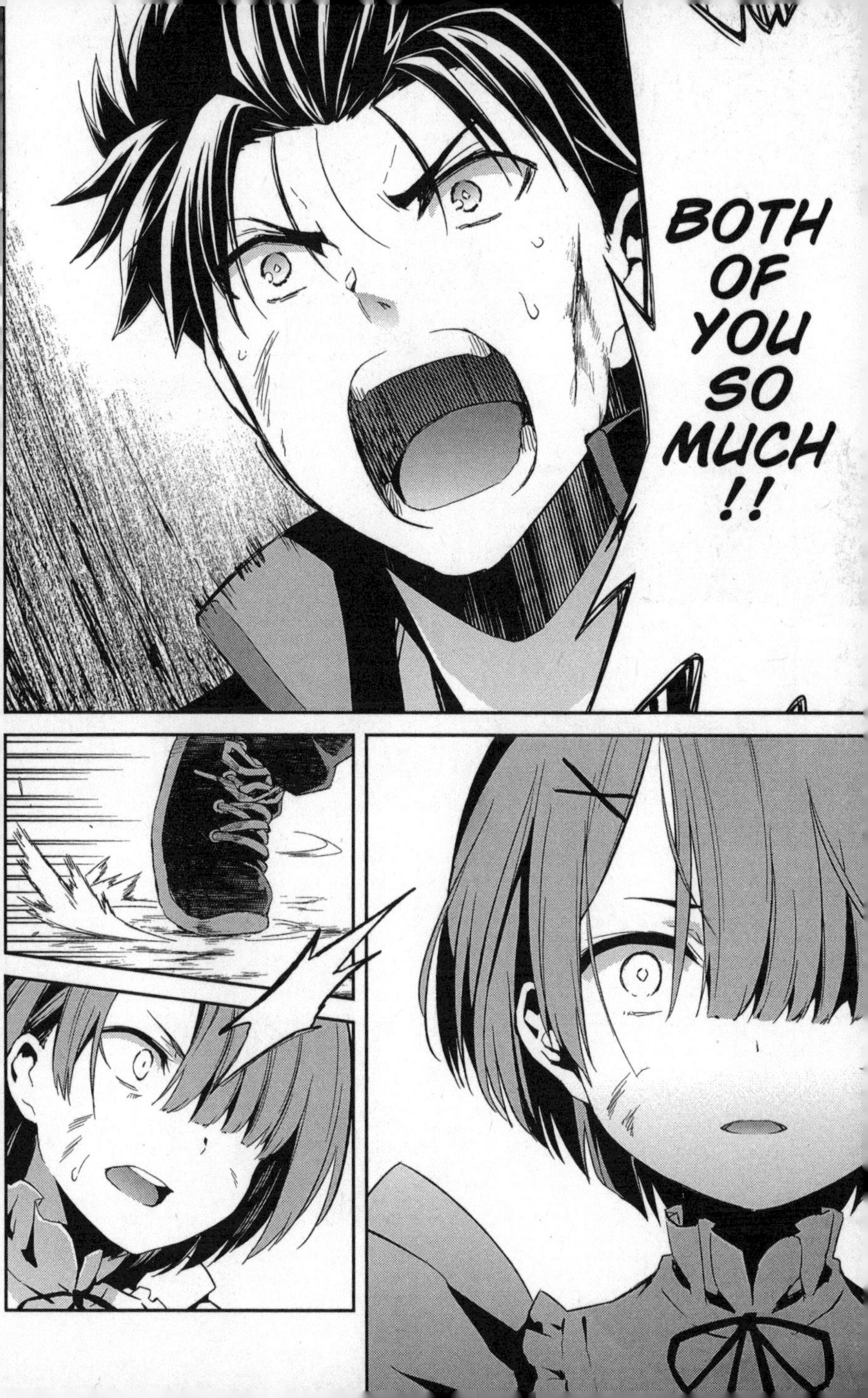
BOTH OF YOU SO MUCH!!

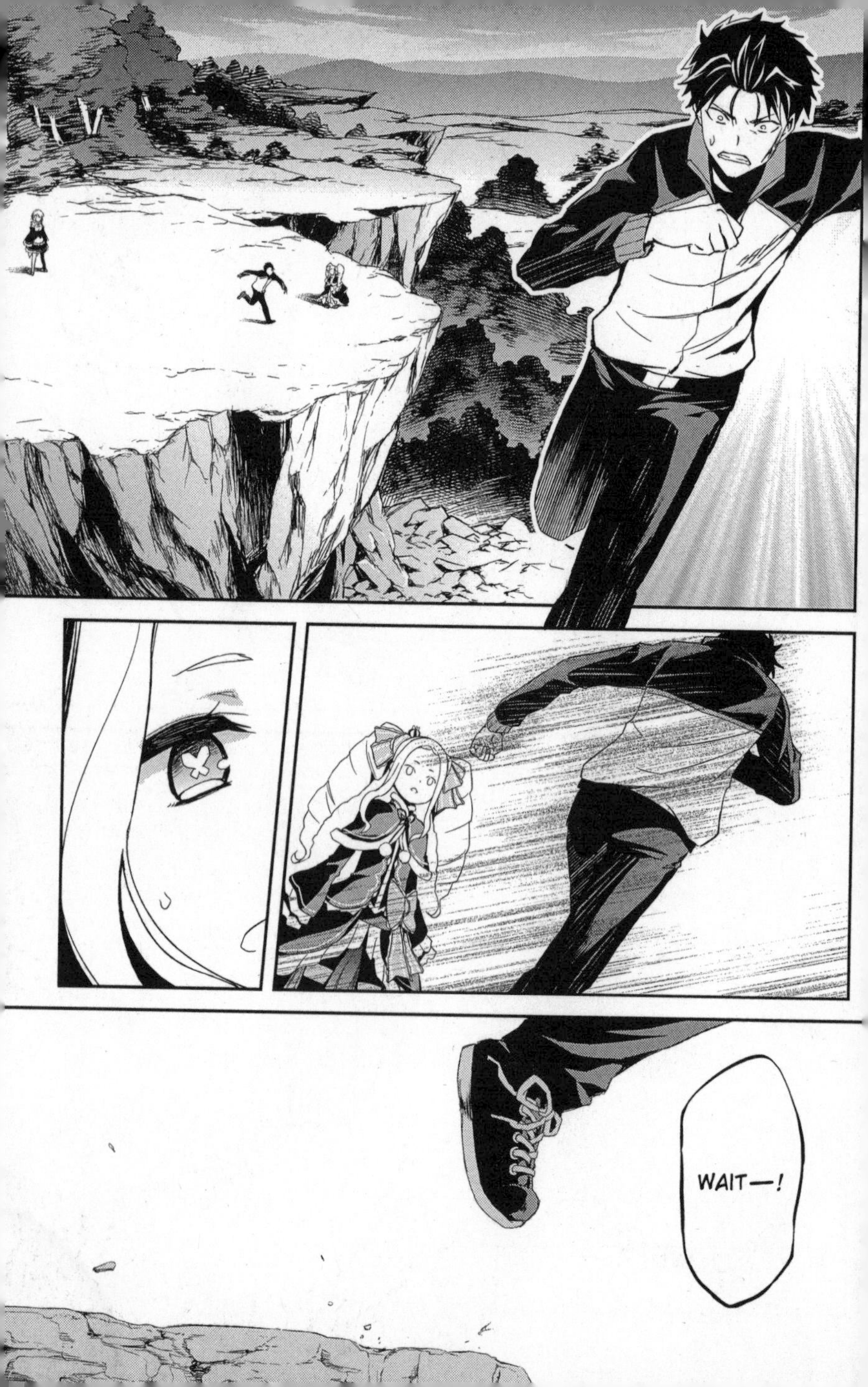
WAIT—!

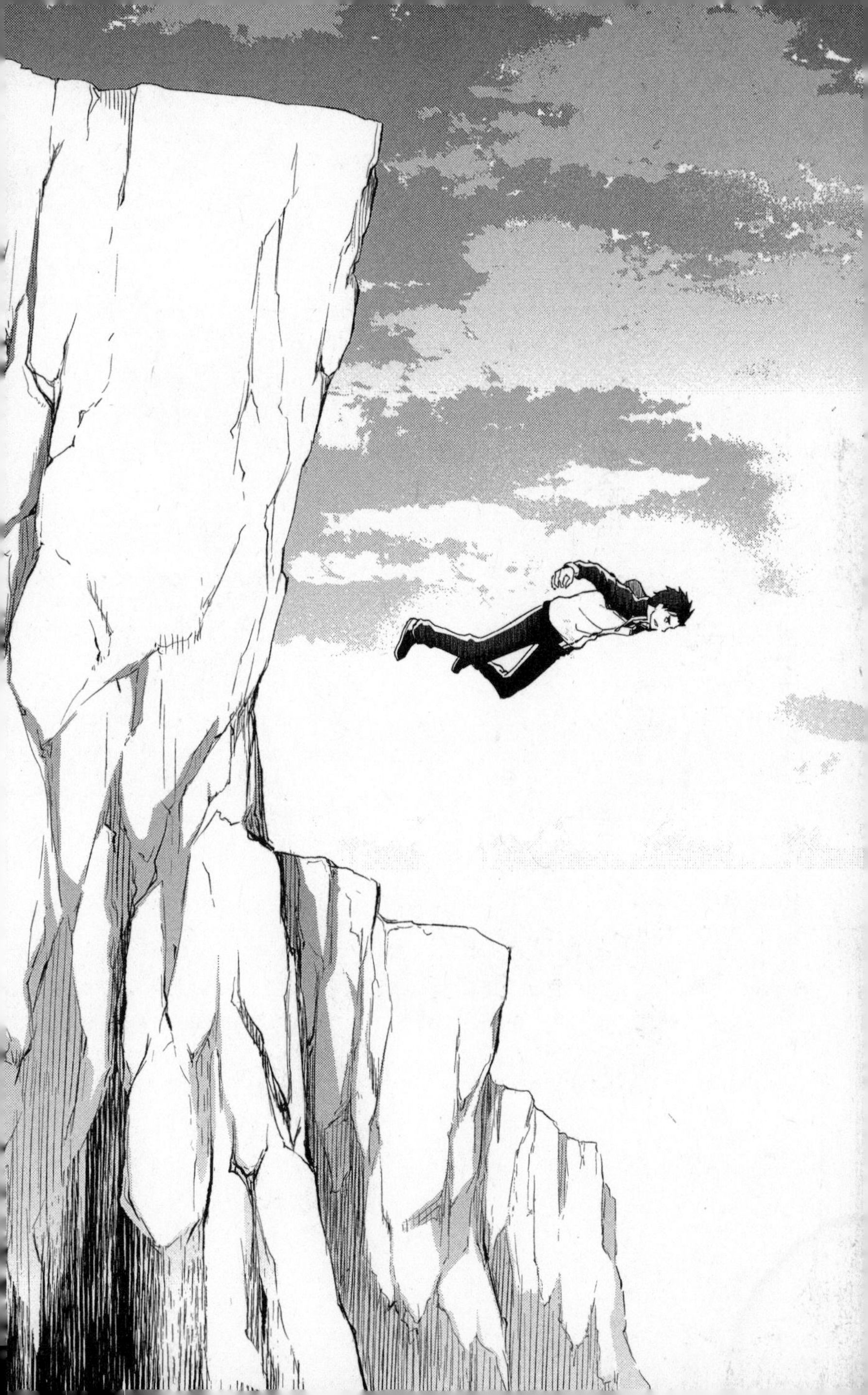

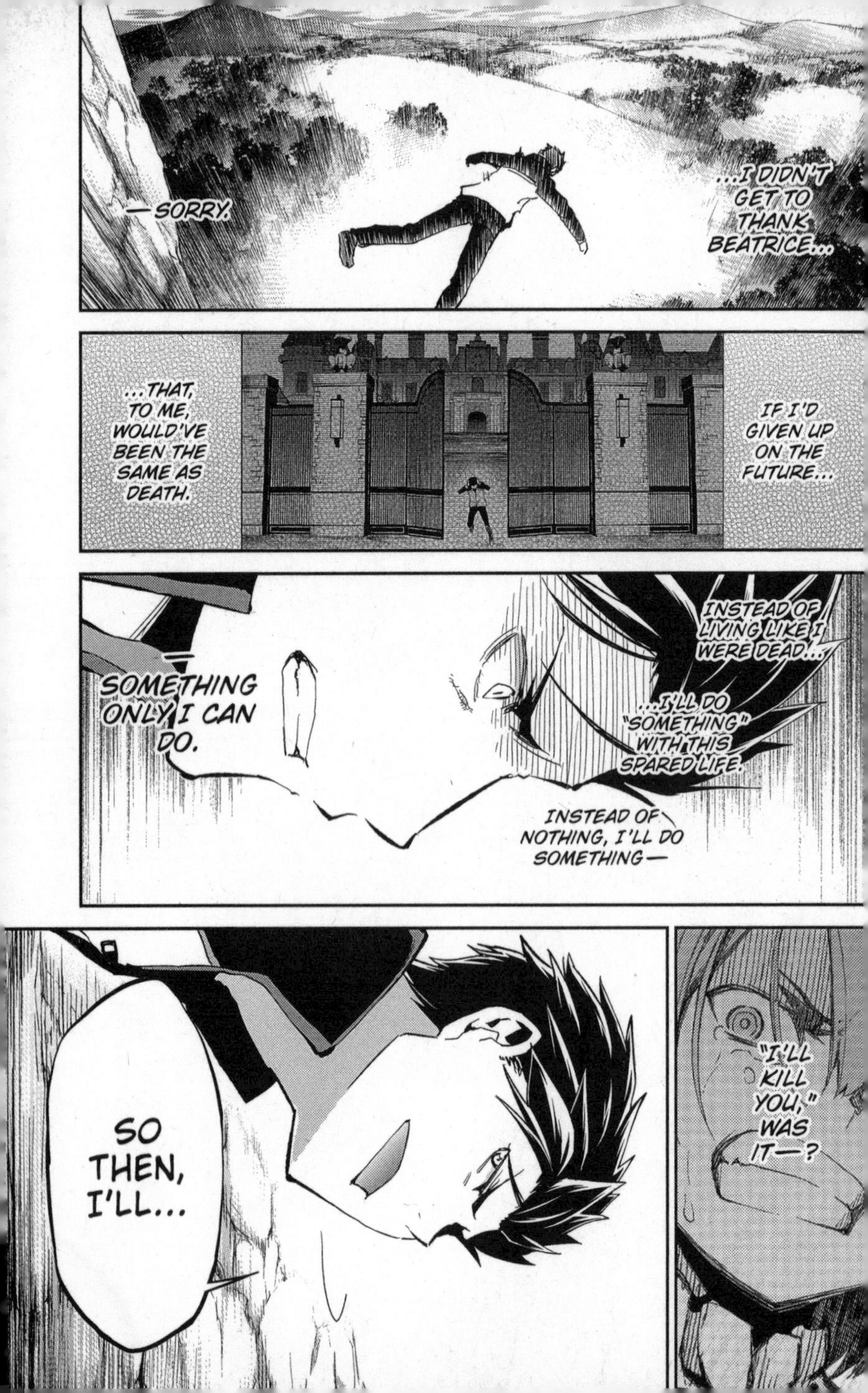
...I DIDN'T GET TO THANK BEATRICE...
—SORRY.
IF I'D GIVEN UP ON THE FUTURE...
...THAT, TO ME, WOULD'VE BEEN THE SAME AS DEATH.
INSTEAD OF LIVING LIKE I WERE DEAD...
...I'LL DO "SOMETHING" WITH THIS SPARED LIFE.
INSTEAD OF NOTHING, I'LL DO SOMETHING—
SOMETHING ONLY I CAN DO.
"I'LL KILL YOU," WAS IT—?
SO THEN, I'LL...

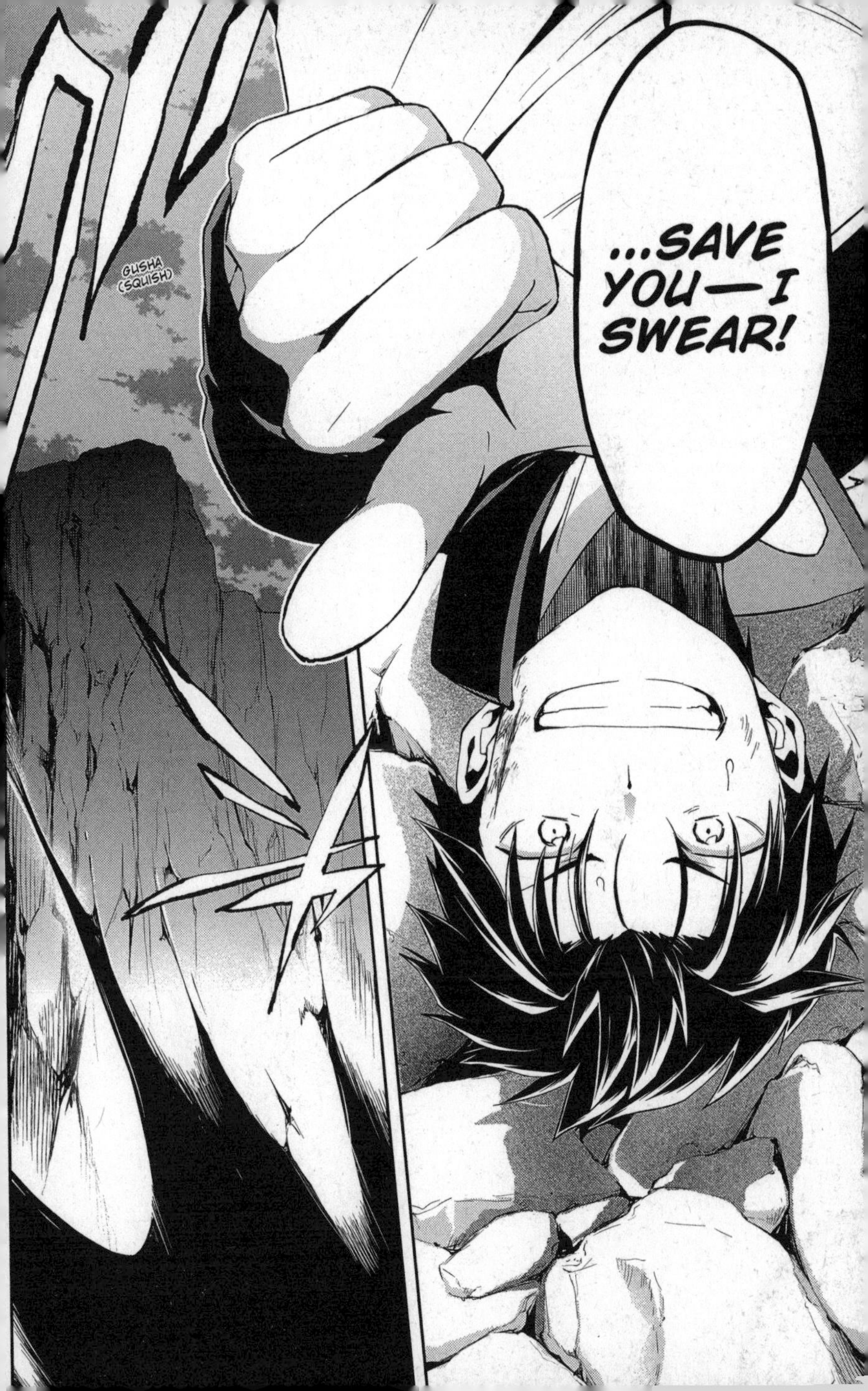
...SAVE YOU—I SWEAR!
GUSHA (SQUISH)

Yes! Subaru has become a main character!

"Suicide"...
I believe this to be the defining image underlying events going forward. Pressed by circumstances, Subaru was seduced by death as an easy escape, but he could not even do that.

Yet, Subaru jumped.

If not for his sake, then for whom—?

This was a forward-looking "suicide," hardening his resolve and embracing "death" to use a future that ought not exist to overcome a seemingly impassable hurdle.

It was a decision only Subaru could make.

Pretty cool, huh?

The only ability Subaru Natsuki gets when he's summoned to another world is time travel via his own death. But to save her, he'll die as many times as it takes.

Re:ZERO -Starting Life in Another World-

A Week at the Mansion

Episode 12 Subaru Natsuki's Restart

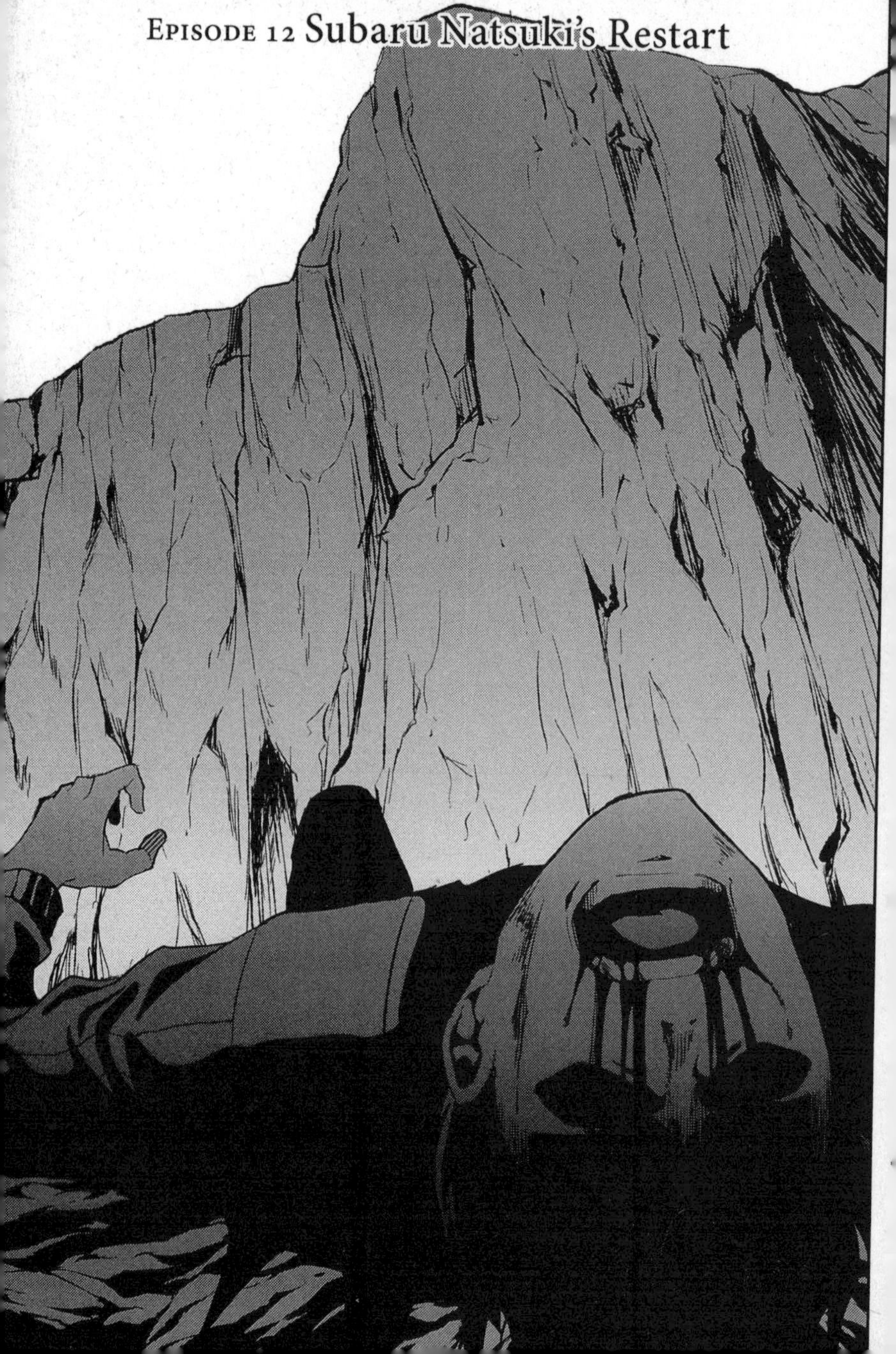

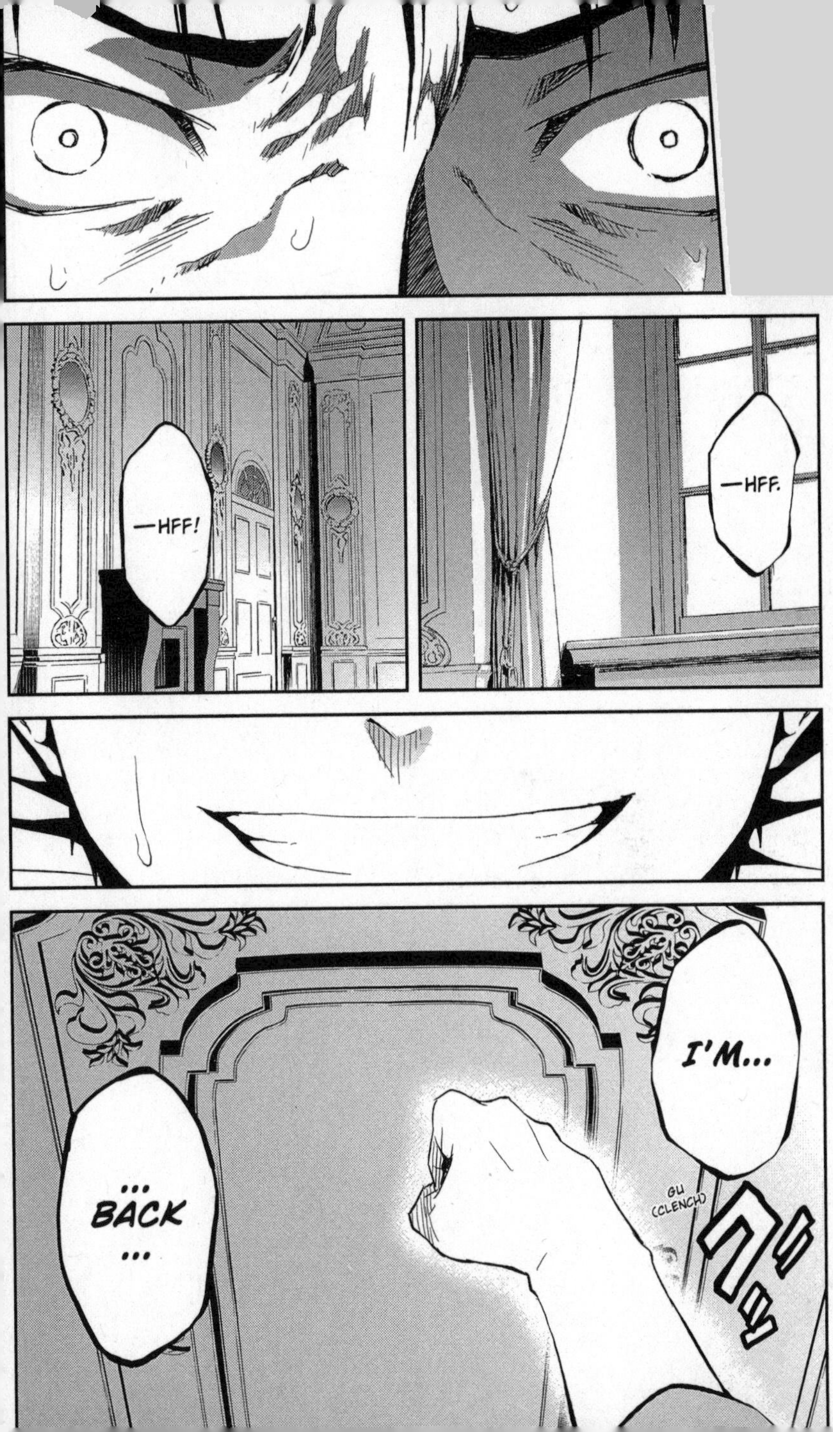
—HFF.
—HFF!
I'M...
GU (CLENCH)
...BACK...

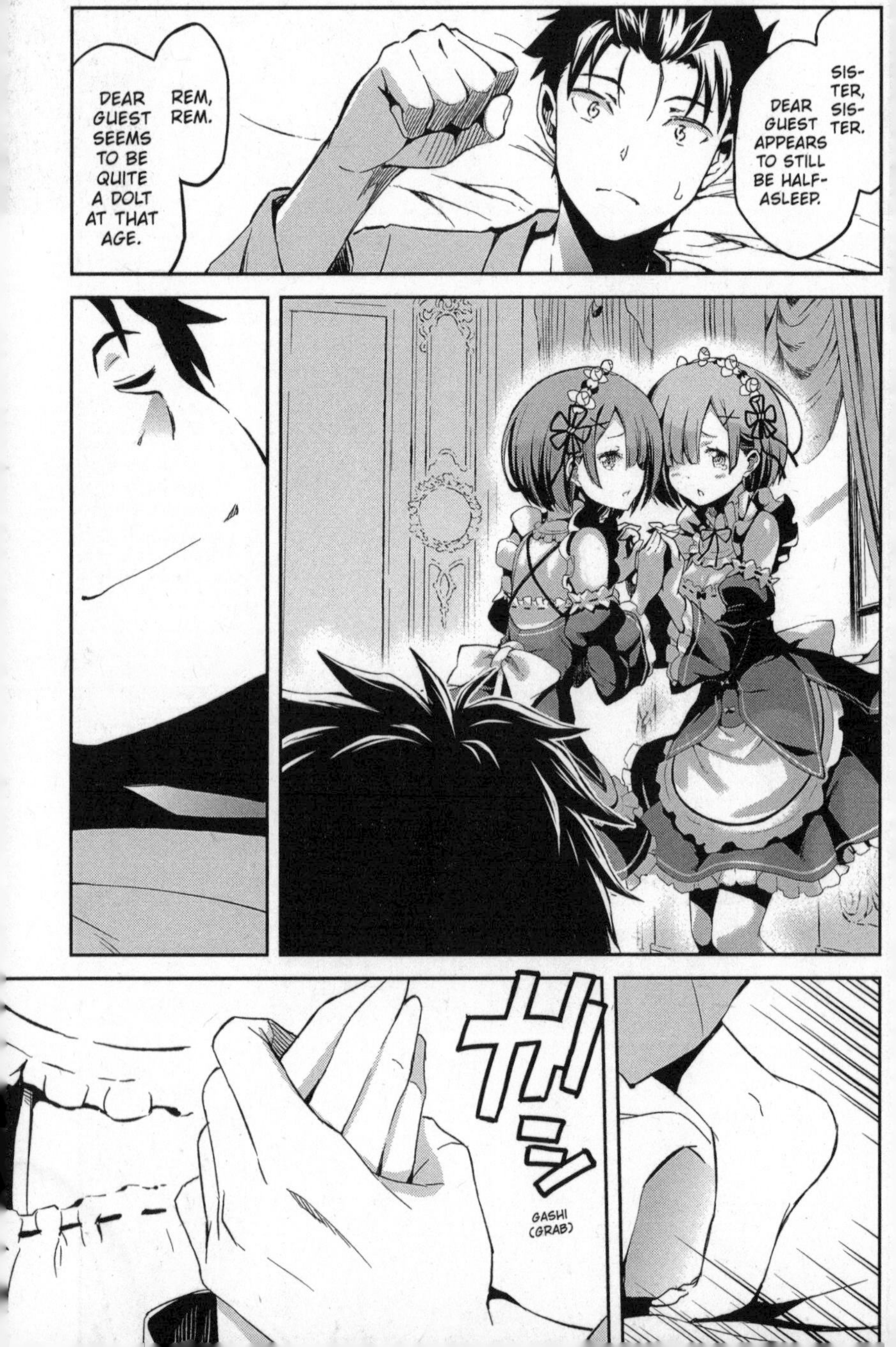
SISTER, SISTER. DEAR GUEST APPEARS TO STILL BE HALF-ASLEEP.
REM, REM. DEAR GUEST SEEMS TO BE QUITE A DOLT AT THAT AGE.
ガシッ
GASHI (GRAB)

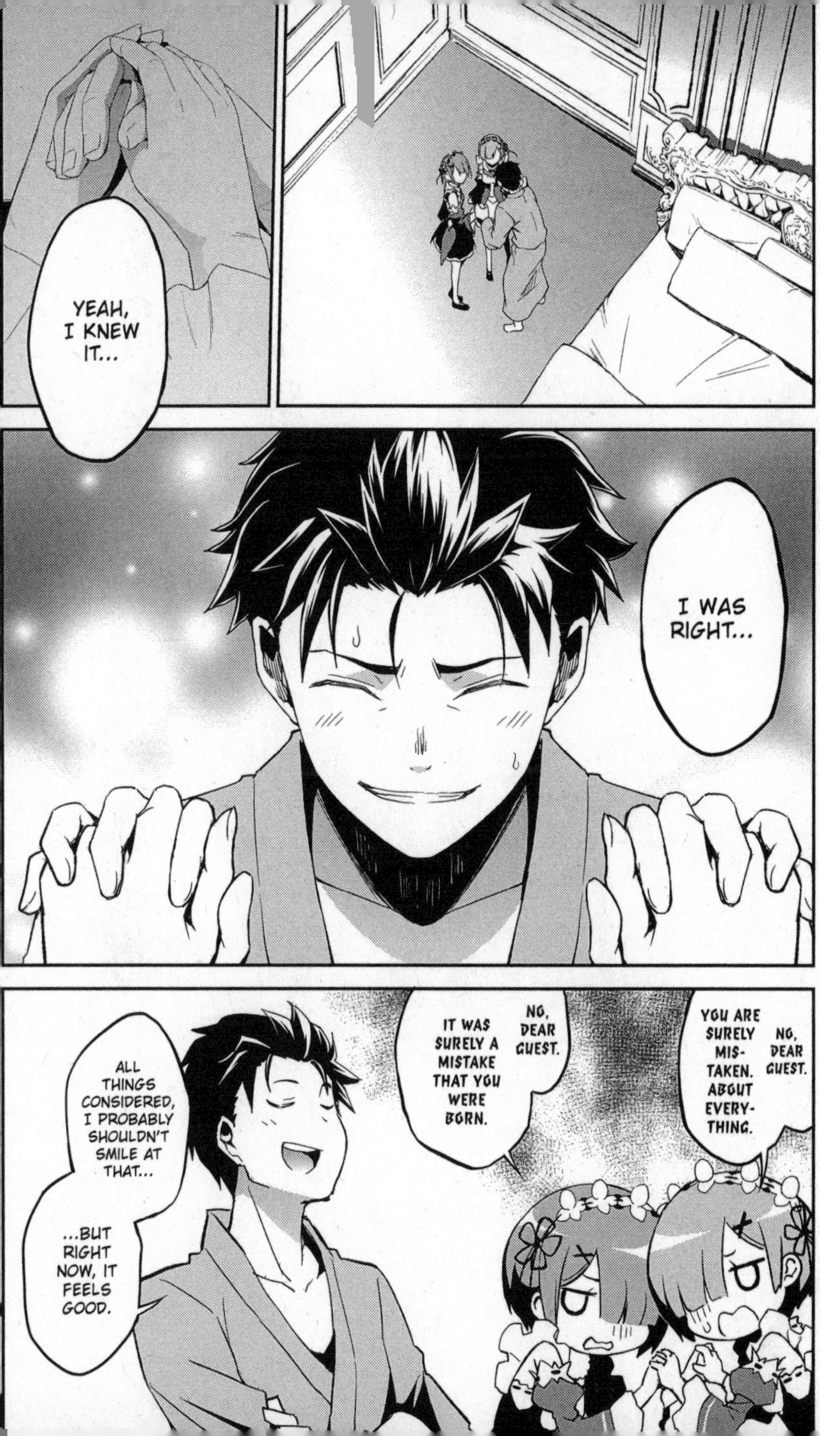
YEAH, I KNEW IT...
I WAS RIGHT...
NO, DEAR GUEST.
YOU ARE SURELY MIS-TAKEN. ABOUT EVERY-THING.
NO, DEAR GUEST.
IT WAS SURELY A MISTAKE THAT YOU WERE BORN.
ALL THINGS CONSIDERED, I PROBABLY SHOULDN'T SMILE AT THAT...
...BUT RIGHT NOW, IT FEELS GOOD.

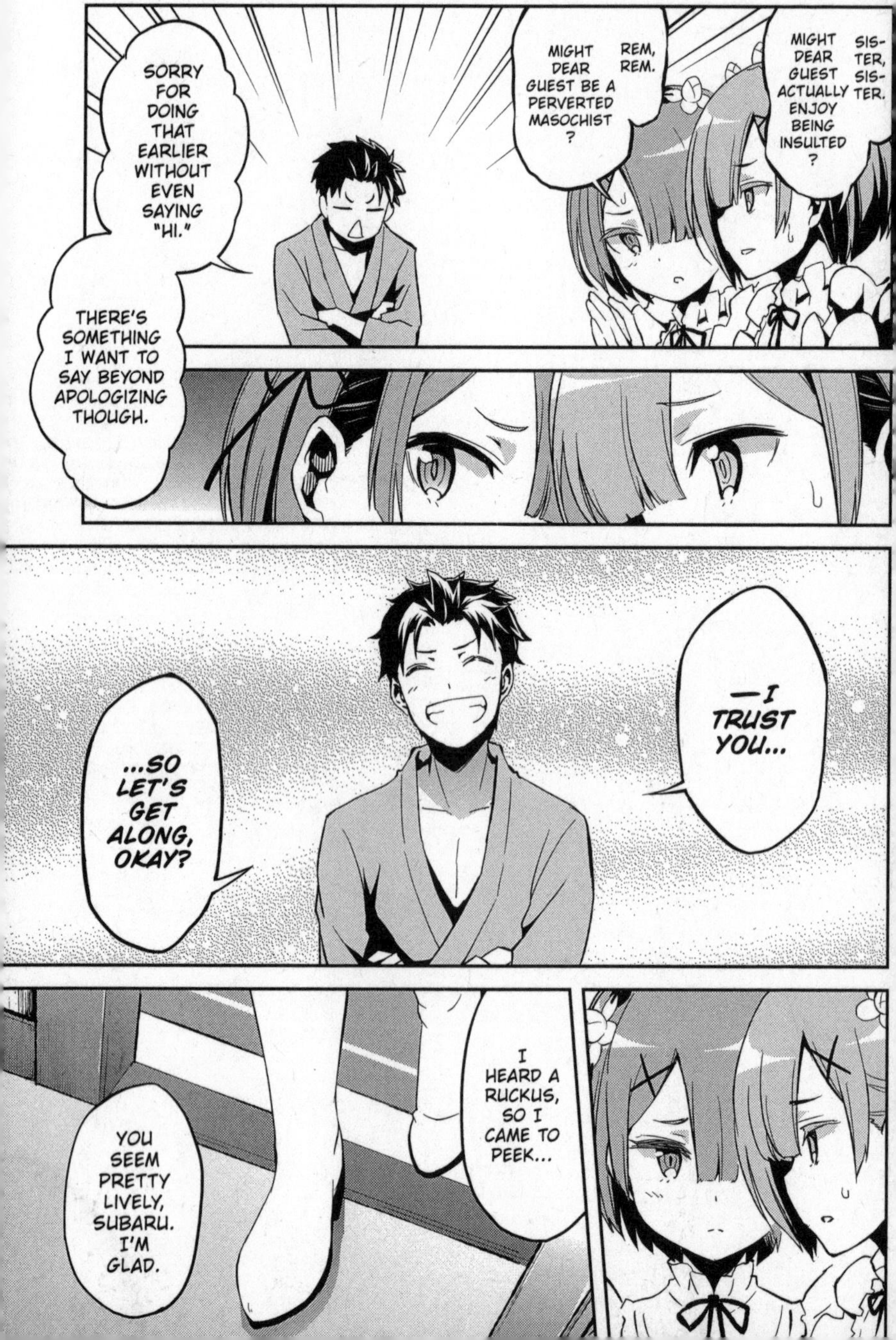
SISTER, SISTER.
MIGHT DEAR GUEST ACTUALLY ENJOY BEING INSULTED?
REM, REM.
MIGHT DEAR GUEST BE A PERVERTED MASOCHIST?
SORRY FOR DOING THAT EARLIER WITHOUT EVEN SAYING "HI."
THERE'S SOMETHING I WANT TO SAY BEYOND APOLOGIZING THOUGH.
—I TRUST YOU...
...SO LET'S GET ALONG, OKAY?
I HEARD A RUCKUS, SO I CAME TO PEEK...
YOU SEEM PRETTY LIVELY, SUBARU. I'M GLAD.

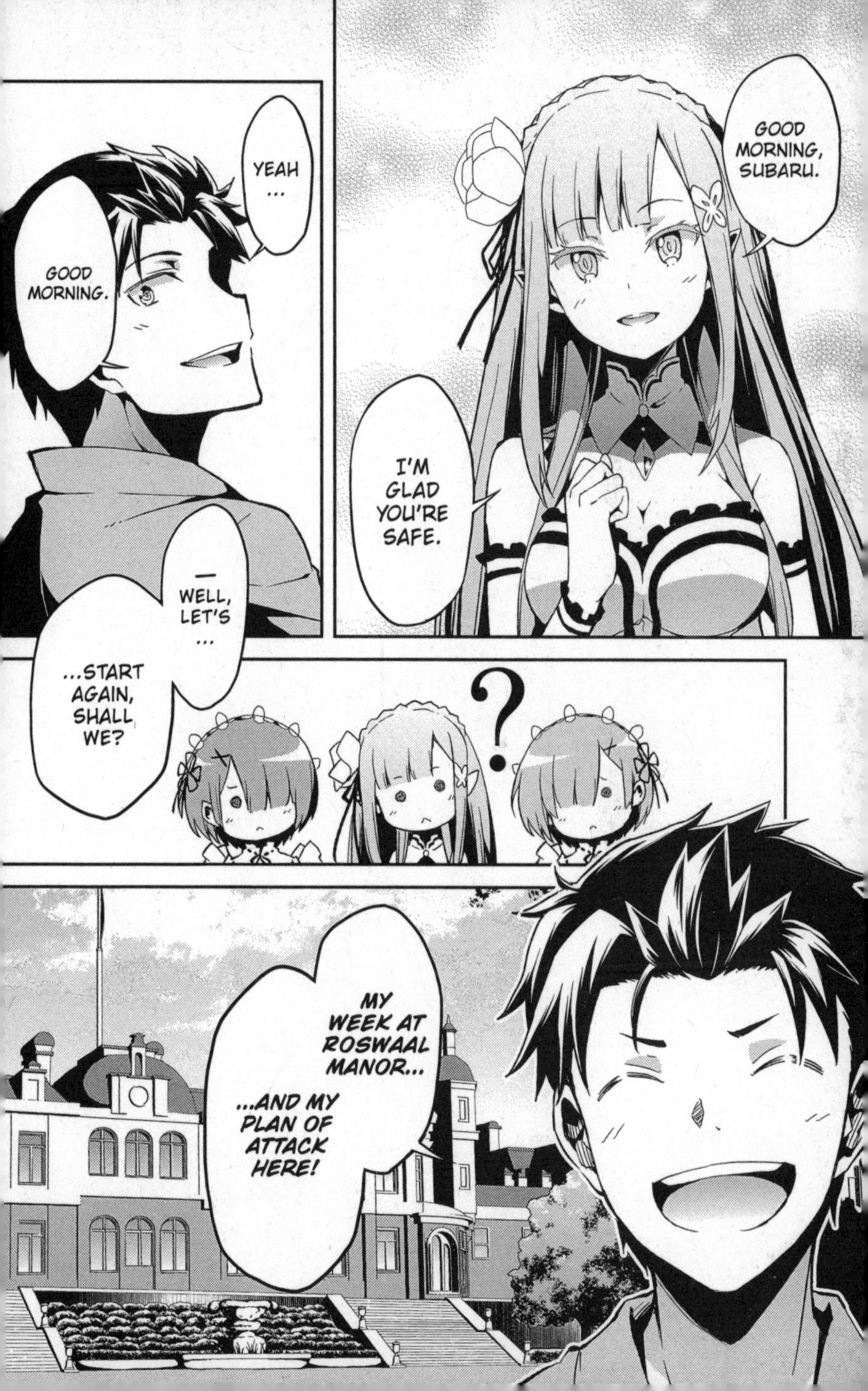
GOOD MORNING, SUBARU.
I'M GLAD YOU'RE SAFE.
YEAH ...
GOOD MORNING.
—WELL, LET'S ...
...START AGAIN, SHALL WE?
?
MY WEEK AT ROSWAAL MANOR...
...AND MY PLAN OF ATTACK HERE!

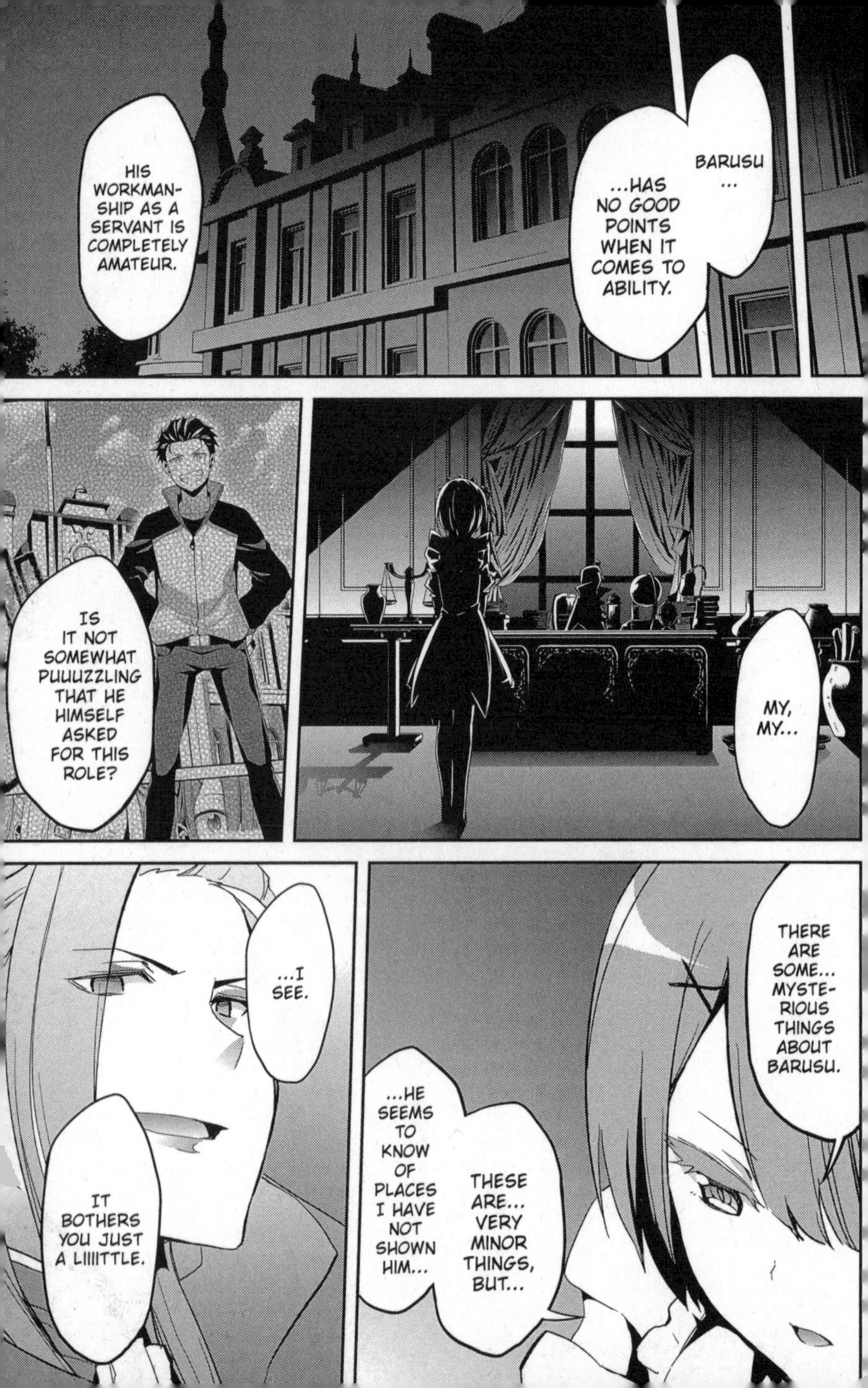
BARUSU…
…HAS NO GOOD POINTS WHEN IT COMES TO ABILITY.
HIS WORKMANSHIP AS A SERVANT IS COMPLETELY AMATEUR.
MY, MY…
IS IT NOT SOMEWHAT PUUUZZLING THAT HE HIMSELF ASKED FOR THIS ROLE?
THERE ARE SOME… MYSTERIOUS THINGS ABOUT BARUSU.
THESE ARE… VERY MINOR THINGS, BUT…
…HE SEEMS TO KNOW OF PLACES I HAVE NOT SHOWN HIM…
…I SEE.
IT BOTHERS YOU JUST A LIIIITTLE.

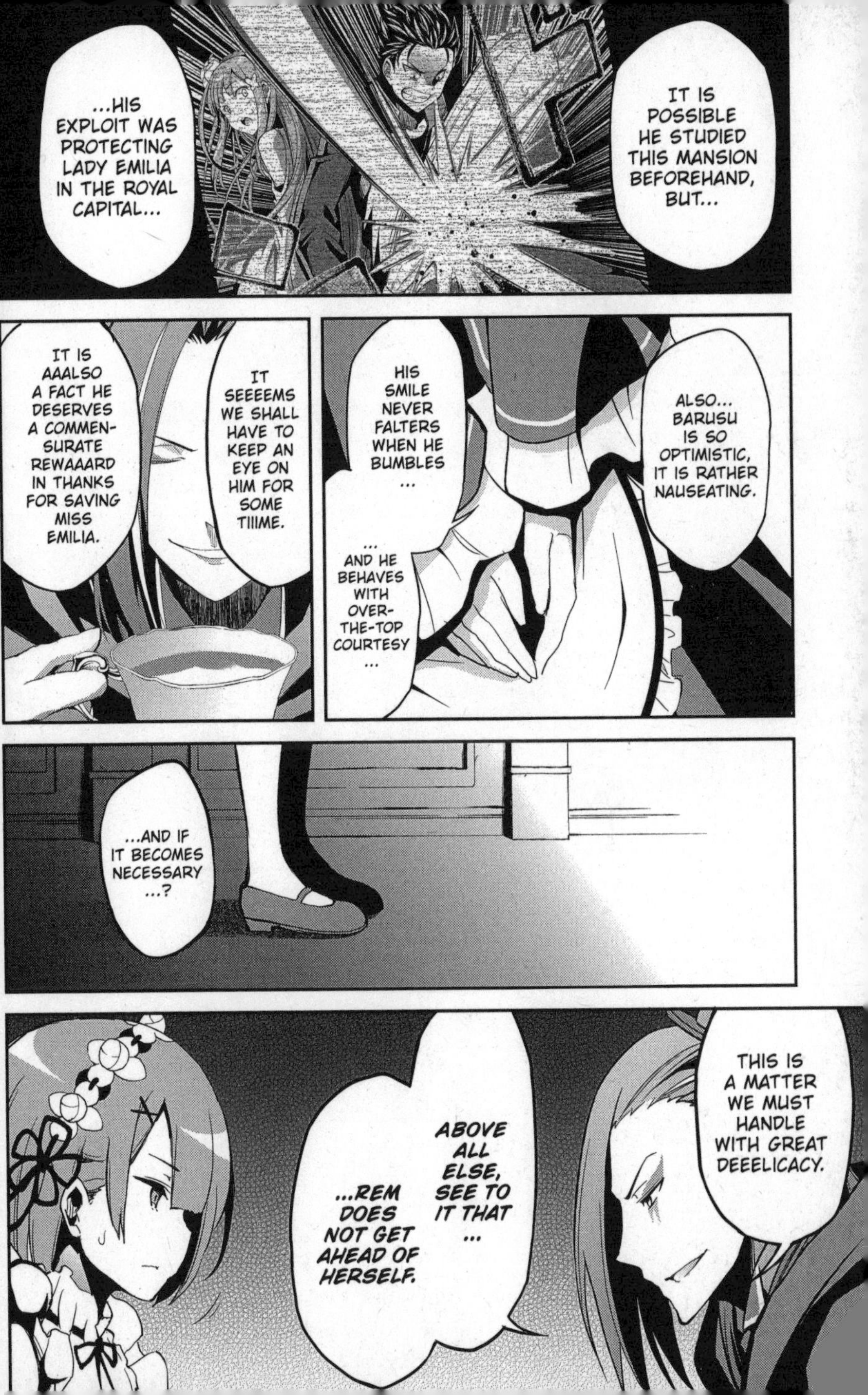
IT IS POSSIBLE HE STUDIED THIS MANSION BEFOREHAND, BUT...
...HIS EXPLOIT WAS PROTECTING LADY EMILIA IN THE ROYAL CAPITAL...
ALSO... BARUSU IS SO OPTIMISTIC, IT IS RATHER NAUSEATING.
HIS SMILE NEVER FALTERS WHEN HE BUMBLES ...
... AND HE BEHAVES WITH OVER-THE-TOP COURTESY ...
IT SEEEEMS WE SHALL HAVE TO KEEP AN EYE ON HIM FOR SOME TIIIME.
IT IS AAALSO A FACT HE DESERVES A COMMEN-SURATE REWAAARD IN THANKS FOR SAVING MISS EMILIA.
...AND IF IT BECOMES NECESSARY ...?
THIS IS A MATTER WE MUST HANDLE WITH GREAT DEEELICACY.
ABOVE ALL ELSE, SEE TO IT THAT ...
...REM DOES NOT GET AHEAD OF HERSELF.

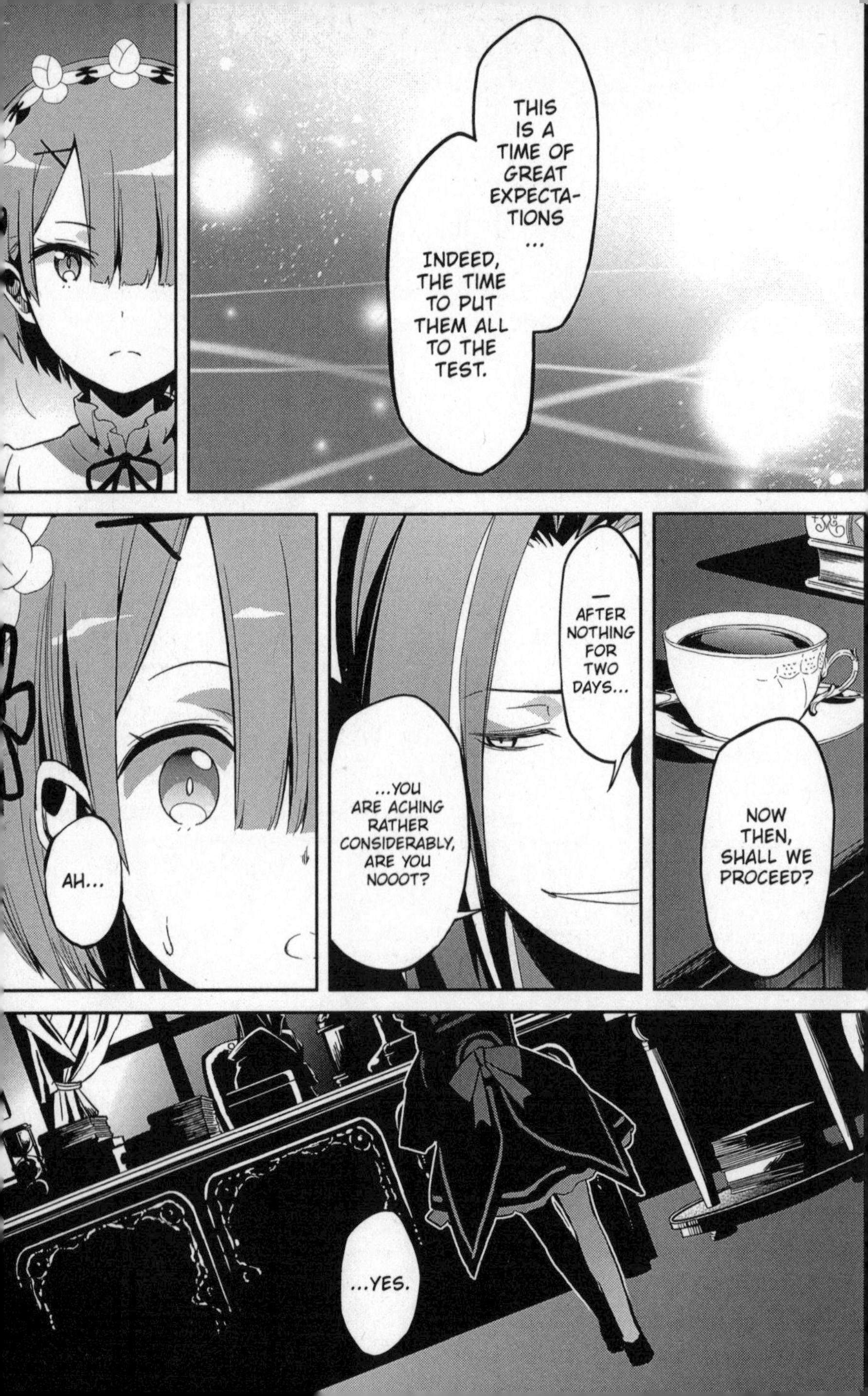
THIS IS A TIME OF GREAT EXPECTATIONS...
INDEED, THE TIME TO PUT THEM ALL TO THE TEST.
NOW THEN, SHALL WE PROCEED?
—AFTER NOTHING FOR TWO DAYS...
...YOU ARE ACHING RATHER CONSIDERABLY, ARE YOU NOOOT?
AH...
...YES.

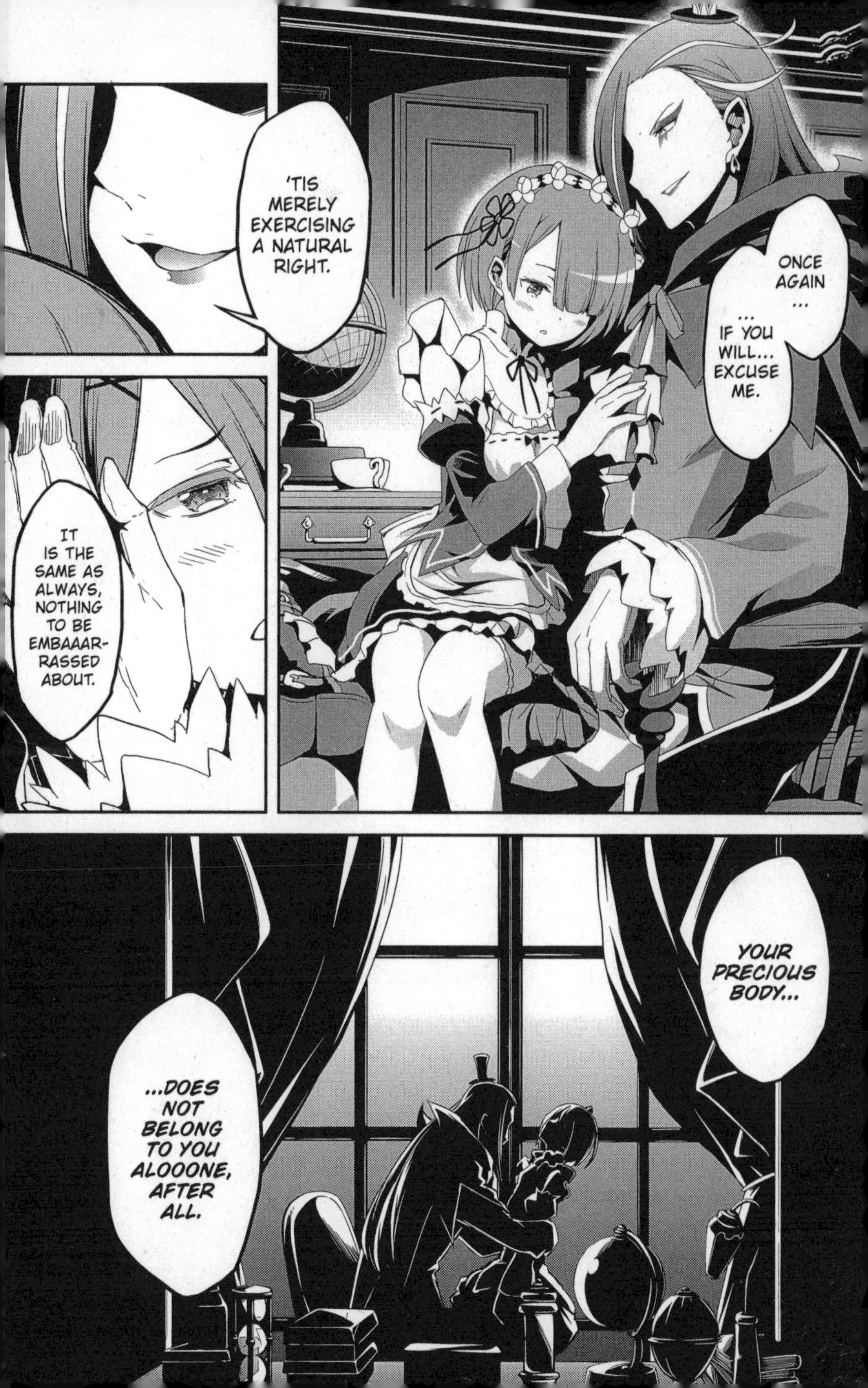
ONCE AGAIN ... ... IF YOU WILL... EXCUSE ME.
'TIS MERELY EXERCISING A NATURAL RIGHT.
IT IS THE SAME AS ALWAYS, NOTHING TO BE EMBAAAR-RASSED ABOUT.
YOUR PRECIOUS BODY...
...DOES NOT BELONG TO YOU ALOOONE, AFTER ALL.

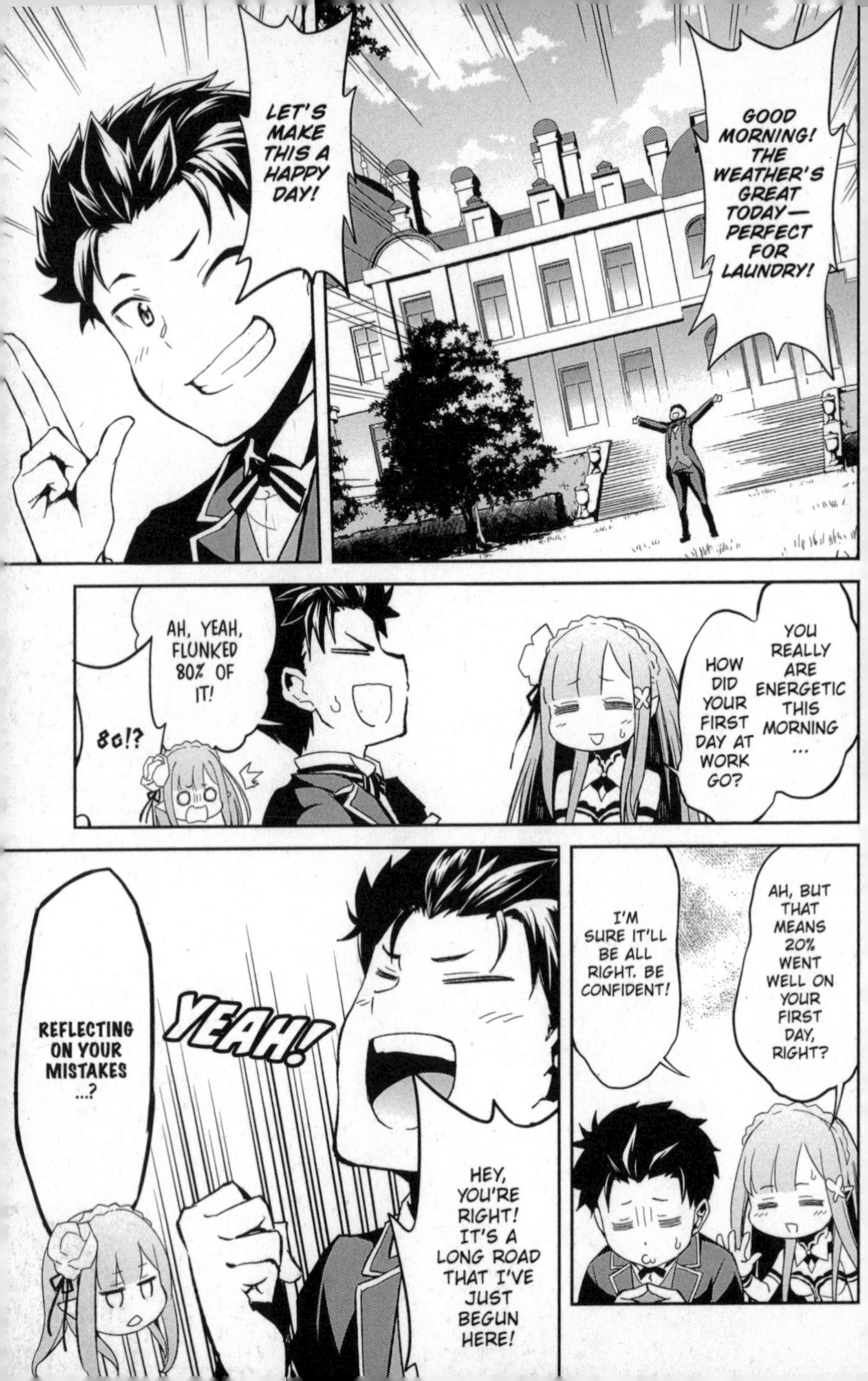
GOOD MORNING! THE WEATHER'S GREAT TODAY—PERFECT FOR LAUNDRY!
LET'S MAKE THIS A HAPPY DAY!
YOU REALLY ARE ENERGETIC THIS MORNING ...
HOW DID YOUR FIRST DAY AT WORK GO?
AH, YEAH, FLUNKED 80% OF IT!
8o!?
AH, BUT THAT MEANS 20% WENT WELL ON YOUR FIRST DAY, RIGHT?
I'M SURE IT'LL BE ALL RIGHT. BE CONFIDENT!
YEAH!
HEY, YOU'RE RIGHT! IT'S A LONG ROAD THAT I'VE JUST BEGUN HERE!
REFLECTING ON YOUR MISTAKES ...?

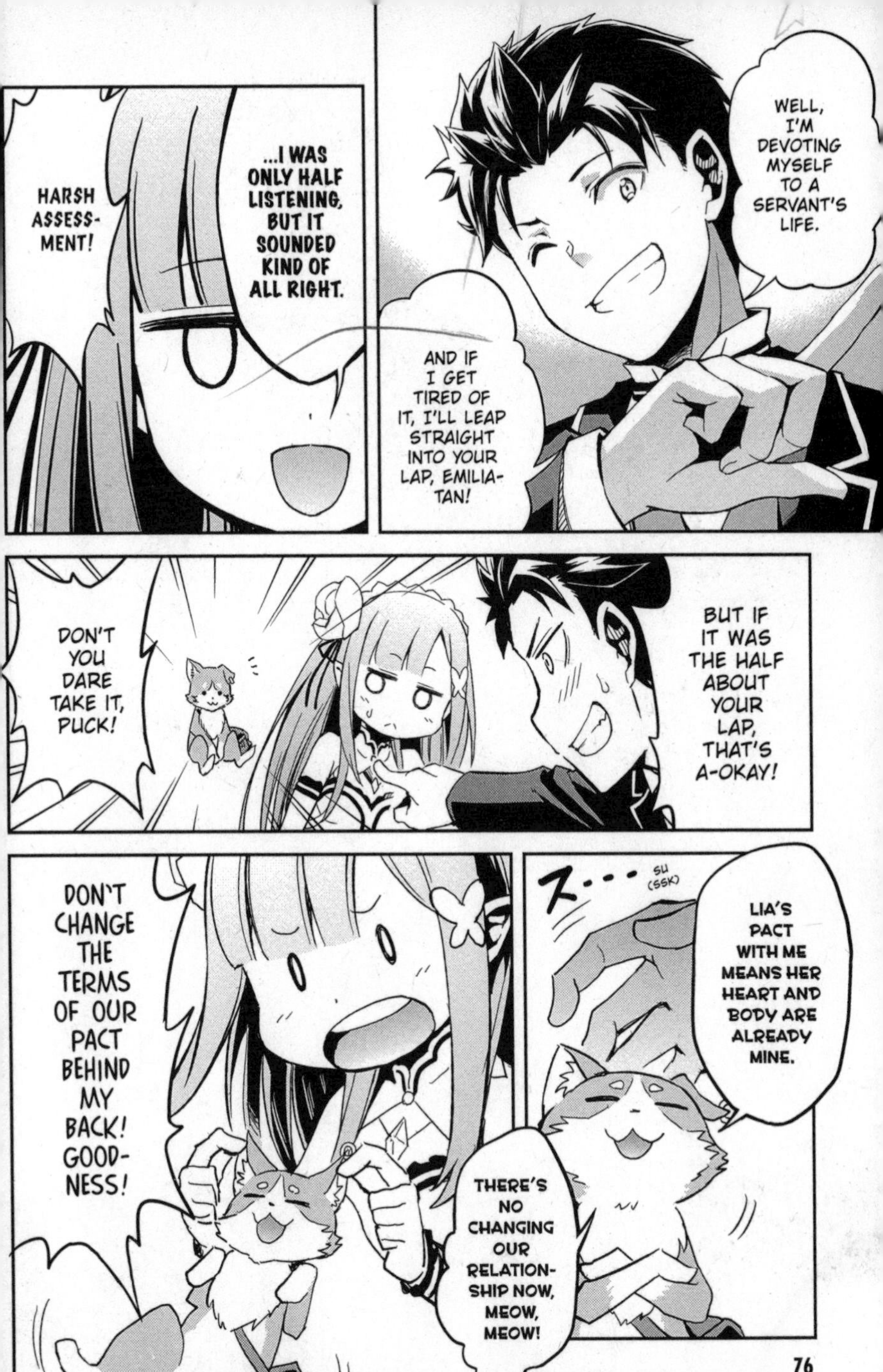
WELL, I'M DEVOTING MYSELF TO A SERVANT'S LIFE.
AND IF I GET TIRED OF IT, I'LL LEAP STRAIGHT INTO YOUR LAP, EMILIA-TAN!
...I WAS ONLY HALF LISTENING, BUT IT SOUNDED KIND OF ALL RIGHT.
HARSH ASSESS-MENT!
BUT IF IT WAS THE HALF ABOUT YOUR LAP, THAT'S A-OKAY!
DON'T YOU DARE TAKE IT, PUCK!
SU (SSK)
LIA'S PACT WITH ME MEANS HER HEART AND BODY ARE ALREADY MINE.
THERE'S NO CHANGING OUR RELATIONSHIP NOW, MEOW, MEOW!
DON'T CHANGE THE TERMS OF OUR PACT BEHIND MY BACK! GOOD-NESS!

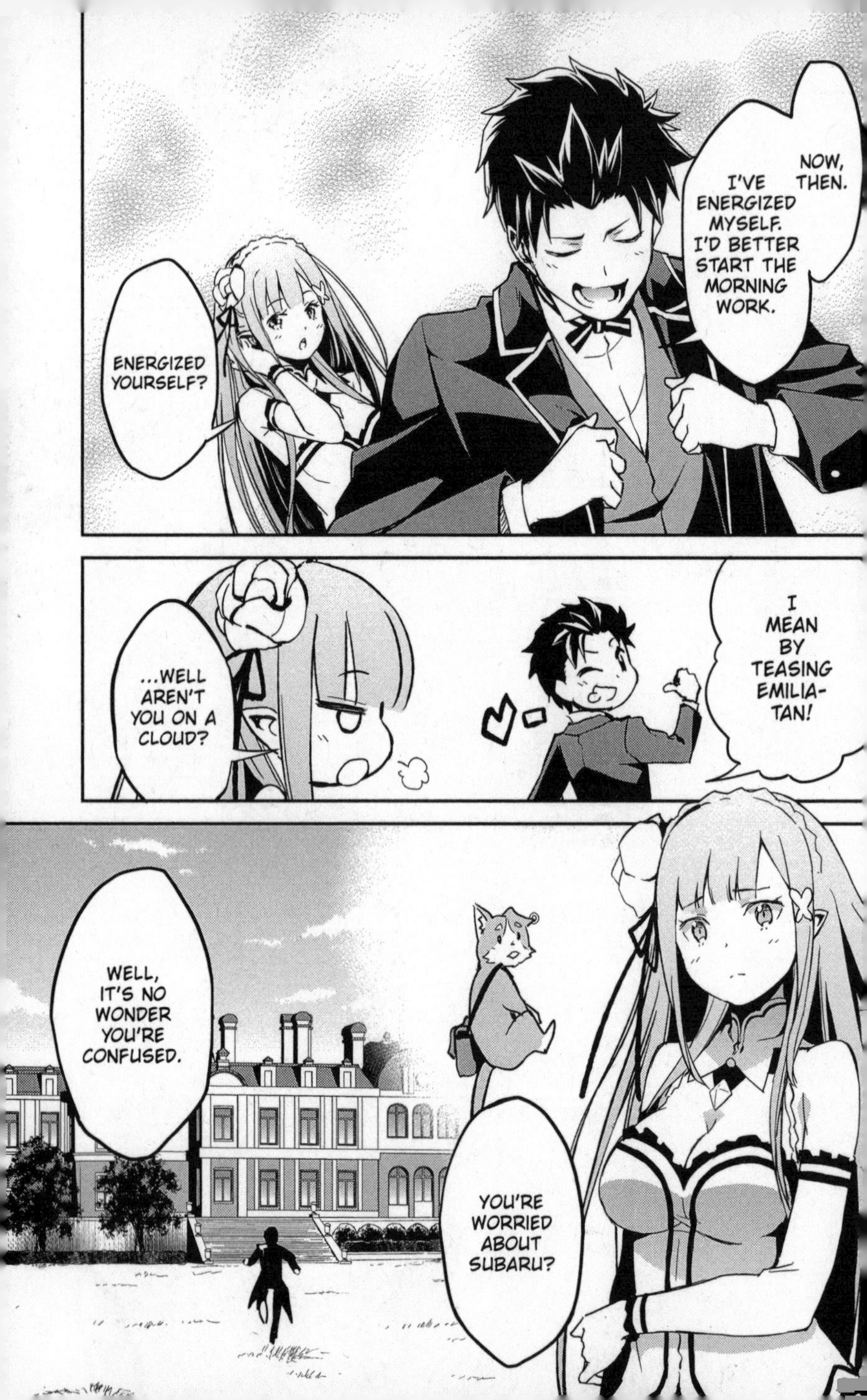
NOW, THEN. I'VE ENERGIZED MYSELF. I'D BETTER START THE MORNING WORK.
ENERGIZED YOURSELF?
I MEAN BY TEASING EMILIA-TAN!
...WELL AREN'T YOU ON A CLOUD?
YOU'RE WORRIED ABOUT SUBARU?
WELL, IT'S NO WONDER YOU'RE CONFUSED.

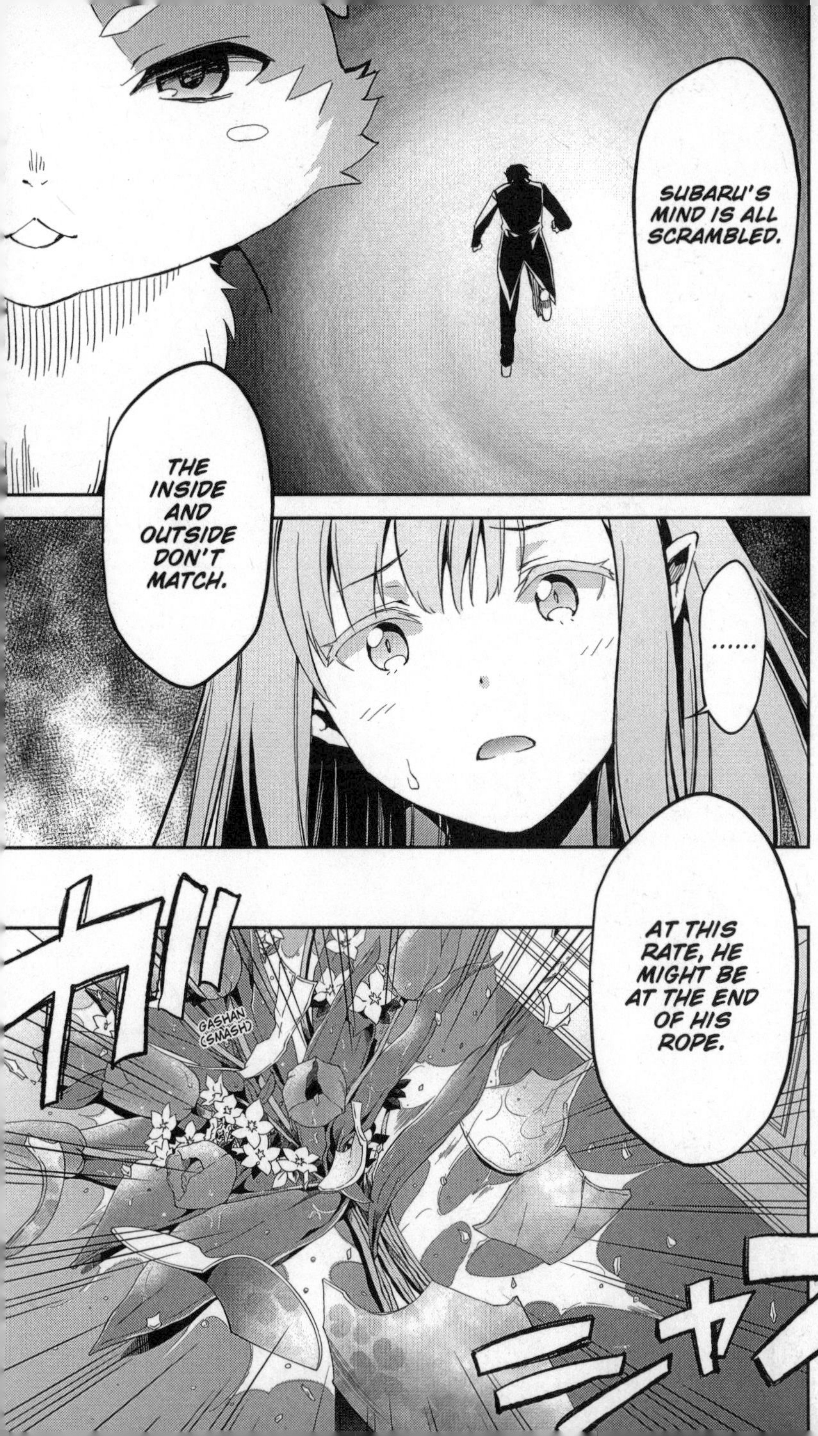
SUBARU'S MIND IS ALL SCRAMBLED.
THE INSIDE AND OUTSIDE DON'T MATCH.
......
AT THIS RATE, HE MIGHT BE AT THE END OF HIS ROPE.
ガシャン
GASHAN (SMASH)

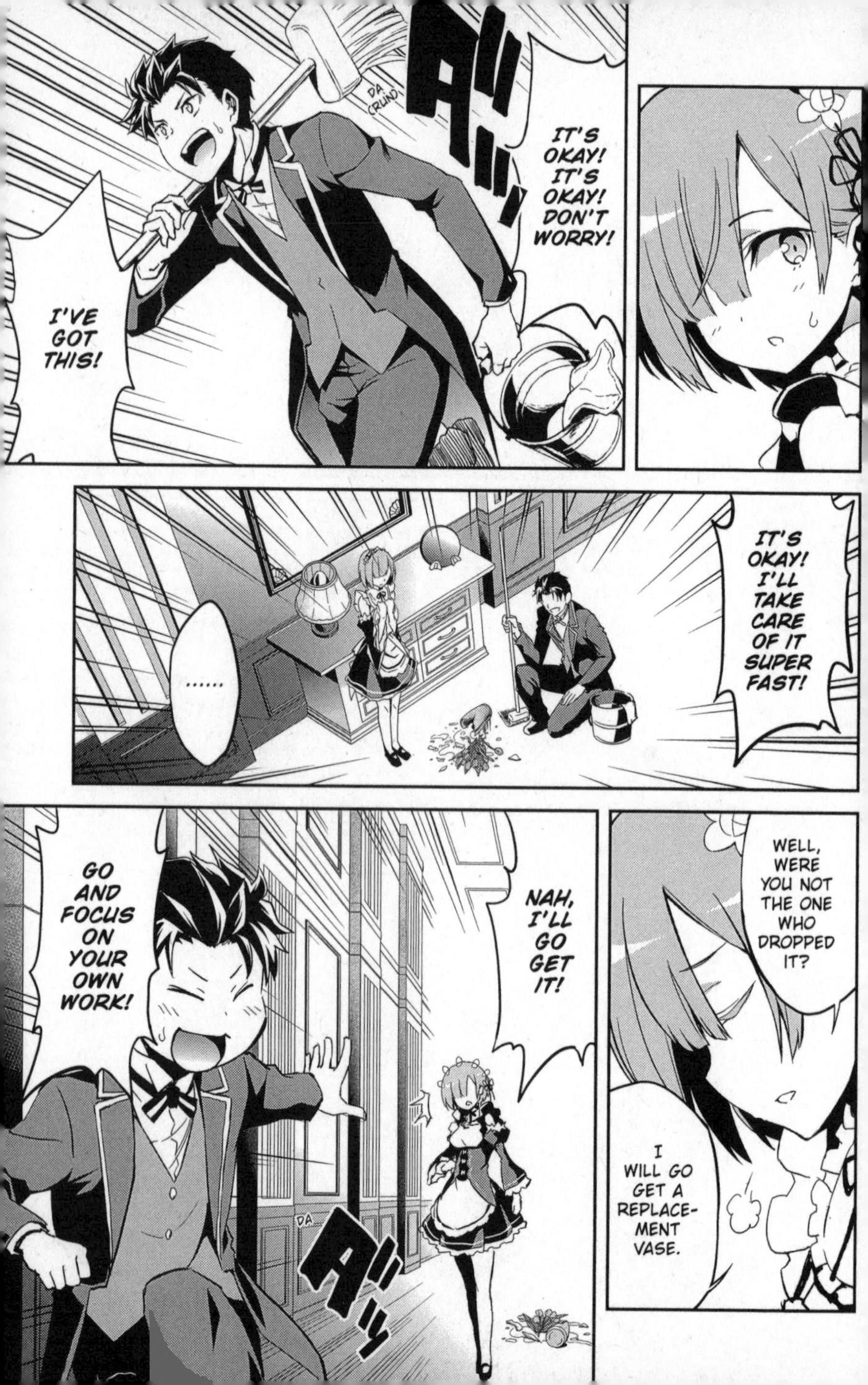

DA CRUND
IT'S OKAY! IT'S OKAY! DON'T WORRY!
I'VE GOT THIS!
IT'S OKAY! I'LL TAKE CARE OF IT SUPER FAST!
......
WELL, WERE YOU NOT THE ONE WHO DROPPED IT?
I WILL GO GET A REPLACE-MENT VASE.
NAH, I'LL GO GET IT!
GO AND FOCUS ON YOUR OWN WORK!
DA

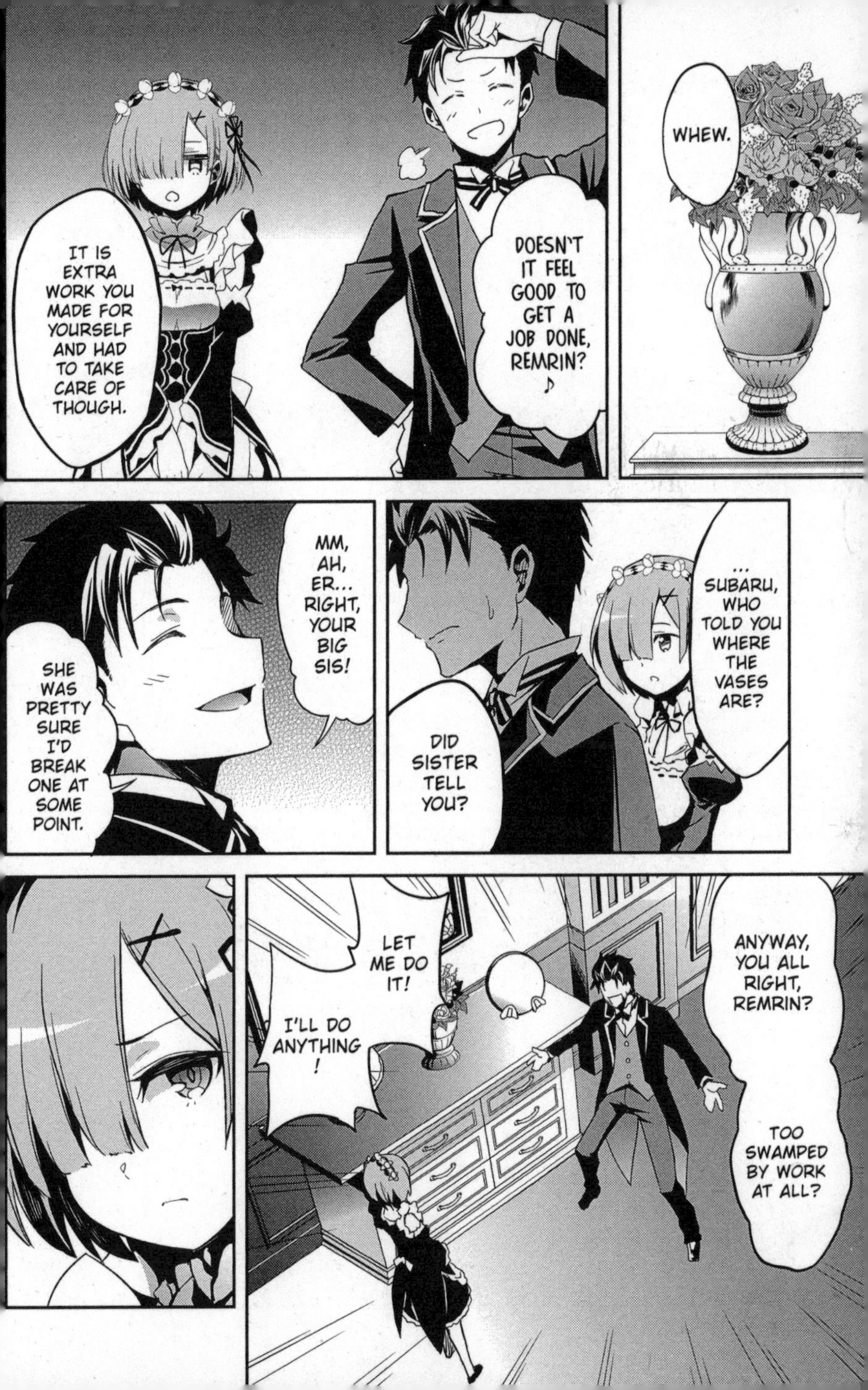
WHEW.
DOESN'T IT FEEL GOOD TO GET A JOB DONE, REMRIN? ♪
IT IS EXTRA WORK YOU MADE FOR YOURSELF AND HAD TO TAKE CARE OF THOUGH.
...SUBARU, WHO TOLD YOU WHERE THE VASES ARE?
DID SISTER TELL YOU?
MM, AH, ER... RIGHT, YOUR BIG SIS!
SHE WAS PRETTY SURE I'D BREAK ONE AT SOME POINT.
ANYWAY, YOU ALL RIGHT, REMRIN?
TOO SWAMPED BY WORK AT ALL?
LET ME DO IT!
I'LL DO ANYTHING!

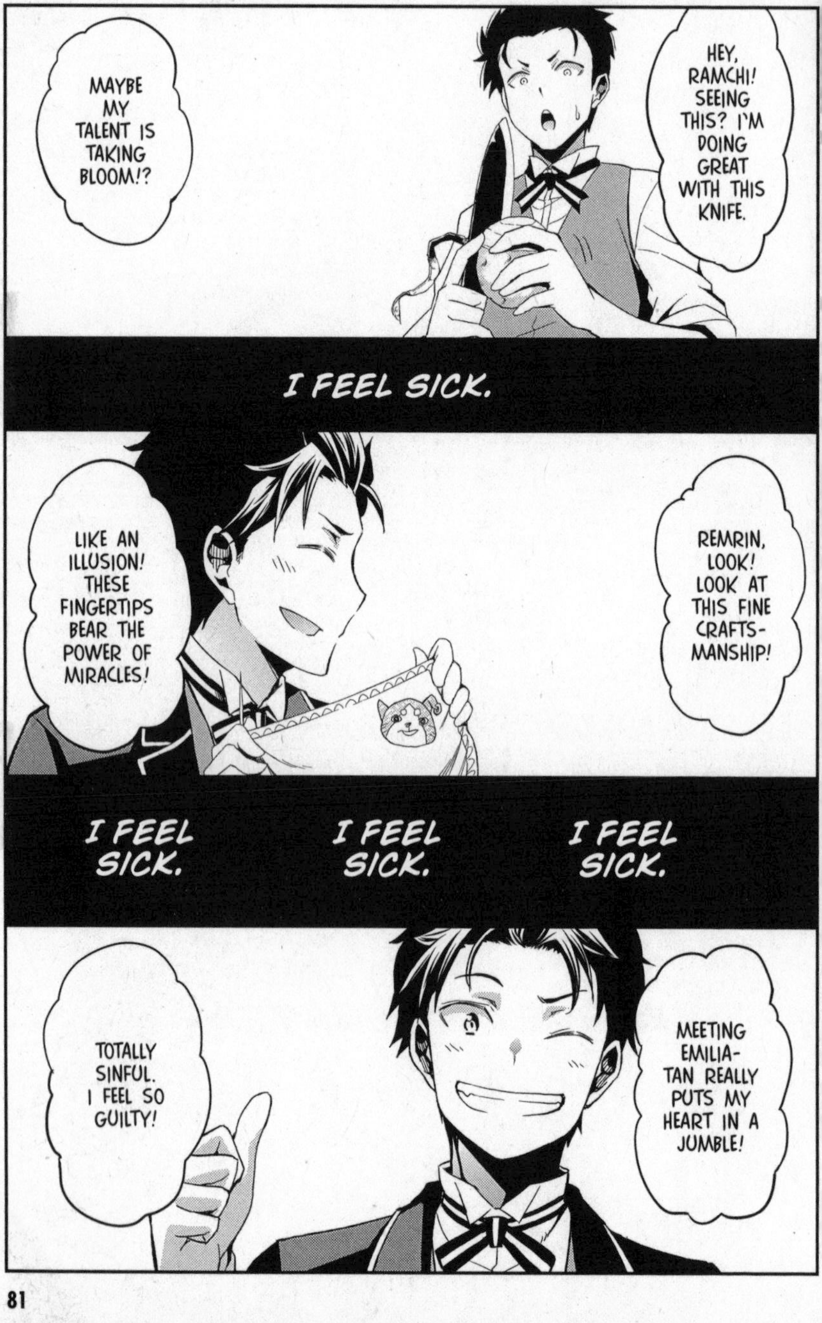
HEY, RAMCHI! SEEING THIS? I'M DOING GREAT WITH THIS KNIFE.
MAYBE MY TALENT IS TAKING BLOOM!?
I FEEL SICK.
REMRIN, LOOK! LOOK AT THIS FINE CRAFTS-MANSHIP!
LIKE AN ILLUSION! THESE FINGERTIPS BEAR THE POWER OF MIRACLES!
I FEEL SICK.
I FEEL SICK.
I FEEL SICK.
MEETING EMILIA-TAN REALLY PUTS MY HEART IN A JUMBLE!
TOTALLY SINFUL. I FEEL SO GUILTY!

DON'T LET ONE THING SLIP—
REMEMBER, THIS IS YOUR FOURTH TIME DOING THIS—
HAVE TO DO EVERYTHING YOU CAN—
YOU HAVE TO DO THIS.
YOU NEED TO DO THIS.
THINK OF IT AS A GAME. DON'T WASTE ONE STEP.
THOROUGHLY MANAGE THE FLAGS— IT'S YOUR SPECIALTY.
MEET EVERYONE AS MUCH AS YOU CAN.
DON'T LET THEM THINK YOU'RE SO STUPID THAT YOU'RE USELESS.
DON'T STOP WHILE YOU THINK. DOESN'T LOOK NATURAL.
DON'T LET YOUR GUARD DOWN FOR ONE SECOND.
MAKE IT SO THAT NO ONE HAS...
...CAUSE TO SUSPECT SUBARU NATSUKI.
NATURALLY ERASE THE UNNATURAL SUBARU.

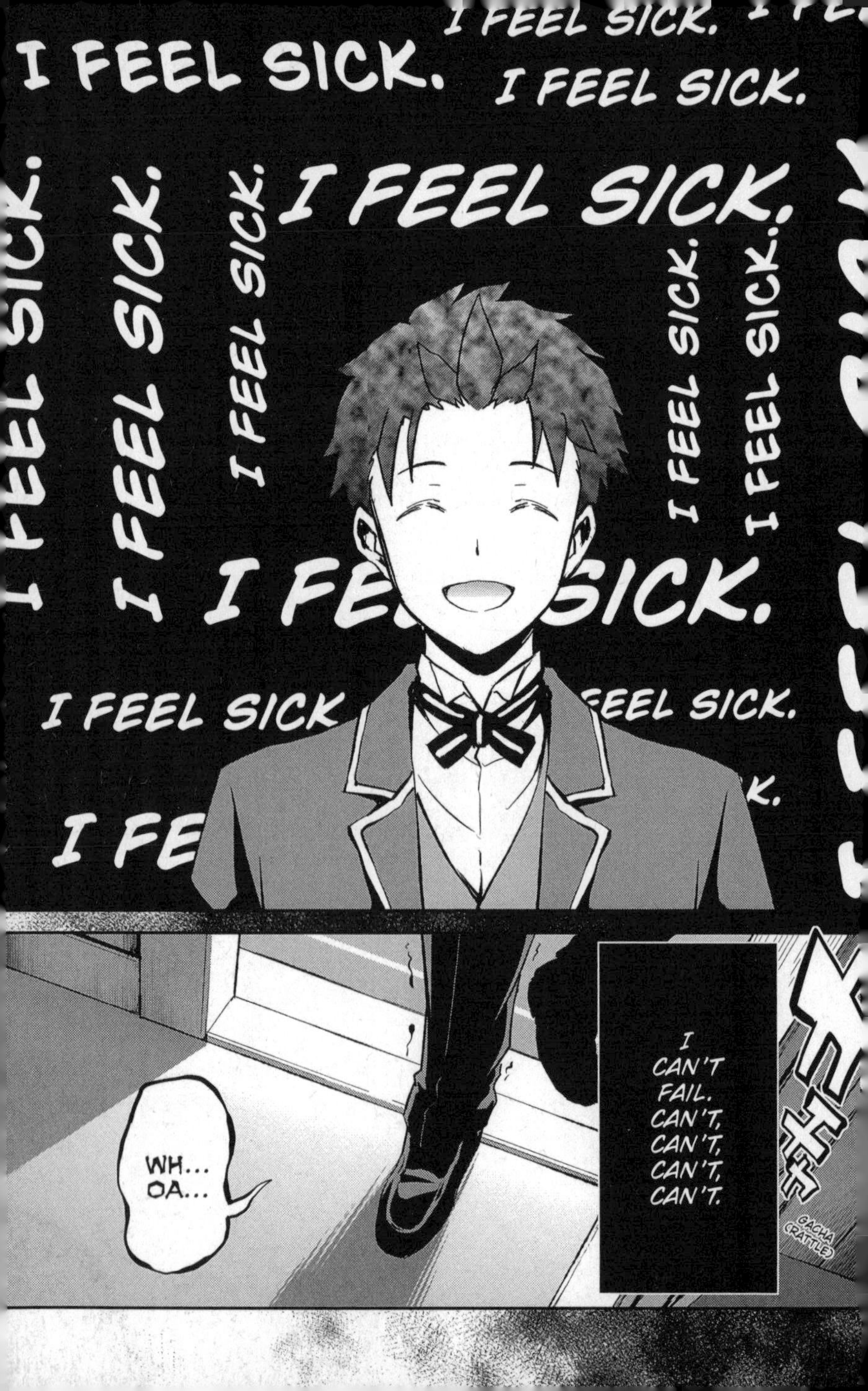
I FEEL SICK.
I FEEL SICK.
I FEEL SICK.
I FEEL SICK.
I FEEL SICK.
I FEEL SICK.
I FEEL SICK.
I FEEL SICK.
I FEEL SICK.
I FE SICK.
EEL SICK.
I FEEL SICK
K.
I FE
I CAN'T FAIL. CAN'T, CAN'T, CAN'T, CAN'T.
GACHA (RATTLE)
WH... OA...

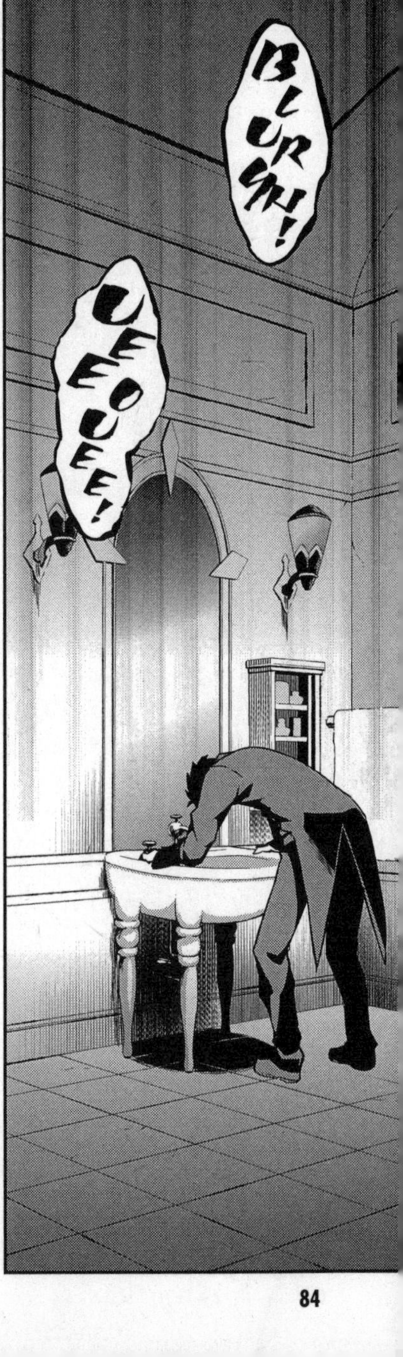
BLURSH!
UEEOUEE!

—AM I REALLY PULLING THIS OFF?

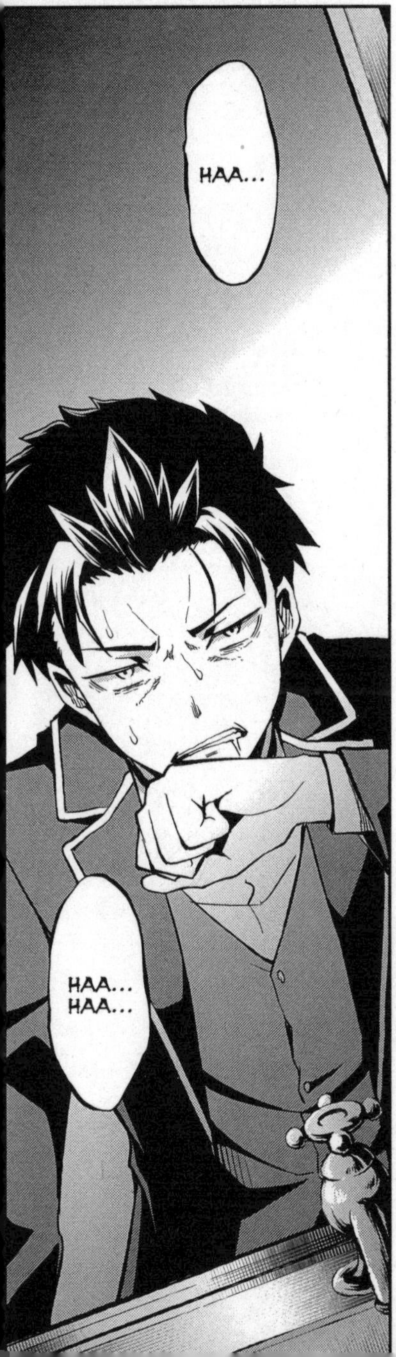
HAA...
HAA...
HAA...

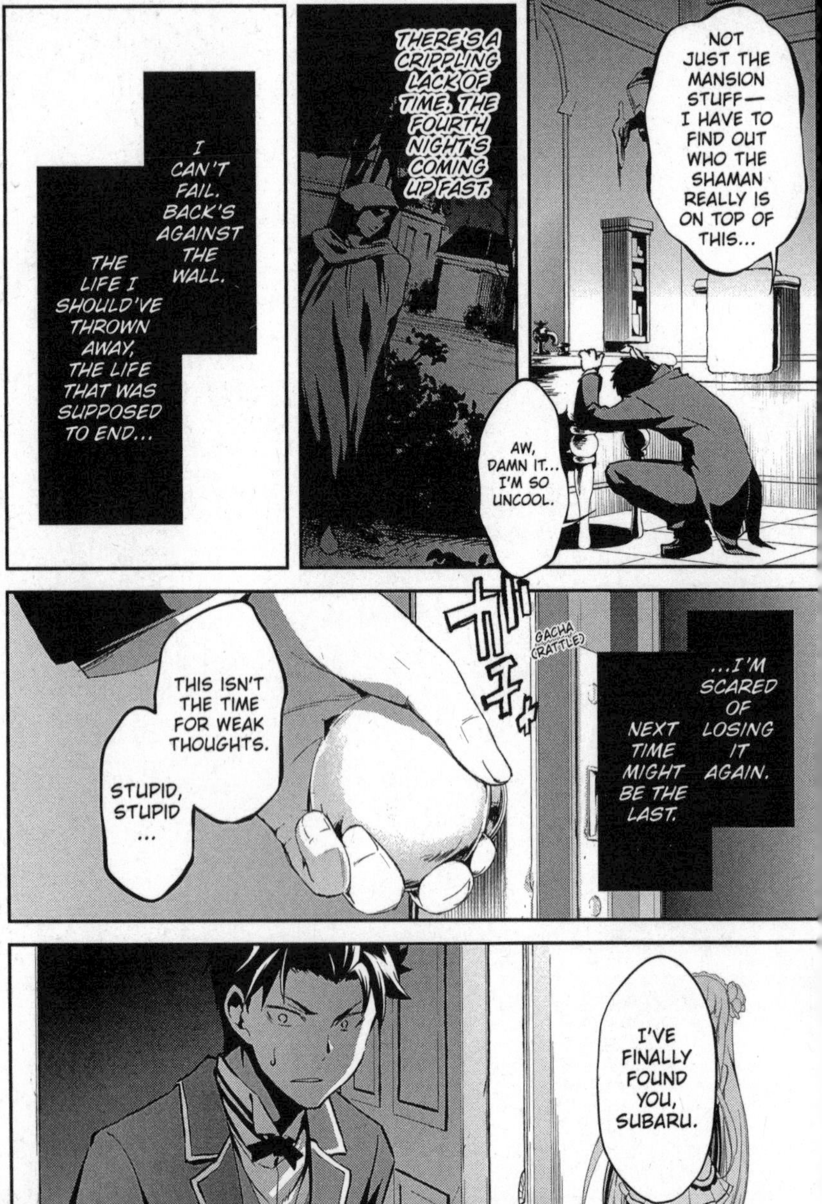
NOT JUST THE MANSION STUFF— I HAVE TO FIND OUT WHO THE SHAMAN REALLY IS ON TOP OF THIS...
AW, DAMN IT... I'M SO UNCOOL.
THERE'S A CRIPPLING LACK OF TIME. THE FOURTH NIGHT'S COMING UP FAST.
I CAN'T FAIL. BACK'S AGAINST THE WALL.
THE LIFE I SHOULD'VE THROWN AWAY, THE LIFE THAT WAS SUPPOSED TO END...
...I'M SCARED OF LOSING IT AGAIN.
NEXT TIME MIGHT BE THE LAST.
GACHA (RATTLE)
THIS ISN'T THE TIME FOR WEAK THOUGHTS.
STUPID, STUPID...
I'VE FINALLY FOUND YOU, SUBARU.

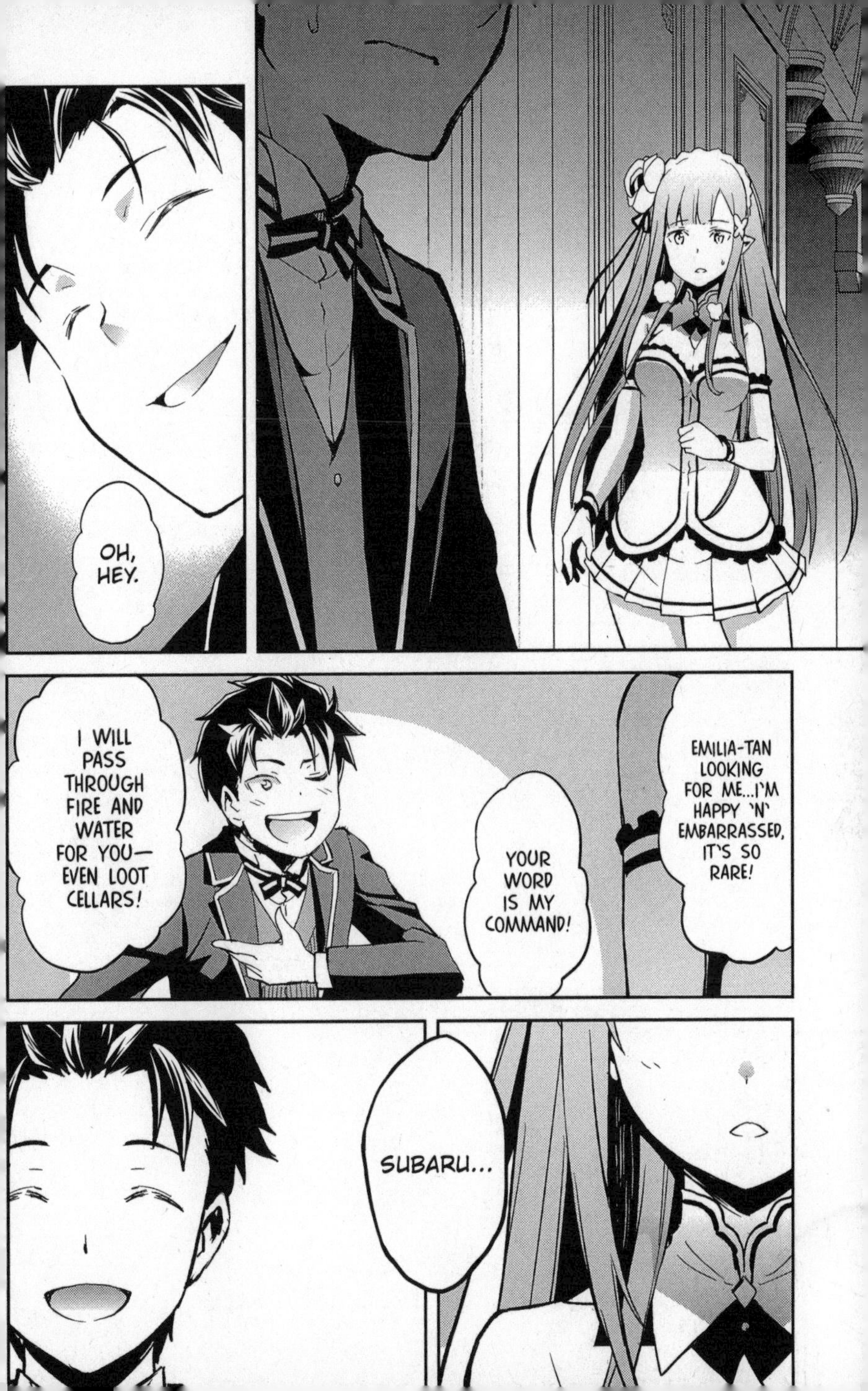
OH, HEY.
EMILIA-TAN LOOKING FOR ME...I'M HAPPY 'N' EMBARRASSED, IT'S SO RARE!
YOUR WORD IS MY COMMAND!
I WILL PASS THROUGH FIRE AND WATER FOR YOU—EVEN LOOT CELLARS!
SUBARU...

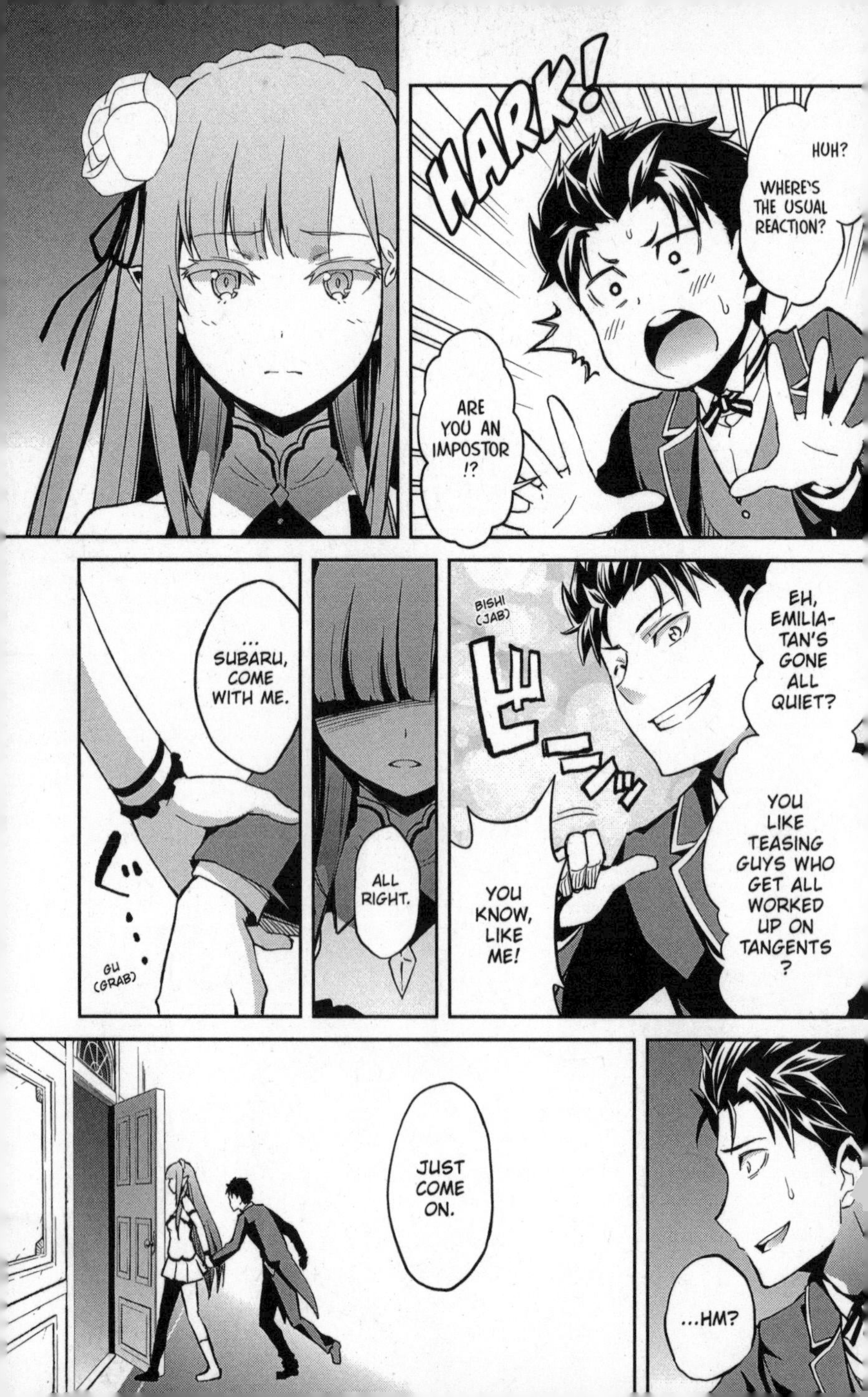
HARK!
HUH?
WHERE'S THE USUAL REACTION?
ARE YOU AN IMPOSTOR!?
EH, EMILIA-TAN'S GONE ALL QUIET?
YOU LIKE TEASING GUYS WHO GET ALL WORKED UP ON TANGENTS?
BISHI (JAB)
YOU KNOW, LIKE ME!
ALL RIGHT.
...SUBARU, COME WITH ME.
GU (GRAB)
...HM?
JUST COME ON.

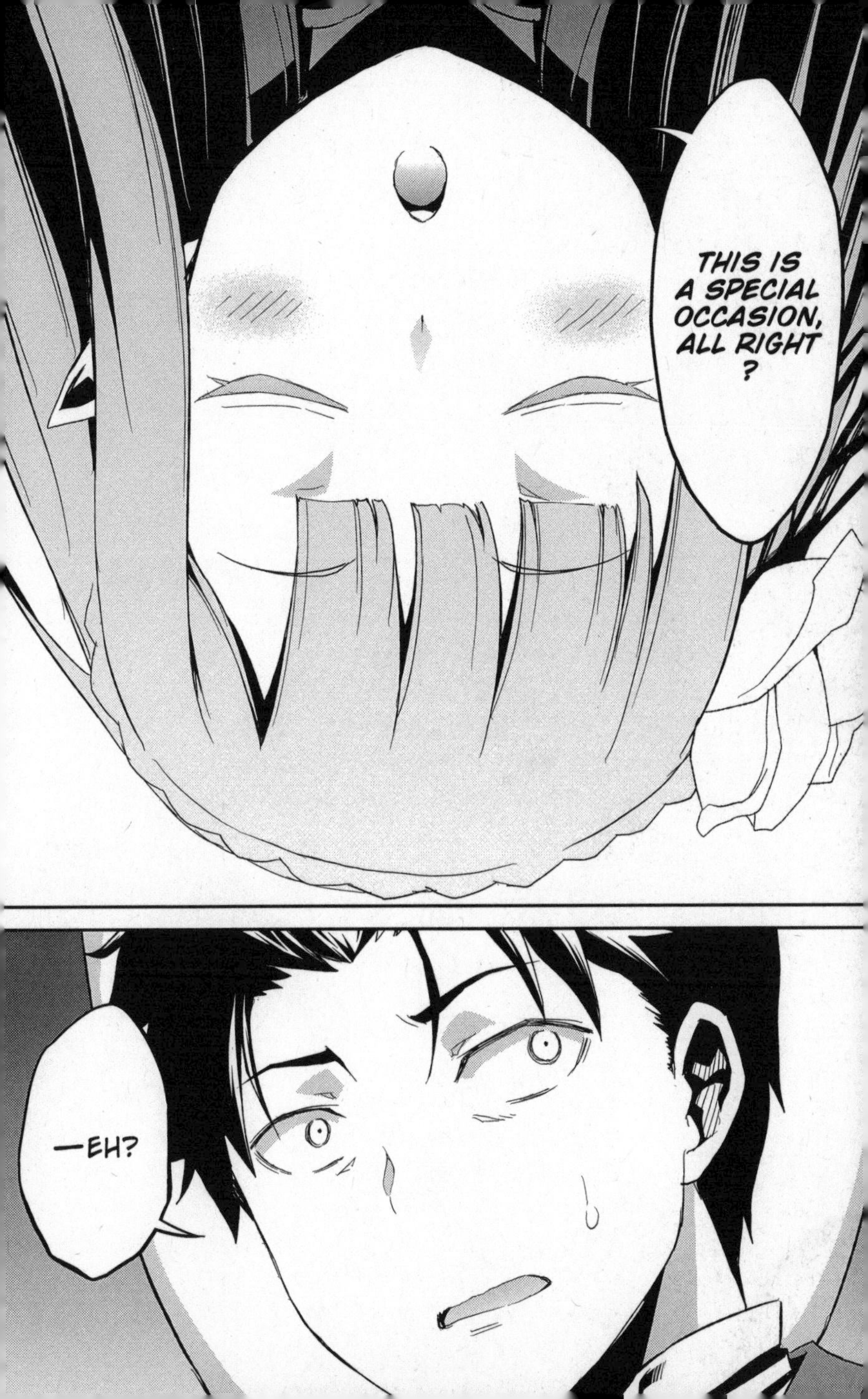
THIS IS A SPECIAL OCCASION, ALL RIGHT?
—EH?

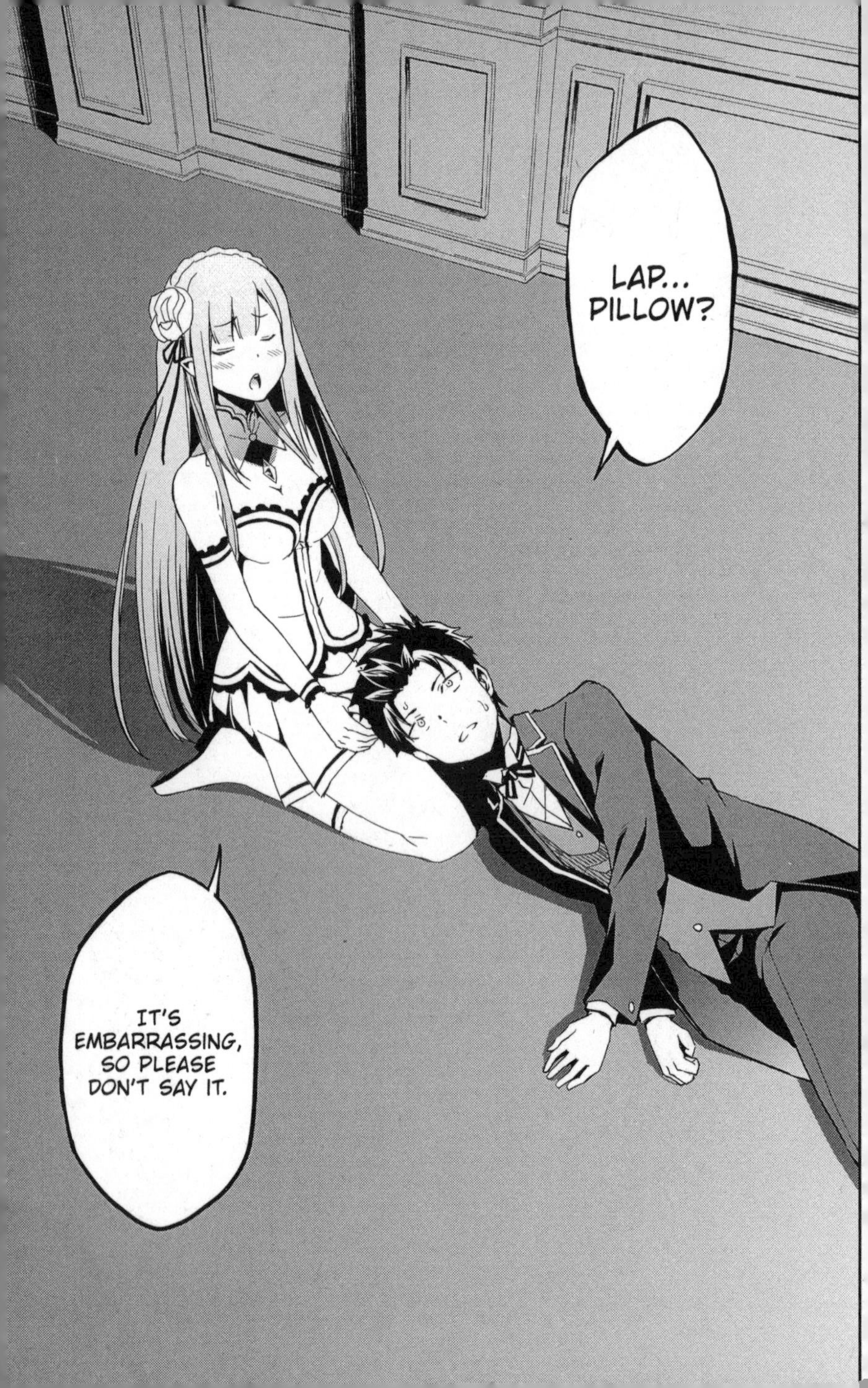
LAP... PILLOW?
IT'S EMBARRASSING, SO PLEASE DON'T SAY IT.

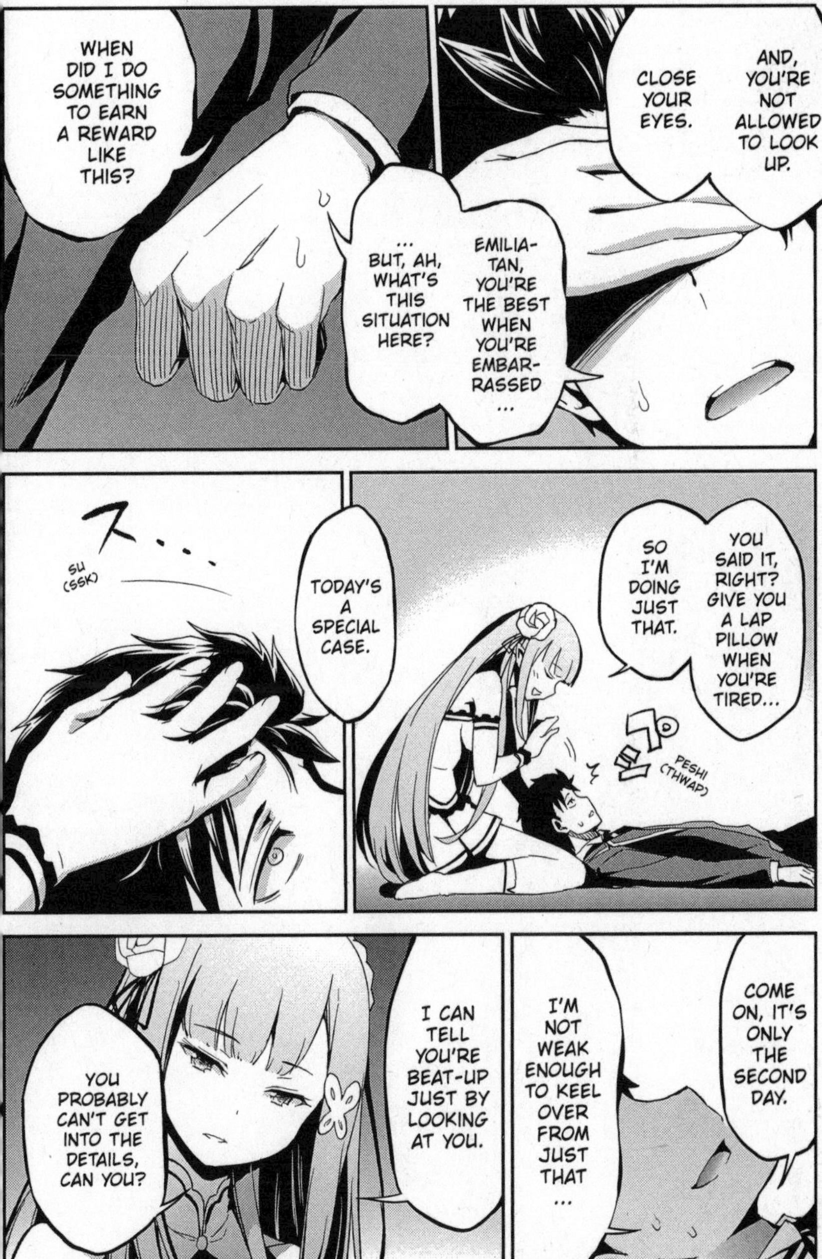
CLOSE YOUR EYES.
AND, YOU'RE NOT ALLOWED TO LOOK UP.
EMILIA-TAN, YOU'RE THE BEST WHEN YOU'RE EMBARRASSED ...
... BUT, AH, WHAT'S THIS SITUATION HERE?
WHEN DID I DO SOMETHING TO EARN A REWARD LIKE THIS?
YOU SAID IT, RIGHT? GIVE YOU A LAP PILLOW WHEN YOU'RE TIRED...
SO I'M DOING JUST THAT.
PESHI (THWAP)
TODAY'S A SPECIAL CASE.
SU (SSK)
COME ON, IT'S ONLY THE SECOND DAY.
I'M NOT WEAK ENOUGH TO KEEL OVER FROM JUST THAT ...
I CAN TELL YOU'RE BEAT-UP JUST BY LOOKING AT YOU.
YOU PROBABLY CAN'T GET INTO THE DETAILS, CAN YOU?

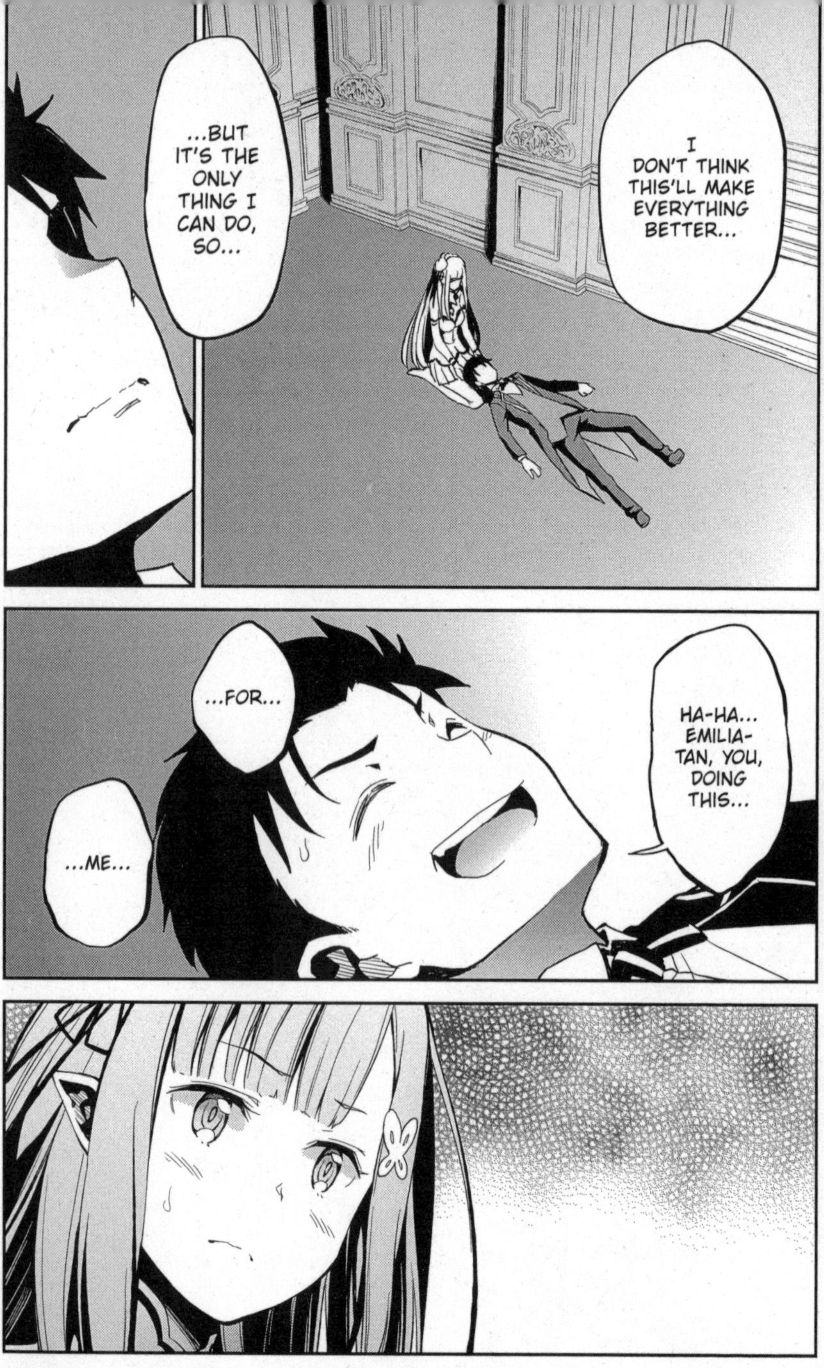
I DON'T THINK THIS'LL MAKE EVERYTHING BETTER...
...BUT IT'S THE ONLY THING I CAN DO, SO...
HA-HA... EMILIA-TAN, YOU, DOING THIS...
...FOR...
...ME...

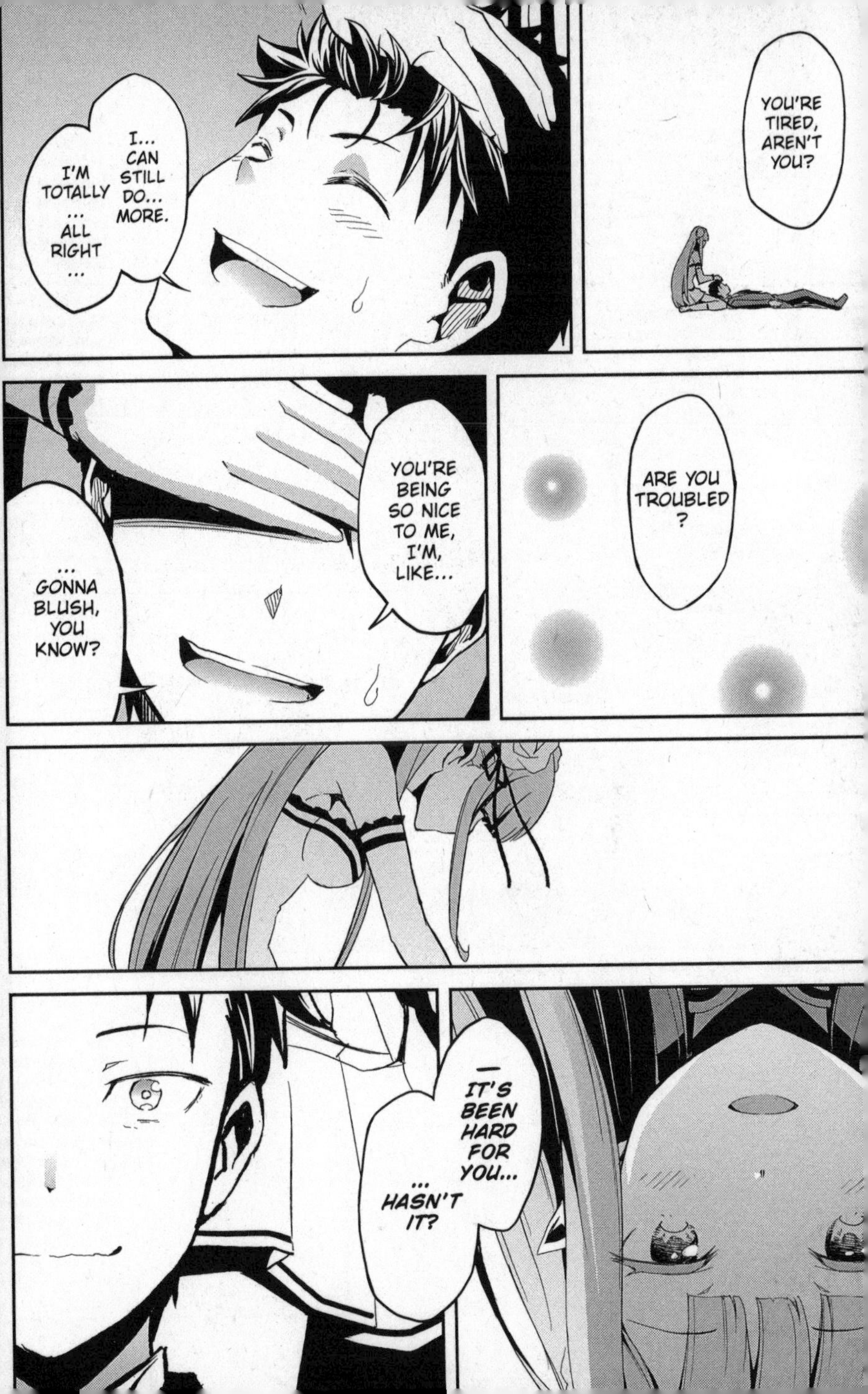
YOU'RE TIRED, AREN'T YOU?
I... CAN STILL DO... MORE.
I'M TOTALLY ... ALL RIGHT ...
ARE YOU TROUBLED?
YOU'RE BEING SO NICE TO ME, I'M, LIKE...
... GONNA BLUSH, YOU KNOW?
— IT'S BEEN HARD FOR YOU... ... HASN'T IT?

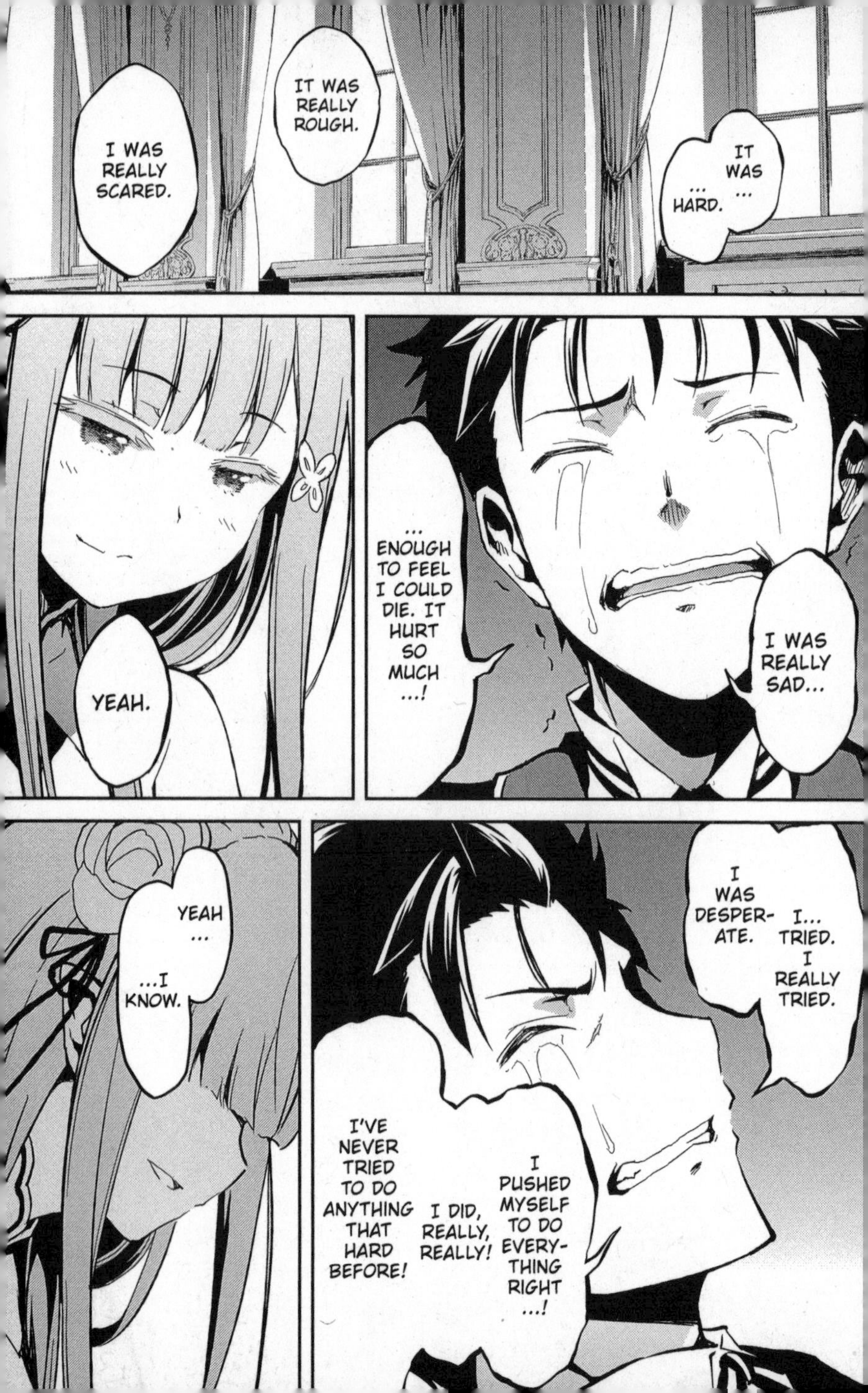
IT WAS ... ... HARD.
IT WAS REALLY ROUGH.
I WAS REALLY SCARED.
I WAS REALLY SAD...
... ENOUGH TO FEEL I COULD DIE. IT HURT SO MUCH ...!
YEAH.
I... TRIED. I REALLY TRIED.
I WAS DESPER-ATE.
I PUSHED MYSELF TO DO EVERY-THING RIGHT ...!
I DID, REALLY, REALLY!
I'VE NEVER TRIED TO DO ANYTHING THAT HARD BEFORE!
YEAH ... ...I KNOW.

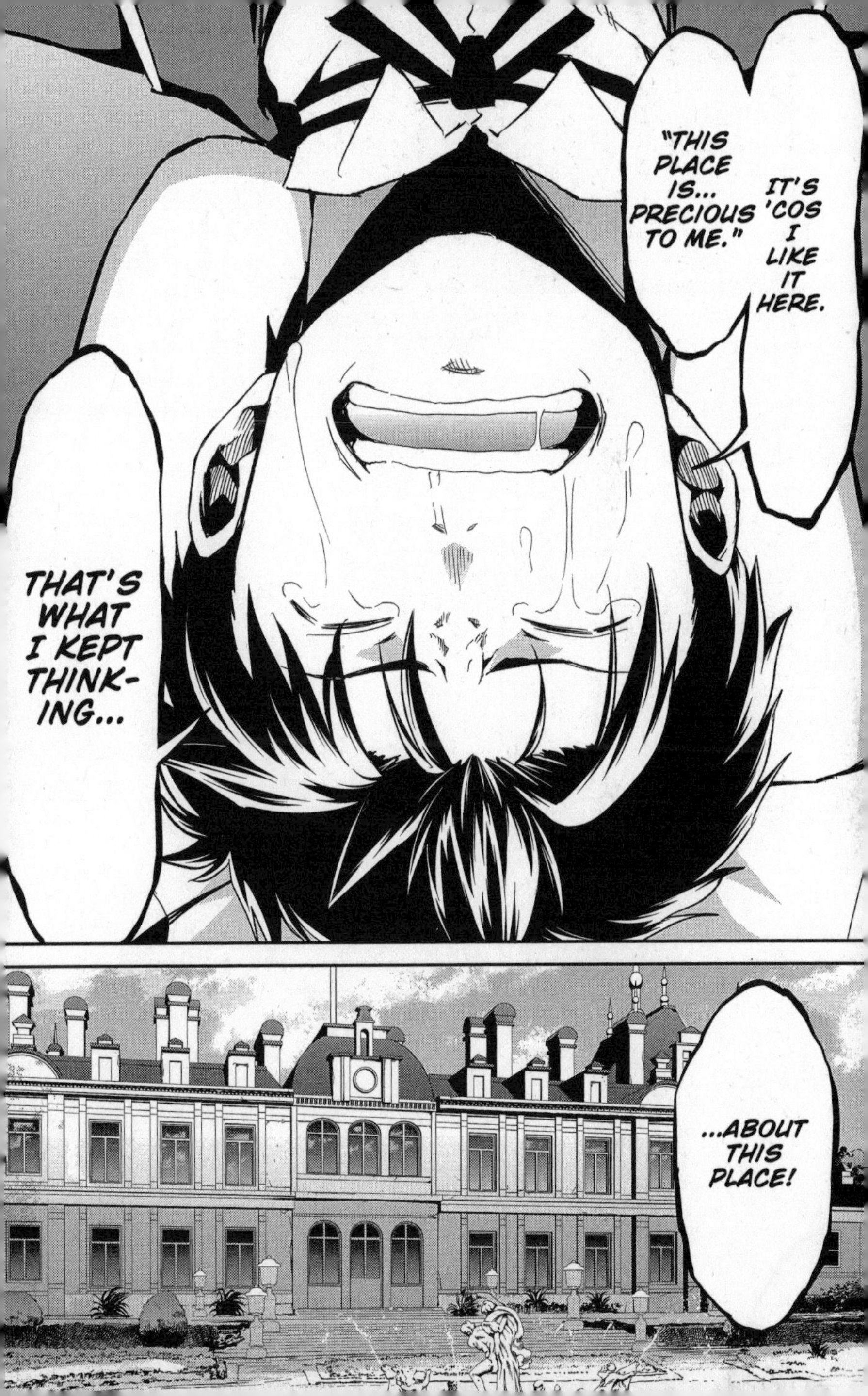
"THIS PLACE IS... PRECIOUS TO ME."
IT'S 'COS I LIKE IT HERE.
THAT'S WHAT I KEPT THINK-ING...
...ABOUT THIS PLACE!

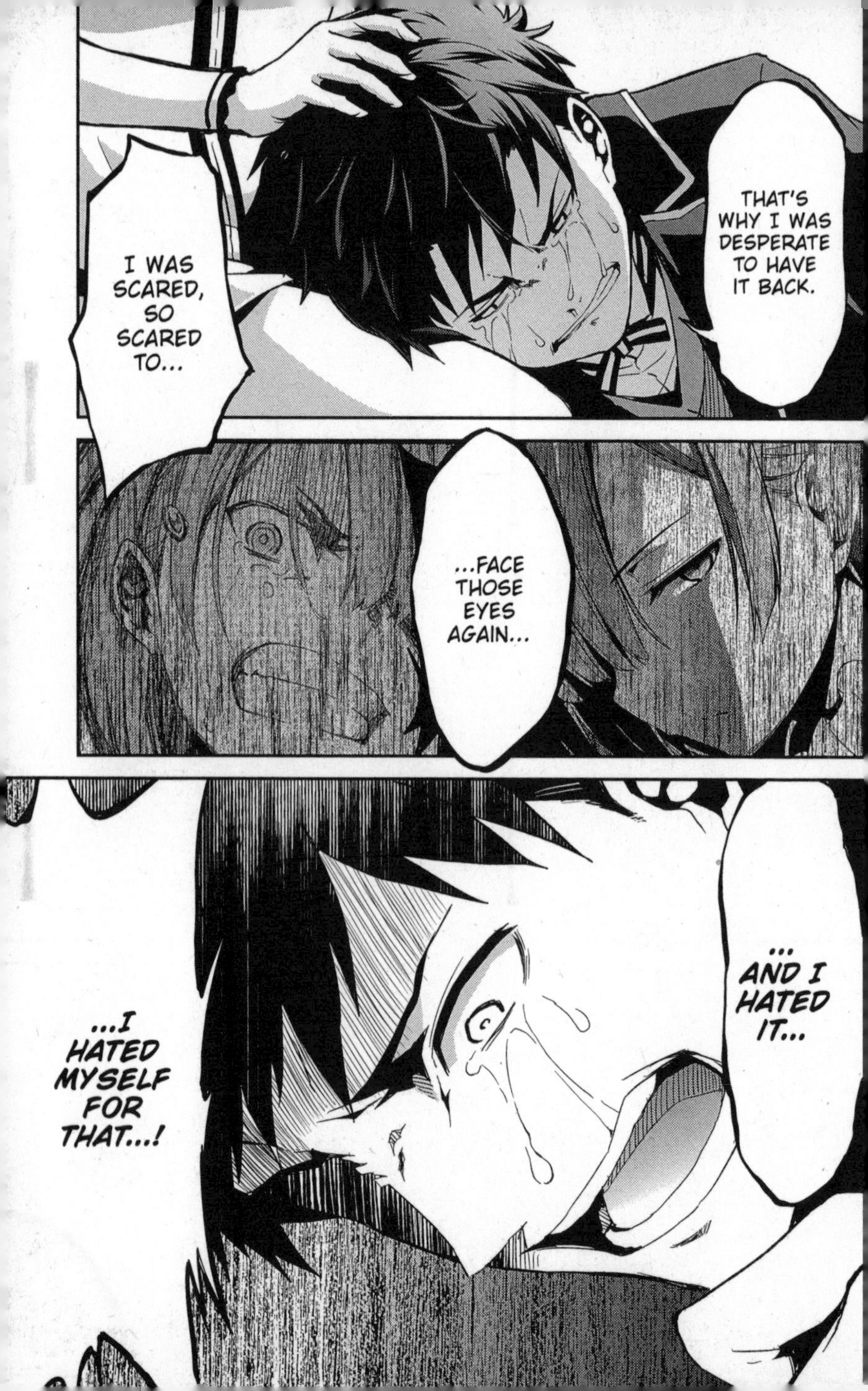
THAT'S WHY I WAS DESPERATE TO HAVE IT BACK.
I WAS SCARED, SO SCARED TO...
...FACE THOSE EYES AGAIN...
...AND I HATED IT...
...I HATED MYSELF FOR THAT...!

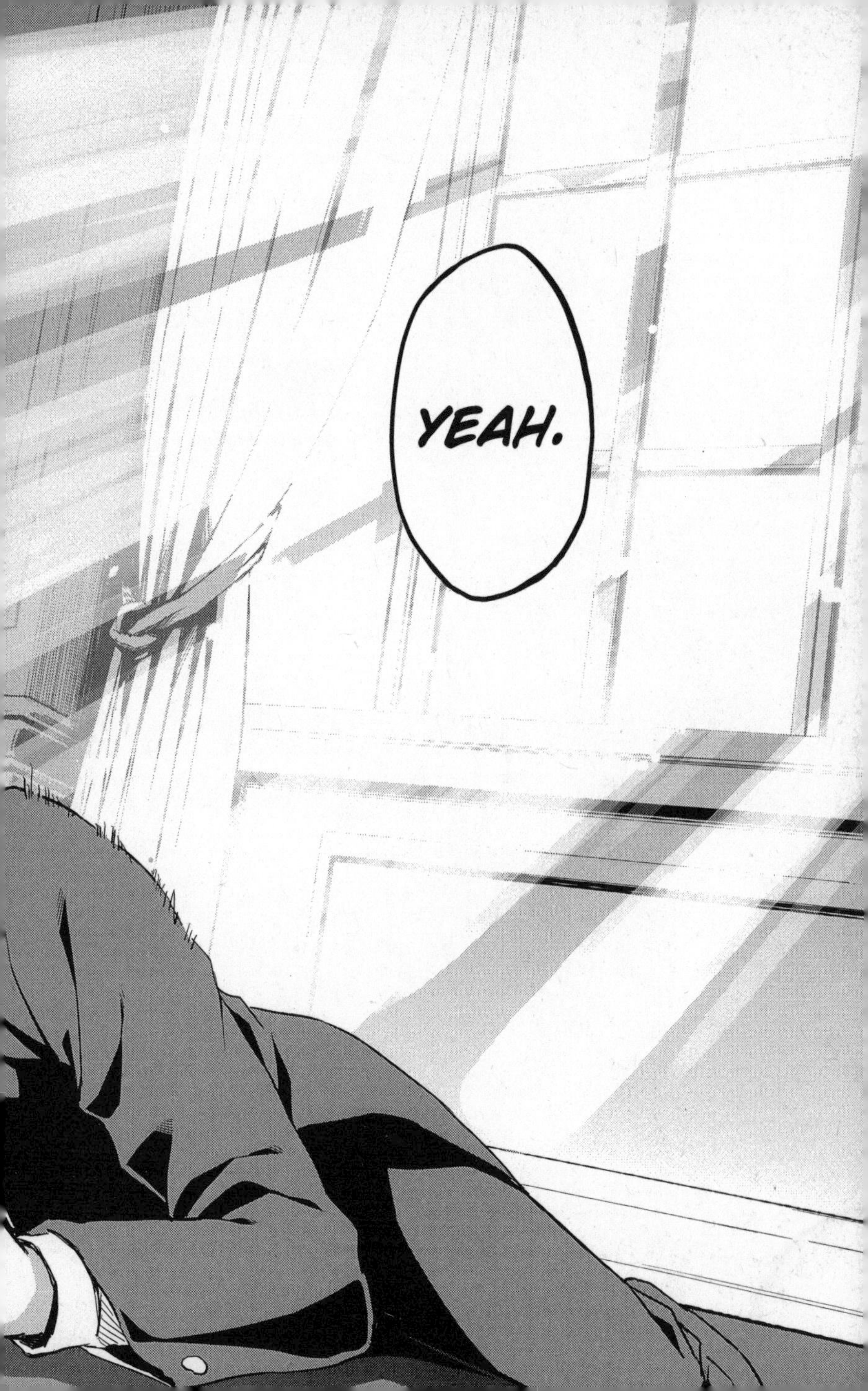
YEAH.

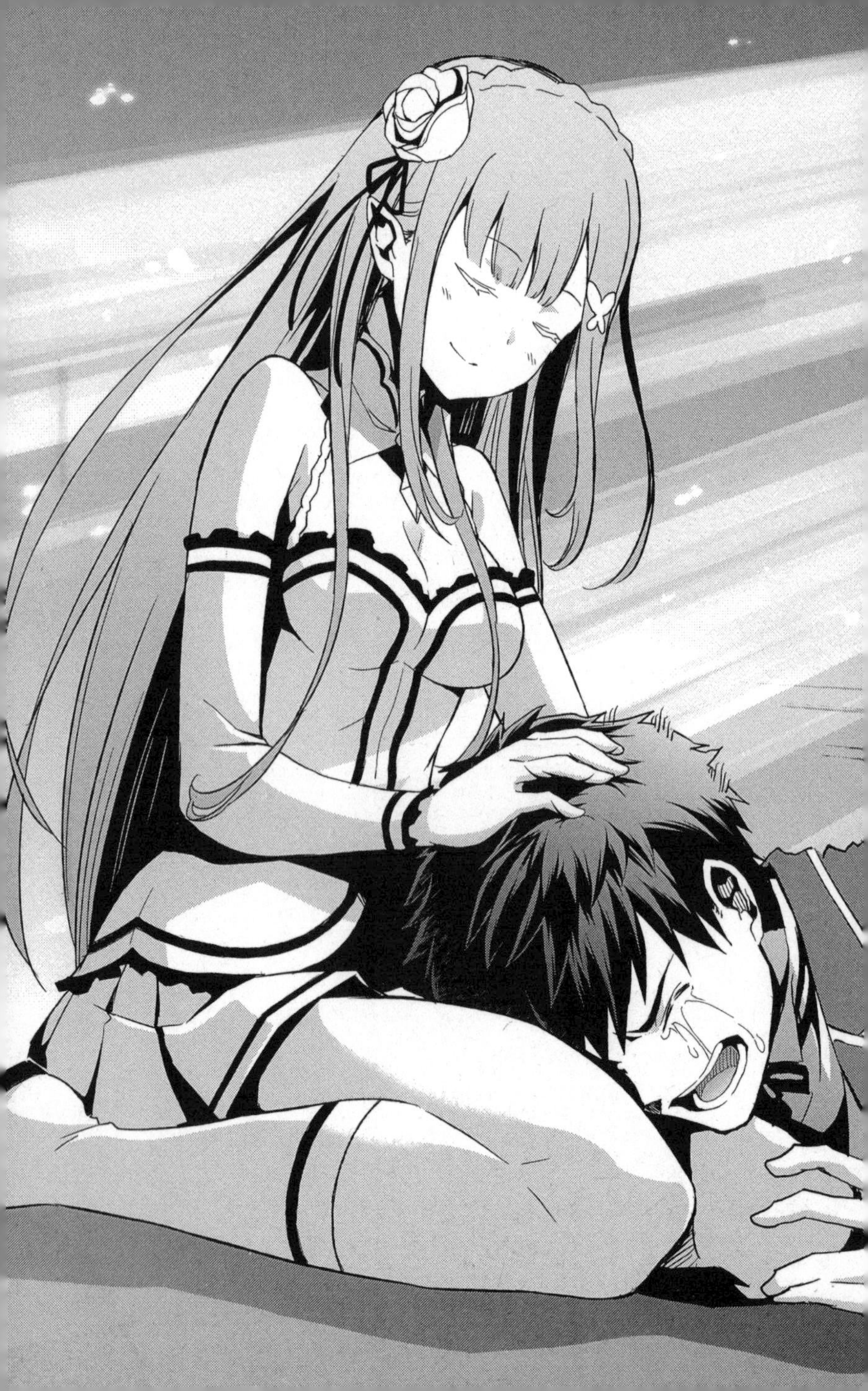

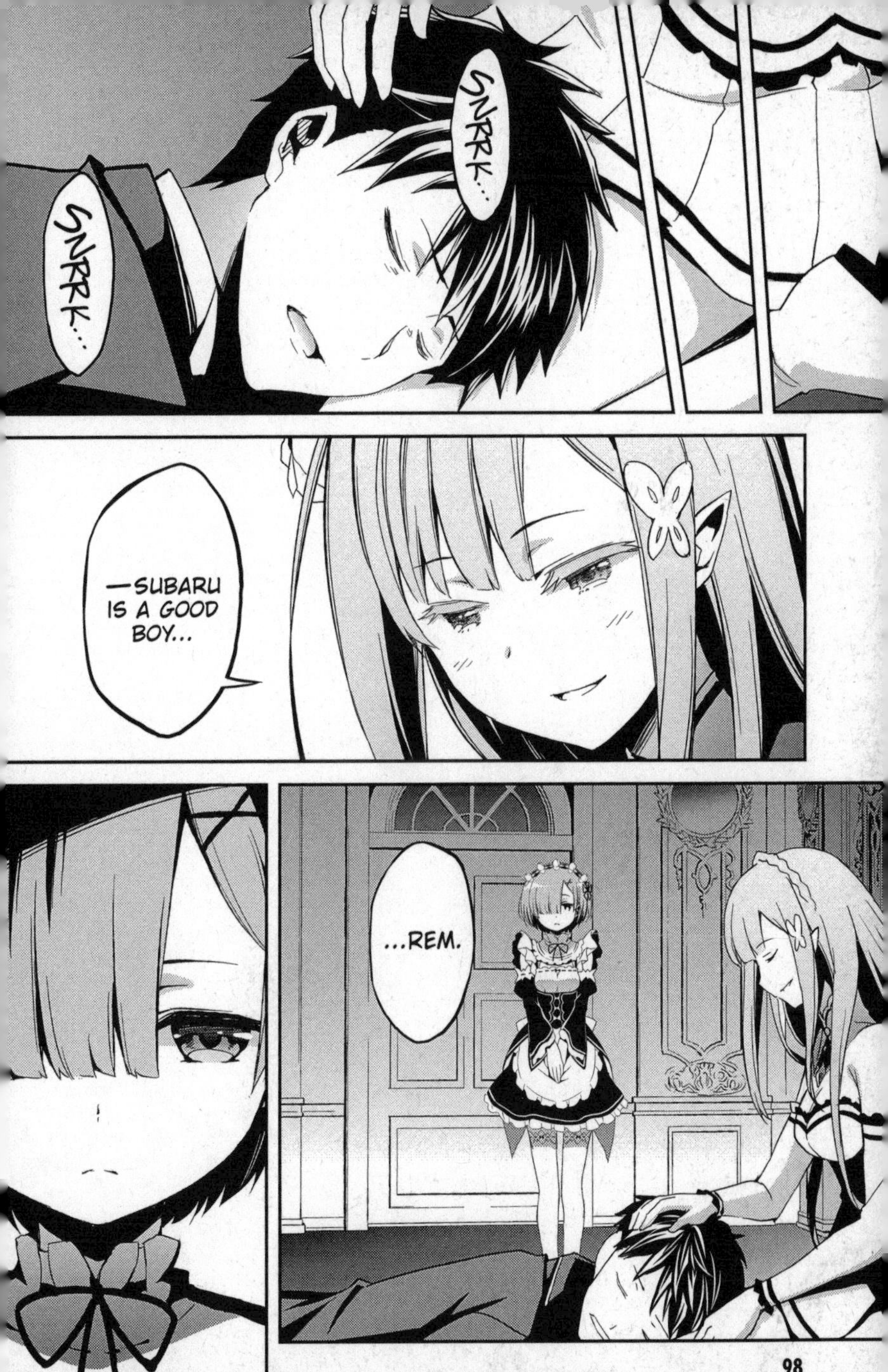
SNRRK...
SNRRK...
—SUBARU IS A GOOD BOY...
...REM.

E.M.T.!!

Re:ZERO -Starting Life in Another World-

A Week at the Mansion

The only ability Subaru Natsuki gets when
he's summoned to another world is time
travel via his own death. But to save her,
he'll die as many times as it takes.

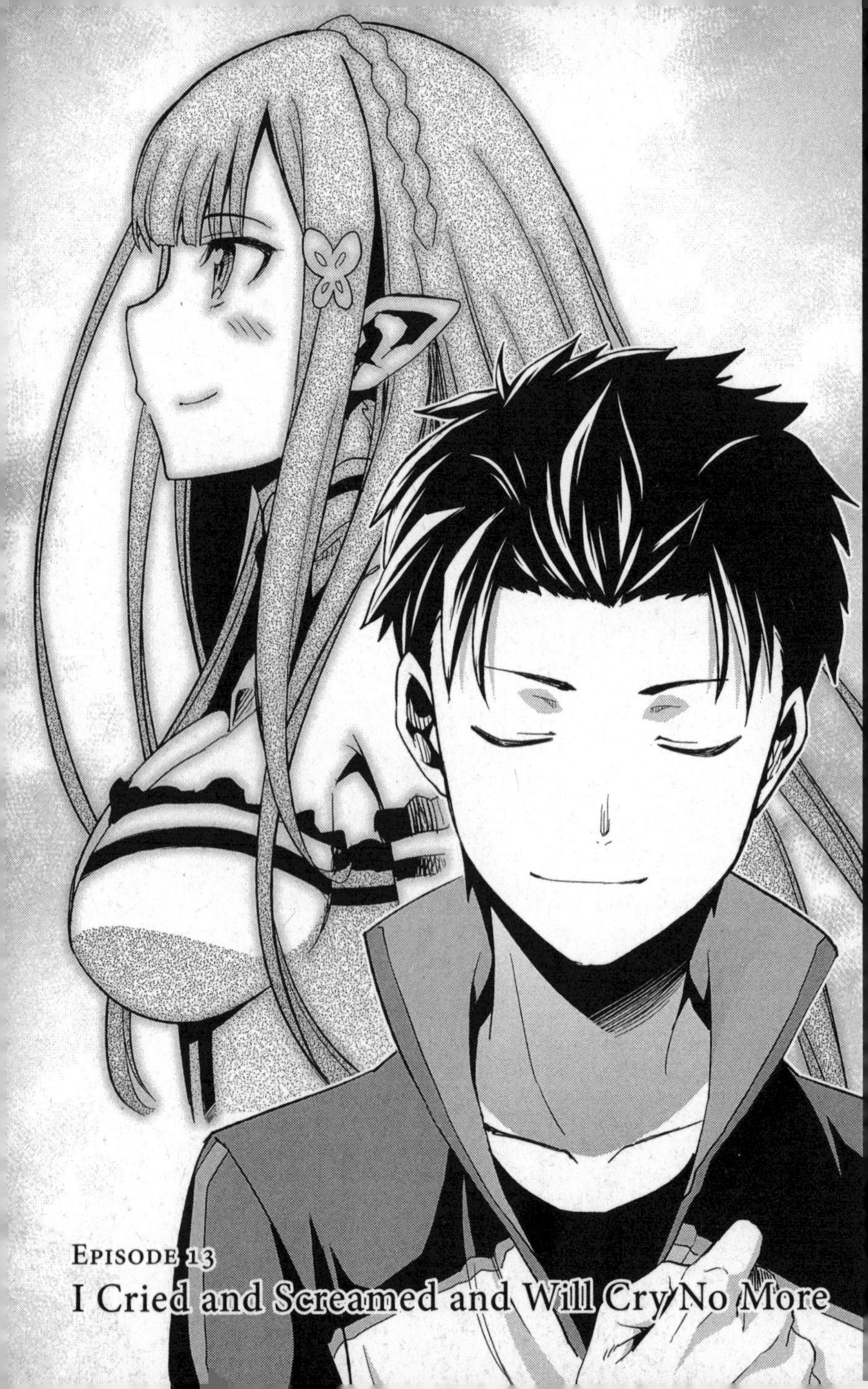

Episode 13

I Cried and Screamed and Will Cry No More

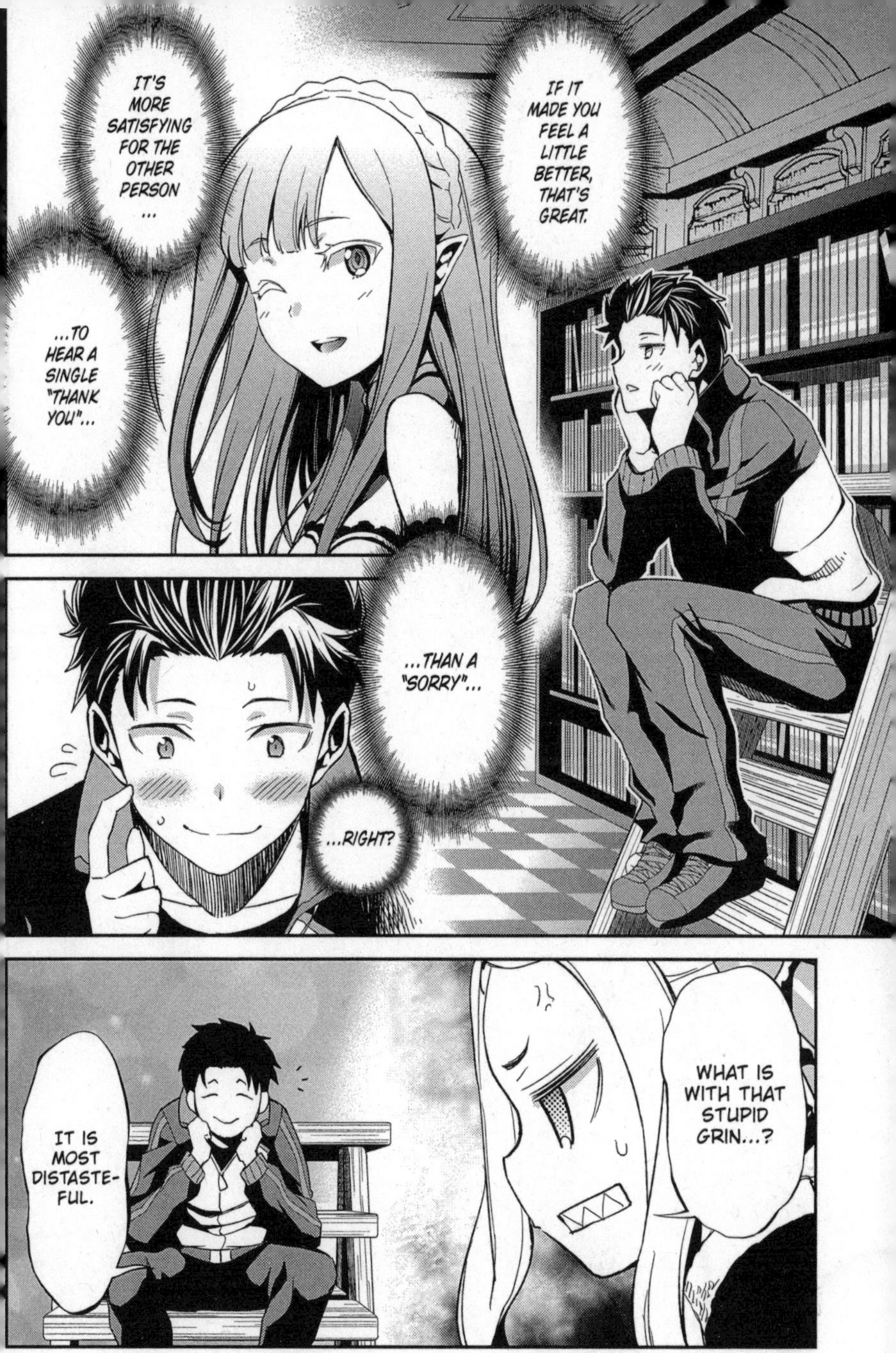
IF IT MADE YOU FEEL A LITTLE BETTER, THAT'S GREAT.
IT'S MORE SATISFYING FOR THE OTHER PERSON ...
...TO HEAR A SINGLE "THANK YOU"...
...THAN A "SORRY"...
...RIGHT?
WHAT IS WITH THAT STUPID GRIN...?
IT IS MOST DISTASTE-FUL.

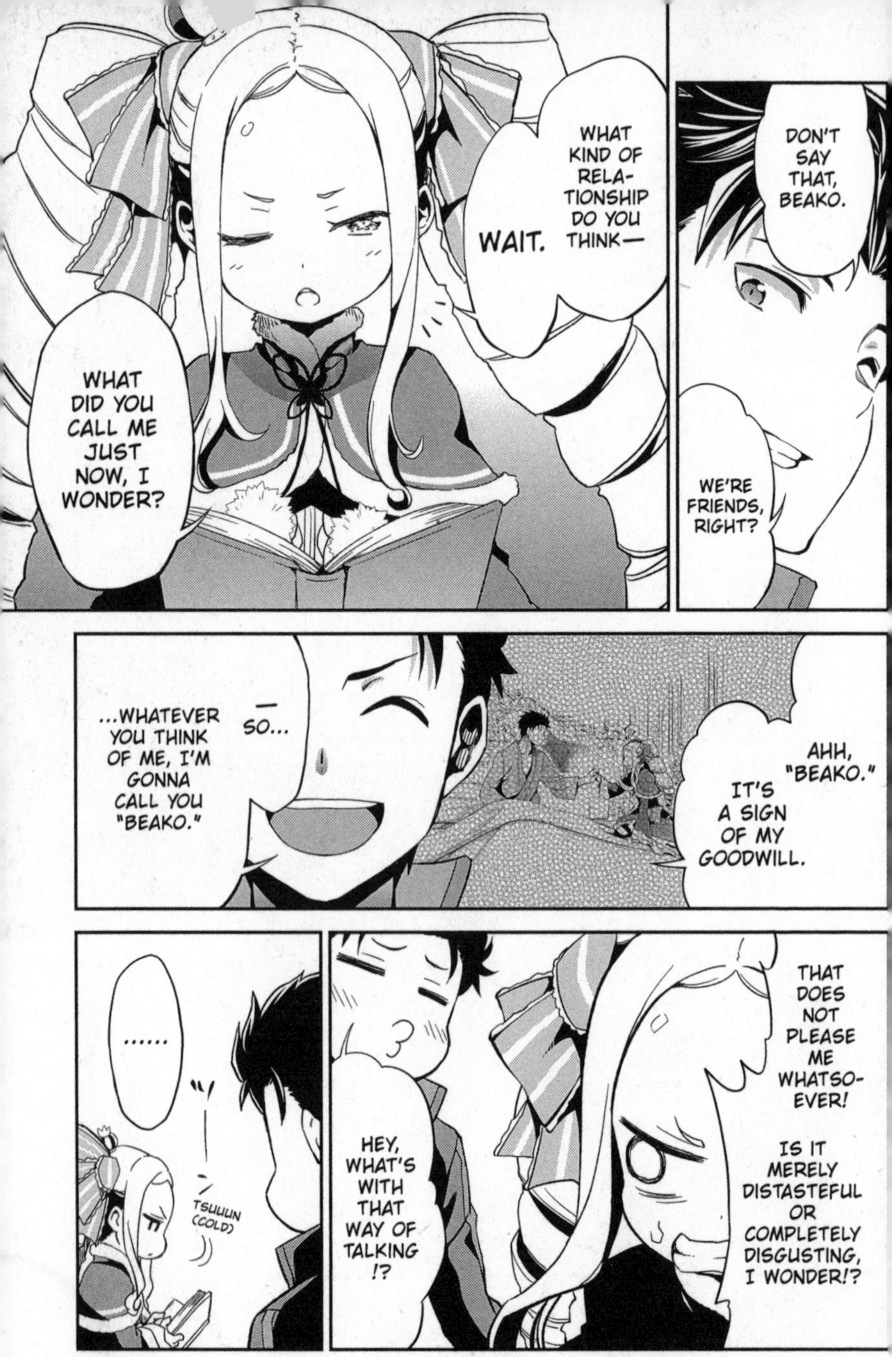
DON'T SAY THAT, BEAKO.
WE'RE FRIENDS, RIGHT?
WHAT KIND OF RELATIONSHIP DO YOU THINK—
WAIT.
WHAT DID YOU CALL ME JUST NOW, I WONDER?
AHH, "BEAKO."
IT'S A SIGN OF MY GOODWILL.
SO...
...WHATEVER YOU THINK OF ME, I'M GONNA CALL YOU "BEAKO."
THAT DOES NOT PLEASE ME WHATSOEVER!
IS IT MERELY DISTASTEFUL OR COMPLETELY DISGUSTING, I WONDER!?
HEY, WHAT'S WITH THAT WAY OF TALKING!?
......
TSUUUN (COLD)

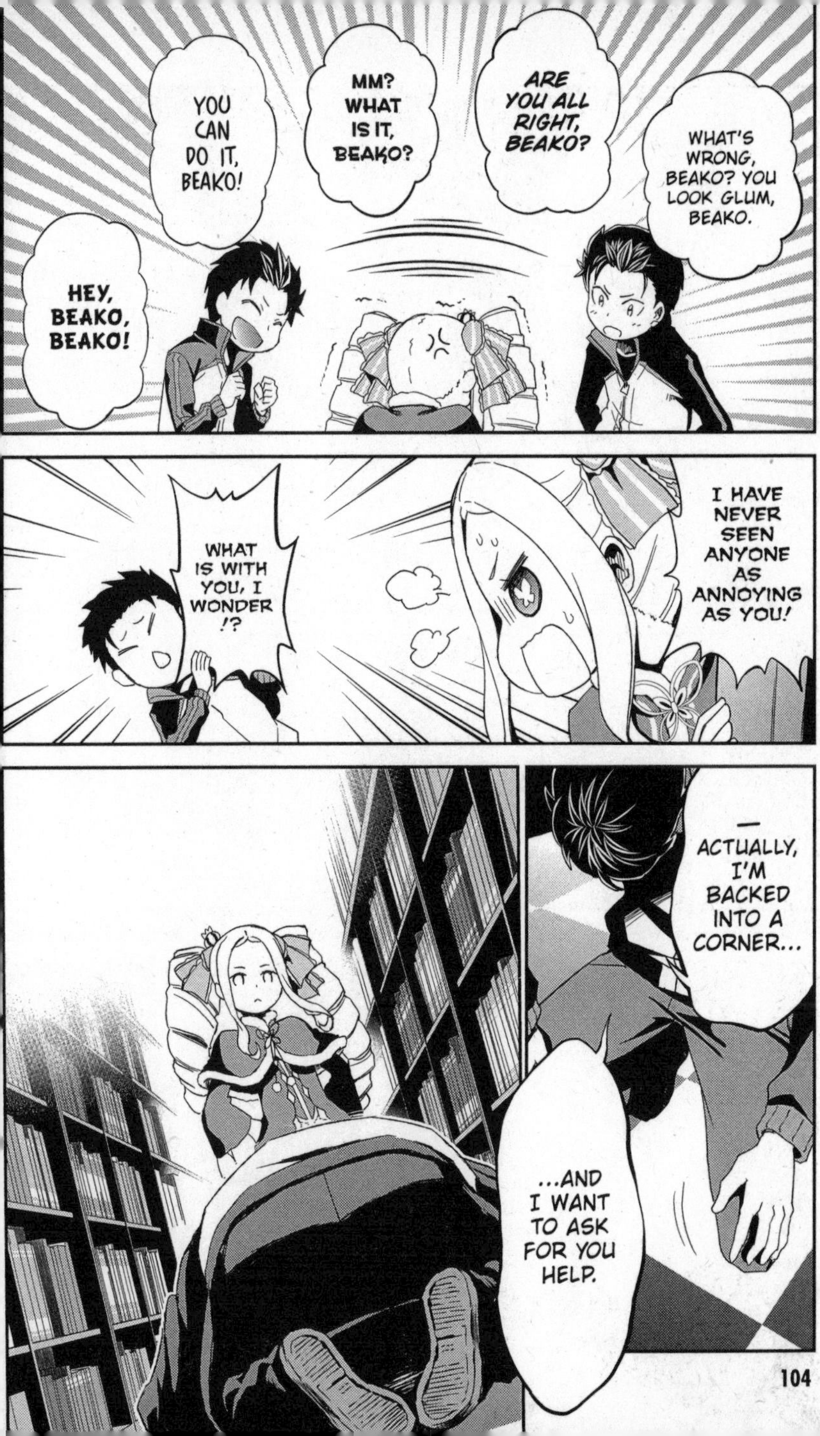
WHAT'S WRONG, BEAKO? YOU LOOK GLUM, BEAKO.
ARE YOU ALL RIGHT, BEAKO?
MM? WHAT IS IT, BEAKO?
YOU CAN DO IT, BEAKO!
HEY, BEAKO, BEAKO!
I HAVE NEVER SEEN ANYONE AS ANNOYING AS YOU!
WHAT IS WITH YOU, I WONDER!?
—ACTUALLY, I'M BACKED INTO A CORNER...
...AND I WANT TO ASK FOR YOU HELP.

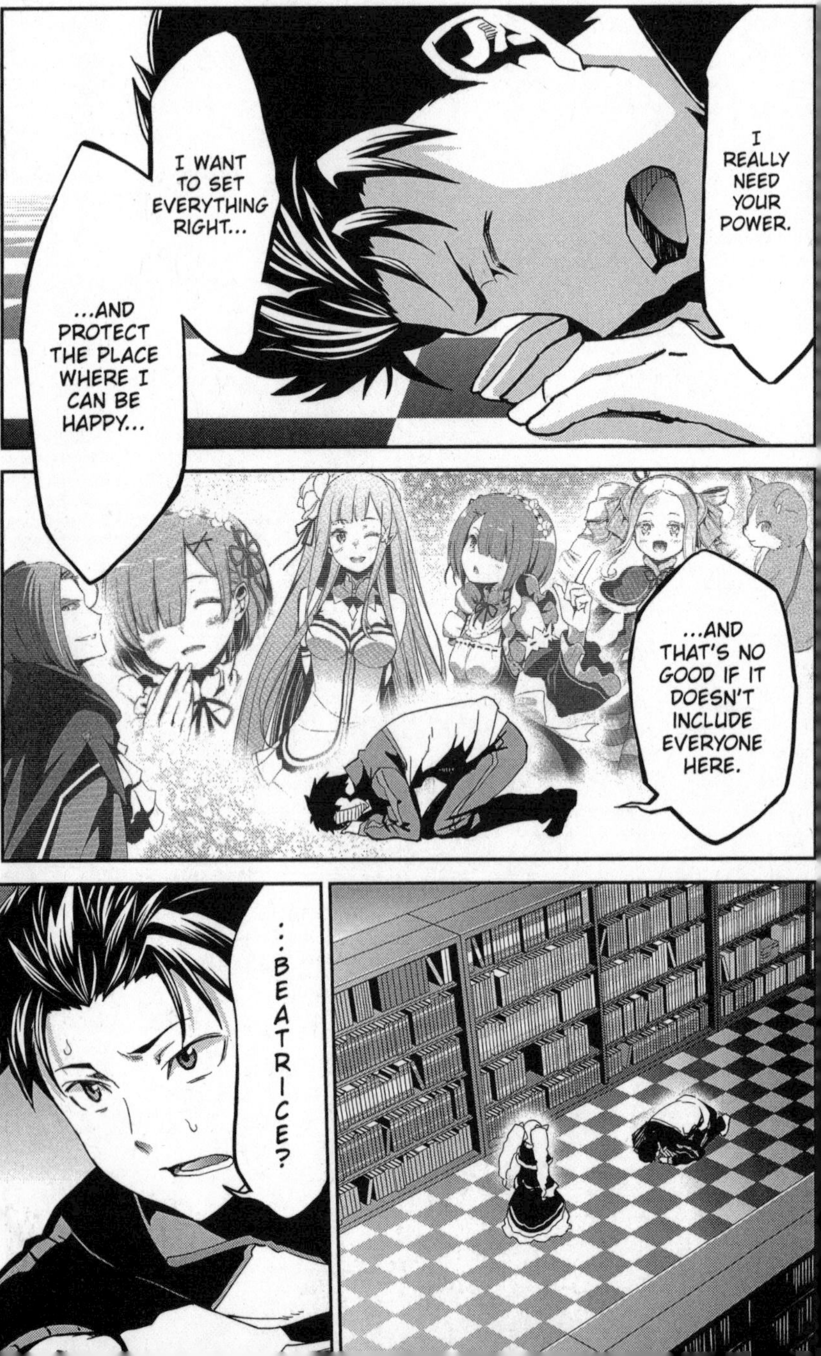
I REALLY NEED YOUR POWER.
I WANT TO SET EVERYTHING RIGHT...
...AND PROTECT THE PLACE WHERE I CAN BE HAPPY...
...AND THAT'S NO GOOD IF IT DOESN'T INCLUDE EVERYONE HERE.
...BEATRICE?

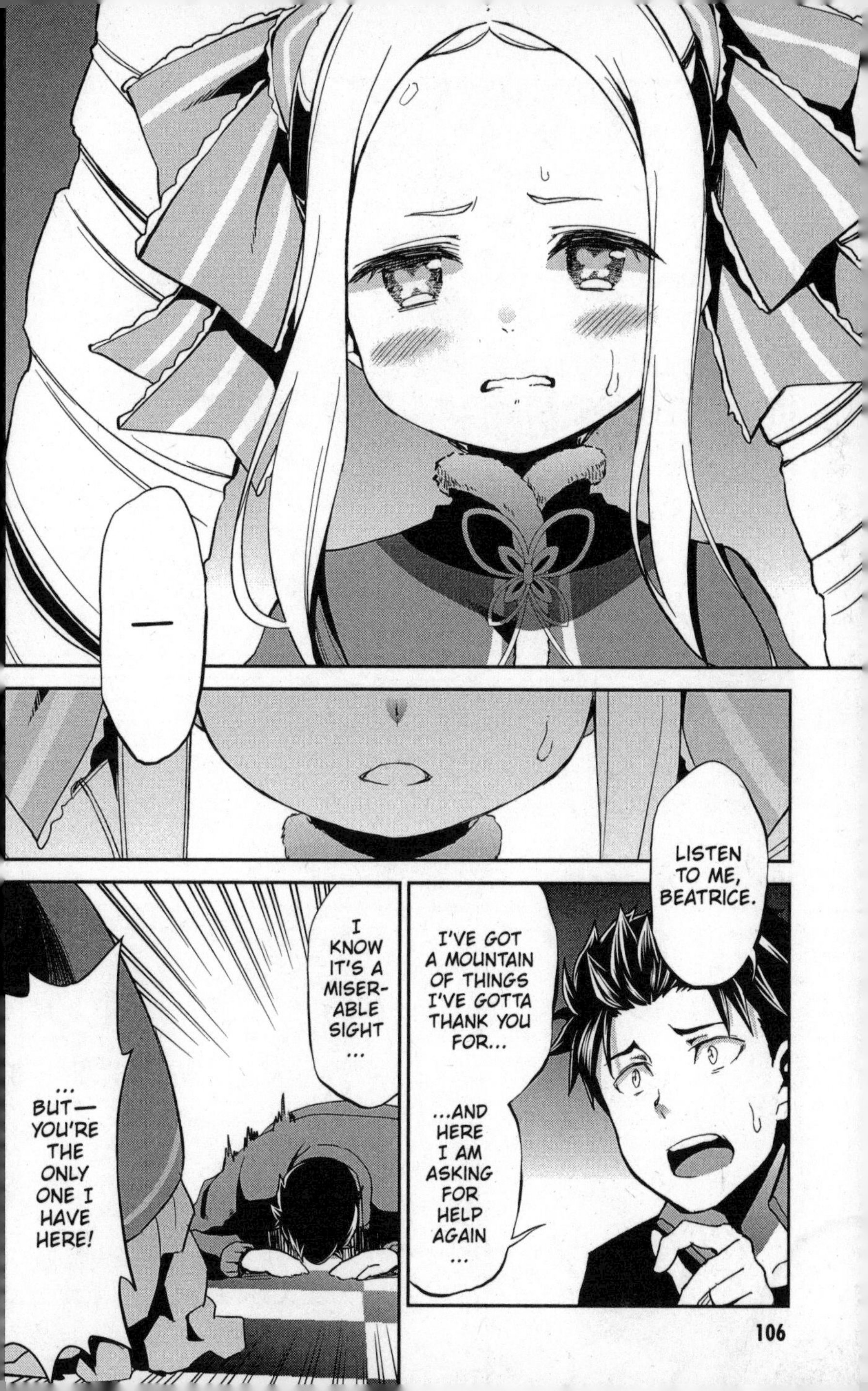
—
LISTEN TO ME, BEATRICE.
I'VE GOT A MOUNTAIN OF THINGS I'VE GOTTA THANK YOU FOR...
...AND HERE I AM ASKING FOR HELP AGAIN...
I KNOW IT'S A MISER-ABLE SIGHT...
...BUT—YOU'RE THE ONLY ONE I HAVE HERE!

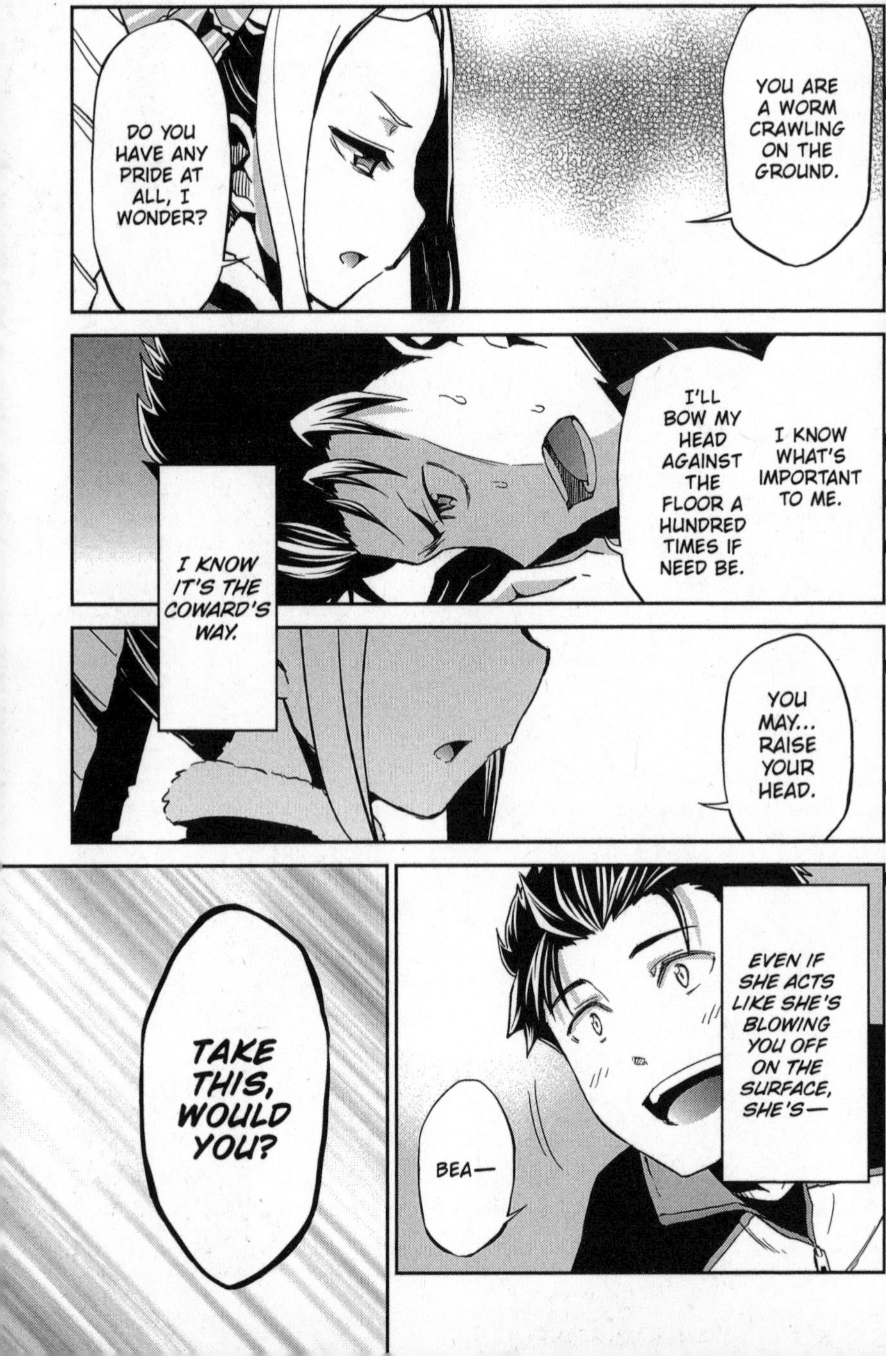
YOU ARE A WORM CRAWLING ON THE GROUND.
DO YOU HAVE ANY PRIDE AT ALL, I WONDER?
I KNOW WHAT'S IMPORTANT TO ME.
I'LL BOW MY HEAD AGAINST THE FLOOR A HUNDRED TIMES IF NEED BE.
I KNOW IT'S THE COWARD'S WAY.
YOU MAY... RAISE YOUR HEAD.
EVEN IF SHE ACTS LIKE SHE'S BLOWING YOU OFF ON THE SURFACE, SHE'S—
BEA—
TAKE THIS, WOULD YOU?

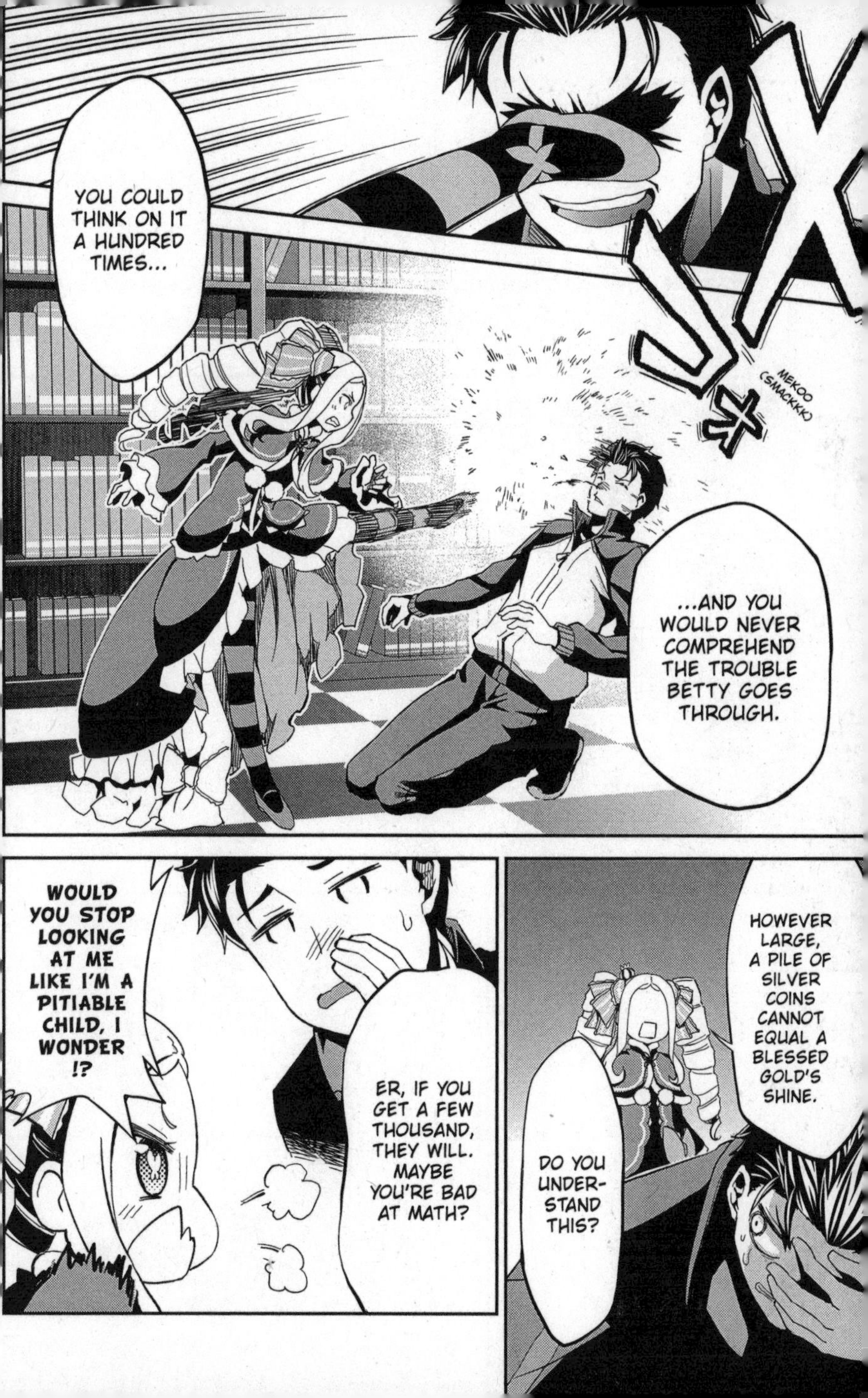
YOU COULD THINK ON IT A HUNDRED TIMES...
MEKOO (SMACKKK)
...AND YOU WOULD NEVER COMPREHEND THE TROUBLE BETTY GOES THROUGH.
HOWEVER LARGE, A PILE OF SILVER COINS CANNOT EQUAL A BLESSED GOLD'S SHINE.
DO YOU UNDER-STAND THIS?
ER, IF YOU GET A FEW THOUSAND, THEY WILL. MAYBE YOU'RE BAD AT MATH?
WOULD YOU STOP LOOKING AT ME LIKE I'M A PITIABLE CHILD, I WONDER!?

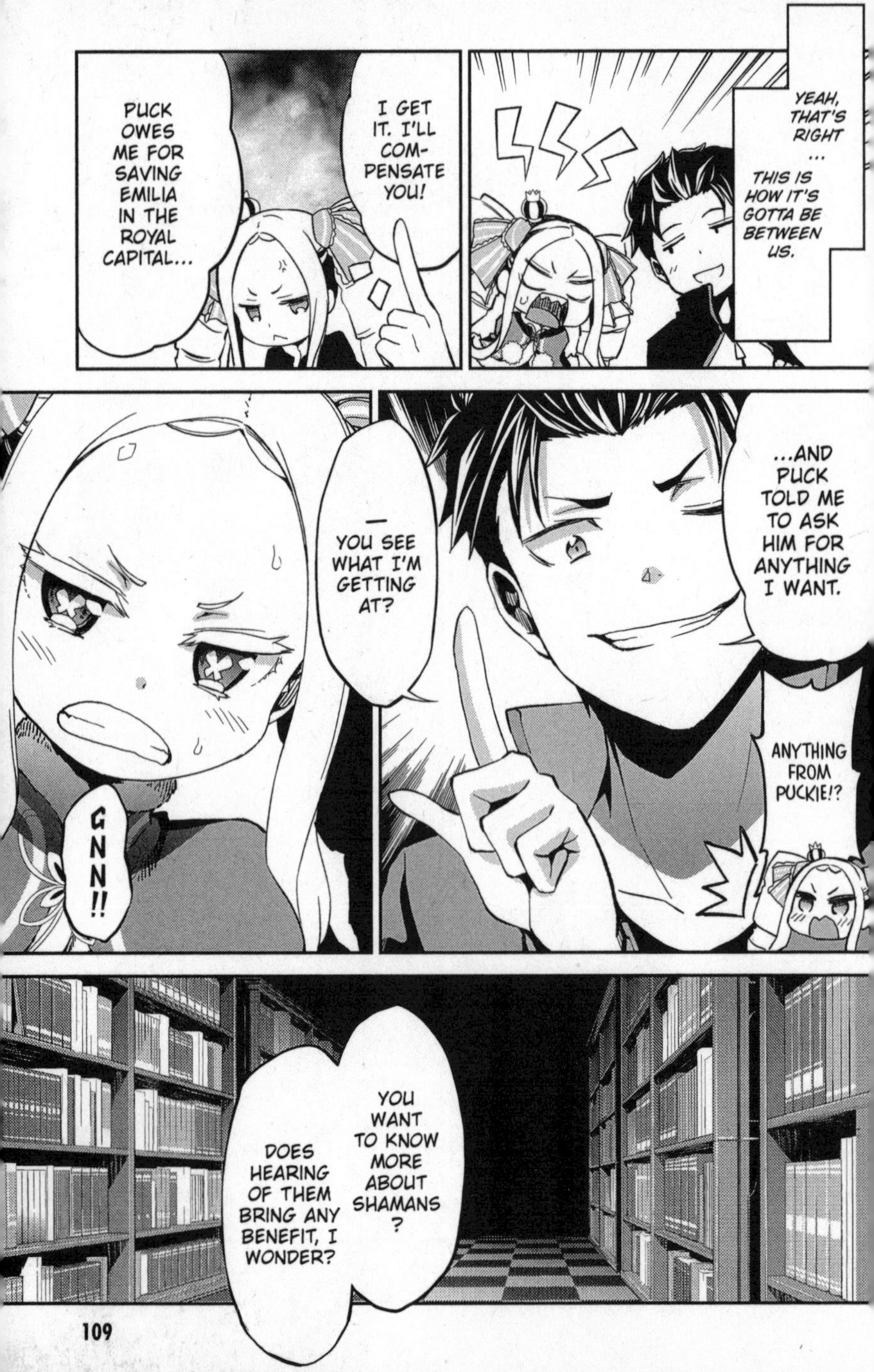
YEAH, THAT'S RIGHT ... THIS IS HOW IT'S GOTTA BE BETWEEN US.
I GET IT. I'LL COM-PENSATE YOU!
PUCK OWES ME FOR SAVING EMILIA IN THE ROYAL CAPITAL...
...AND PUCK TOLD ME TO ASK HIM FOR ANYTHING I WANT.
ANYTHING FROM PUCKIE!?
— YOU SEE WHAT I'M GETTING AT?
GNN!!
YOU WANT TO KNOW MORE ABOUT SHAMANS?
DOES HEARING OF THEM BRING ANY BENEFIT, I WONDER?

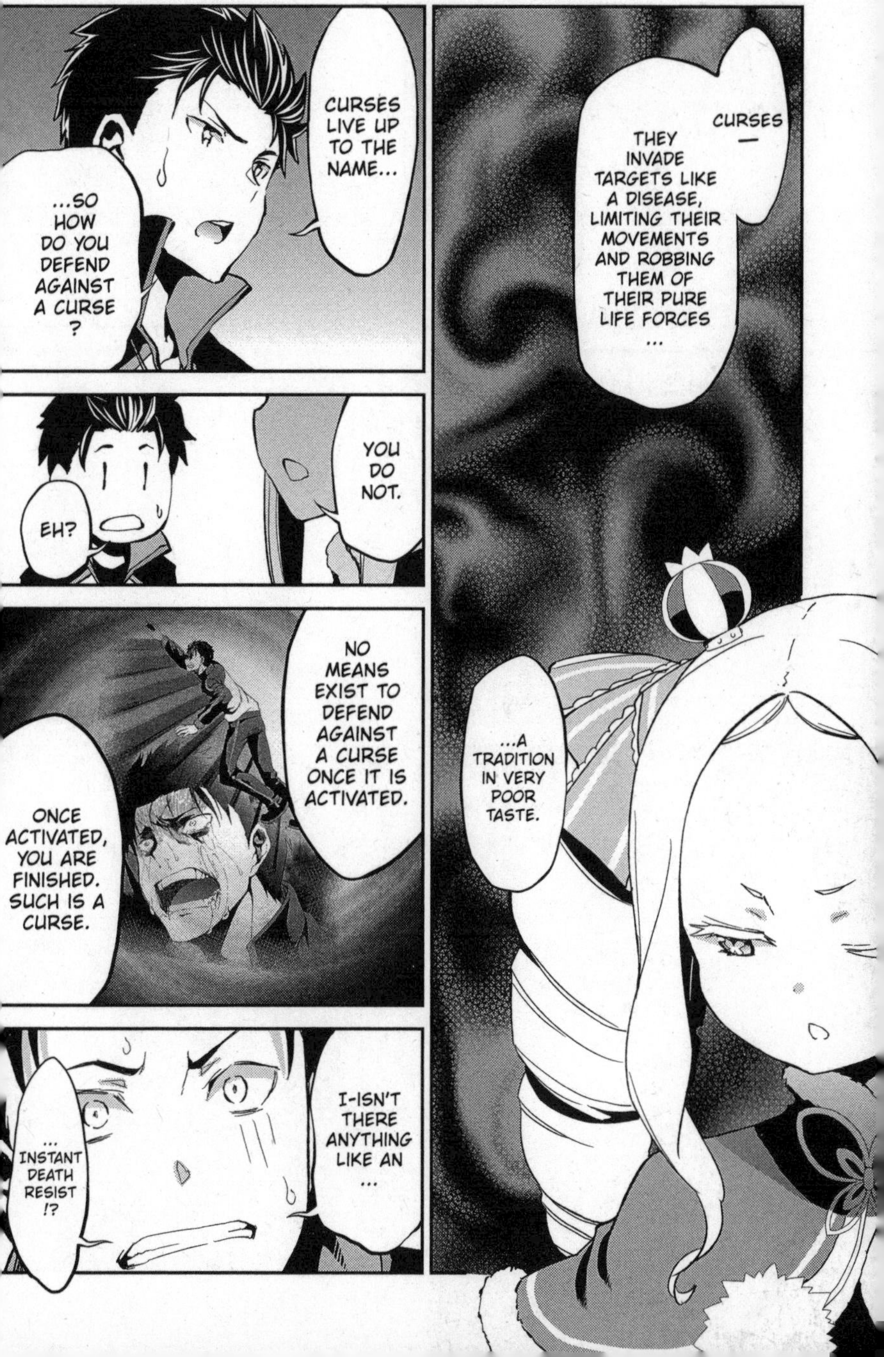
CURSES— THEY INVADE TARGETS LIKE A DISEASE, LIMITING THEIR MOVEMENTS AND ROBBING THEM OF THEIR PURE LIFE FORCES...
...A TRADITION IN VERY POOR TASTE.
CURSES LIVE UP TO THE NAME...
...SO HOW DO YOU DEFEND AGAINST A CURSE?
YOU DO NOT.
EH?
NO MEANS EXIST TO DEFEND AGAINST A CURSE ONCE IT IS ACTIVATED.
ONCE ACTIVATED, YOU ARE FINISHED. SUCH IS A CURSE.
I-ISN'T THERE ANYTHING LIKE AN...
...INSTANT DEATH RESIST!?

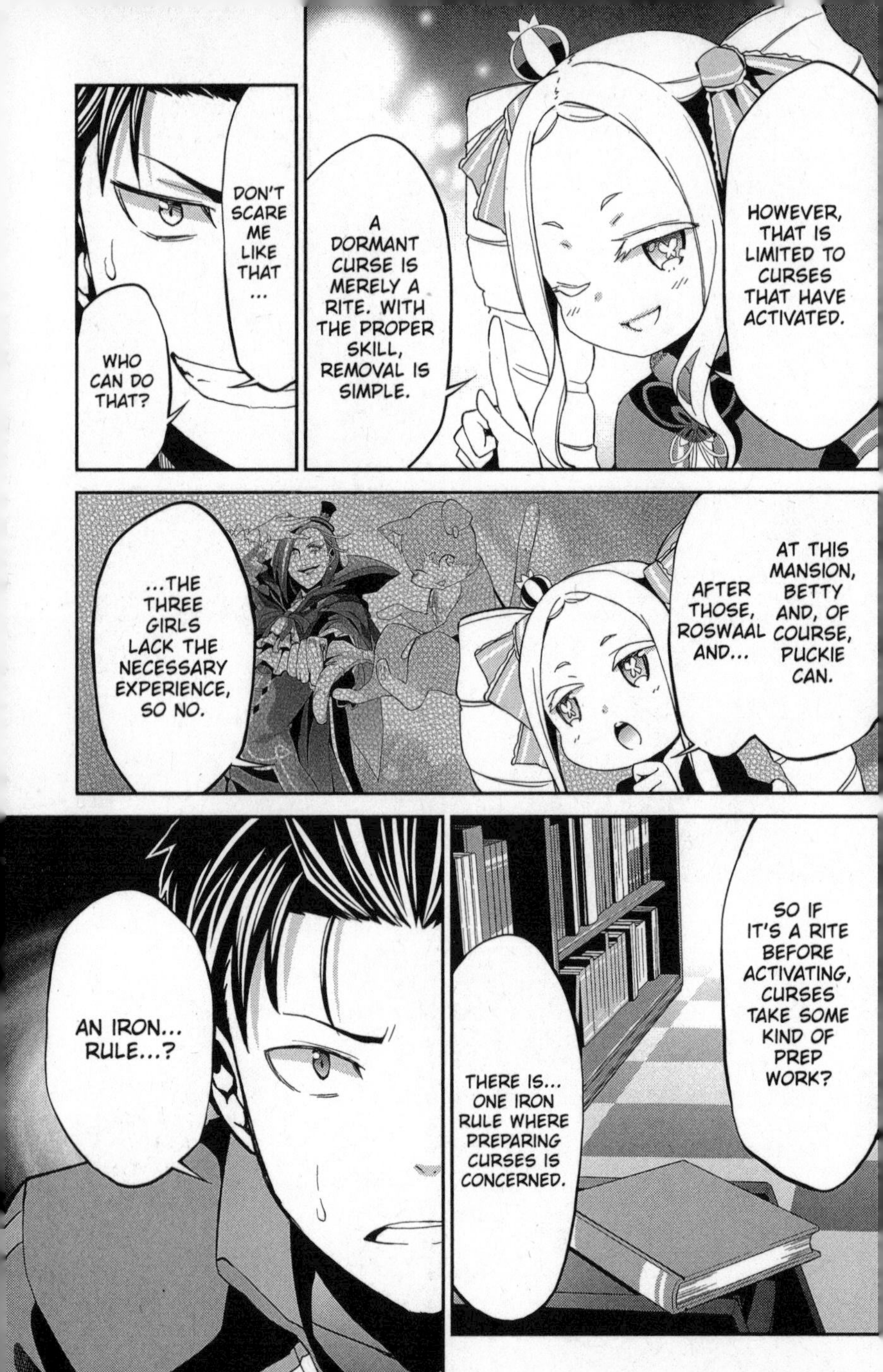
HOWEVER, THAT IS LIMITED TO CURSES THAT HAVE ACTIVATED.
A DORMANT CURSE IS MERELY A RITE. WITH THE PROPER SKILL, REMOVAL IS SIMPLE.
DON'T SCARE ME LIKE THAT...
WHO CAN DO THAT?
AT THIS MANSION, BETTY AND, OF COURSE, PUCKIE CAN.
AFTER THOSE, ROSWAAL AND...
...THE THREE GIRLS LACK THE NECESSARY EXPERIENCE, SO NO.
SO IF IT'S A RITE BEFORE ACTIVATING, CURSES TAKE SOME KIND OF PREP WORK?
THERE IS... ONE IRON RULE WHERE PREPARING CURSES IS CONCERNED.
AN IRON... RULE...?

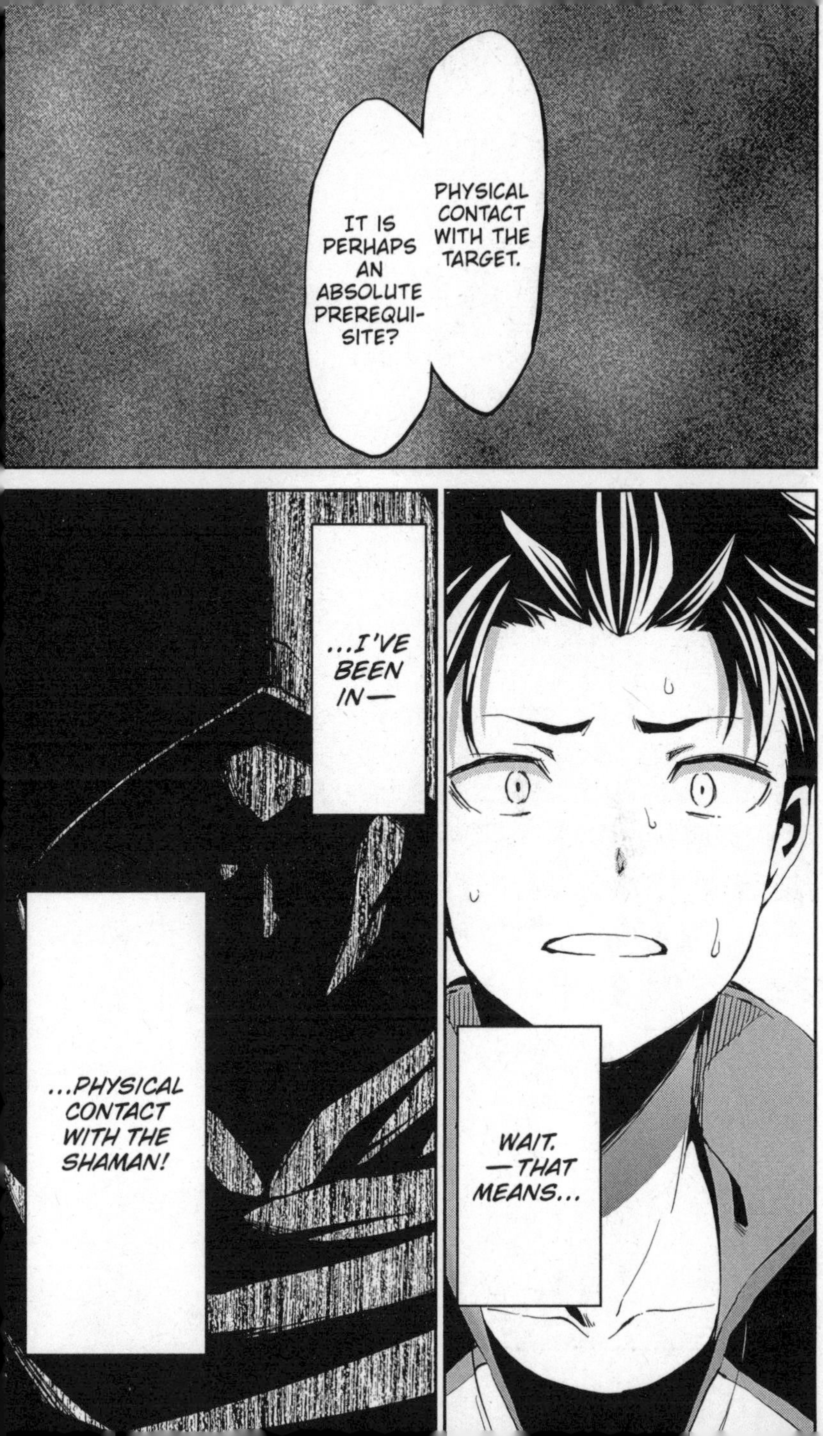
PHYSICAL CONTACT WITH THE TARGET.
IT IS PERHAPS AN ABSOLUTE PREREQUI-SITE?
WAIT. —THAT MEANS...
...I'VE BEEN IN—
...PHYSICAL CONTACT WITH THE SHAMAN!

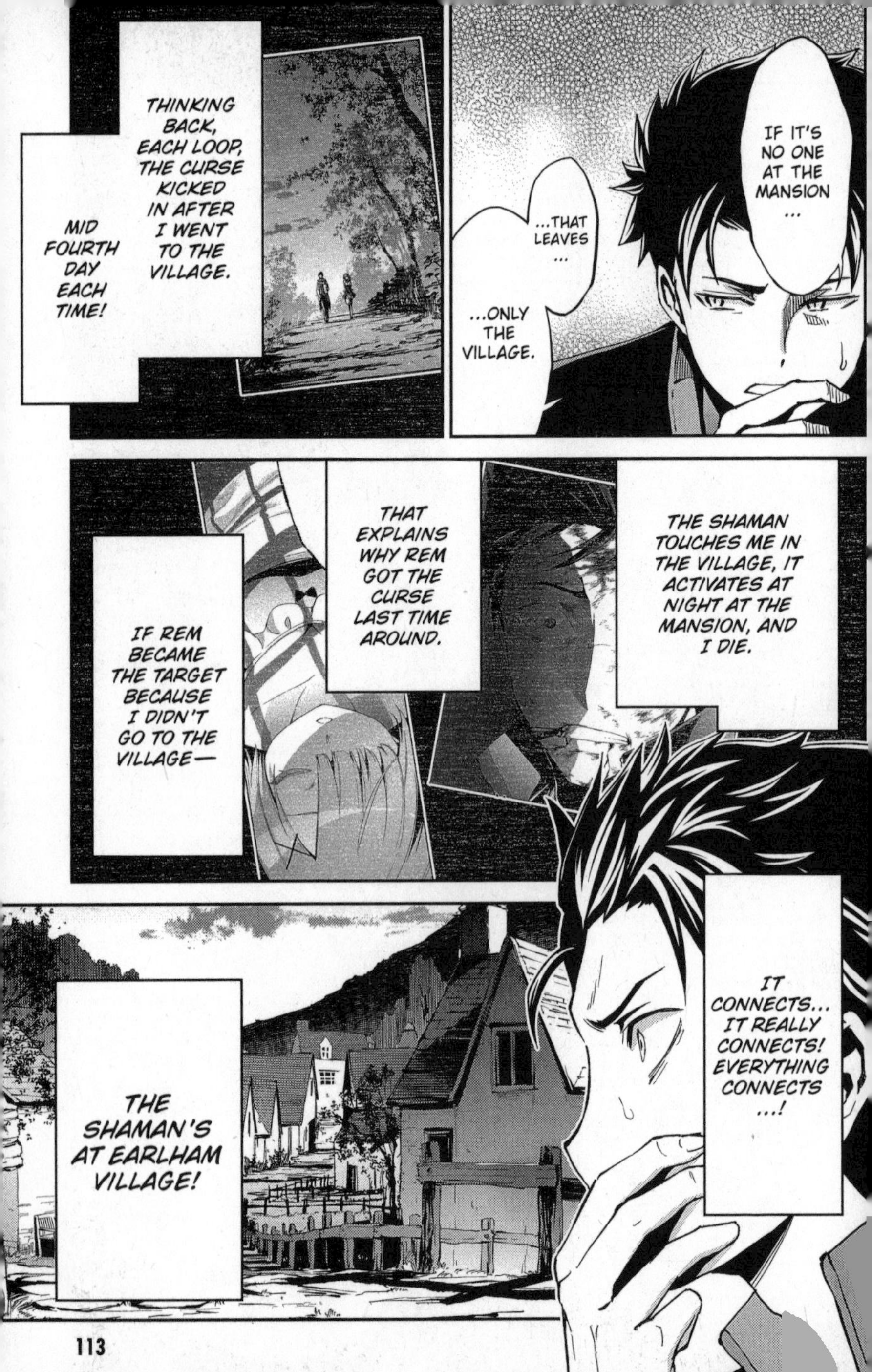
IF IT'S NO ONE AT THE MANSION ...
...THAT LEAVES ...
...ONLY THE VILLAGE.
THINKING BACK, EACH LOOP, THE CURSE KICKED IN AFTER I WENT TO THE VILLAGE.
MID FOURTH DAY EACH TIME!
THE SHAMAN TOUCHES ME IN THE VILLAGE, IT ACTIVATES AT NIGHT AT THE MANSION, AND I DIE.
THAT EXPLAINS WHY REM GOT THE CURSE LAST TIME AROUND.
IF REM BECAME THE TARGET BECAUSE I DIDN'T GO TO THE VILLAGE—
IT CONNECTS... IT REALLY CONNECTS! EVERYTHING CONNECTS ...!
THE SHAMAN'S AT EARLHAM VILLAGE!

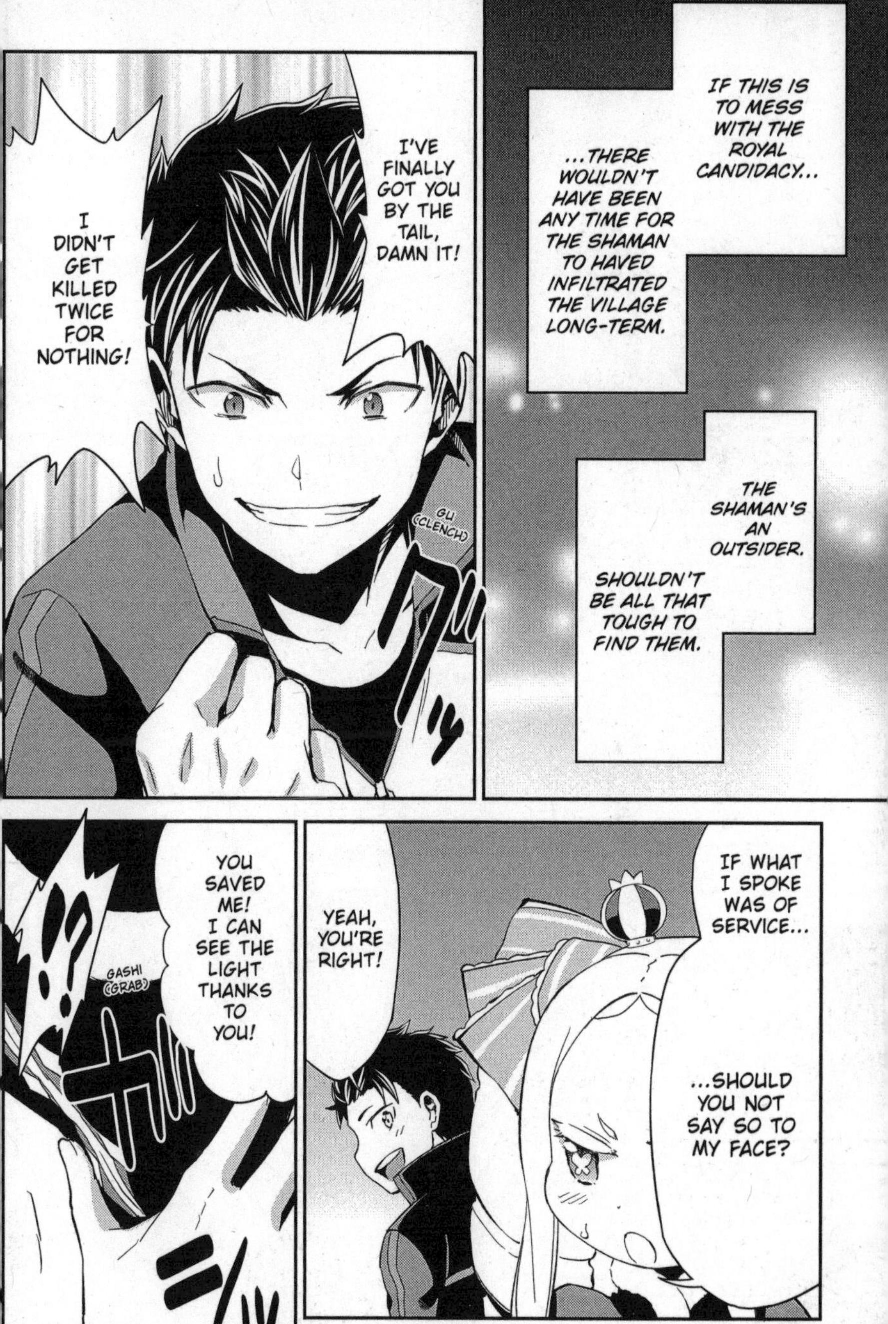
IF THIS IS TO MESS WITH THE ROYAL CANDIDACY...
...THERE WOULDN'T HAVE BEEN ANY TIME FOR THE SHAMAN TO HAVED INFILTRATED THE VILLAGE LONG-TERM.
THE SHAMAN'S AN OUTSIDER.
SHOULDN'T BE ALL THAT TOUGH TO FIND THEM.
I'VE FINALLY GOT YOU BY THE TAIL, DAMN IT!
I DIDN'T GET KILLED TWICE FOR NOTHING!
GU (CLENCH)
IF WHAT I SPOKE WAS OF SERVICE...
...SHOULD YOU NOT SAY SO TO MY FACE?
YEAH, YOU'RE RIGHT!
YOU SAVED ME! I CAN SEE THE LIGHT THANKS TO YOU!
!?
GASHI (GRAB)

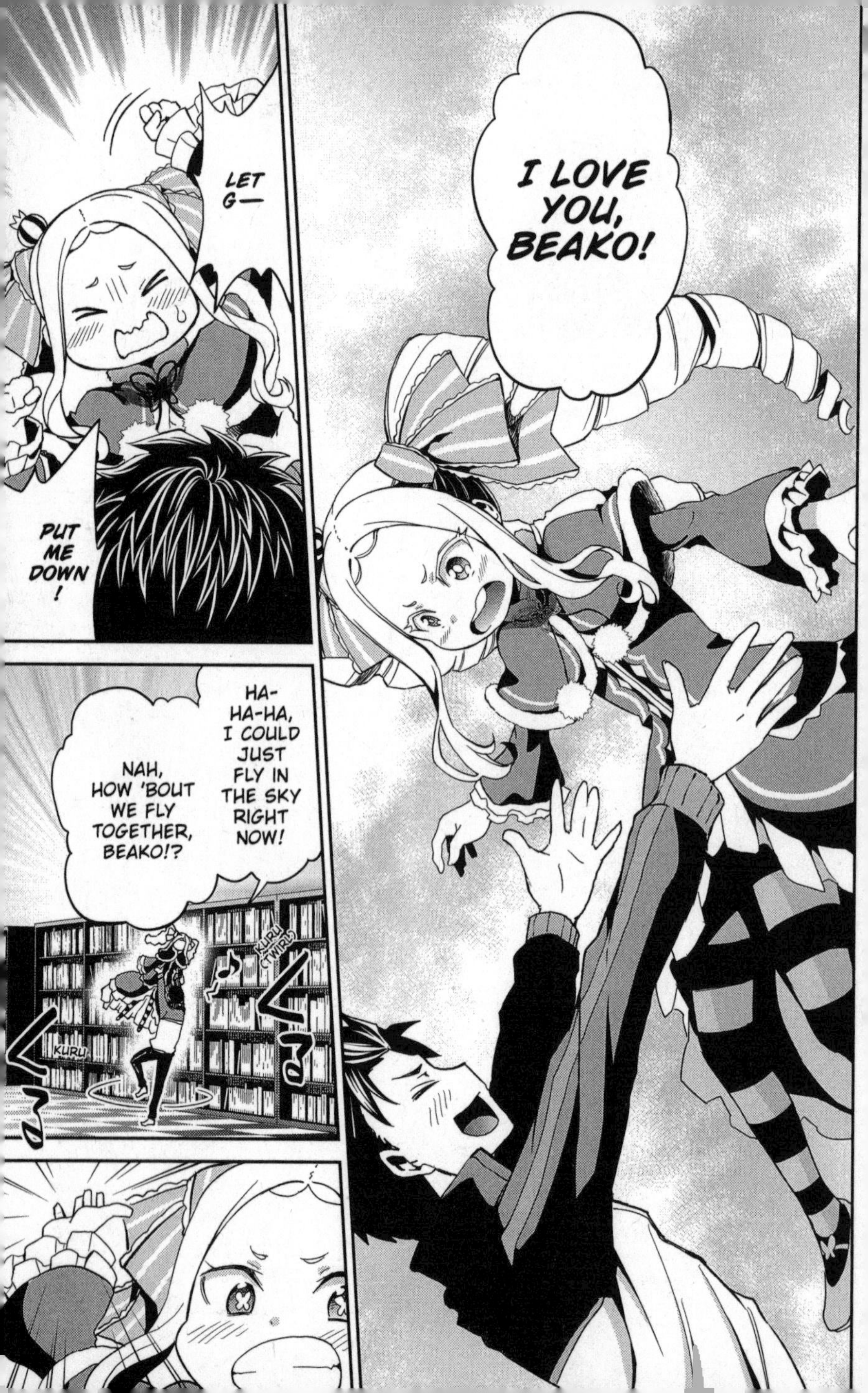
I LOVE YOU, BEAKO!
LET G—
PUT ME DOWN!
HA-HA-HA, I COULD JUST FLY IN THE SKY RIGHT NOW!
NAH, HOW 'BOUT WE FLY TOGETHER, BEAKO!?
KURU (TWIRL)
KURU

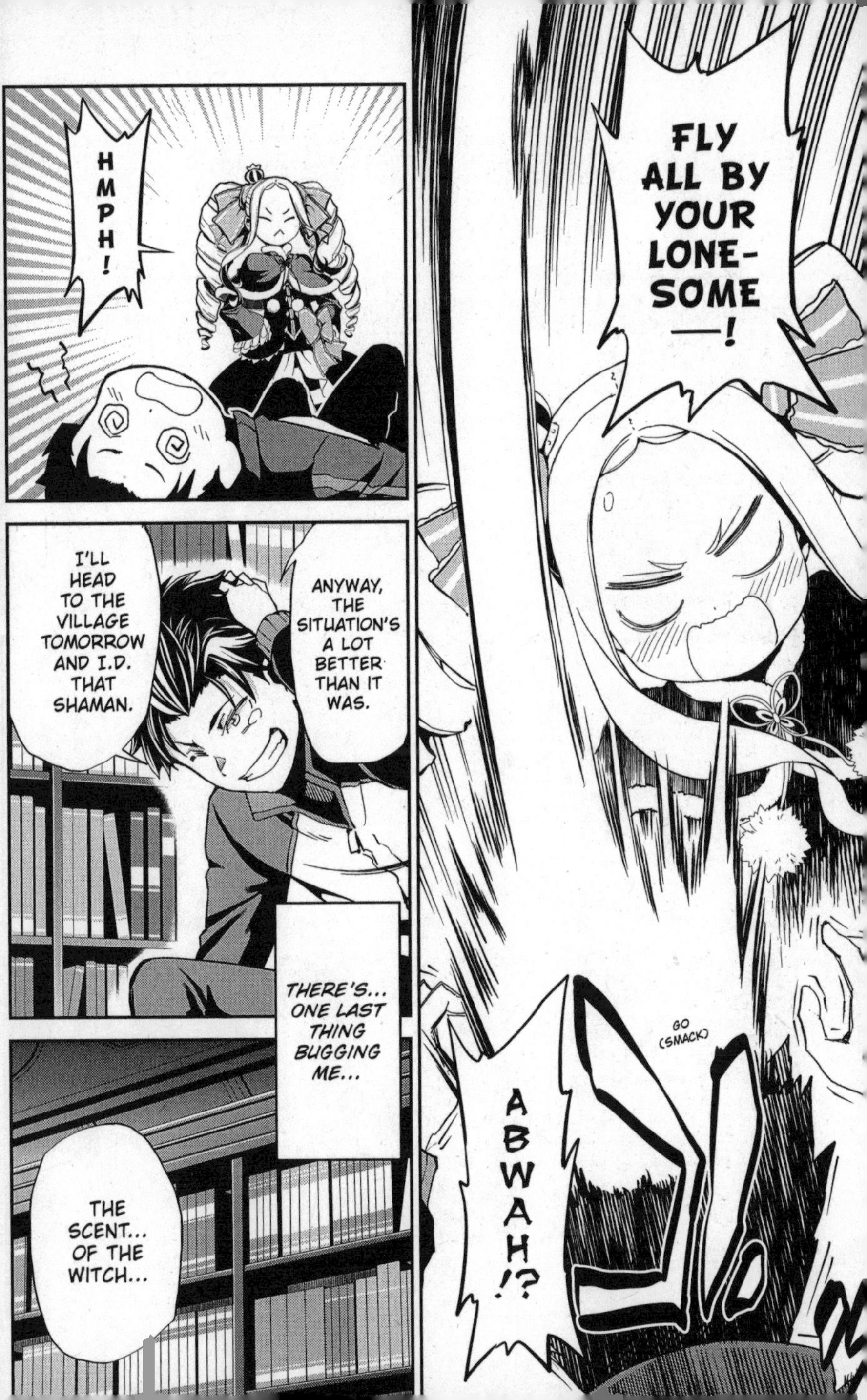
FLY ALL BY YOUR LONESOME—!
GO (SMACK)
ABWAH!?
HMPH!
ANYWAY, THE SITUATION'S A LOT BETTER THAN IT WAS.
I'LL HEAD TO THE VILLAGE TOMORROW AND I.D. THAT SHAMAN.
THERE'S... ONE LAST THING BUGGING ME...
THE SCENT... OF THE WITCH...

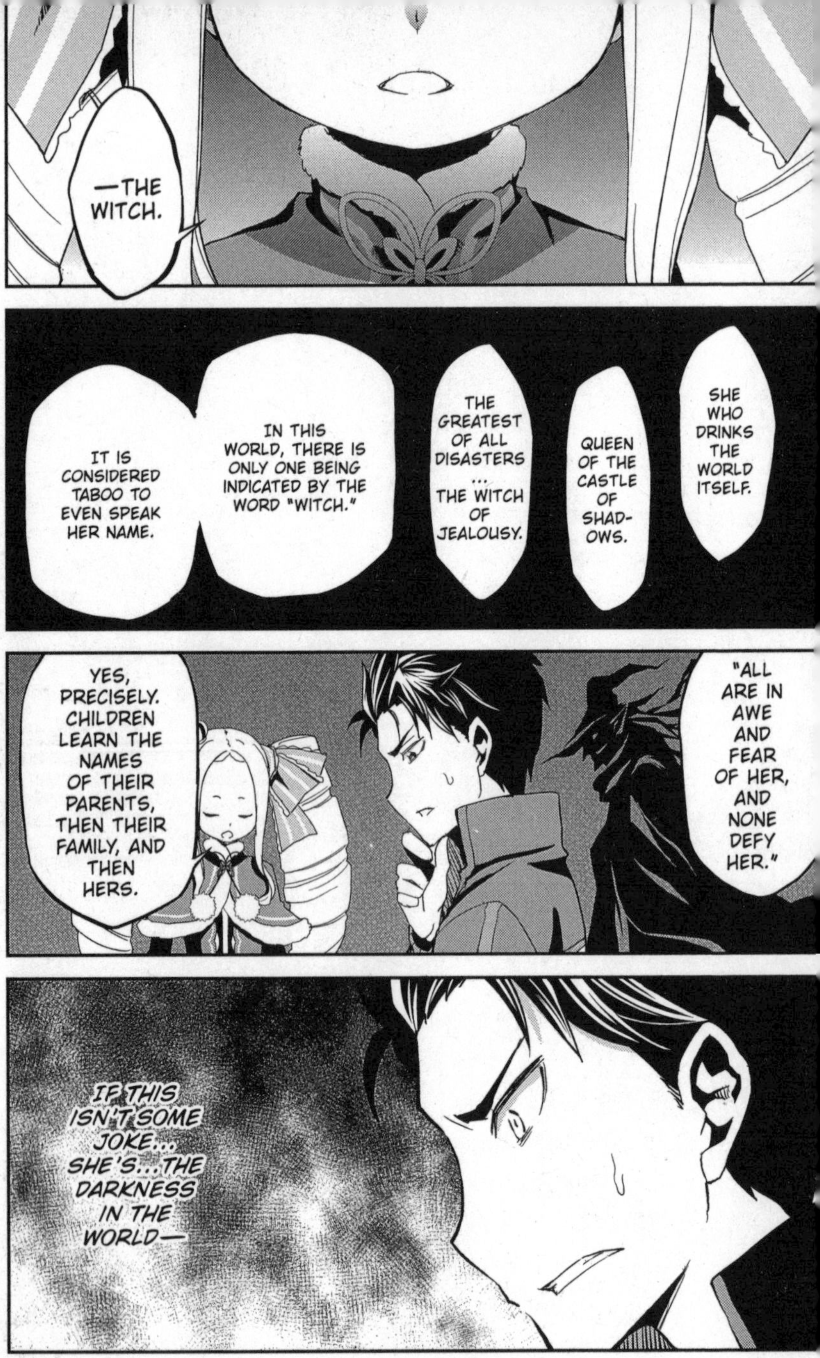
—THE WITCH.
SHE WHO DRINKS THE WORLD ITSELF.
QUEEN OF THE CASTLE OF SHAD-OWS.
THE GREATEST OF ALL DISASTERS ... THE WITCH OF JEALOUSY.
IN THIS WORLD, THERE IS ONLY ONE BEING INDICATED BY THE WORD "WITCH."
IT IS CONSIDERED TABOO TO EVEN SPEAK HER NAME.
"ALL ARE IN AWE AND FEAR OF HER, AND NONE DEFY HER."
YES, PRECISELY. CHILDREN LEARN THE NAMES OF THEIR PARENTS, THEN THEIR FAMILY, AND THEN HERS.
IF THIS ISN'T SOME JOKE... SHE'S...THE DARKNESS IN THE WORLD—

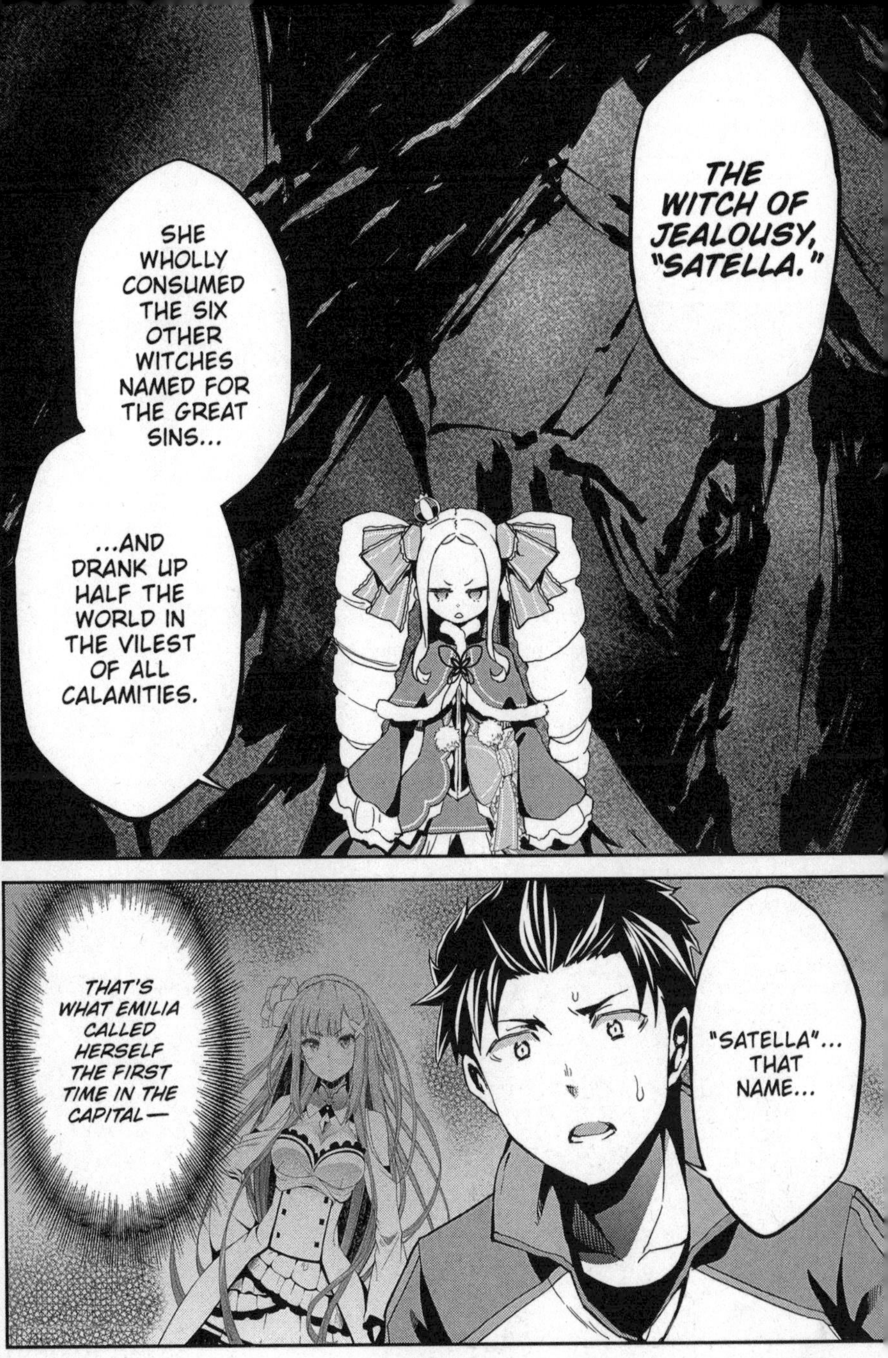
THE WITCH OF JEALOUSY, "SATELLA."
SHE WHOLLY CONSUMED THE SIX OTHER WITCHES NAMED FOR THE GREAT SINS...
...AND DRANK UP HALF THE WORLD IN THE VILEST OF ALL CALAMITIES.
"SATELLA"... THAT NAME...
THAT'S WHAT EMILIA CALLED HERSELF THE FIRST TIME IN THE CAPITAL—

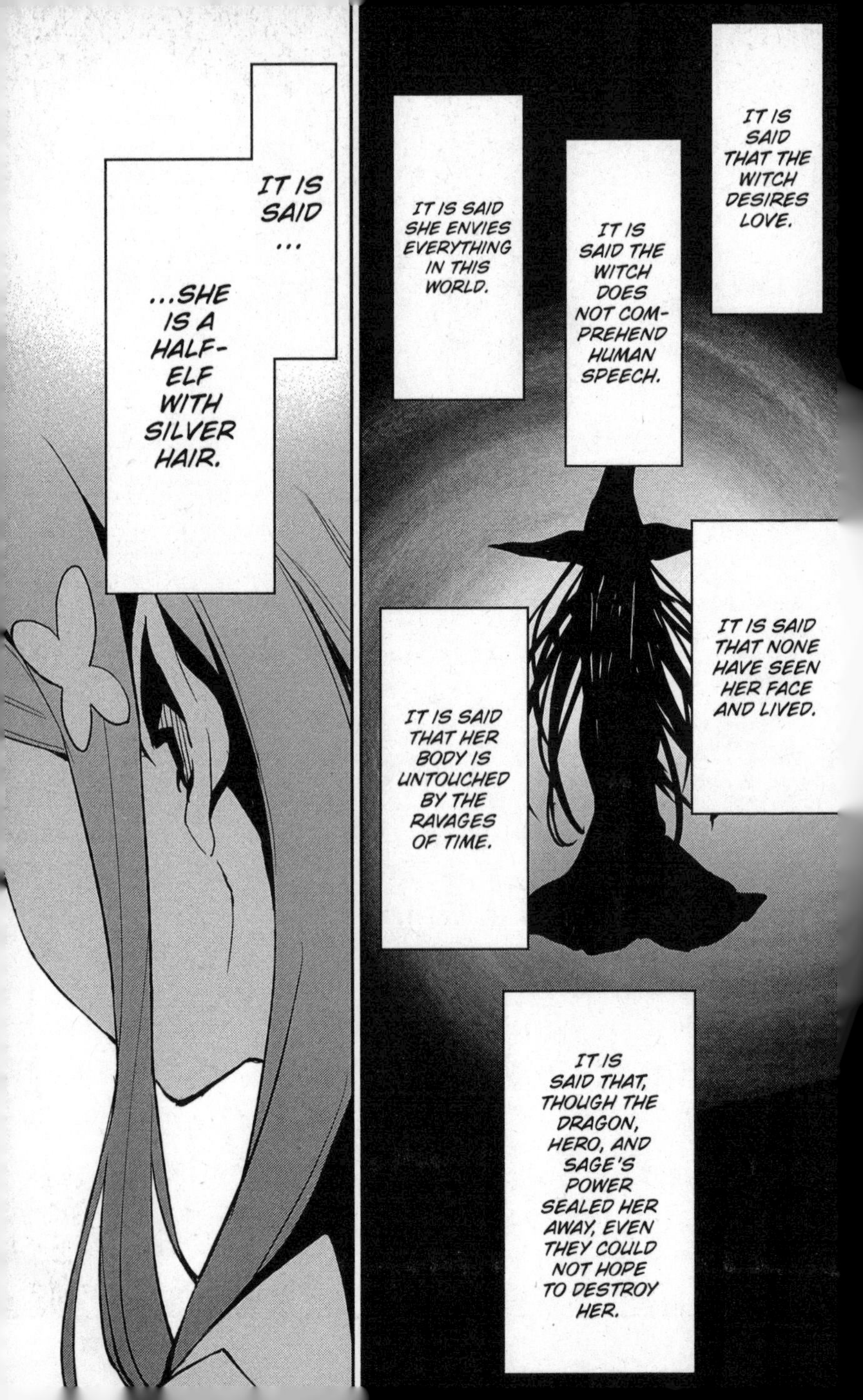
IT IS SAID THAT THE WITCH DESIRES LOVE.
IT IS SAID THE WITCH DOES NOT COMPREHEND HUMAN SPEECH.
IT IS SAID SHE ENVIES EVERYTHING IN THIS WORLD.
IT IS SAID THAT NONE HAVE SEEN HER FACE AND LIVED.
IT IS SAID THAT HER BODY IS UNTOUCHED BY THE RAVAGES OF TIME.
IT IS SAID THAT, THOUGH THE DRAGON, HERO, AND SAGE'S POWER SEALED HER AWAY, EVEN THEY COULD NOT HOPE TO DESTROY HER.
IT IS SAID...
...SHE IS A HALF-ELF WITH SILVER HAIR.

Episode 14
Earlham Village, for the Third Time

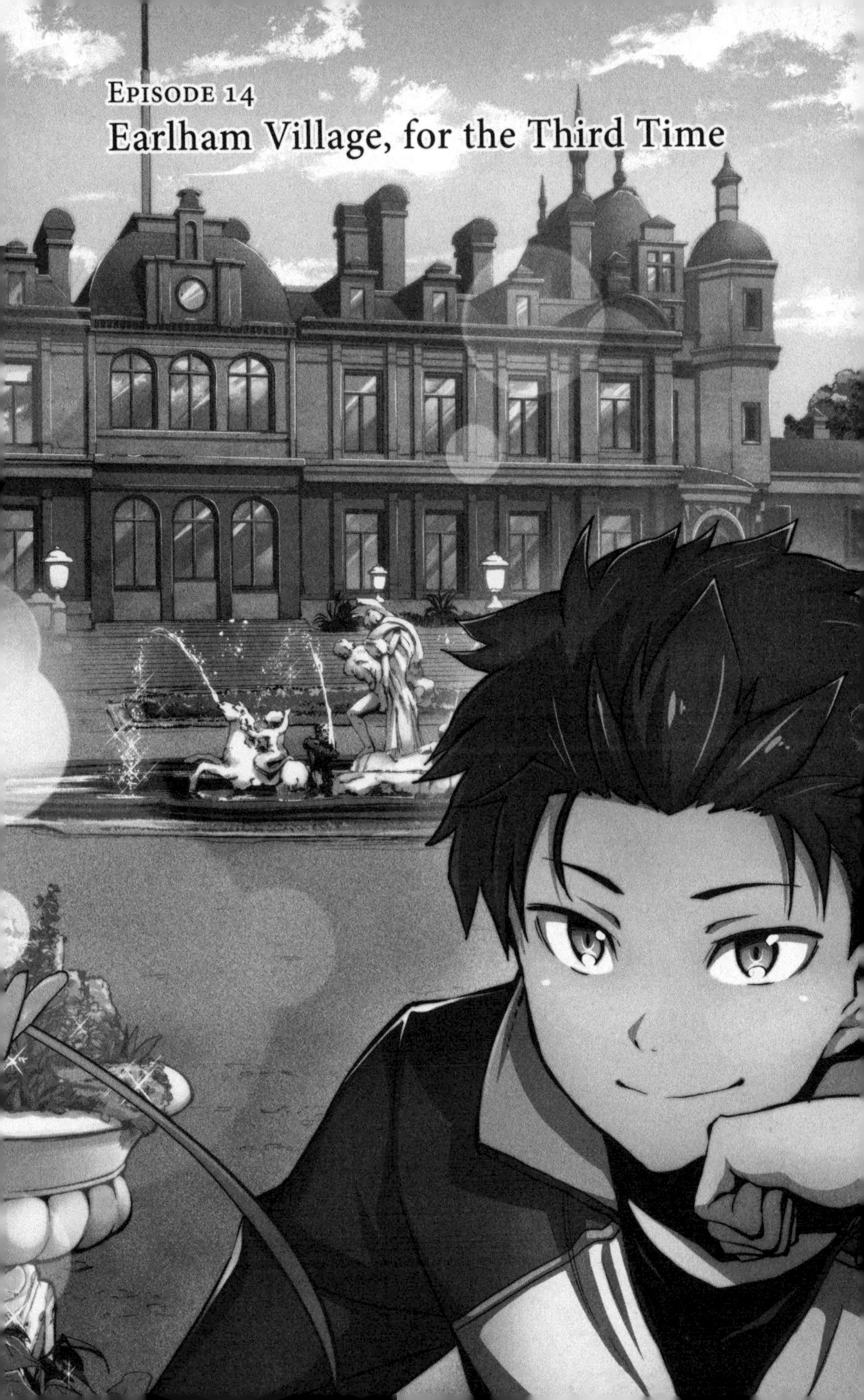

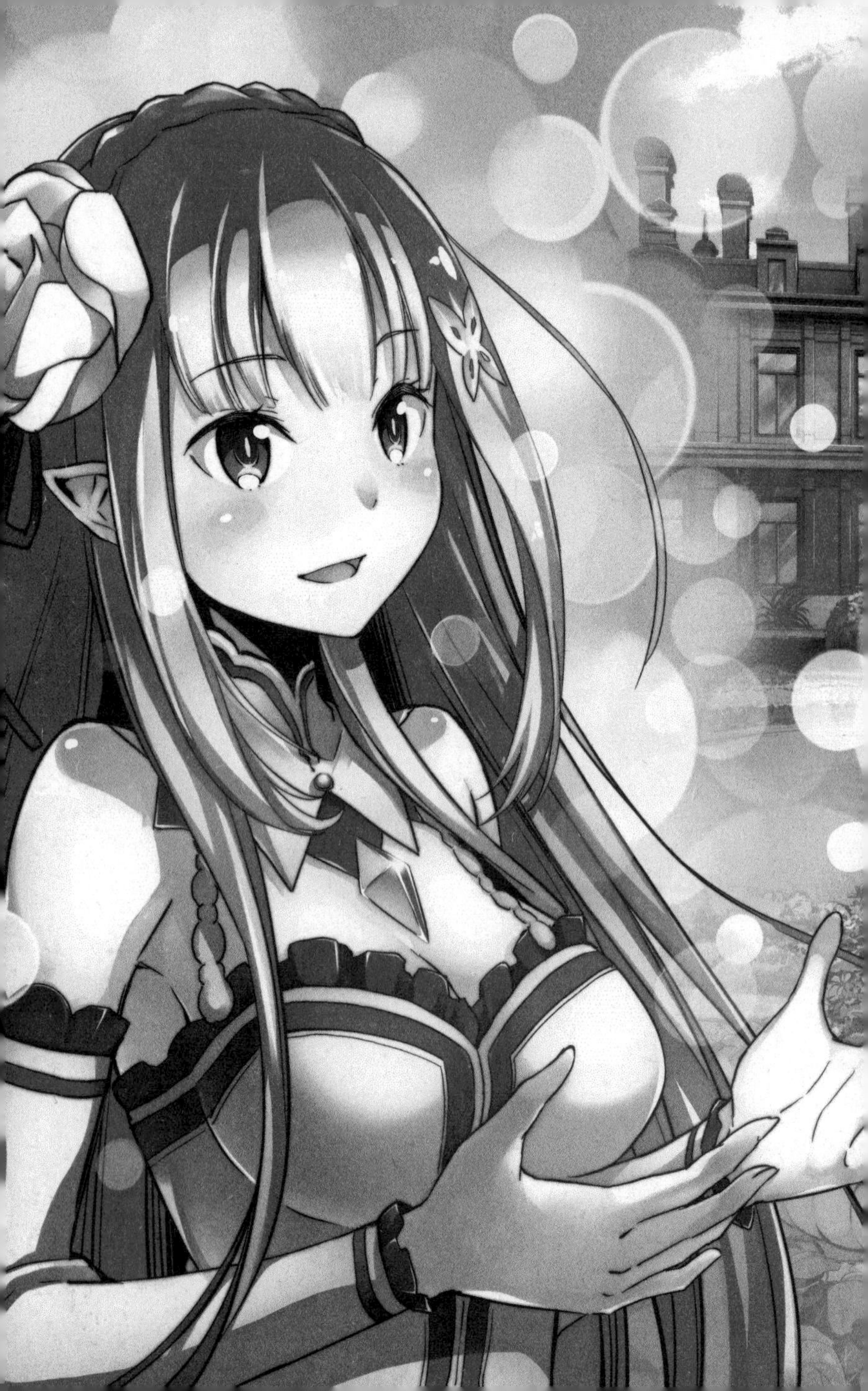

Re:ZeRo

-Starting Life in Another World-

A Week at the Mansion

The only ability Subaru Natsuki gets when he's summoned to another world is time travel via his own death. But to save her, he'll die as many times as it takes.

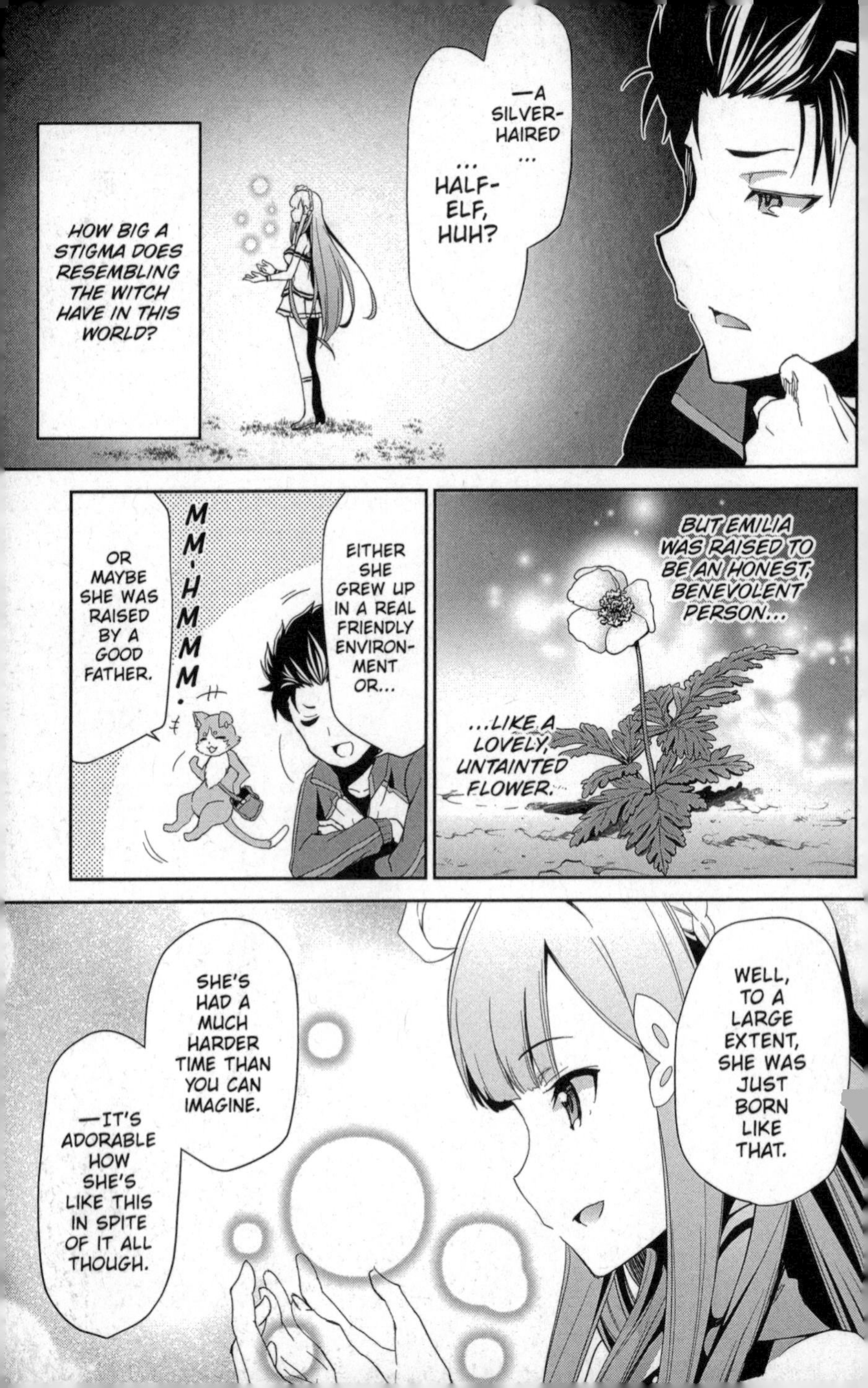
—A SILVER-HAIRED ... ...HALF-ELF, HUH?
HOW BIG A STIGMA DOES RESEMBLING THE WITCH HAVE IN THIS WORLD?
BUT EMILIA WAS RAISED TO BE AN HONEST, BENEVOLENT PERSON...
...LIKE A LOVELY, UNTAINTED FLOWER.
EITHER SHE GREW UP IN A REAL FRIENDLY ENVIRONMENT OR...
MM-HMMMM.
OR MAYBE SHE WAS RAISED BY A GOOD FATHER.
WELL, TO A LARGE EXTENT, SHE WAS JUST BORN LIKE THAT.
SHE'S HAD A MUCH HARDER TIME THAN YOU CAN IMAGINE.
—IT'S ADORABLE HOW SHE'S LIKE THIS IN SPITE OF IT ALL THOUGH.

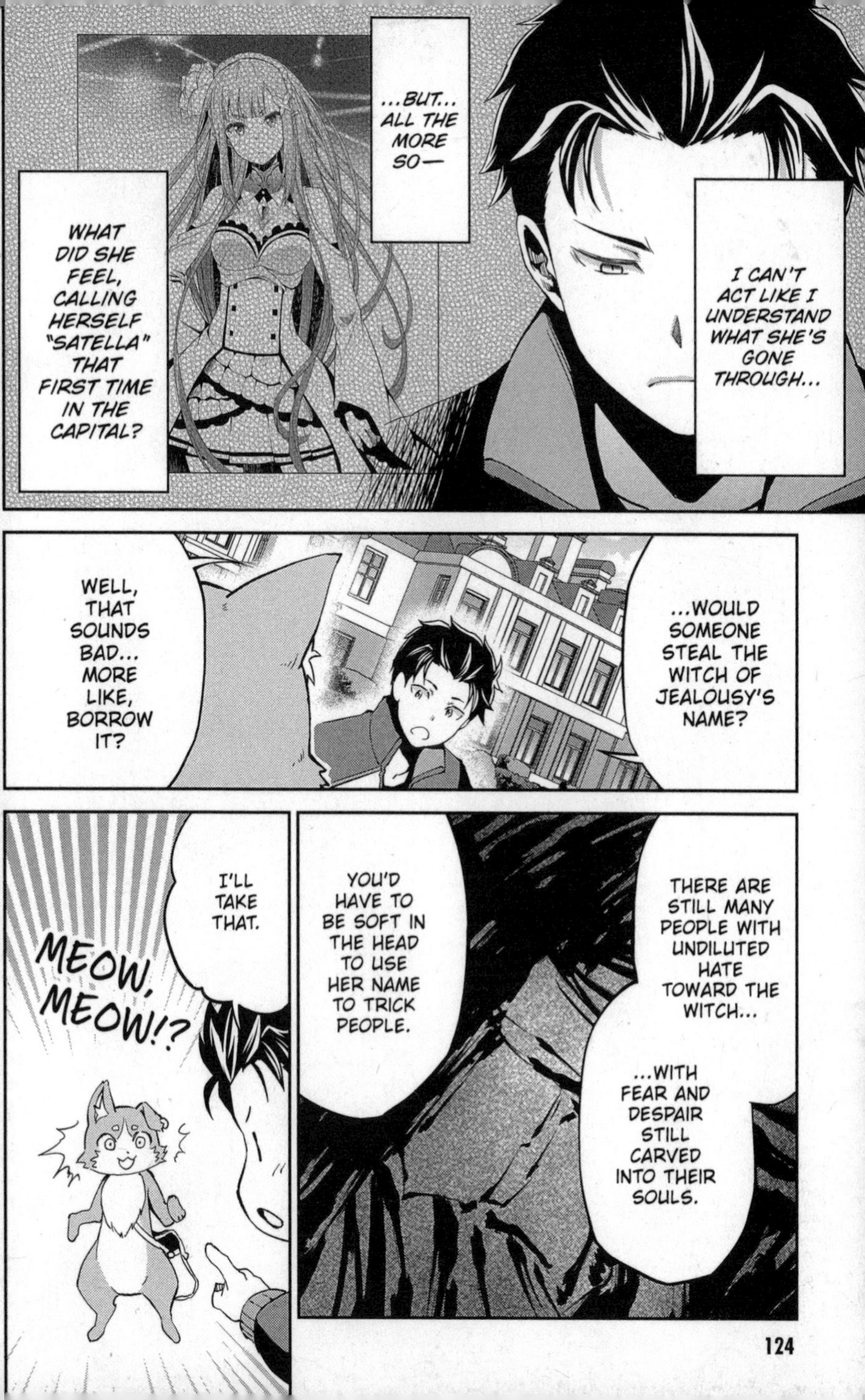

I CAN'T ACT LIKE I UNDERSTAND WHAT SHE'S GONE THROUGH...
...BUT... ALL THE MORE SO—
WHAT DID SHE FEEL, CALLING HERSELF "SATELLA" THAT FIRST TIME IN THE CAPITAL?
...WOULD SOMEONE STEAL THE WITCH OF JEALOUSY'S NAME?
WELL, THAT SOUNDS BAD... MORE LIKE, BORROW IT?
THERE ARE STILL MANY PEOPLE WITH UNDILUTED HATE TOWARD THE WITCH...
...WITH FEAR AND DESPAIR STILL CARVED INTO THEIR SOULS.
YOU'D HAVE TO BE SOFT IN THE HEAD TO USE HER NAME TO TRICK PEOPLE.
I'LL TAKE THAT.
MEOW, MEOW!?

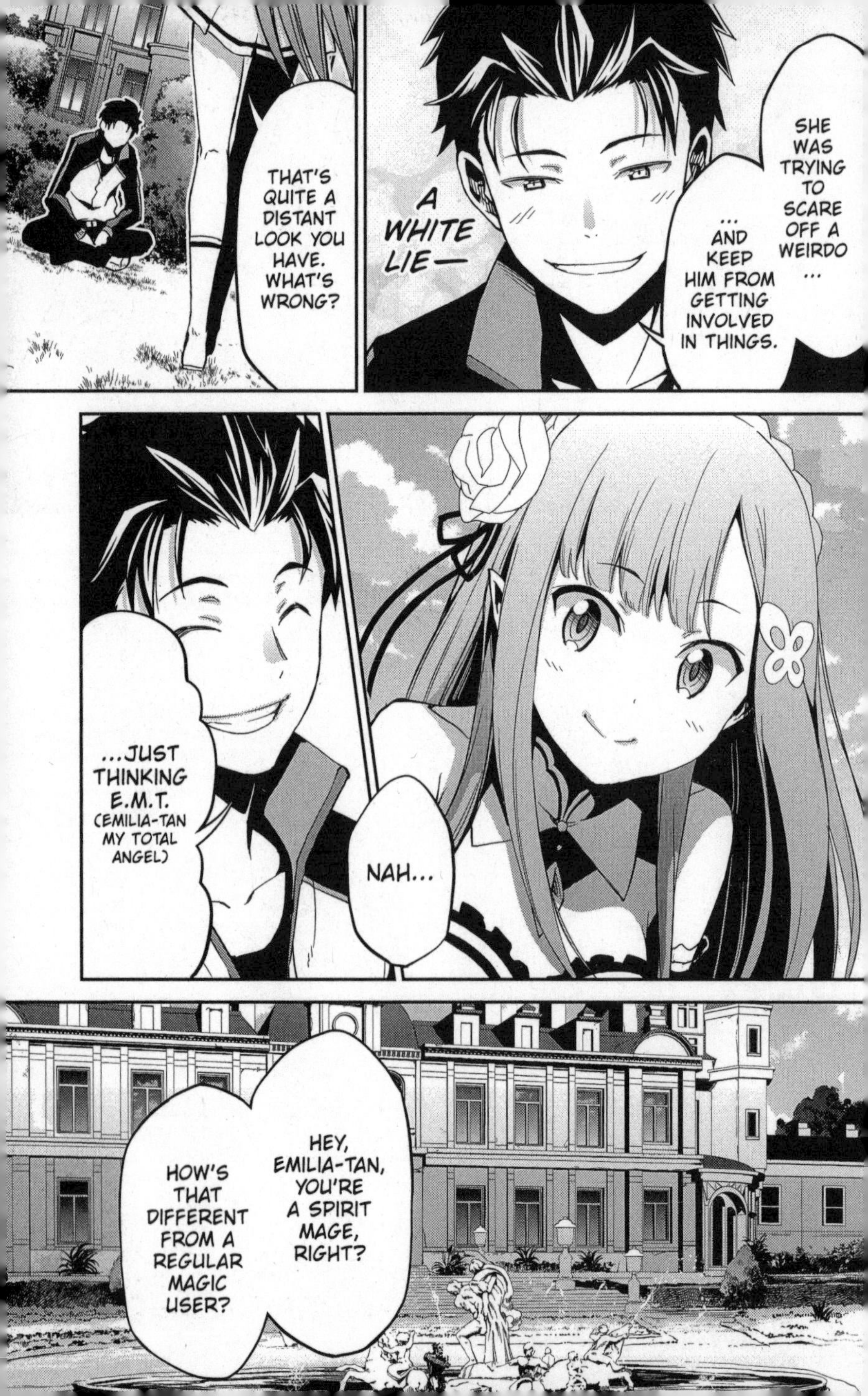
SHE WAS TRYING TO SCARE OFF A WEIRDO ...
... AND KEEP HIM FROM GETTING INVOLVED IN THINGS.
A WHITE LIE—
THAT'S QUITE A DISTANT LOOK YOU HAVE. WHAT'S WRONG?
NAH...
...JUST THINKING E.M.T. (EMILIA-TAN MY TOTAL ANGEL)
HEY, EMILIA-TAN, YOU'RE A SPIRIT MAGE, RIGHT?
HOW'S THAT DIFFERENT FROM A REGULAR MAGIC USER?

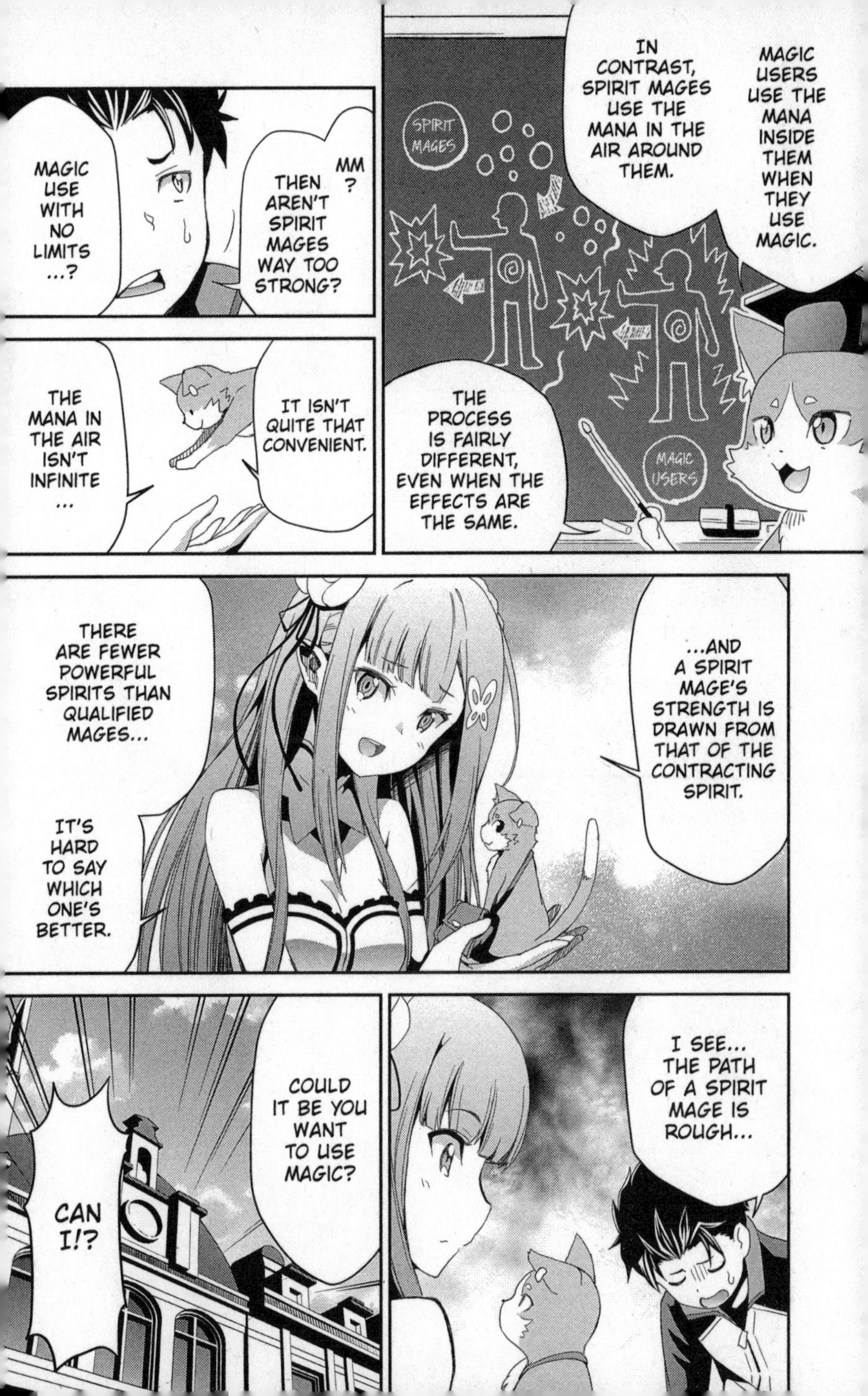
MAGIC USERS USE THE MANA INSIDE THEM WHEN THEY USE MAGIC.
IN CONTRAST, SPIRIT MAGES USE THE MANA IN THE AIR AROUND THEM.
SPIRIT MAGES
MAGIC USERS
THE PROCESS IS FAIRLY DIFFERENT, EVEN WHEN THE EFFECTS ARE THE SAME.
MM? THEN AREN'T SPIRIT MAGES WAY TOO STRONG?
MAGIC USE WITH NO LIMITS...?
IT ISN'T QUITE THAT CONVENIENT.
THE MANA IN THE AIR ISN'T INFINITE...
...AND A SPIRIT MAGE'S STRENGTH IS DRAWN FROM THAT OF THE CONTRACTING SPIRIT.
THERE ARE FEWER POWERFUL SPIRITS THAN QUALIFIED MAGES...
IT'S HARD TO SAY WHICH ONE'S BETTER.
I SEE... THE PATH OF A SPIRIT MAGE IS ROUGH...
COULD IT BE YOU WANT TO USE MAGIC?
CAN I!?

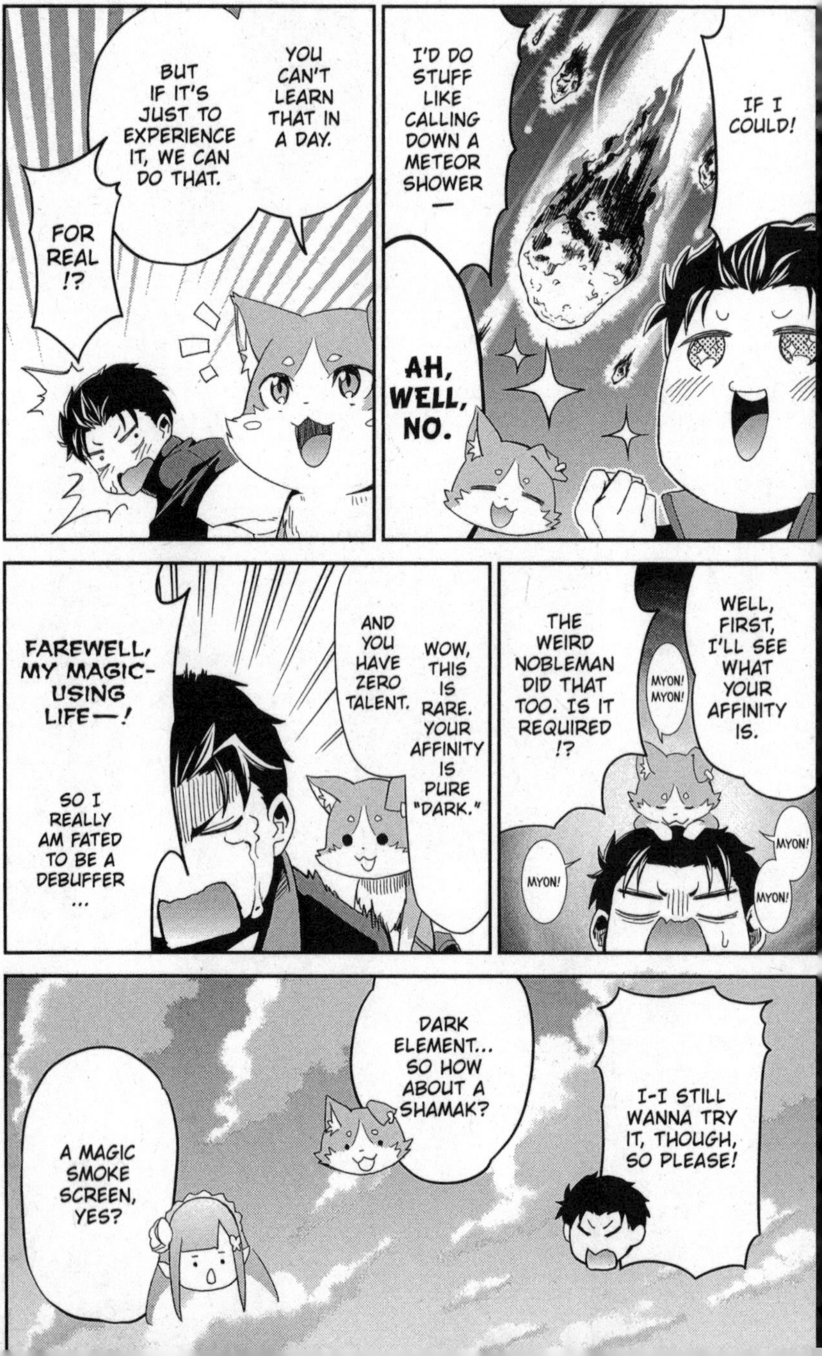
IF I COULD!
I'D DO STUFF LIKE CALLING DOWN A METEOR SHOWER —
AH, WELL, NO.
YOU CAN'T LEARN THAT IN A DAY.
BUT IF IT'S JUST TO EXPERIENCE IT, WE CAN DO THAT.
FOR REAL !?
WELL, FIRST, I'LL SEE WHAT YOUR AFFINITY IS.
MYON! MYON!
THE WEIRD NOBLEMAN DID THAT TOO. IS IT REQUIRED !?
MYON!
MYON!
MYON!
WOW, THIS IS RARE. YOUR AFFINITY IS PURE "DARK."
AND YOU HAVE ZERO TALENT.
FAREWELL, MY MAGIC-USING LIFE—!
SO I REALLY AM FATED TO BE A DEBUFFER ...
I-I STILL WANNA TRY IT, THOUGH, SO PLEASE!
DARK ELEMENT... SO HOW ABOUT A SHAMAK?
A MAGIC SMOKE SCREEN, YES?

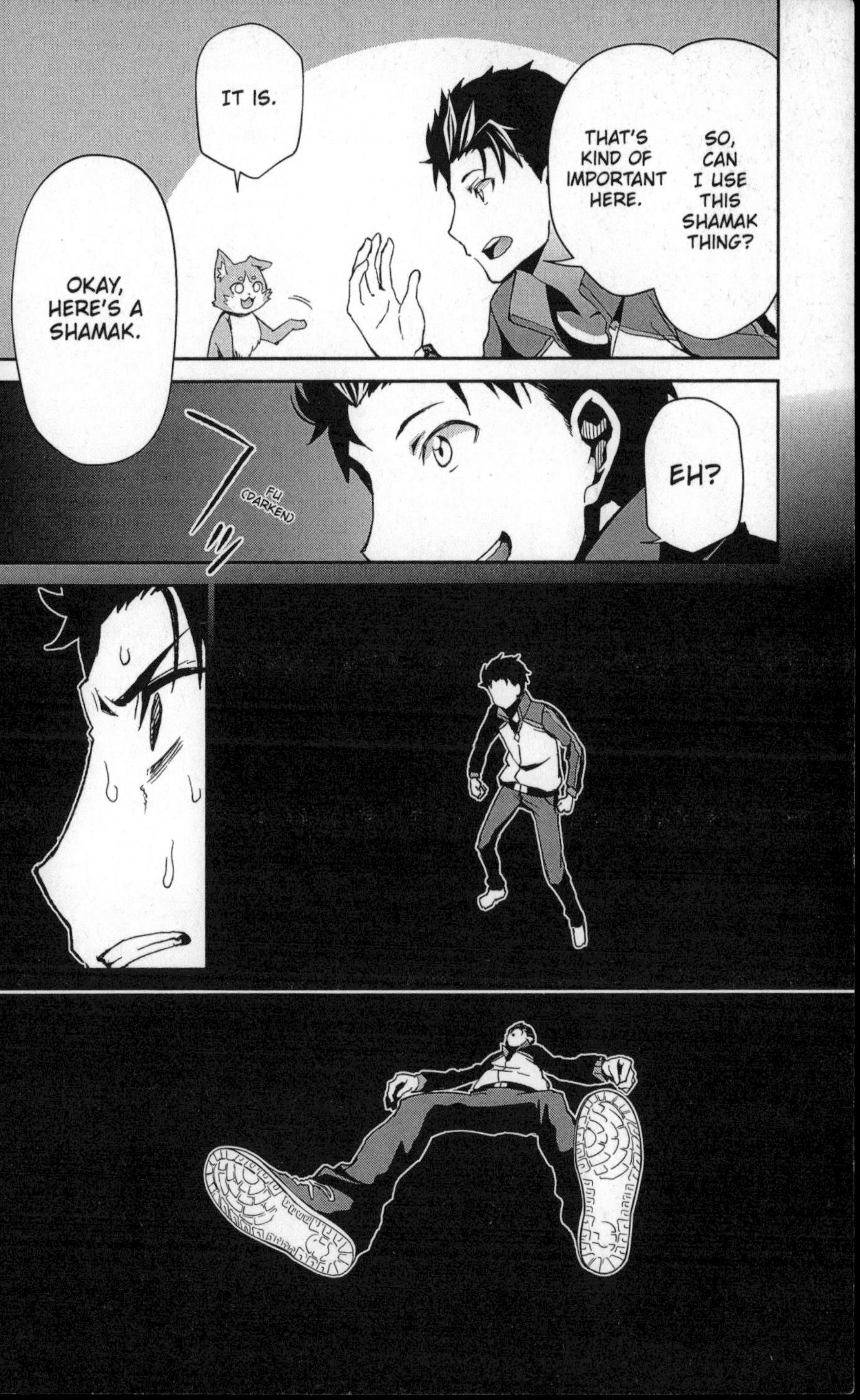
SO, CAN I USE THIS SHAMAK THING?
THAT'S KIND OF IMPORTANT HERE.
IT IS.
OKAY, HERE'S A SHAMAK.
EH?
FU (DARKEN)

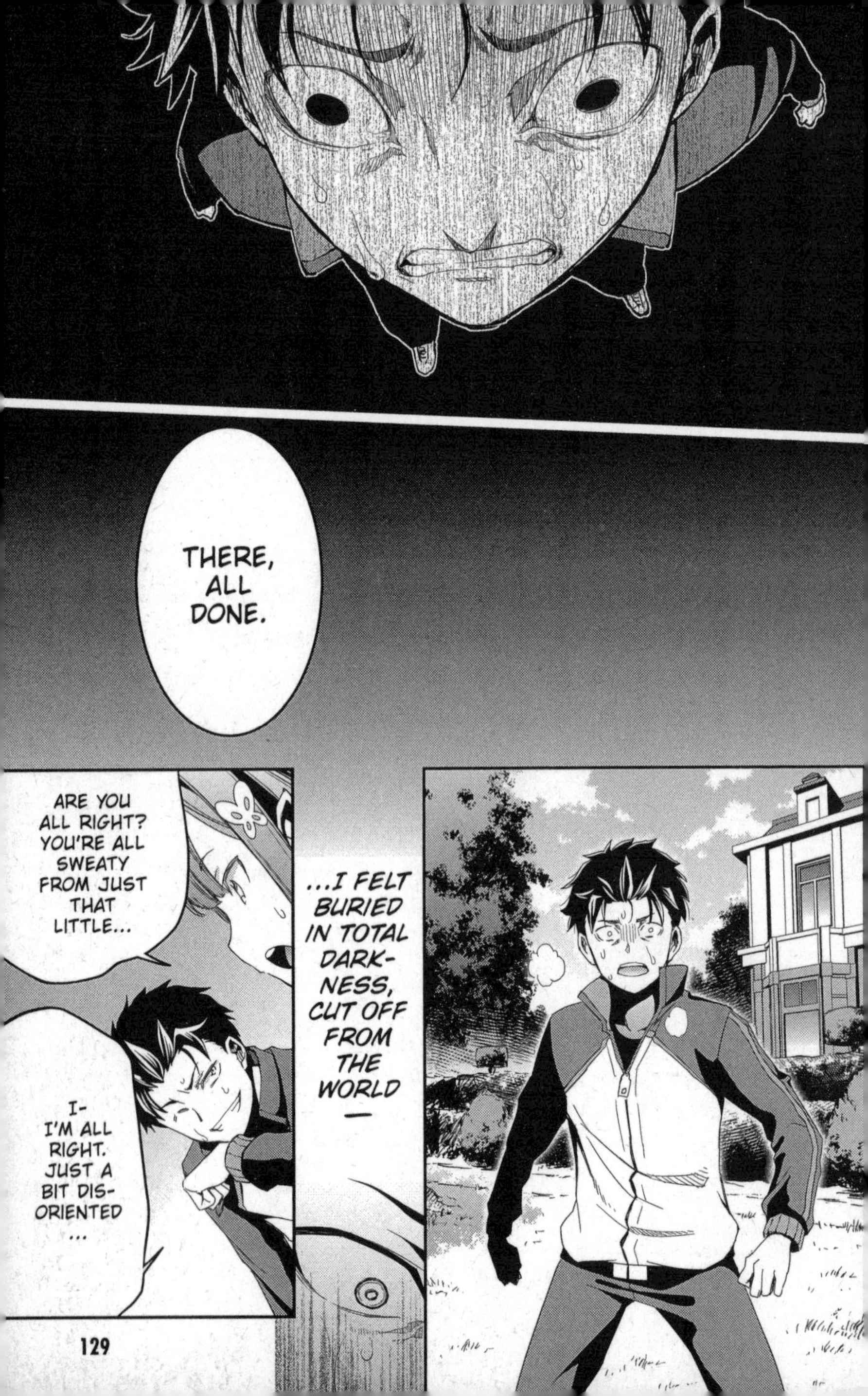
THERE, ALL DONE.
...I FELT BURIED IN TOTAL DARKNESS, CUT OFF FROM THE WORLD—
ARE YOU ALL RIGHT? YOU'RE ALL SWEATY FROM JUST THAT LITTLE...
I- I'M ALL RIGHT. JUST A BIT DISORIENTED...

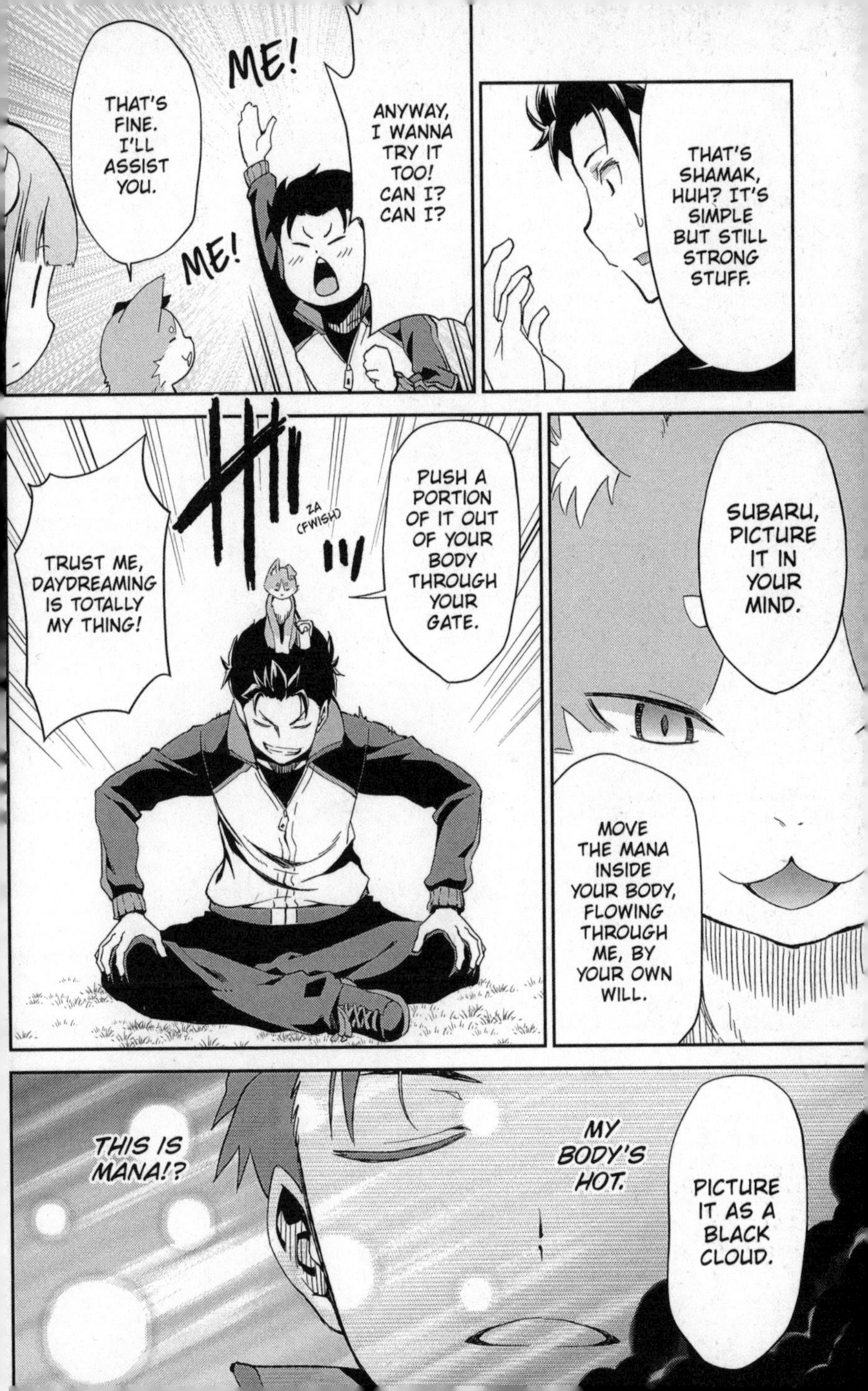
THAT'S SHAMAK, HUH? IT'S SIMPLE BUT STILL STRONG STUFF.
ANYWAY, I WANNA TRY IT TOO! CAN I? CAN I?
ME!
ME!
THAT'S FINE. I'LL ASSIST YOU.
SUBARU, PICTURE IT IN YOUR MIND.
MOVE THE MANA INSIDE YOUR BODY, FLOWING THROUGH ME, BY YOUR OWN WILL.
PUSH A PORTION OF IT OUT OF YOUR BODY THROUGH YOUR GATE.
ZA (FWISH)
TRUST ME, DAYDREAMING IS TOTALLY MY THING!
PICTURE IT AS A BLACK CLOUD.
MY BODY'S HOT.
THIS IS MANA!?

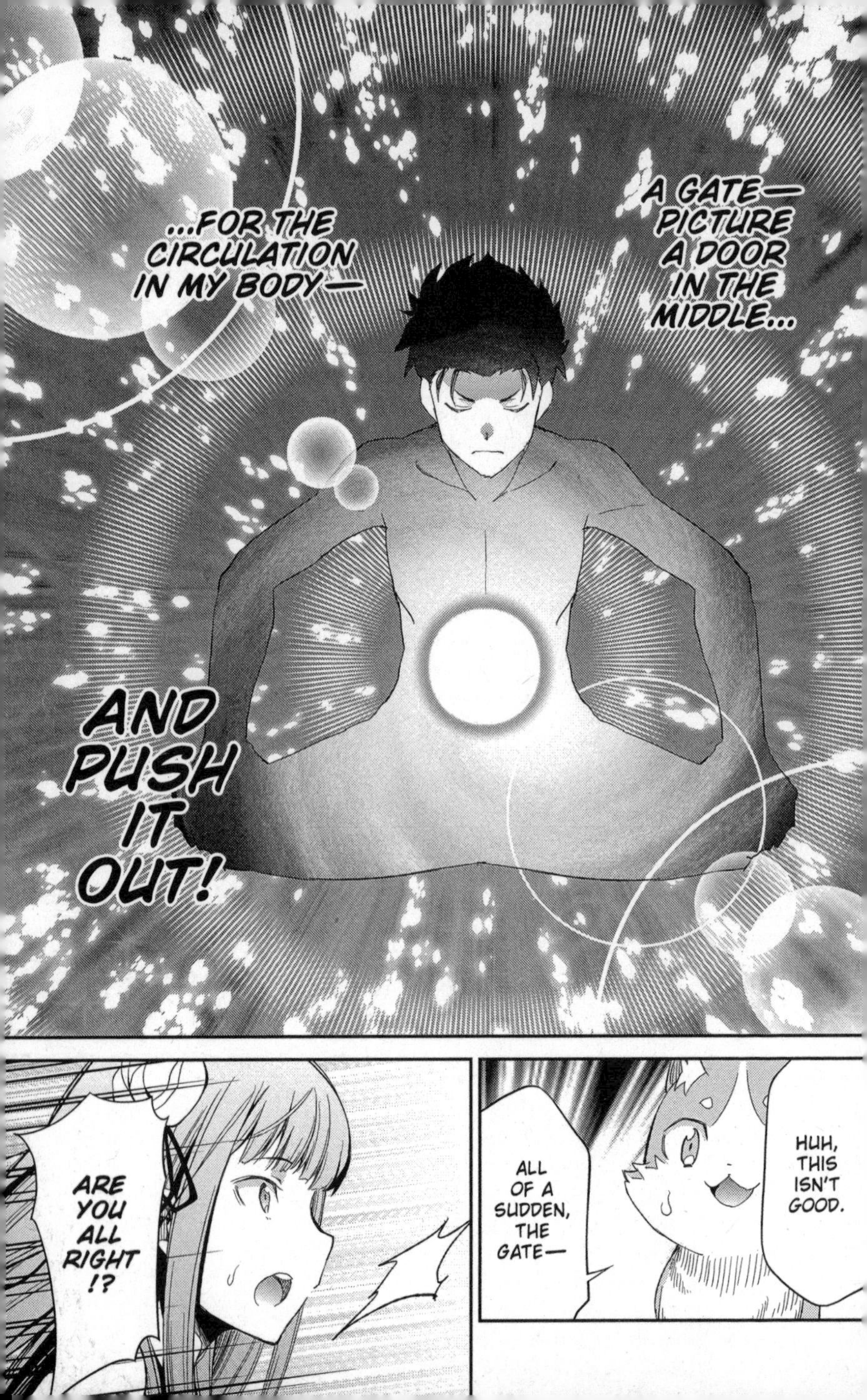
A GATE—PICTURE A DOOR IN THE MIDDLE...
...FOR THE CIRCULATION IN MY BODY—
AND PUSH IT OUT!
HUH, THIS ISN'T GOOD.
ALL OF A SUDDEN, THE GATE—
ARE YOU ALL RIGHT!?

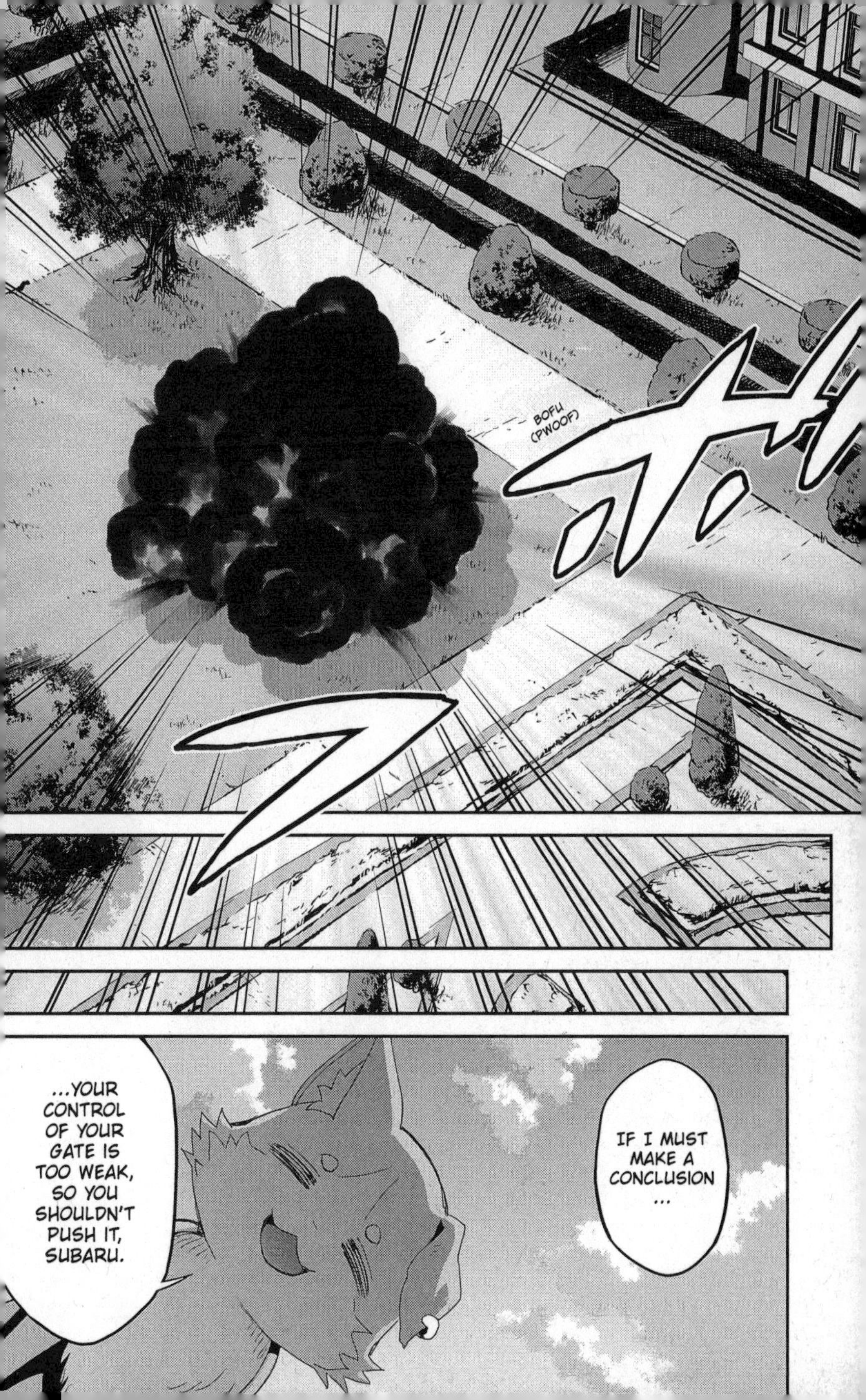
BOFU (PWOOF)
IF I MUST MAKE A CONCLUSION ...
...YOUR CONTROL OF YOUR GATE IS TOO WEAK, SO YOU SHOULDN'T PUSH IT, SUBARU.

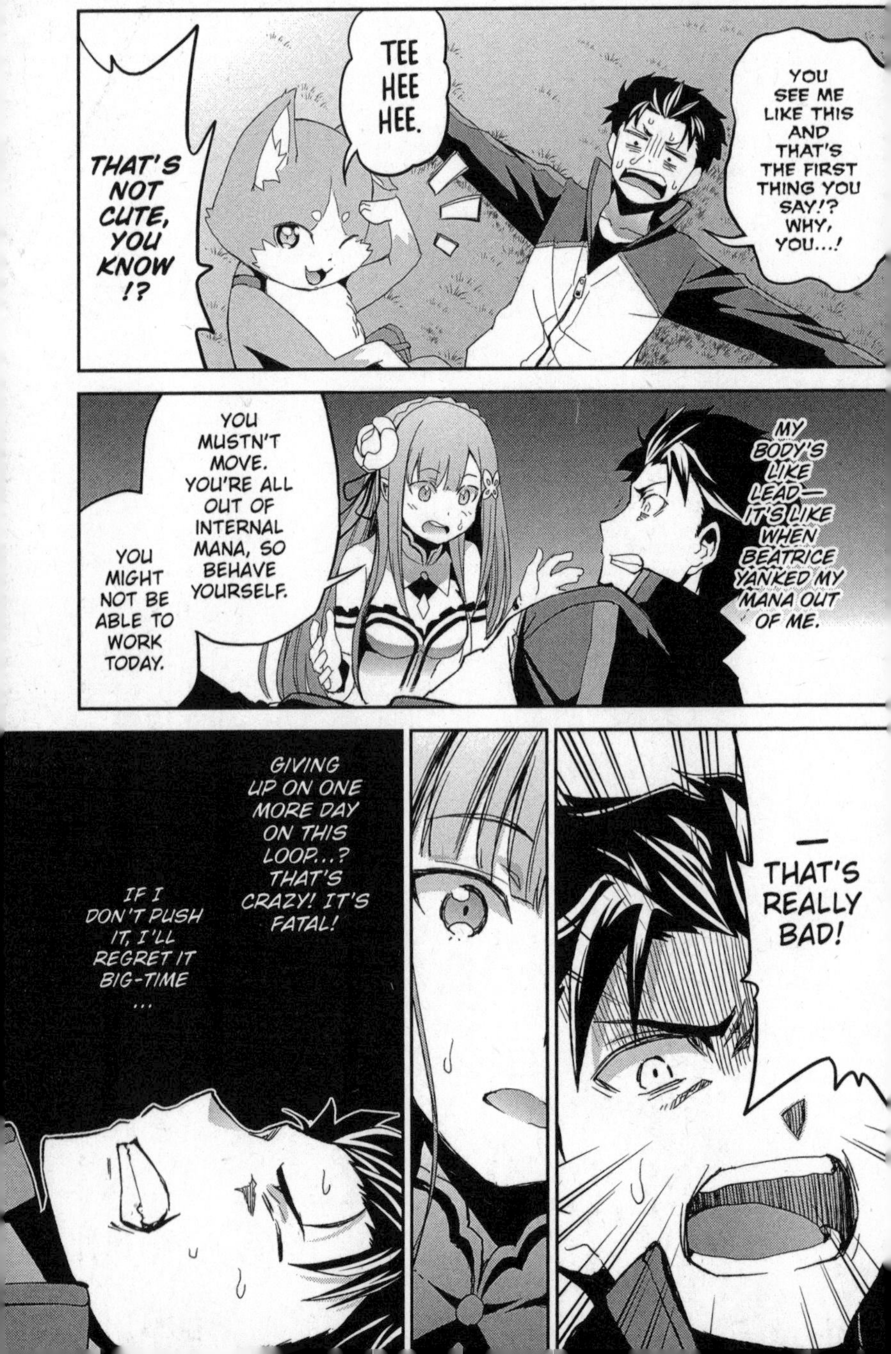
YOU SEE ME LIKE THIS AND THAT'S THE FIRST THING YOU SAY!? WHY, YOU...!
TEE HEE HEE.
THAT'S NOT CUTE, YOU KNOW!?
MY BODY'S LIKE LEAD—IT'S LIKE WHEN BEATRICE YANKED MY MANA OUT OF ME.
YOU MUSTN'T MOVE. YOU'RE ALL OUT OF INTERNAL MANA, SO BEHAVE YOURSELF.
YOU MIGHT NOT BE ABLE TO WORK TODAY.
—THAT'S REALLY BAD!
GIVING UP ON ONE MORE DAY ON THIS LOOP...? THAT'S CRAZY! IT'S FATAL!
IF I DON'T PUSH IT, I'LL REGRET IT BIG-TIME...

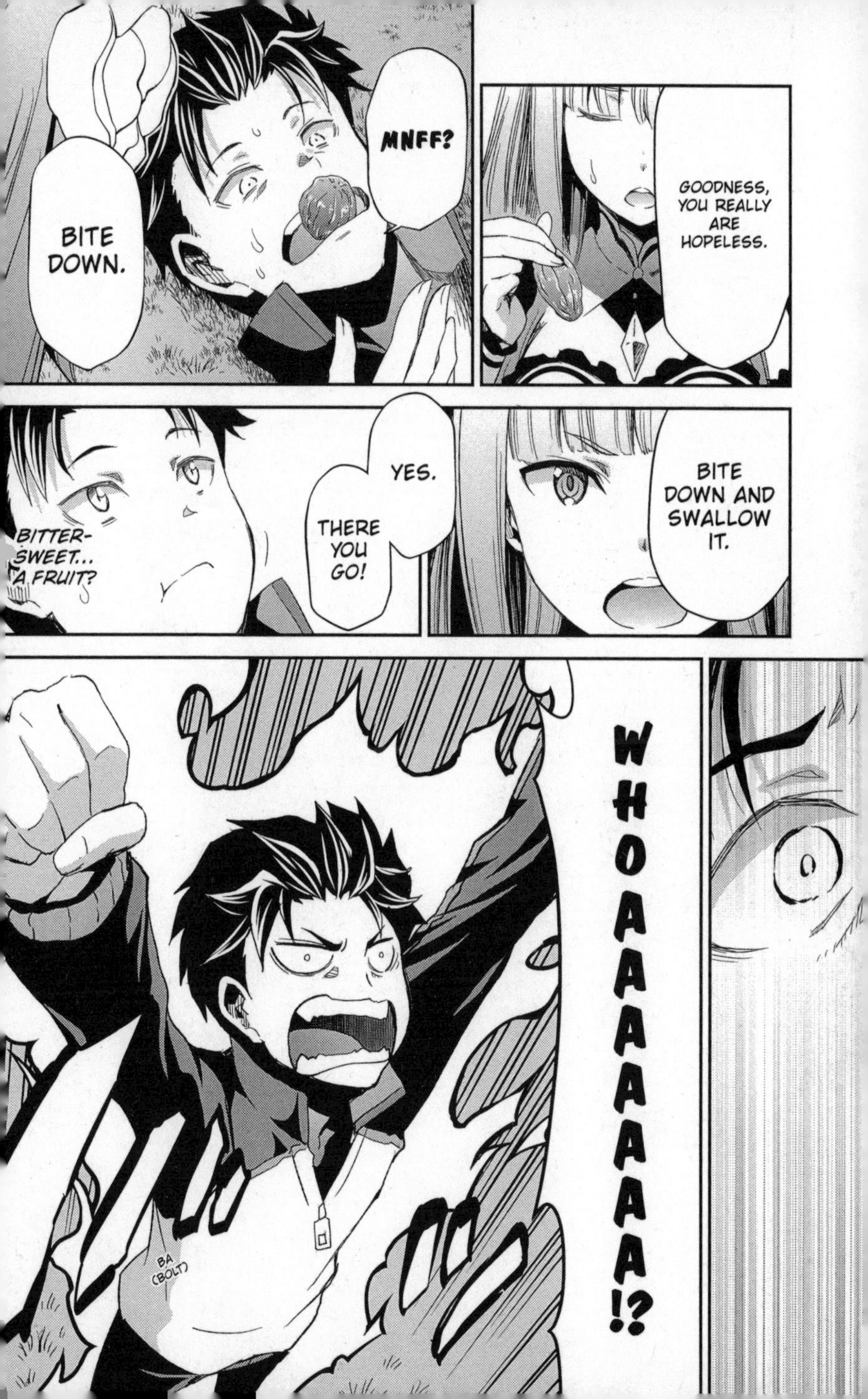
GOODNESS, YOU REALLY ARE HOPELESS.
MNFF?
BITE DOWN.
BITE DOWN AND SWALLOW IT.
YES.
THERE YOU GO!
BITTER-SWEET... A FRUIT?
WHOAAAAAAA!?
BA (BOLT)

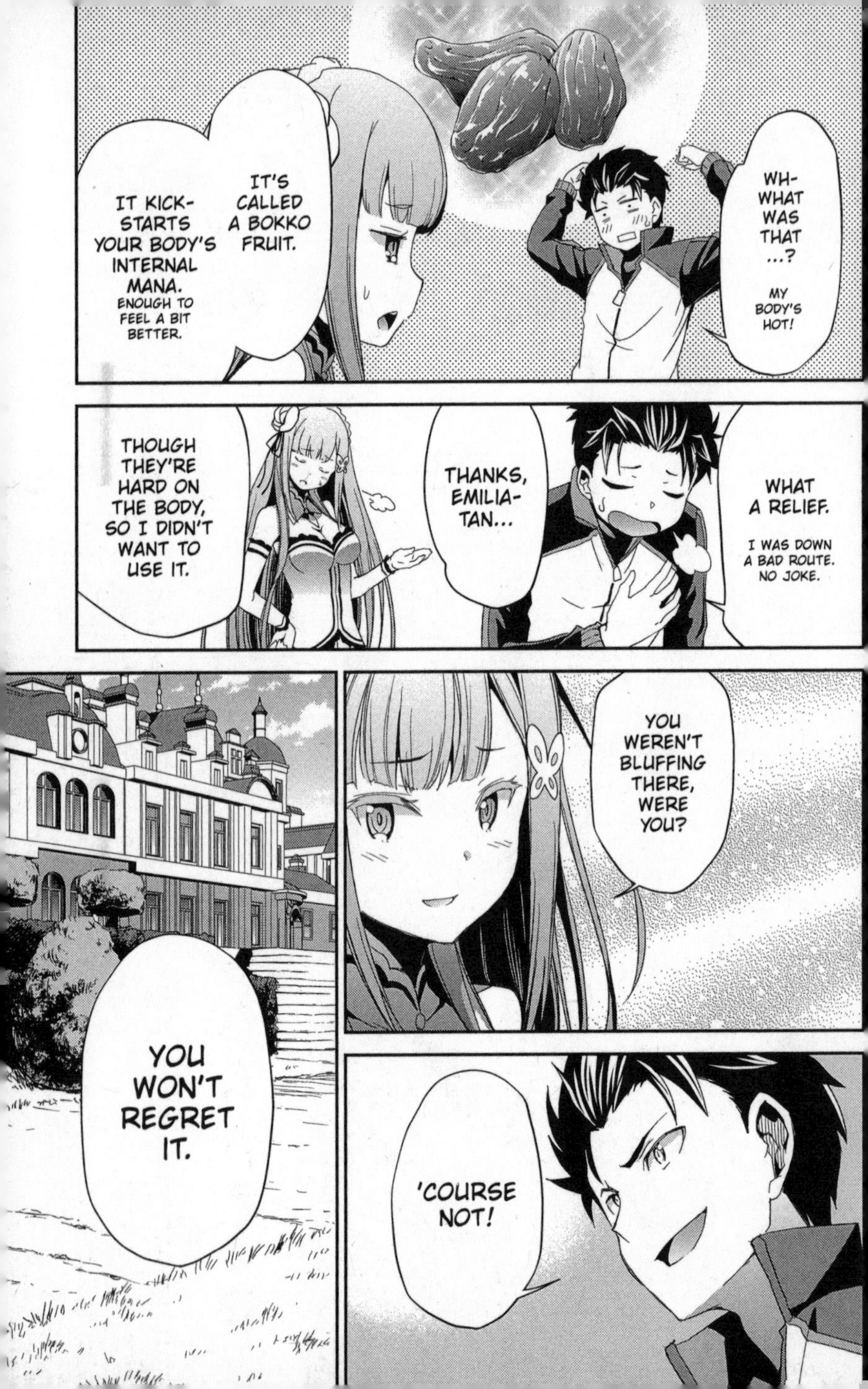
WH-WHAT WAS THAT...?
MY BODY'S HOT!
IT'S CALLED A BOKKO FRUIT.
IT KICK-STARTS YOUR BODY'S INTERNAL MANA.
ENOUGH TO FEEL A BIT BETTER.
WHAT A RELIEF.
I WAS DOWN A BAD ROUTE. NO JOKE.
THANKS, EMILIA-TAN...
THOUGH THEY'RE HARD ON THE BODY, SO I DIDN'T WANT TO USE IT.
YOU WEREN'T BLUFFING THERE, WERE YOU?
'COURSE NOT!
YOU WON'T REGRET IT.

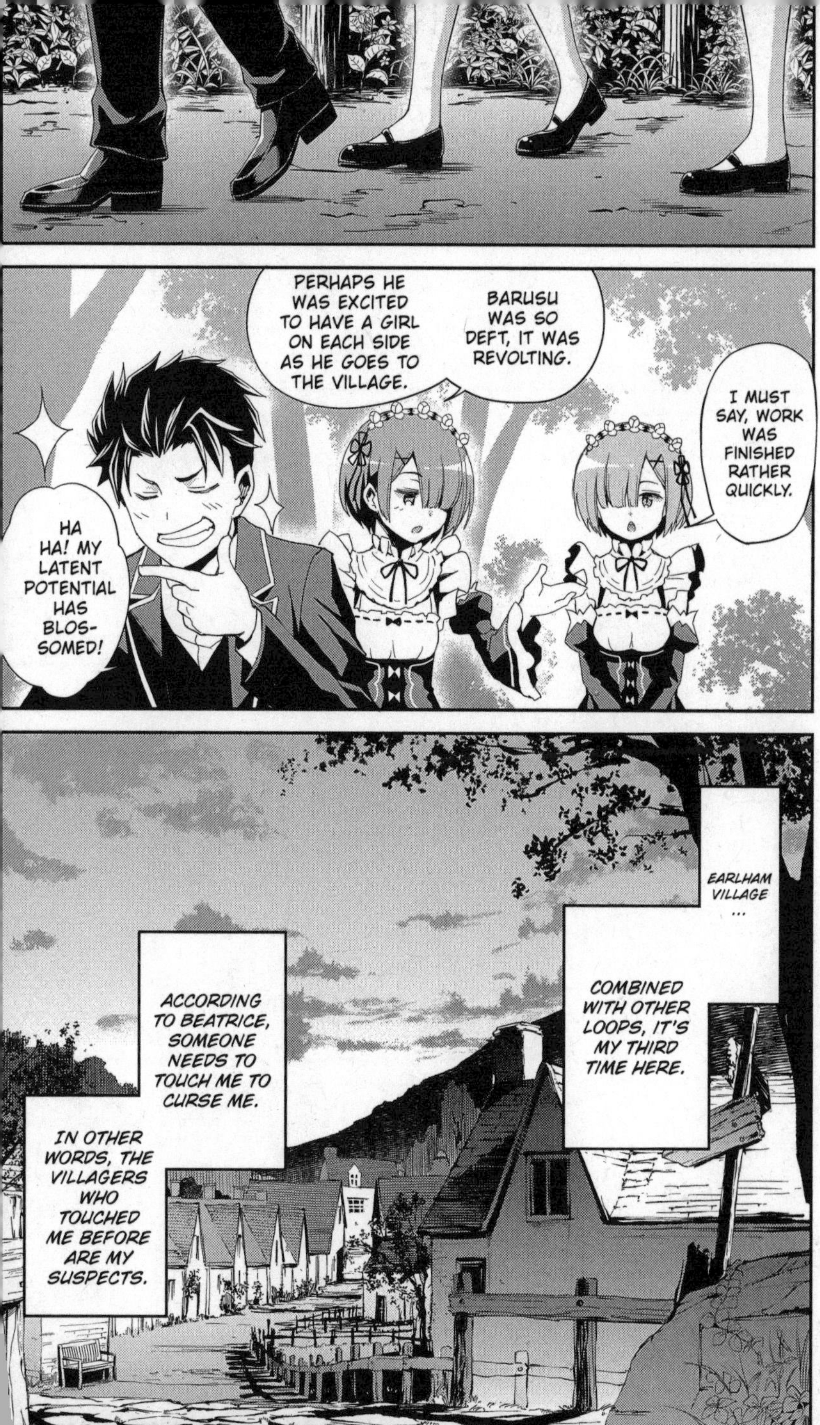
I MUST SAY, WORK WAS FINISHED RATHER QUICKLY.
BARUSU WAS SO DEFT, IT WAS REVOLTING.
PERHAPS HE WAS EXCITED TO HAVE A GIRL ON EACH SIDE AS HE GOES TO THE VILLAGE.
HA HA! MY LATENT POTENTIAL HAS BLOS-SOMED!
EARLHAM VILLAGE ...
COMBINED WITH OTHER LOOPS, IT'S MY THIRD TIME HERE.
ACCORDING TO BEATRICE, SOMEONE NEEDS TO TOUCH ME TO CURSE ME.
IN OTHER WORDS, THE VILLAGERS WHO TOUCHED ME BEFORE ARE MY SUSPECTS.

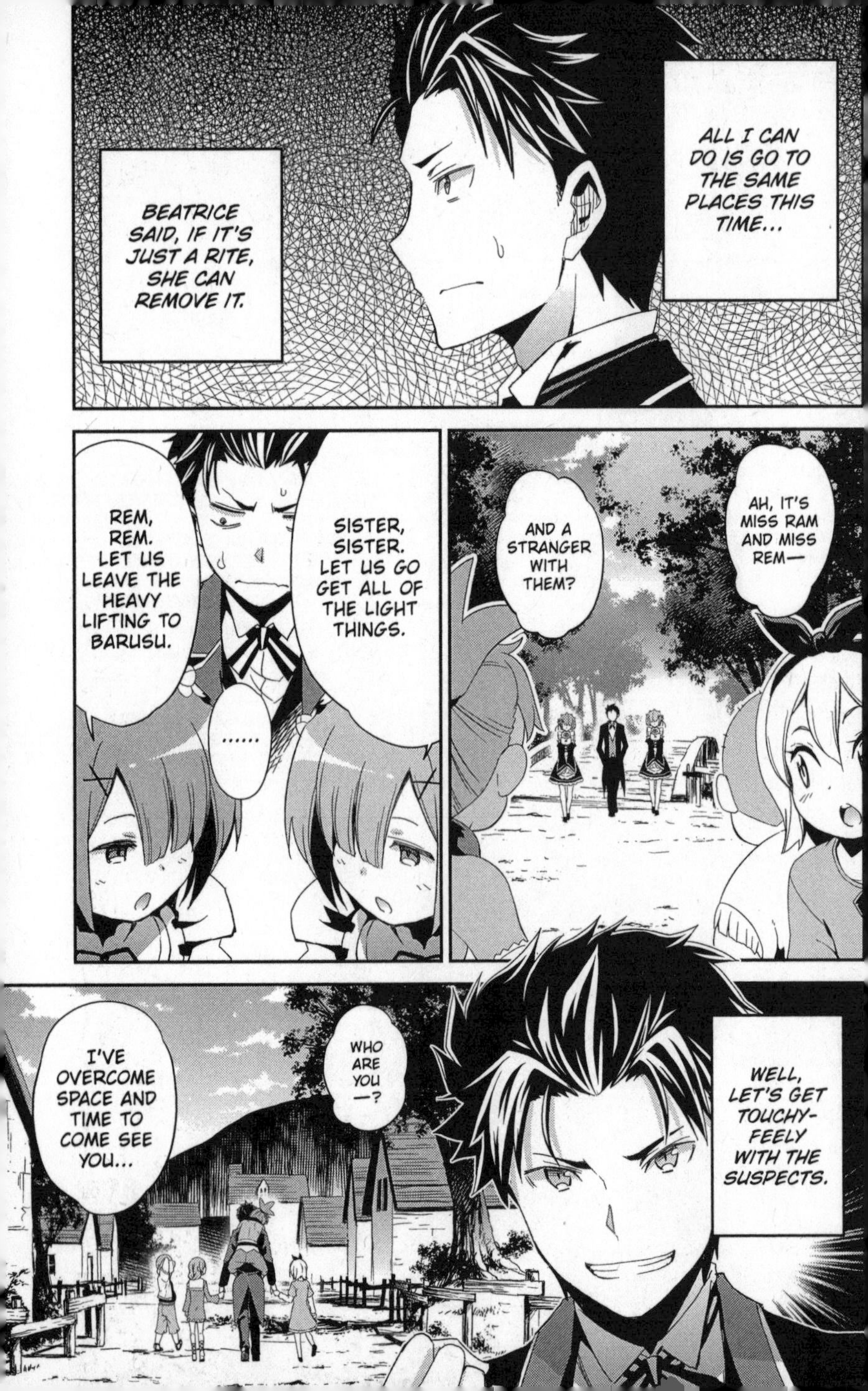
ALL I CAN DO IS GO TO THE SAME PLACES THIS TIME...
BEATRICE SAID, IF IT'S JUST A RITE, SHE CAN REMOVE IT.
AH, IT'S MISS RAM AND MISS REM—
AND A STRANGER WITH THEM?
SISTER, SISTER. LET US GO GET ALL OF THE LIGHT THINGS.
REM, REM. LET US LEAVE THE HEAVY LIFTING TO BARUSU.
......
WELL, LET'S GET TOUCHY-FEELY WITH THE SUSPECTS.
WHO ARE YOU—?
I'VE OVERCOME SPACE AND TIME TO COME SEE YOU...

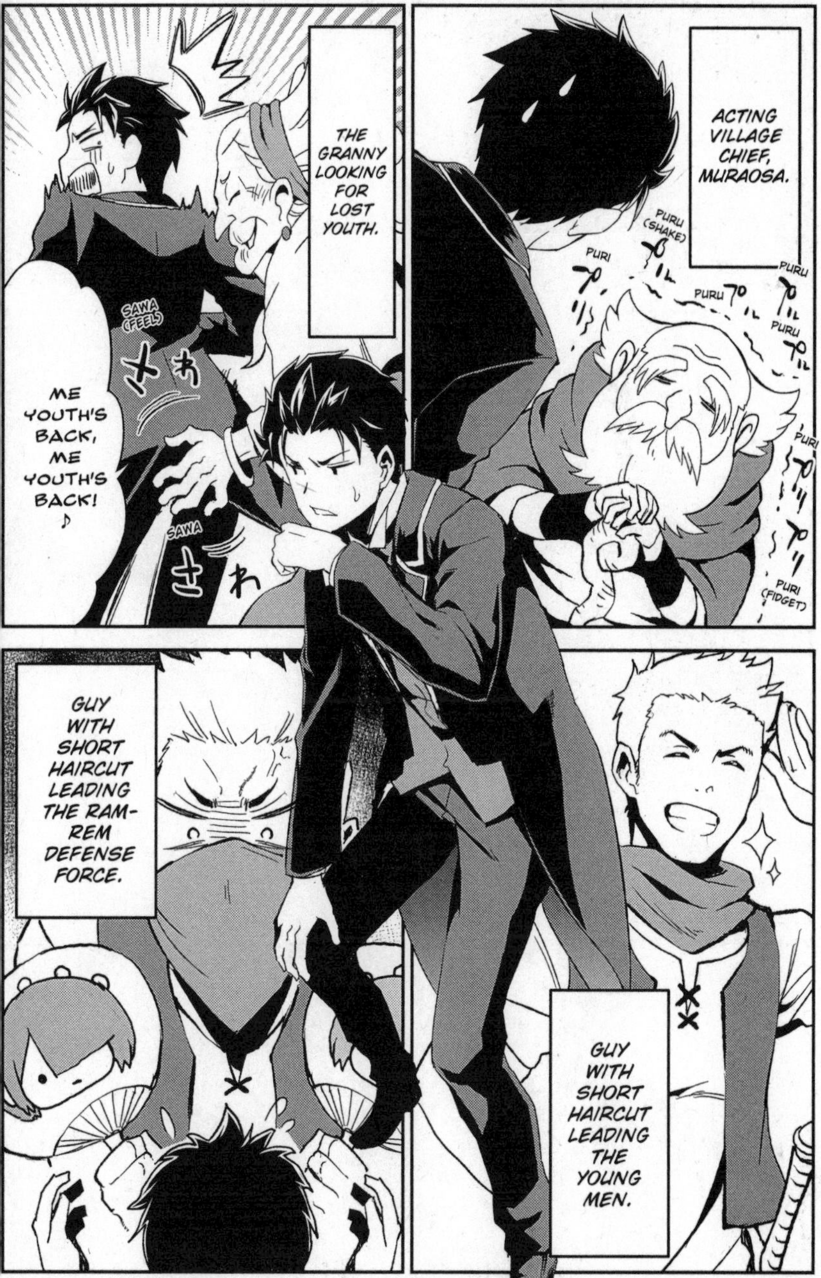
ACTING VILLAGE CHIEF, MURAOSA.
PURU (SHAKE)
PURI
PURU
PURU
PURU
PURI
PURI (FIDGET)
THE GRANNY LOOKING FOR LOST YOUTH.
SAWA (FEEL)
SAWA
ME YOUTH'S BACK, ME YOUTH'S BACK! ♪
GUY WITH SHORT HAIRCUT LEADING THE YOUNG MEN.
GUY WITH SHORT HAIRCUT LEADING THE RAM-REM DEFENSE FORCE.

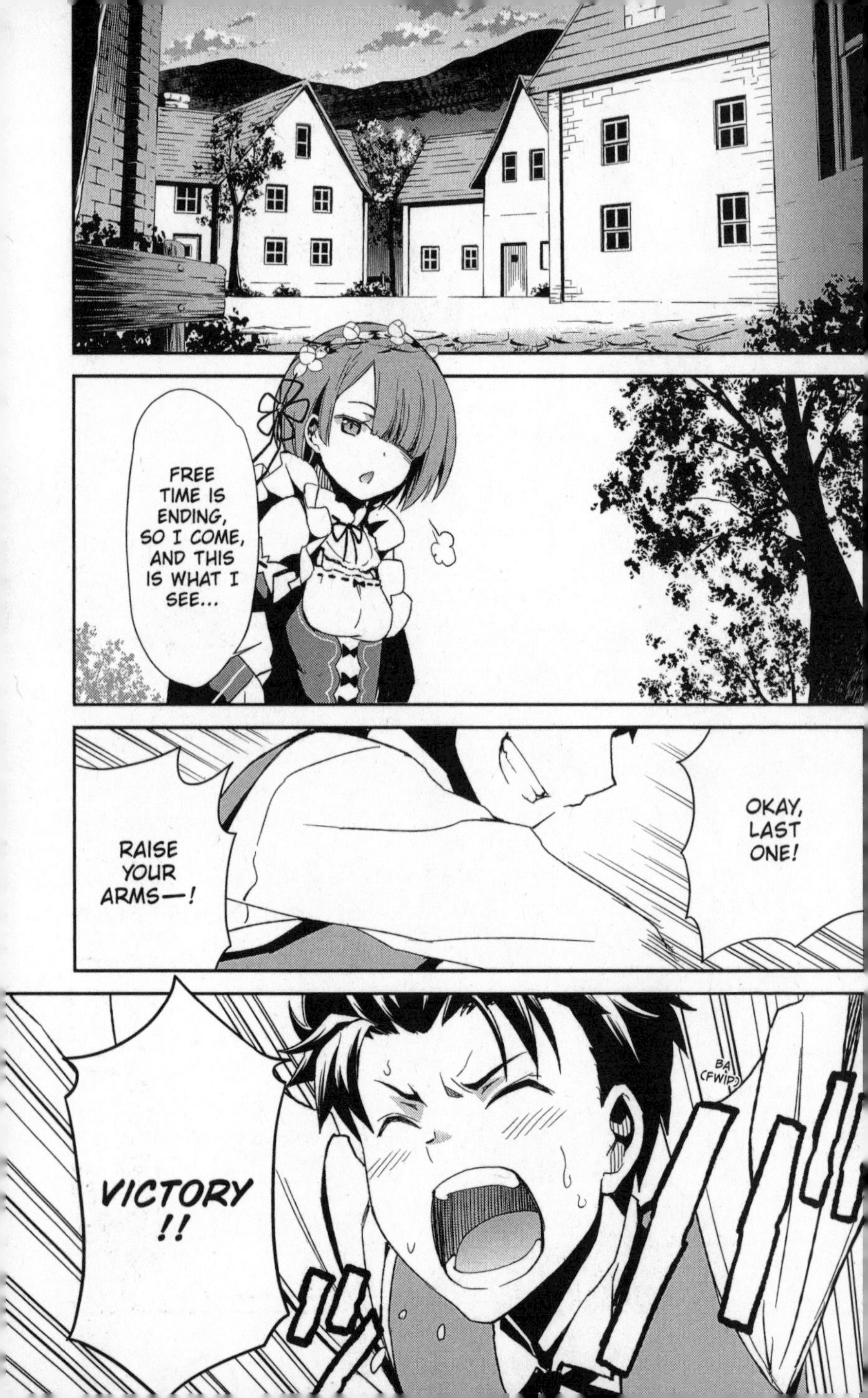
FREE TIME IS ENDING, SO I COME, AND THIS IS WHAT I SEE...
OKAY, LAST ONE!
RAISE YOUR ARMS—!
BA (FWIP)
VICTORY !!

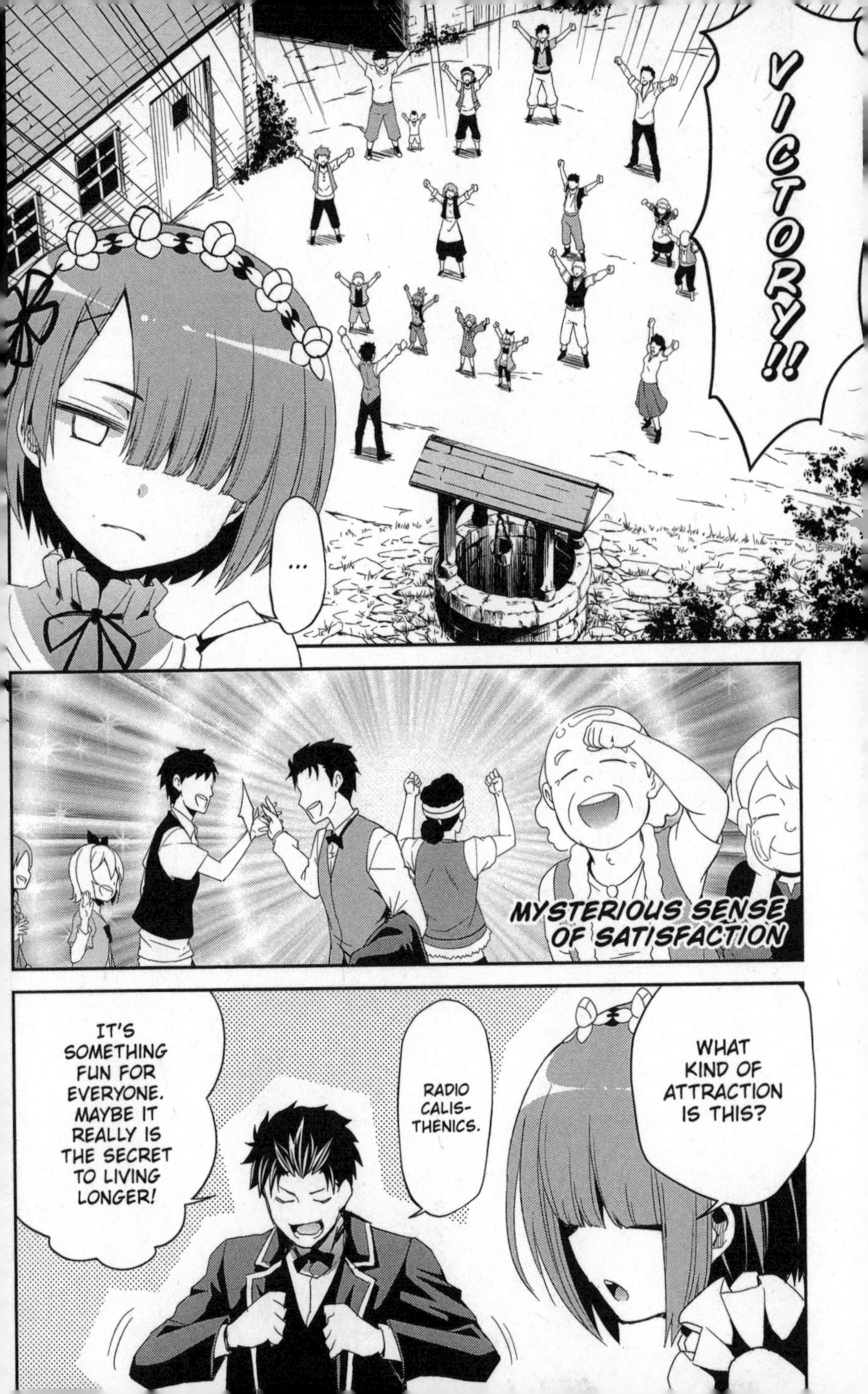
VICTORY!!
...
MYSTERIOUS SENSE OF SATISFACTION
WHAT KIND OF ATTRACTION IS THIS?
RADIO CALIS-THENICS.
IT'S SOMETHING FUN FOR EVERYONE. MAYBE IT REALLY IS THE SECRET TO LIVING LONGER!

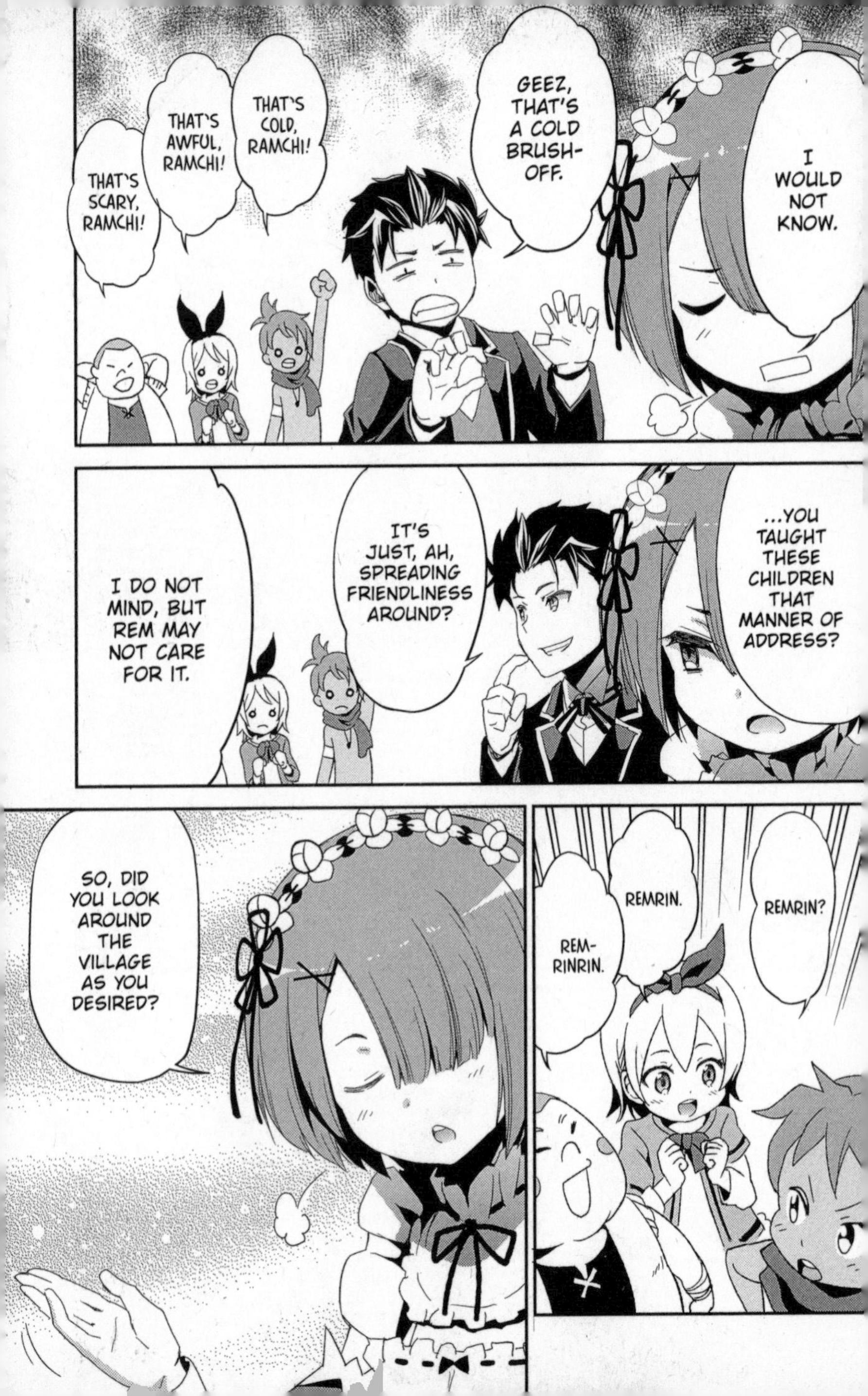
I WOULD NOT KNOW.
GEEZ, THAT'S A COLD BRUSH-OFF.
THAT'S COLD, RAMCHI!
THAT'S AWFUL, RAMCHI!
THAT'S SCARY, RAMCHI!
...YOU TAUGHT THESE CHILDREN THAT MANNER OF ADDRESS?
IT'S JUST, AH, SPREADING FRIENDLINESS AROUND?
I DO NOT MIND, BUT REM MAY NOT CARE FOR IT.
REMRIN?
REMRIN.
REM-RINRIN.
SO, DID YOU LOOK AROUND THE VILLAGE AS YOU DESIRED?

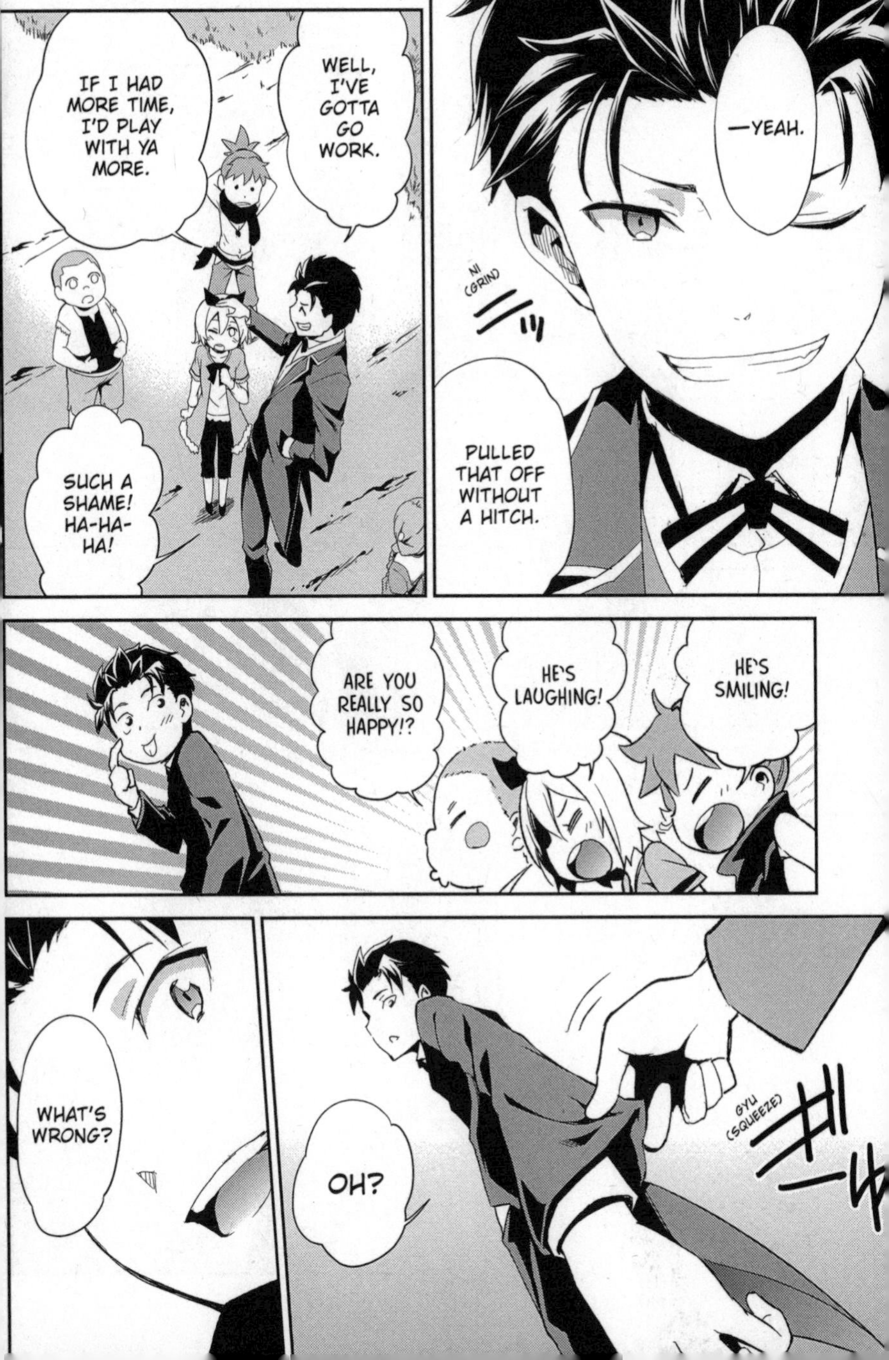
—YEAH.
NI (GRIN)
PULLED THAT OFF WITHOUT A HITCH.
WELL, I'VE GOTTA GO WORK.
IF I HAD MORE TIME, I'D PLAY WITH YA MORE.
SUCH A SHAME! HA-HA-HA!
HE'S SMILING!
HE'S LAUGHING!
ARE YOU REALLY SO HAPPY!?
GYU (SQUEEZE)
OH?
WHAT'S WRONG?

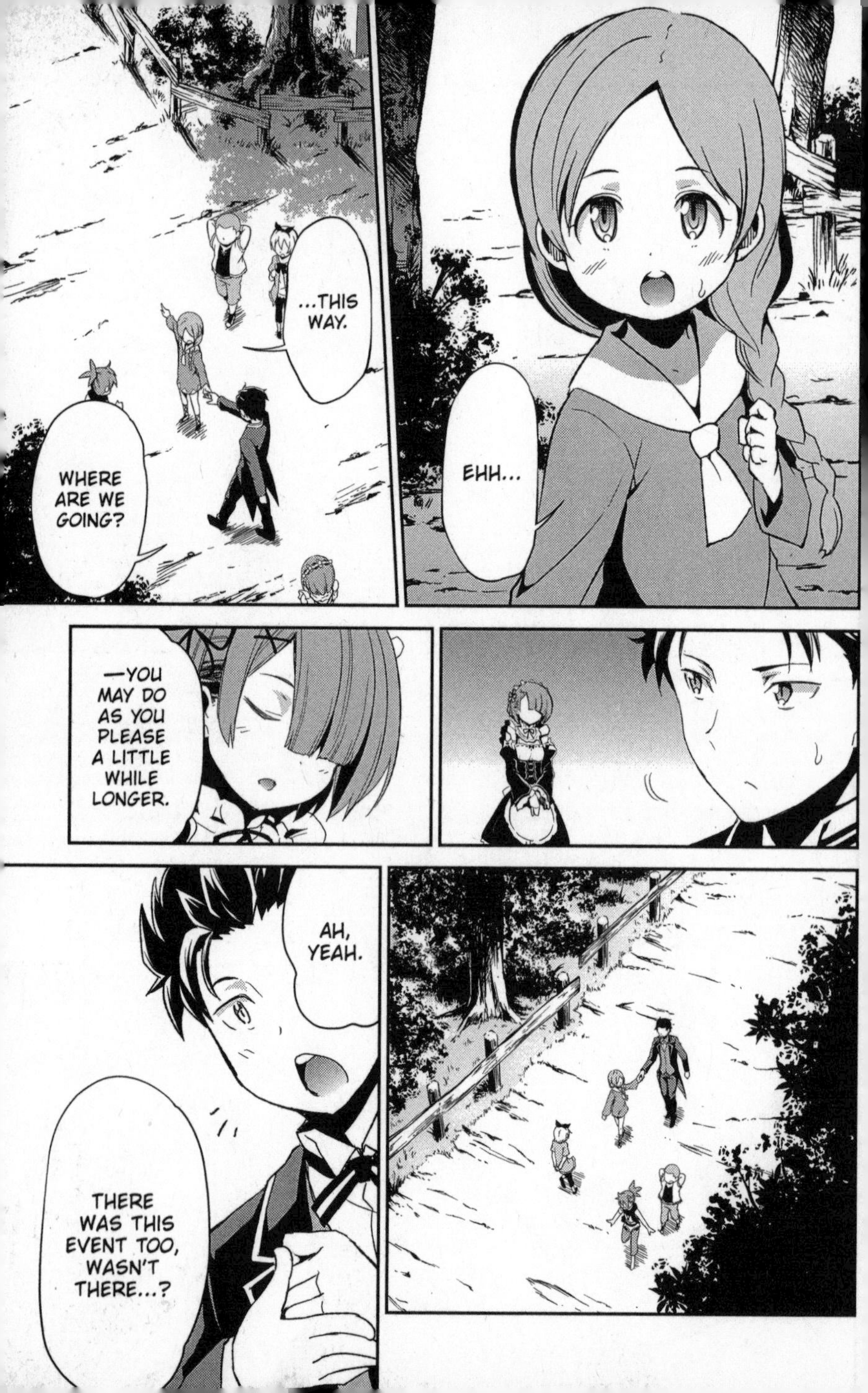
EHH...
...THIS WAY.
WHERE ARE WE GOING?
—YOU MAY DO AS YOU PLEASE A LITTLE WHILE LONGER.
AH, YEAH.
THERE WAS THIS EVENT TOO, WASN'T THERE...?

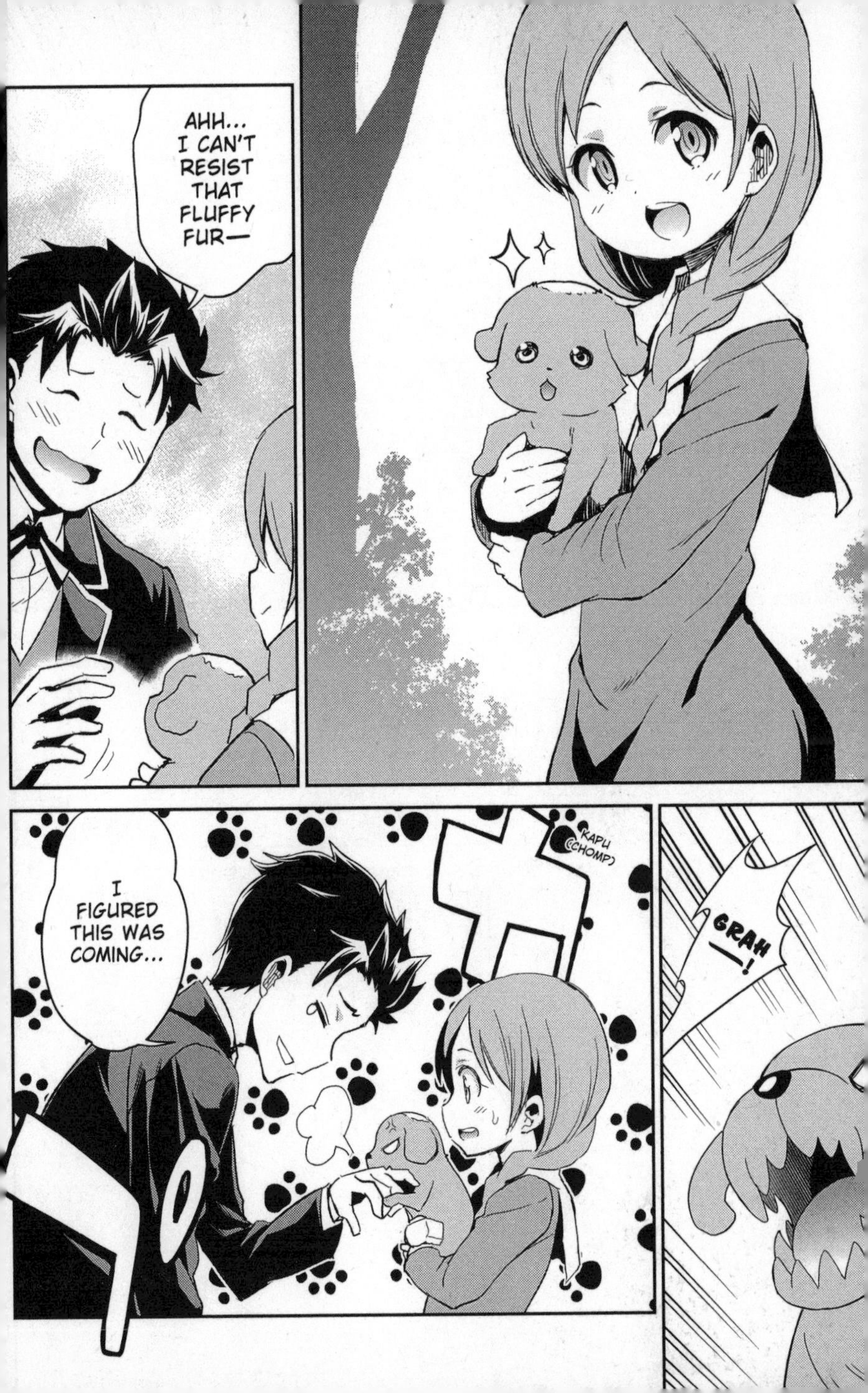
AHH... I CAN'T RESIST THAT FLUFFY FUR—
GRAH—!
KAPU (CHOMP)
I FIGURED THIS WAS COMING...

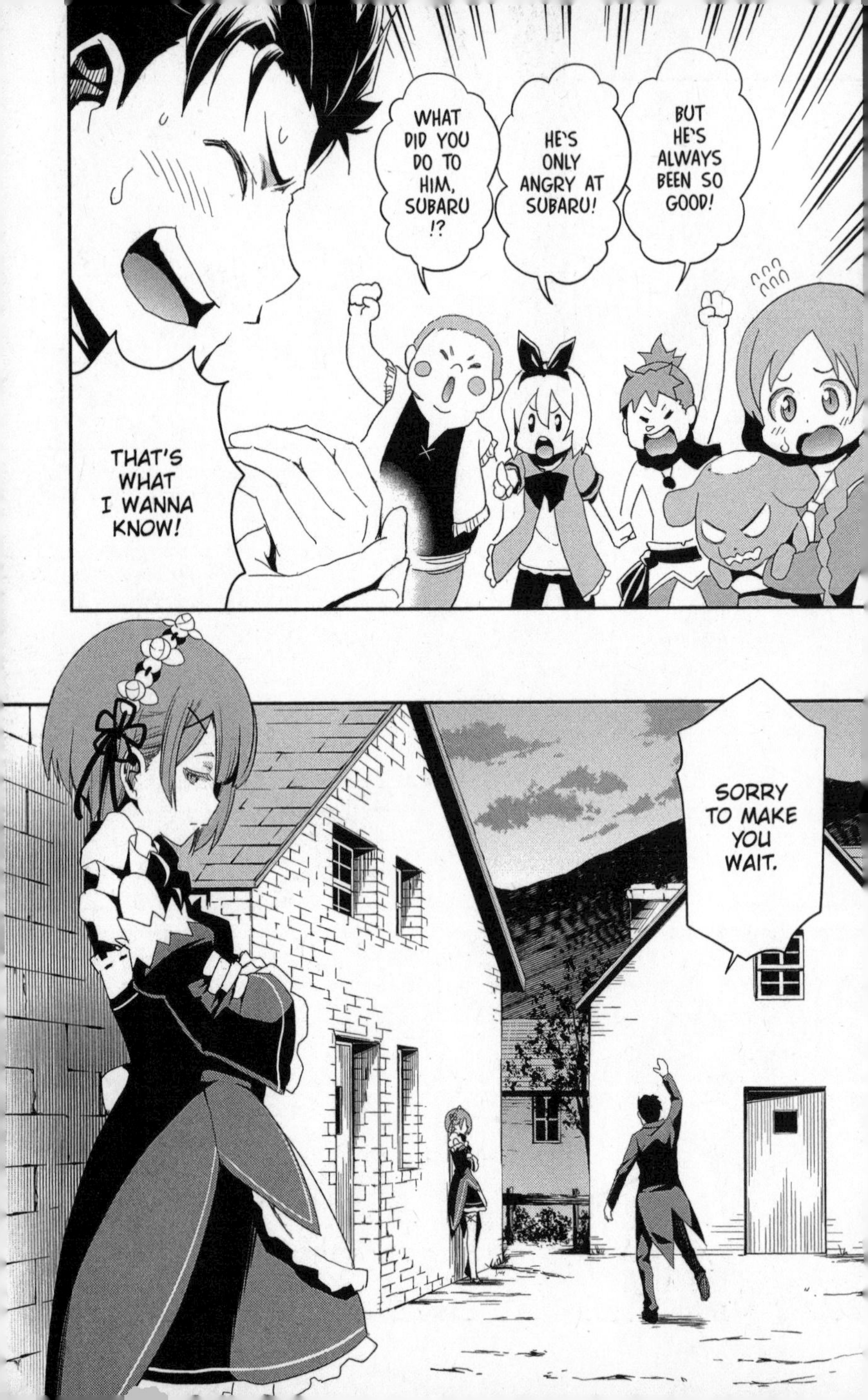
BUT HE'S ALWAYS BEEN SO GOOD!
HE'S ONLY ANGRY AT SUBARU!
WHAT DID YOU DO TO HIM, SUBARU!?
THAT'S WHAT I WANNA KNOW!
SORRY TO MAKE YOU WAIT.

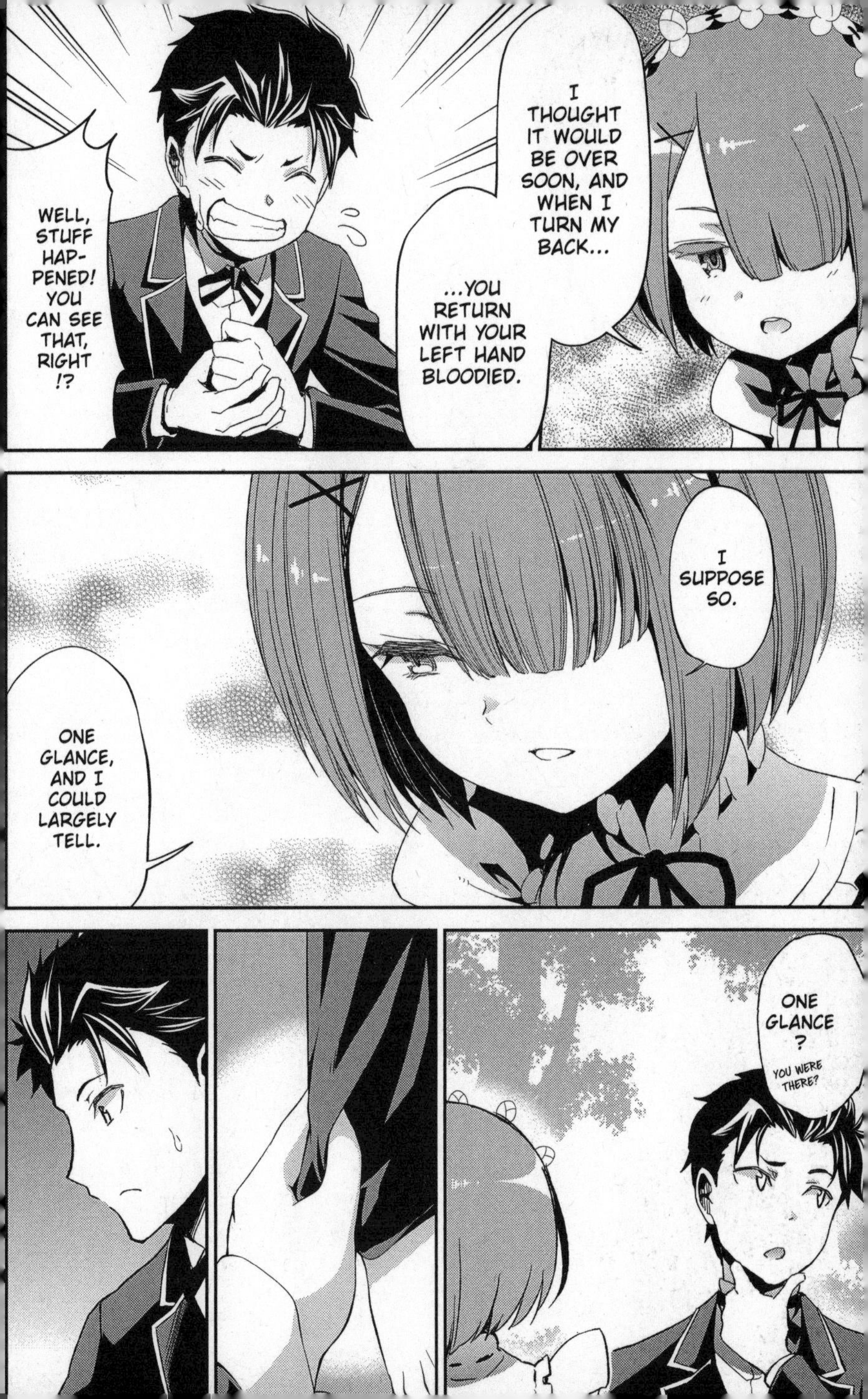
I THOUGHT IT WOULD BE OVER SOON, AND WHEN I TURN MY BACK...
...YOU RETURN WITH YOUR LEFT HAND BLOODIED.
WELL, STUFF HAP-PENED! YOU CAN SEE THAT, RIGHT!?
I SUPPOSE SO.
ONE GLANCE, AND I COULD LARGELY TELL.
ONE GLANCE?
YOU WERE THERE?

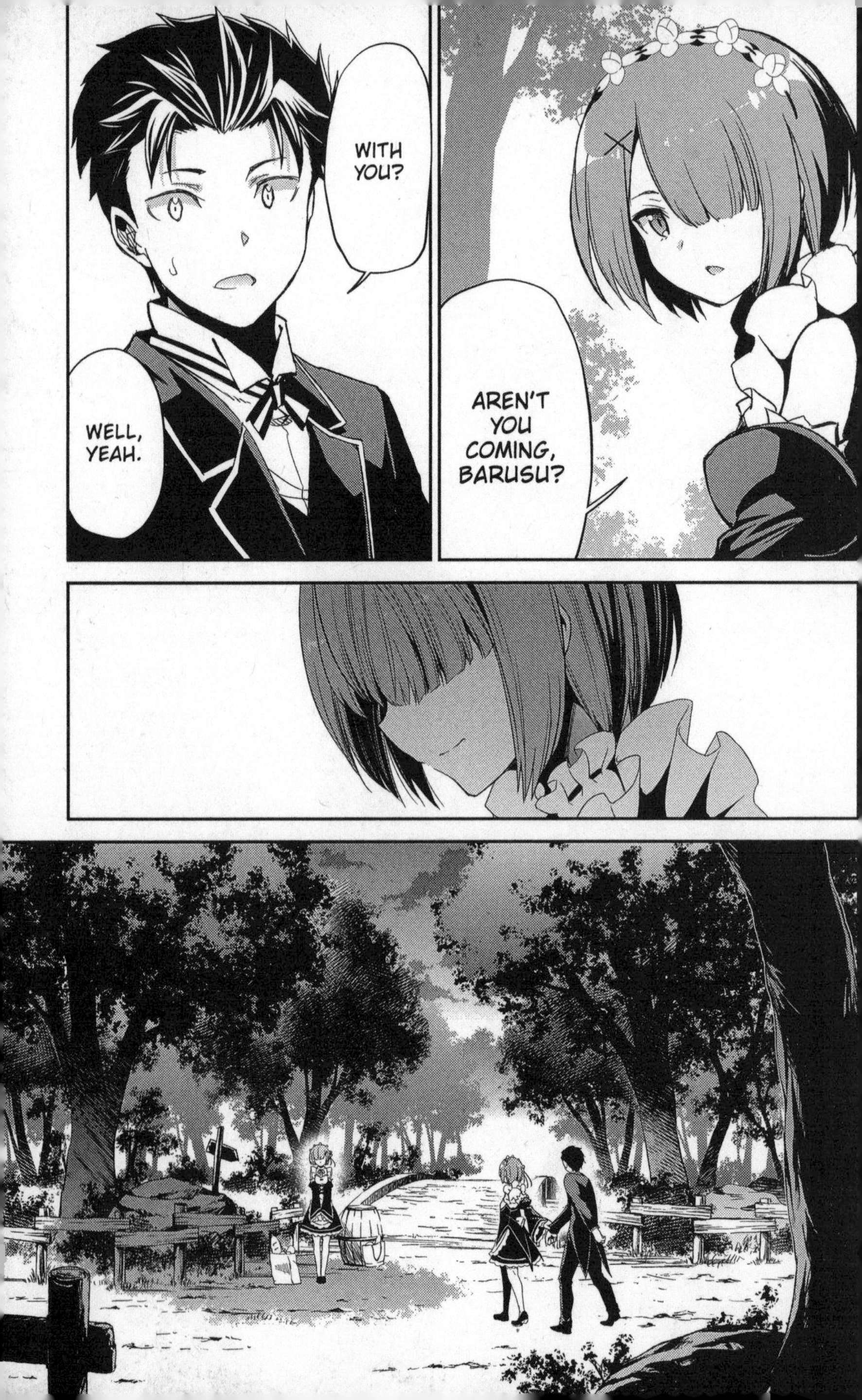
AREN'T YOU COMING, BARUSU?
WITH YOU?
WELL, YEAH.

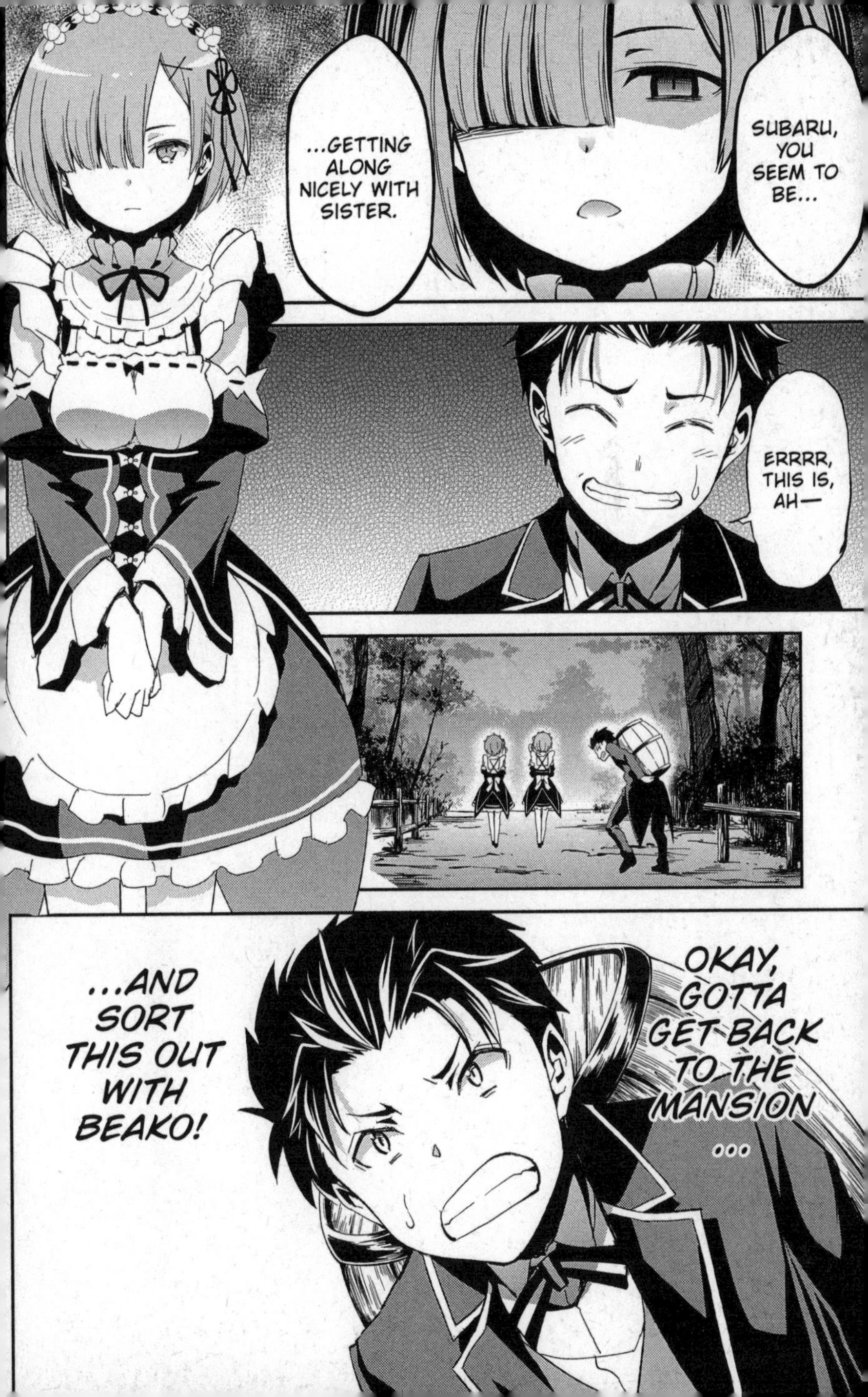
SUBARU, YOU SEEM TO BE...
...GETTING ALONG NICELY WITH SISTER.
ERRRR, THIS IS, AH—
OKAY, GOTTA GET BACK TO THE MANSION...
...AND SORT THIS OUT WITH BEAKO!

The children of Earlham Village.
The girl with the ribbon is cute.
Very cute.
I want to dress her in a maid outfit…

Let us meet again in Volume 4.

Re:ZERO -Starting Life in Another World-

A Week at the Mansion

The only ability Subaru Natsuki gets when he's summoned to another world is time travel via his own death. But to save her, he'll die as many times as it takes.

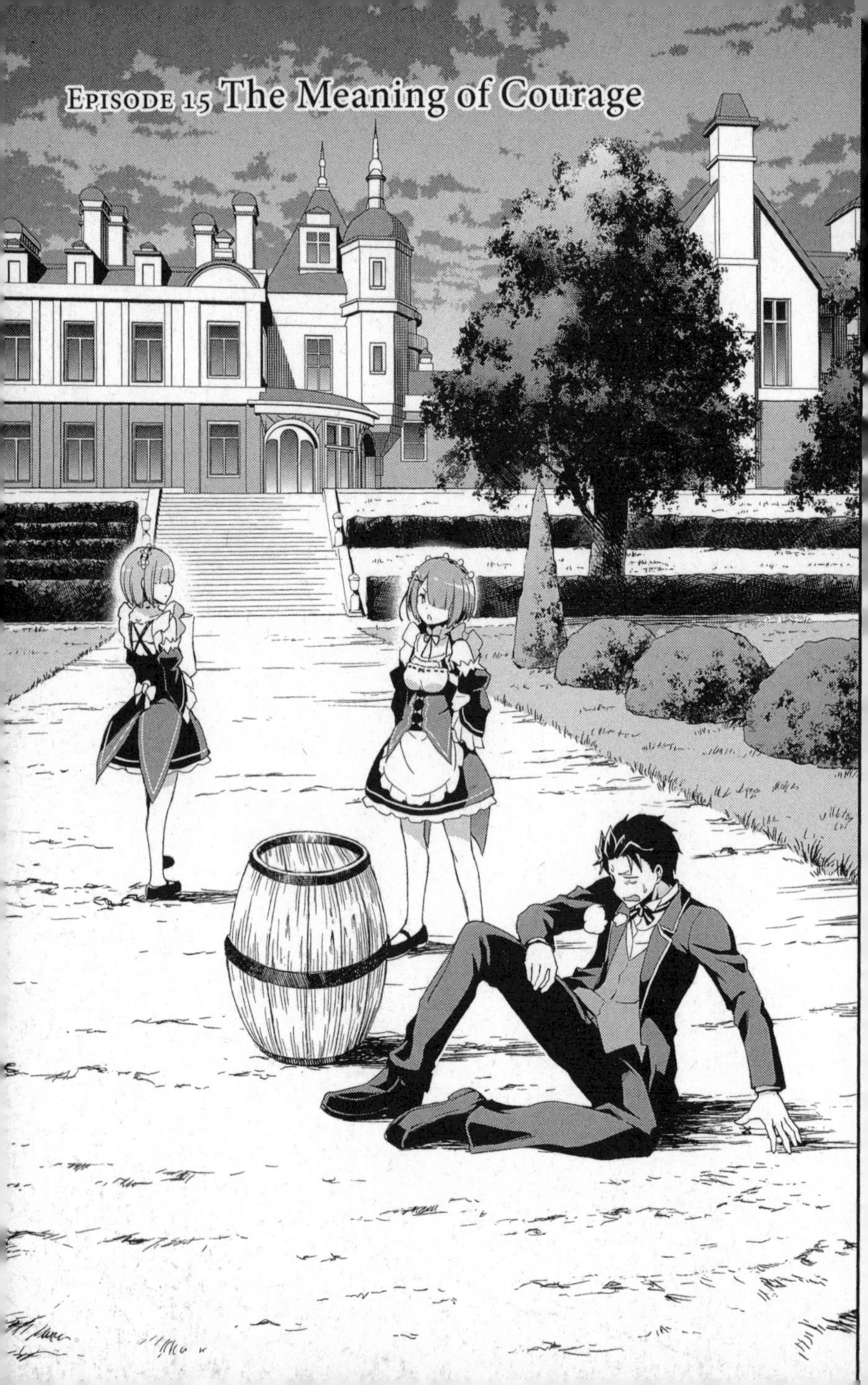
EPISODE 15 The Meaning of Courage

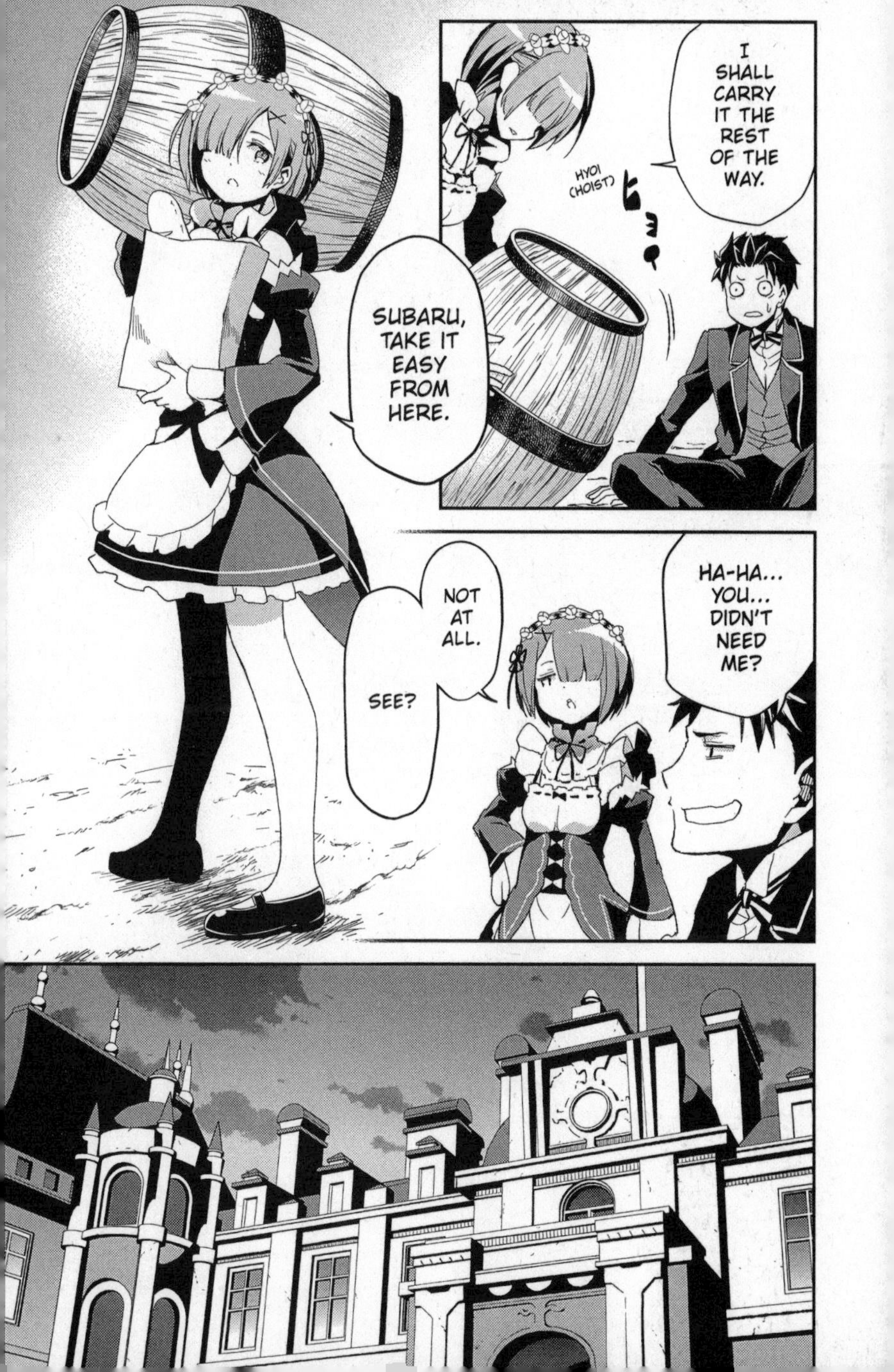
I SHALL CARRY IT THE REST OF THE WAY.
HYOI (HOIST)
SUBARU, TAKE IT EASY FROM HERE.
HA-HA... YOU... DIDN'T NEED ME?
NOT AT ALL.
SEE?

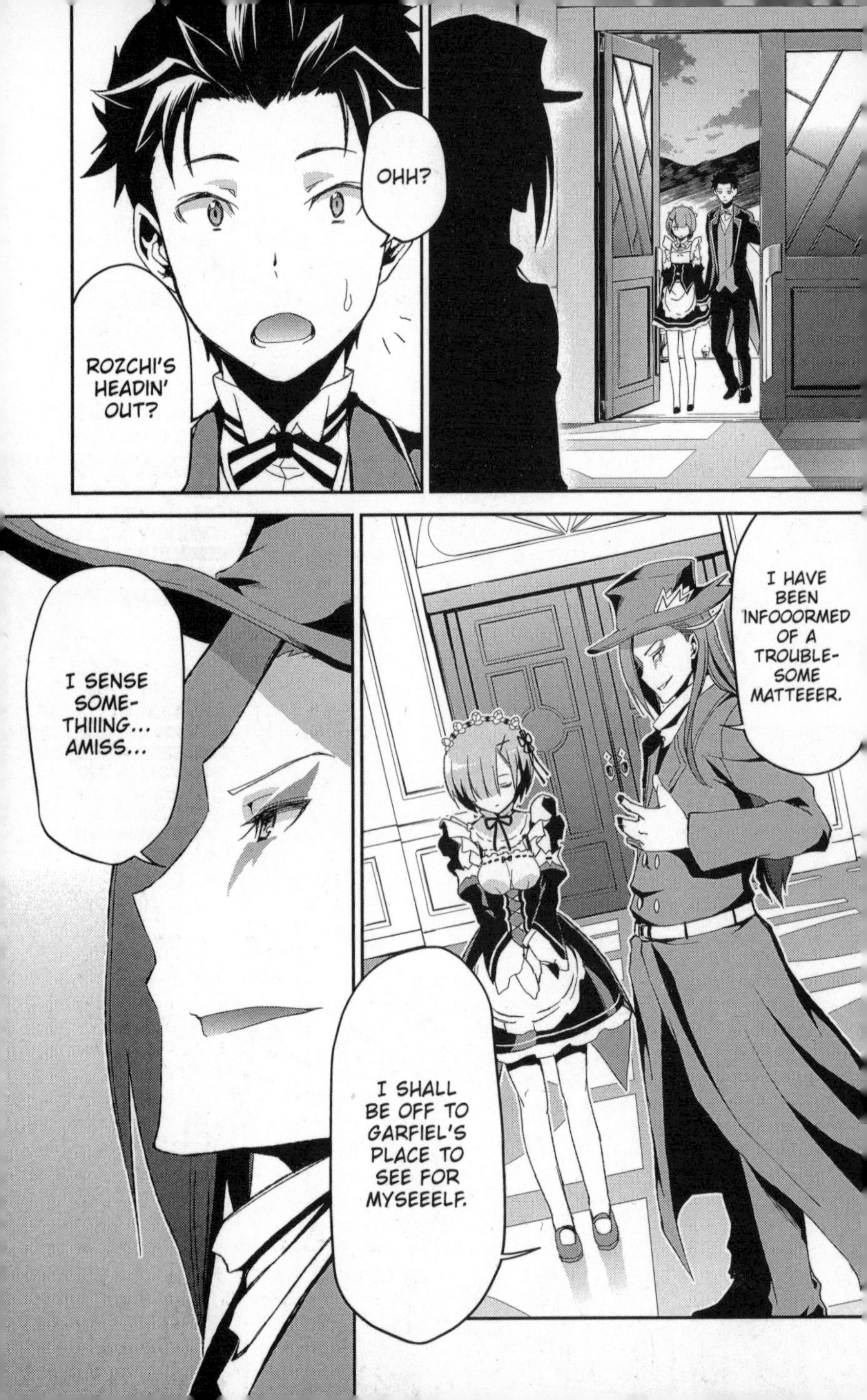
OHH?
ROZCHI'S HEADIN' OUT?
I HAVE BEEN INFOOORMED OF A TROUBLE-SOME MATTEEER.
I SHALL BE OFF TO GARFIEL'S PLACE TO SEE FOR MYSEEELF.
I SENSE SOME-THIIING... AMISS...

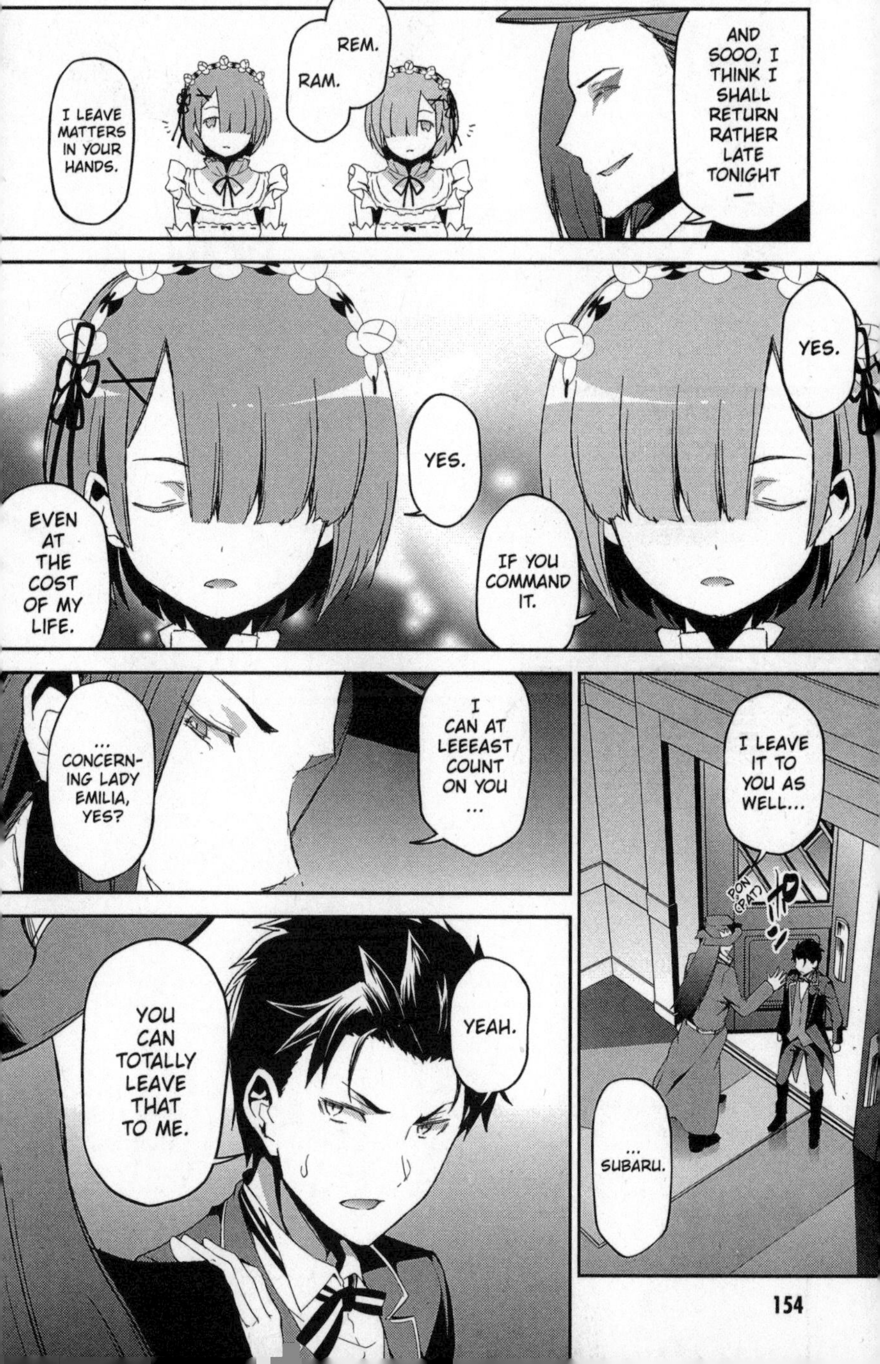
AND SOOO, I THINK I SHALL RETURN RATHER LATE TONIGHT—
REM.
RAM.
I LEAVE MATTERS IN YOUR HANDS.
YES.
YES.
IF YOU COMMAND IT.
EVEN AT THE COST OF MY LIFE.
I LEAVE IT TO YOU AS WELL...
PON (PAT)
... SUBARU.
I CAN AT LEEEAST COUNT ON YOU ...
... CONCERNING LADY EMILIA, YES?
YEAH.
YOU CAN TOTALLY LEAVE THAT TO ME.

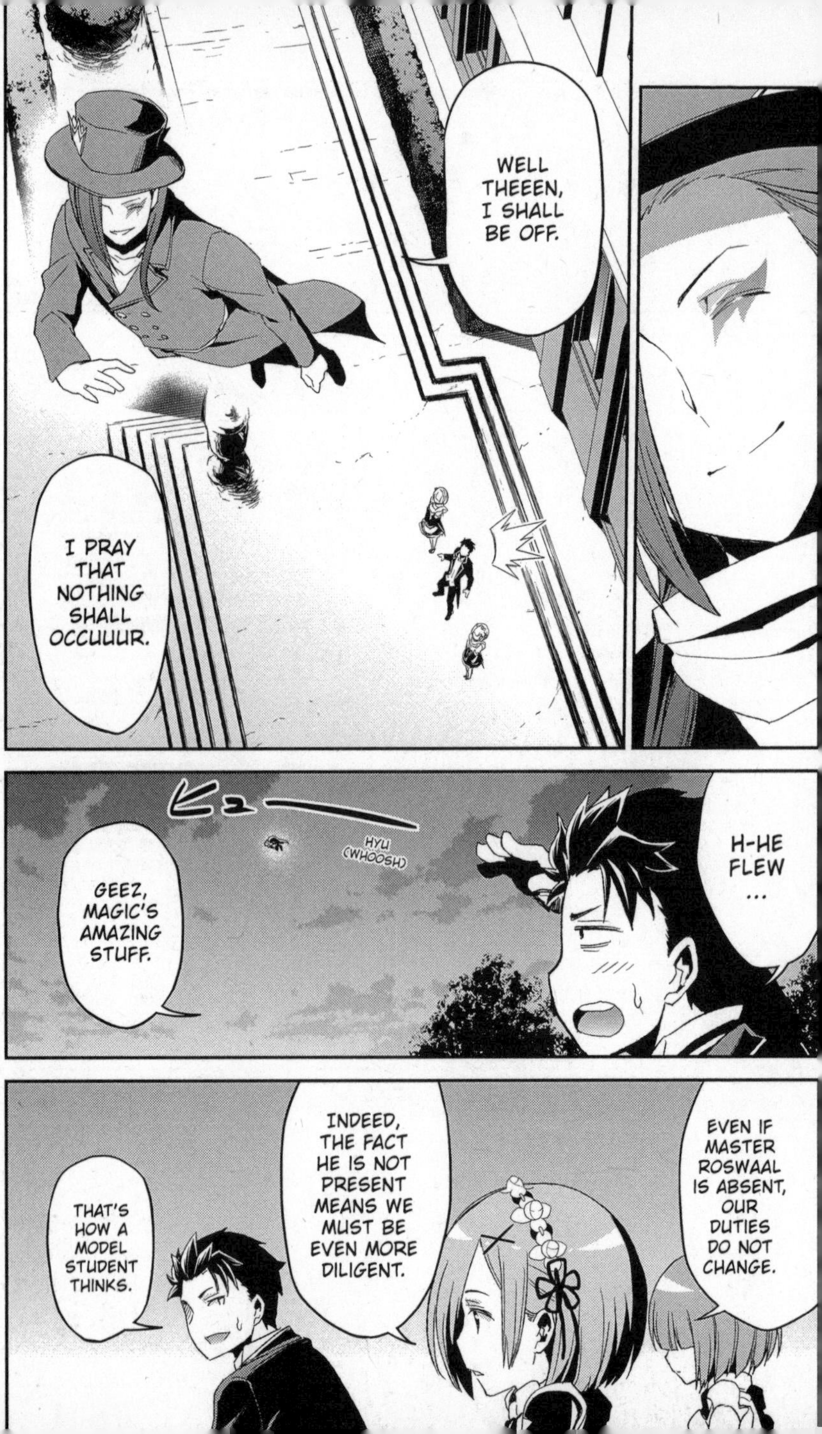
WELL THEEEN, I SHALL BE OFF.
I PRAY THAT NOTHING SHALL OCCUUUR.
H-HE FLEW ...
HYU (WHOOSH)
GEEZ, MAGIC'S AMAZING STUFF.
EVEN IF MASTER ROSWAAL IS ABSENT, OUR DUTIES DO NOT CHANGE.
INDEED, THE FACT HE IS NOT PRESENT MEANS WE MUST BE EVEN MORE DILIGENT.
THAT'S HOW A MODEL STUDENT THINKS.

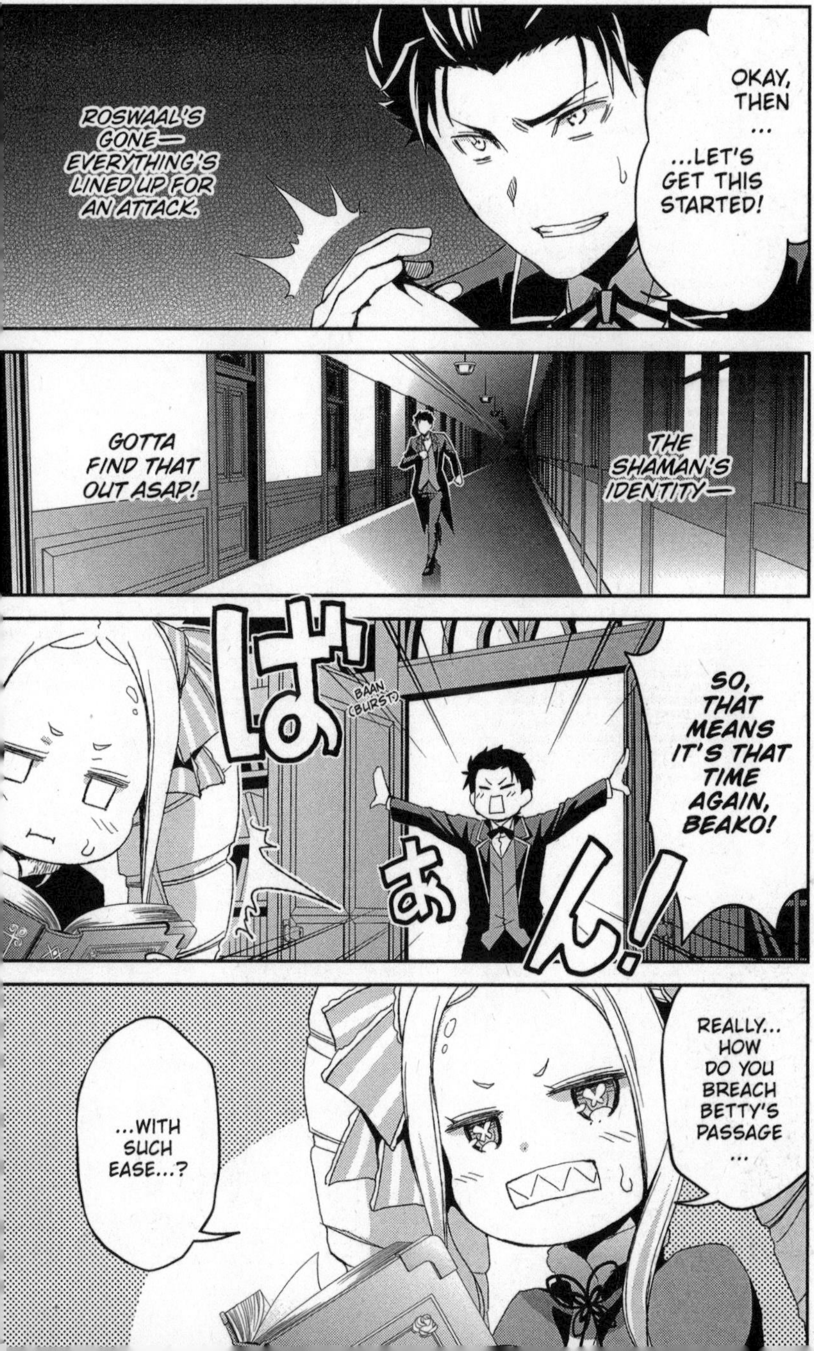
OKAY, THEN ...
...LET'S GET THIS STARTED!
ROSWAAL'S GONE—EVERYTHING'S LINED UP FOR AN ATTACK.
THE SHAMAN'S IDENTITY—
GOTTA FIND THAT OUT ASAP!
SO, THAT MEANS IT'S THAT TIME AGAIN, BEAKO!
ばあん!
BAAN (BURST)
REALLY... HOW DO YOU BREACH BETTY'S PASSAGE ...
...WITH SUCH EASE...?

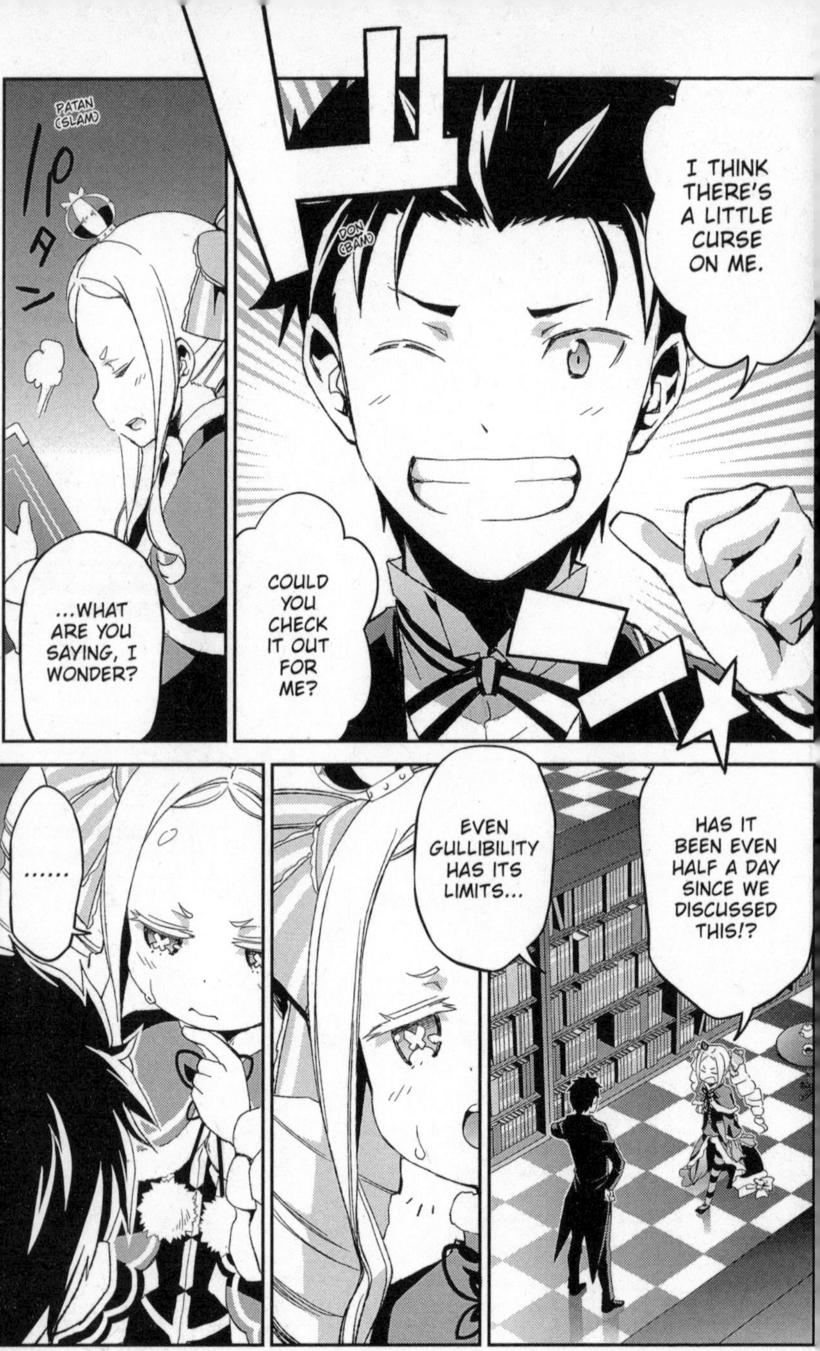
DON (BAM)
I THINK THERE'S A LITTLE CURSE ON ME.
COULD YOU CHECK IT OUT FOR ME?
PATAN (SLAM)
...WHAT ARE YOU SAYING, I WONDER?
HAS IT BEEN EVEN HALF A DAY SINCE WE DISCUSSED THIS!?
EVEN GULLIBILITY HAS ITS LIMITS...
......

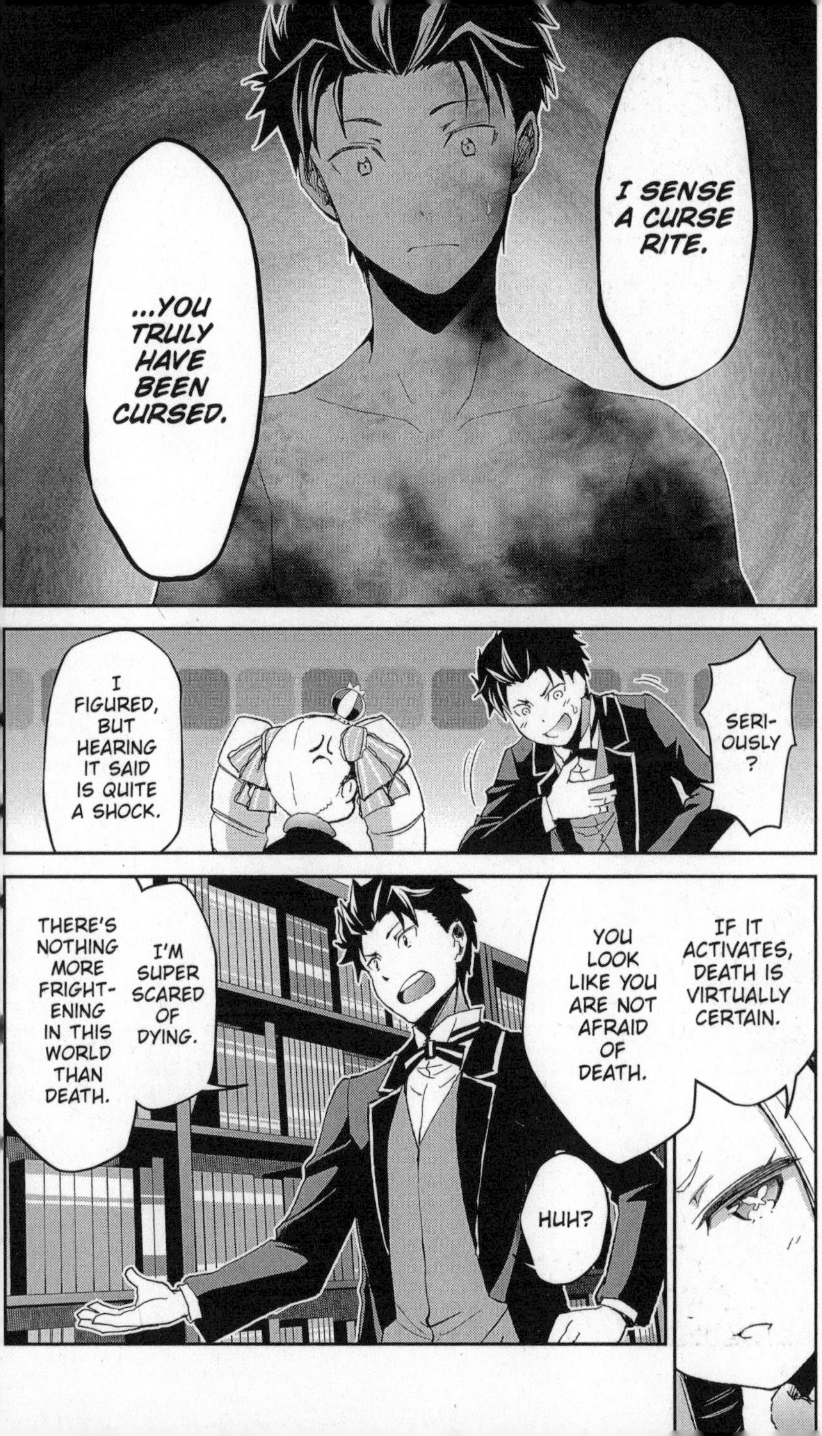
I SENSE A CURSE RITE.
...YOU TRULY HAVE BEEN CURSED.
SERI-OUSLY?
I FIGURED, BUT HEARING IT SAID IS QUITE A SHOCK.
IF IT ACTIVATES, DEATH IS VIRTUALLY CERTAIN.
YOU LOOK LIKE YOU ARE NOT AFRAID OF DEATH.
HUH?
I'M SUPER SCARED OF DYING.
THERE'S NOTHING MORE FRIGHT-ENING IN THIS WORLD THAN DEATH.

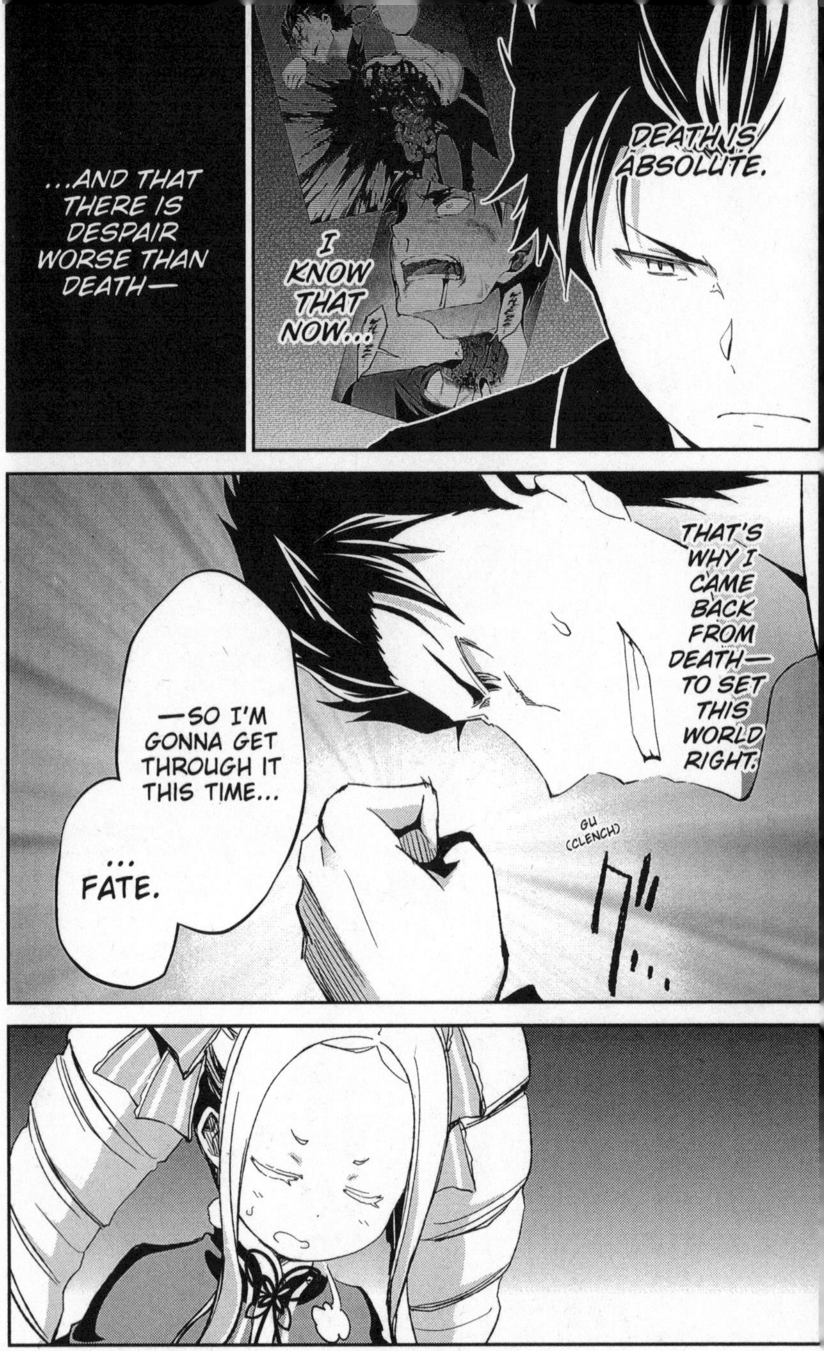
DEATH IS ABSOLUTE.
I KNOW THAT NOW...
...AND THAT THERE IS DESPAIR WORSE THAN DEATH—
THAT'S WHY I CAME BACK FROM DEATH—TO SET THIS WORLD RIGHT.
—SO I'M GONNA GET THROUGH IT THIS TIME...
...FATE.
GU (CLENCH)

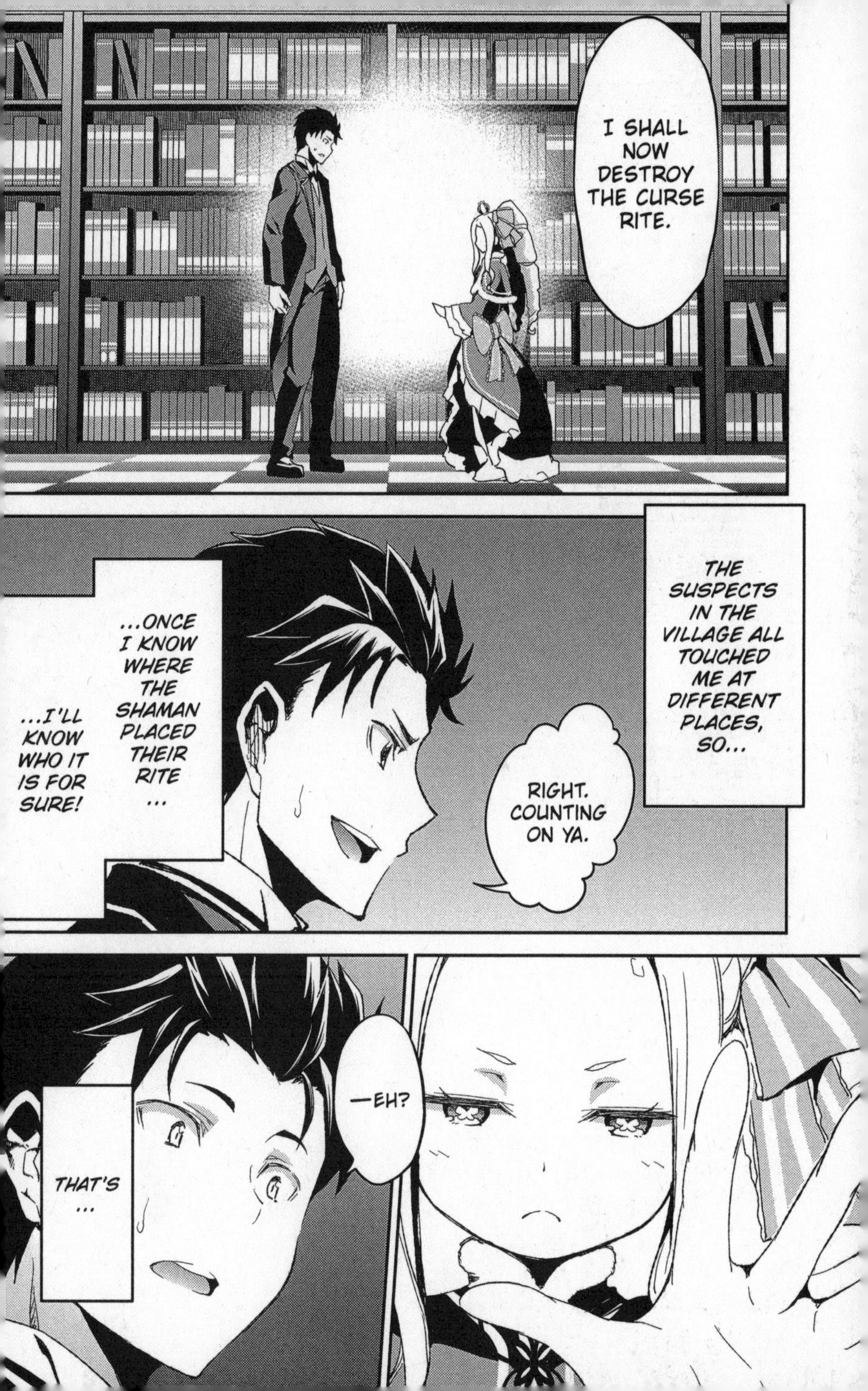
I SHALL NOW DESTROY THE CURSE RITE.
THE SUSPECTS IN THE VILLAGE ALL TOUCHED ME AT DIFFERENT PLACES, SO...
RIGHT. COUNTING ON YA.
...ONCE I KNOW WHERE THE SHAMAN PLACED THEIR RITE...
...I'LL KNOW WHO IT IS FOR SURE!
—EH?
THAT'S...

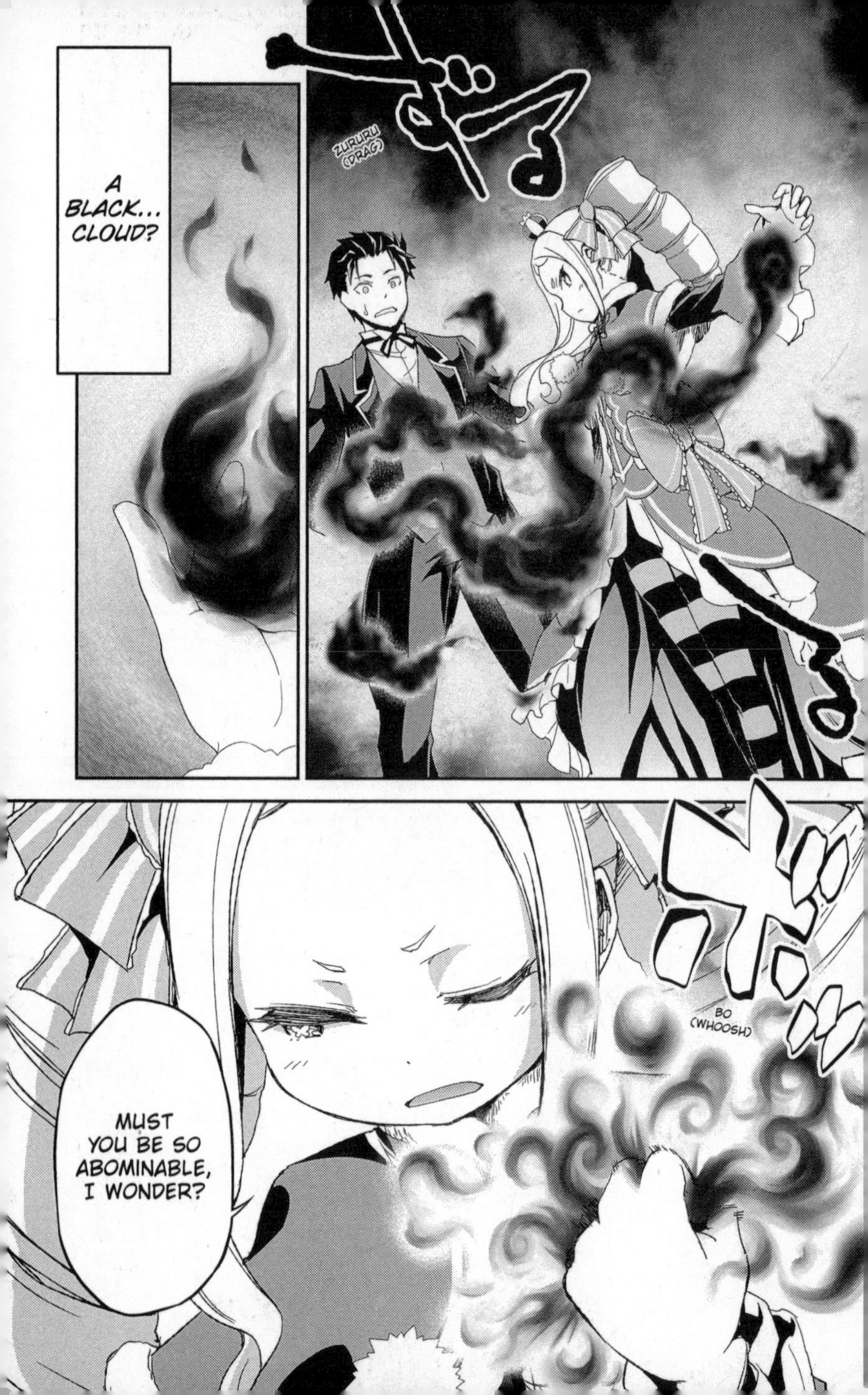
ZURURU (DRAG)
A BLACK... CLOUD?
BO (WHOOSH)
MUST YOU BE SO ABOMINABLE, I WONDER?

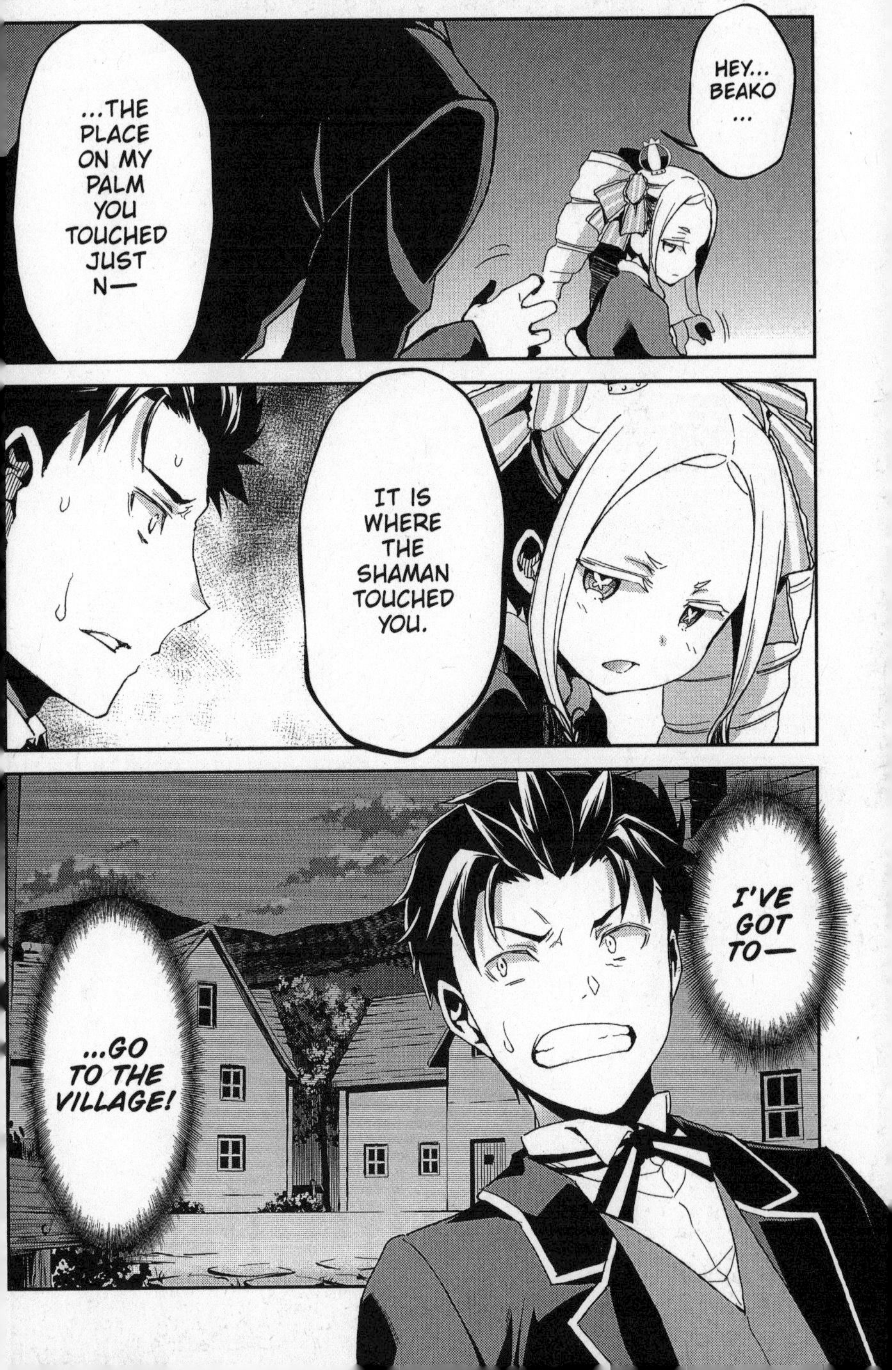
HEY... BEAKO ...
...THE PLACE ON MY PALM YOU TOUCHED JUST N—
IT IS WHERE THE SHAMAN TOUCHED YOU.
I'VE GOT TO—
...GO TO THE VILLAGE!

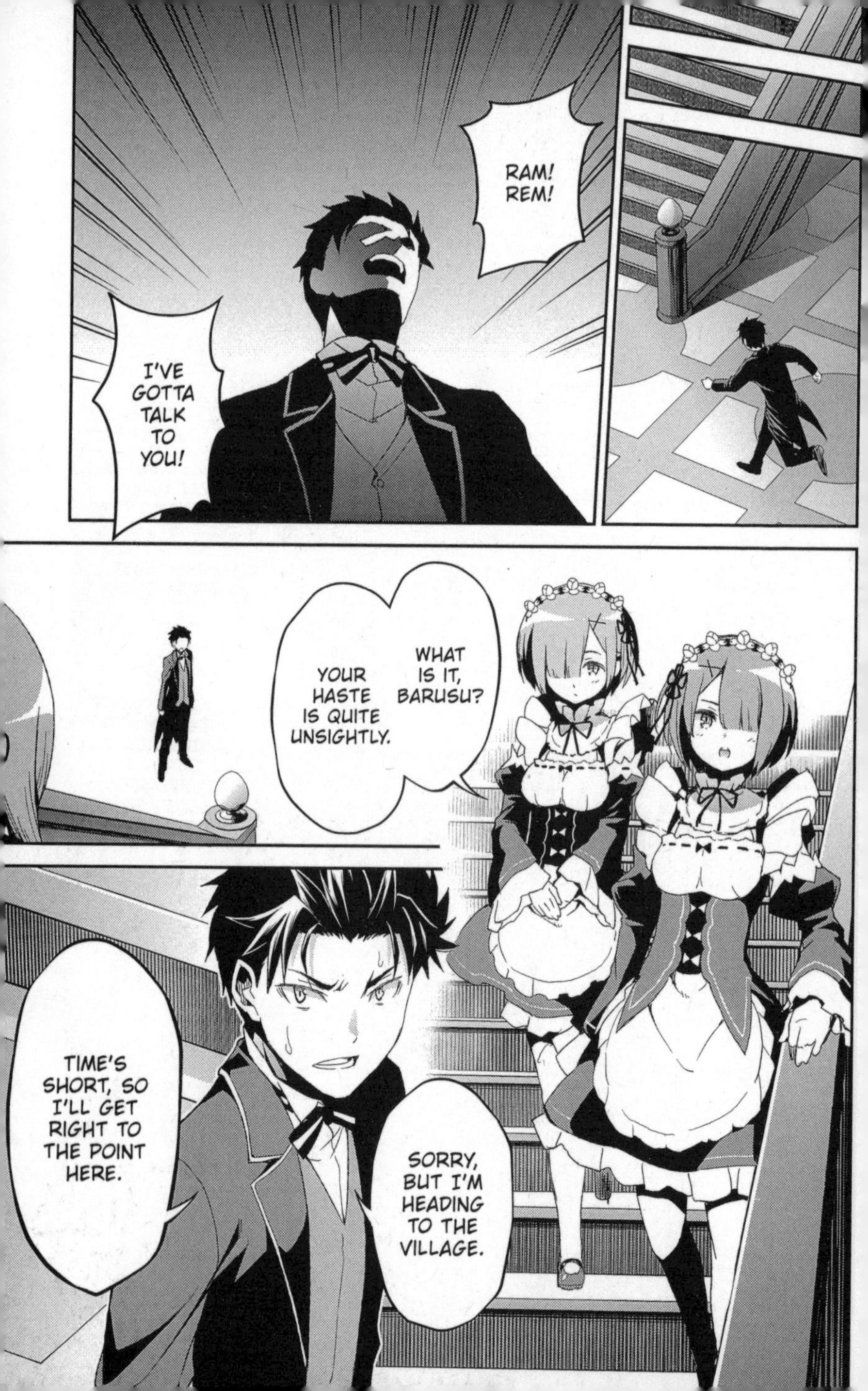
RAM! REM!
I'VE GOTTA TALK TO YOU!
WHAT IS IT, BARUSU?
YOUR HASTE IS QUITE UNSIGHTLY.
SORRY, BUT I'M HEADING TO THE VILLAGE.
TIME'S SHORT, SO I'LL GET RIGHT TO THE POINT HERE.

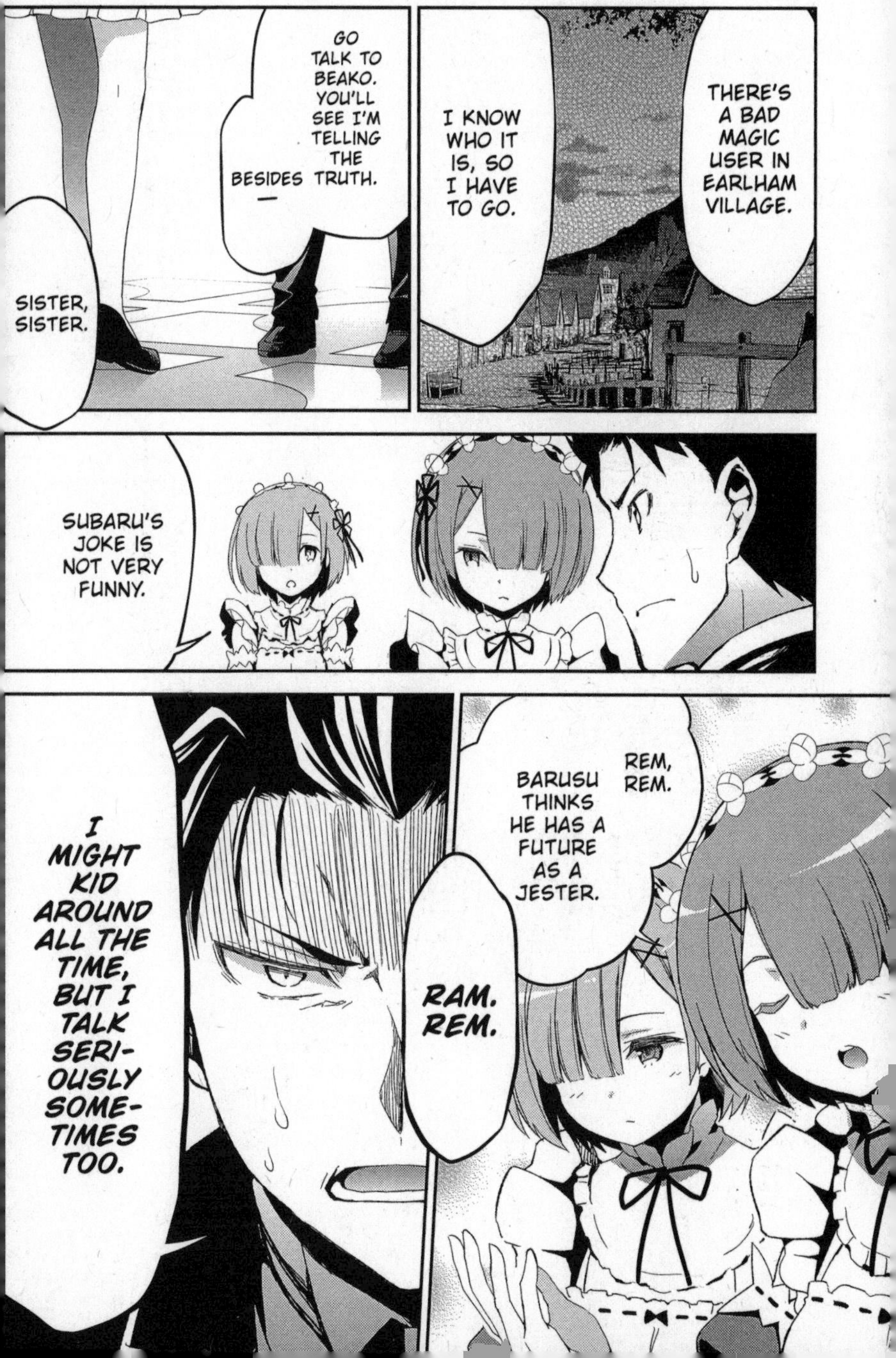
THERE'S A BAD MAGIC USER IN EARLHAM VILLAGE.
I KNOW WHO IT IS, SO I HAVE TO GO.
GO TALK TO BEAKO. YOU'LL SEE I'M TELLING THE TRUTH.
BESIDES—
SISTER, SISTER.
SUBARU'S JOKE IS NOT VERY FUNNY.
REM, REM.
BARUSU THINKS HE HAS A FUTURE AS A JESTER.
RAM. REM.
I MIGHT KID AROUND ALL THE TIME, BUT I TALK SERIOUSLY SOMETIMES TOO.

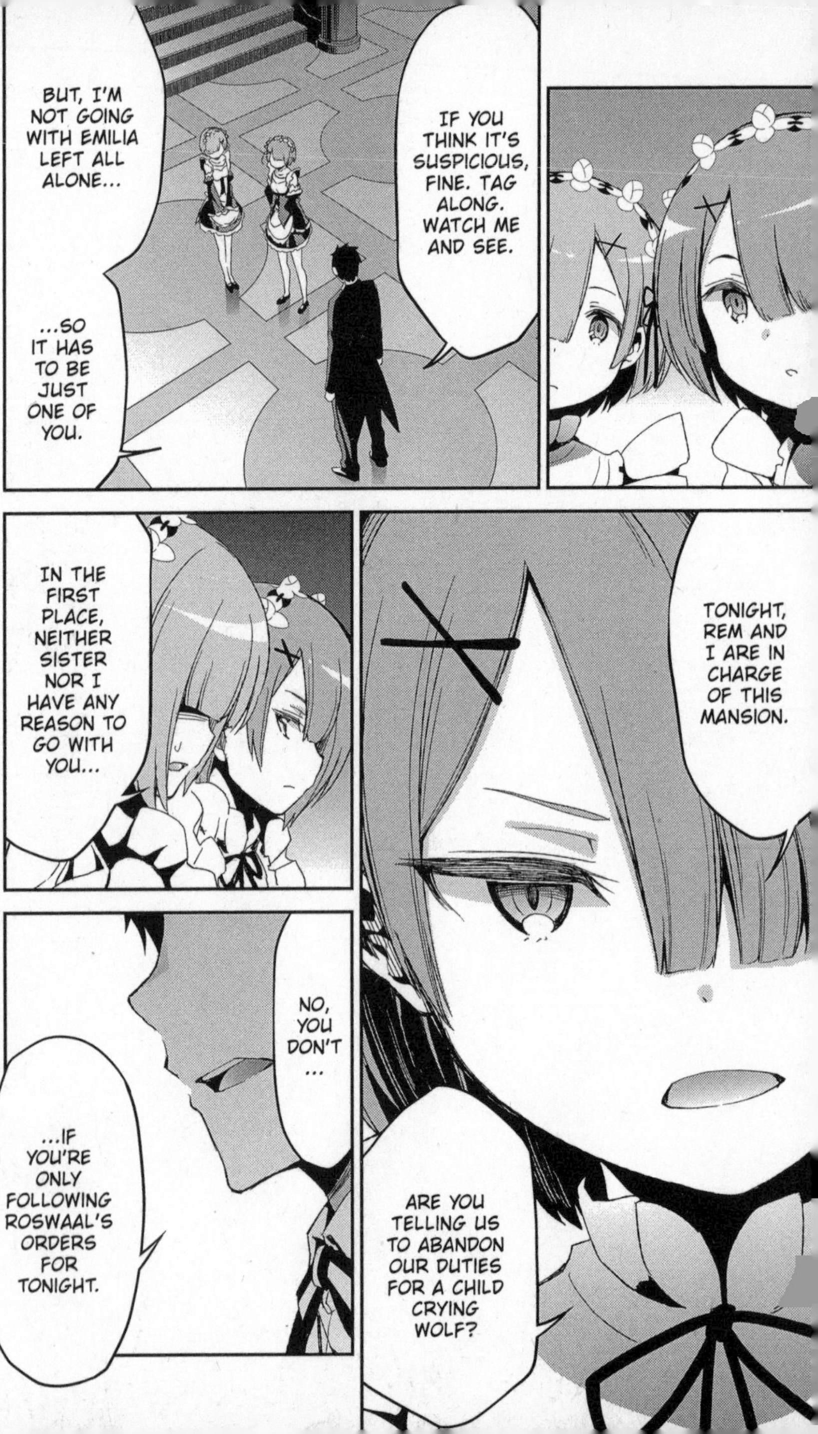
IF YOU THINK IT'S SUSPICIOUS, FINE. TAG ALONG. WATCH ME AND SEE.
BUT, I'M NOT GOING WITH EMILIA LEFT ALL ALONE...
...SO IT HAS TO BE JUST ONE OF YOU.
TONIGHT, REM AND I ARE IN CHARGE OF THIS MANSION.
ARE YOU TELLING US TO ABANDON OUR DUTIES FOR A CHILD CRYING WOLF?
IN THE FIRST PLACE, NEITHER SISTER NOR I HAVE ANY REASON TO GO WITH YOU...
NO, YOU DON'T ...
...IF YOU'RE ONLY FOLLOWING ROSWAAL'S ORDERS FOR TONIGHT.

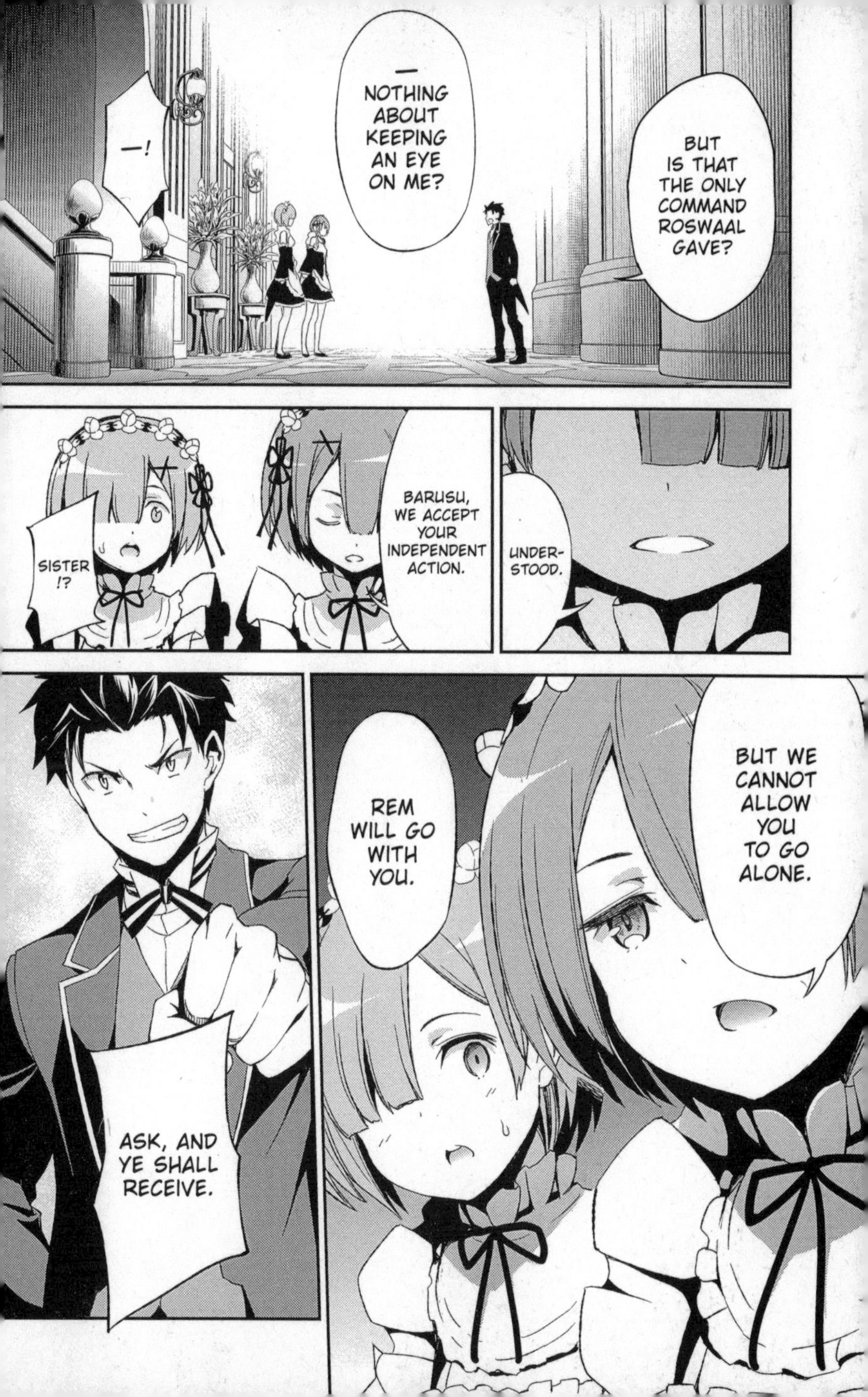
BUT IS THAT THE ONLY COMMAND ROSWAAL GAVE?
— NOTHING ABOUT KEEPING AN EYE ON ME?
—!
UNDER-STOOD.
BARUSU, WE ACCEPT YOUR INDEPENDENT ACTION.
SISTER!?
BUT WE CANNOT ALLOW YOU TO GO ALONE.
REM WILL GO WITH YOU.
ASK, AND YE SHALL RECEIVE.

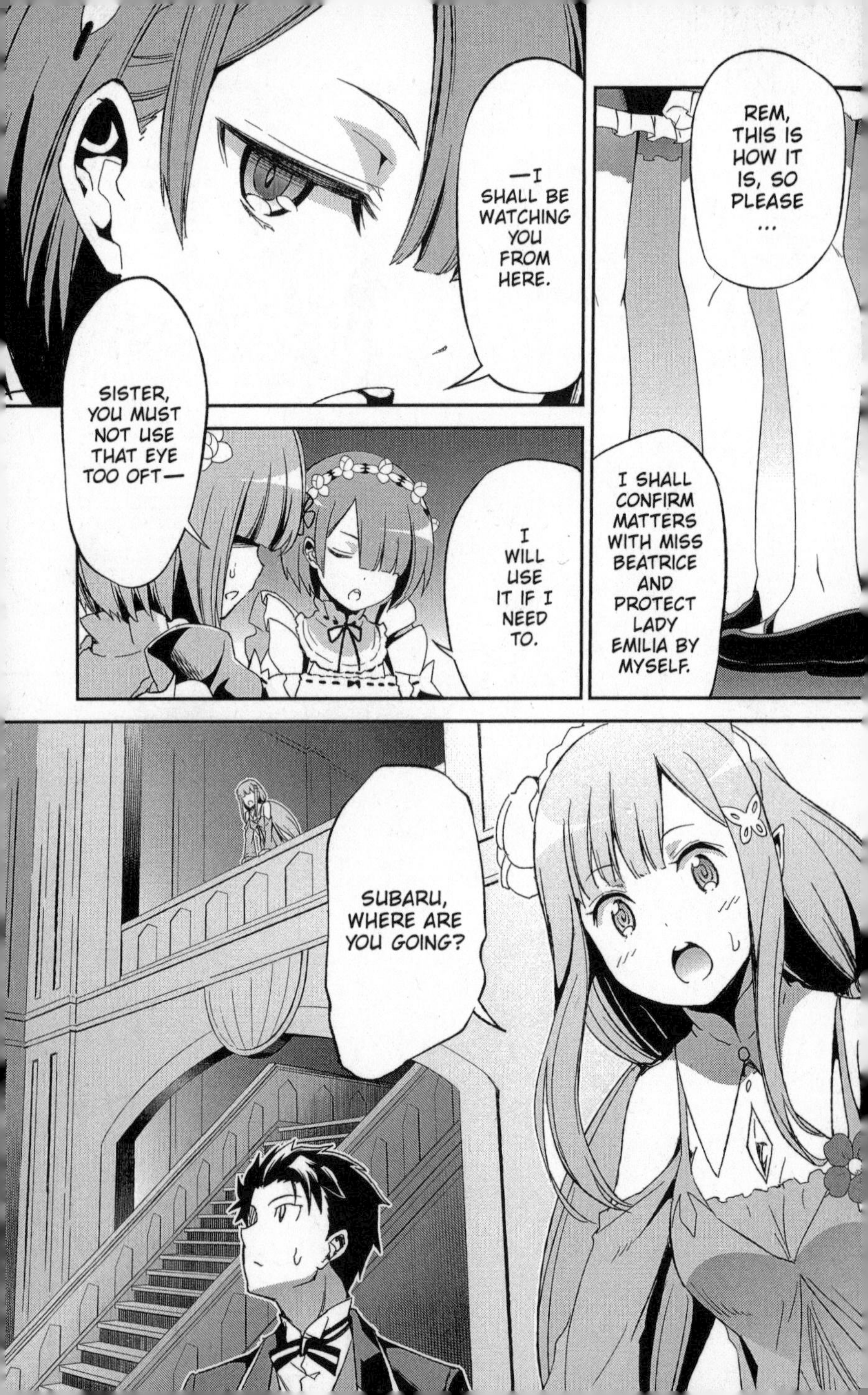
REM, THIS IS HOW IT IS, SO PLEASE ...
I SHALL CONFIRM MATTERS WITH MISS BEATRICE AND PROTECT LADY EMILIA BY MYSELF.
—I SHALL BE WATCHING YOU FROM HERE.
SISTER, YOU MUST NOT USE THAT EYE TOO OFT—
I WILL USE IT IF I NEED TO.
SUBARU, WHERE ARE YOU GOING?

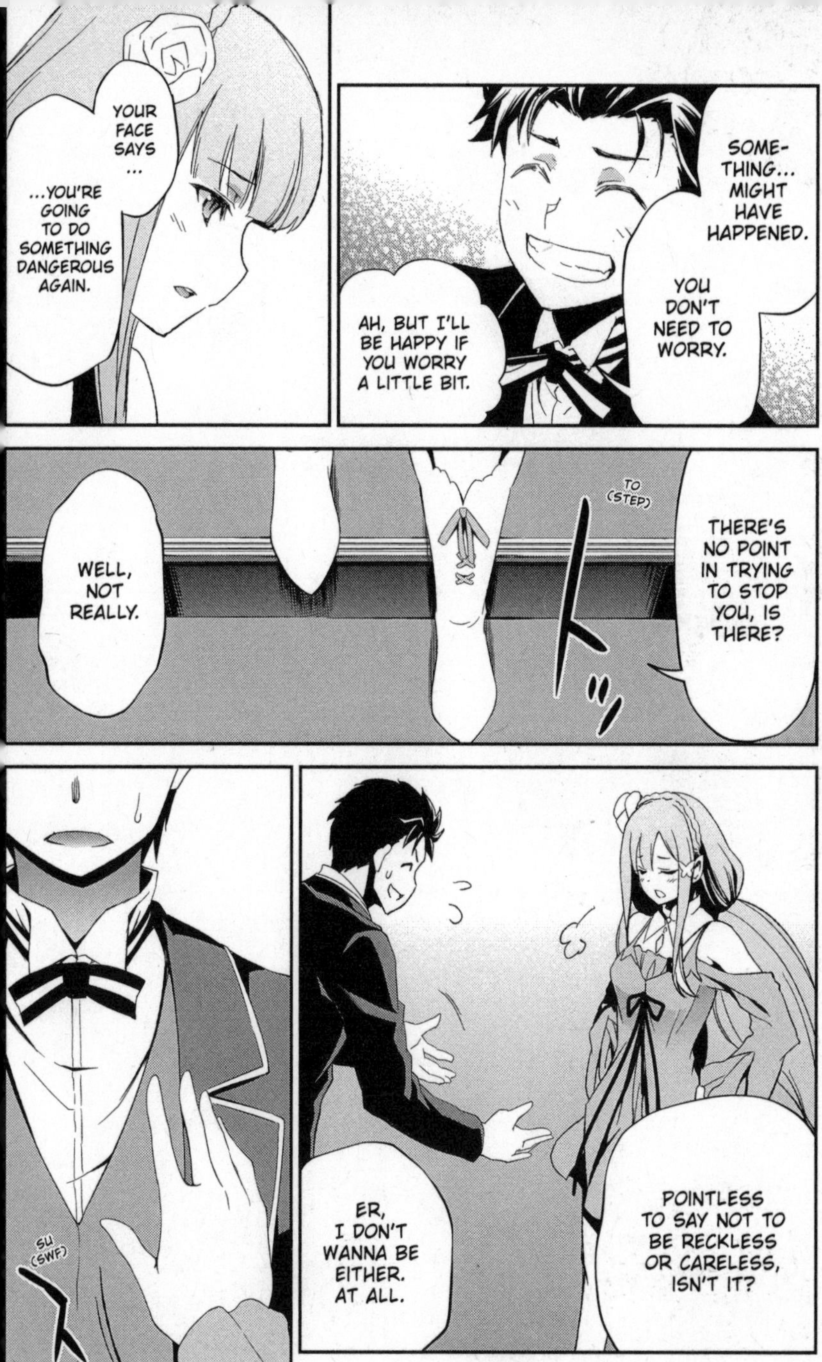
SOME-THING... MIGHT HAVE HAPPENED.
YOU DON'T NEED TO WORRY.
AH, BUT I'LL BE HAPPY IF YOU WORRY A LITTLE BIT.
YOUR FACE SAYS ...
...YOU'RE GOING TO DO SOMETHING DANGEROUS AGAIN.
THERE'S NO POINT IN TRYING TO STOP YOU, IS THERE?
TO (STEP)
WELL, NOT REALLY.
POINTLESS TO SAY NOT TO BE RECKLESS OR CARELESS, ISN'T IT?
ER, I DON'T WANNA BE EITHER. AT ALL.
SU (SWF)

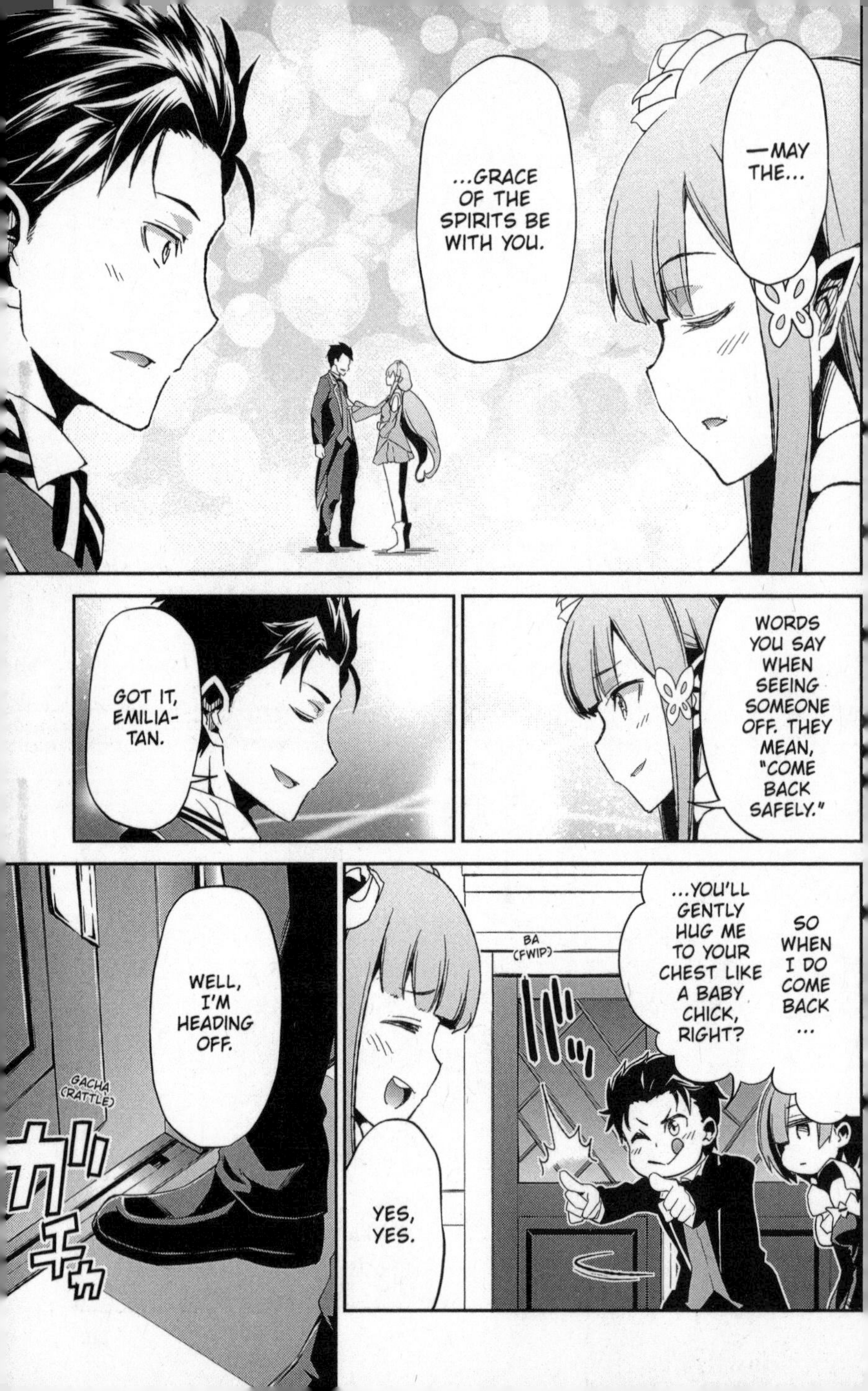
—MAY THE...
...GRACE OF THE SPIRITS BE WITH YOU.
WORDS YOU SAY WHEN SEEING SOMEONE OFF. THEY MEAN, "COME BACK SAFELY."
GOT IT, EMILIA-TAN.
SO WHEN I DO COME BACK...
...YOU'LL GENTLY HUG ME TO YOUR CHEST LIKE A BABY CHICK, RIGHT?
BA (FWIP)
YES, YES.
WELL, I'M HEADING OFF.
GACHA (RATTLE)

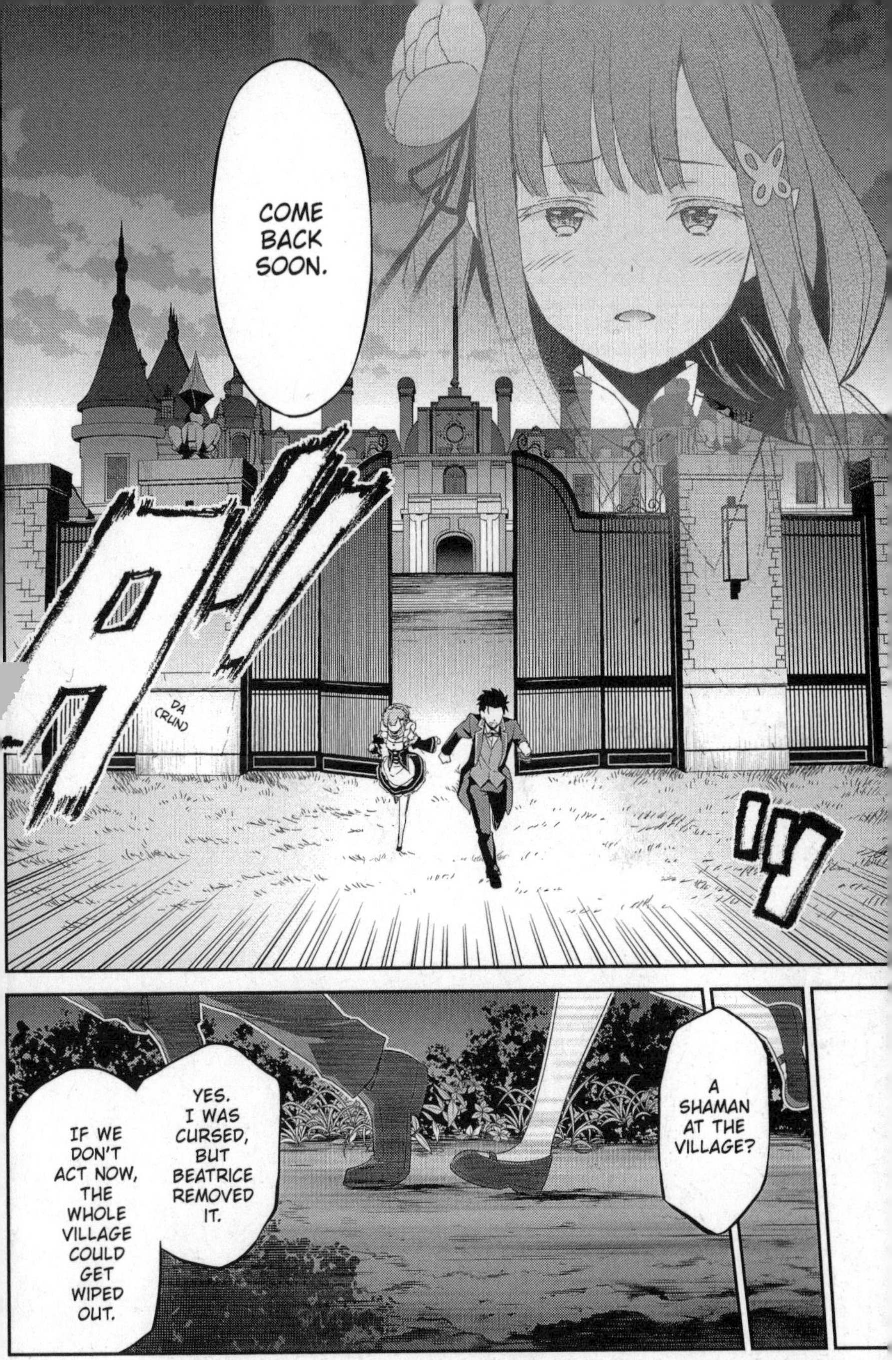
COME BACK SOON.
DA CRUN
A SHAMAN AT THE VILLAGE?
YES. I WAS CURSED, BUT BEATRICE REMOVED IT.
IF WE DON'T ACT NOW, THE WHOLE VILLAGE COULD GET WIPED OUT.

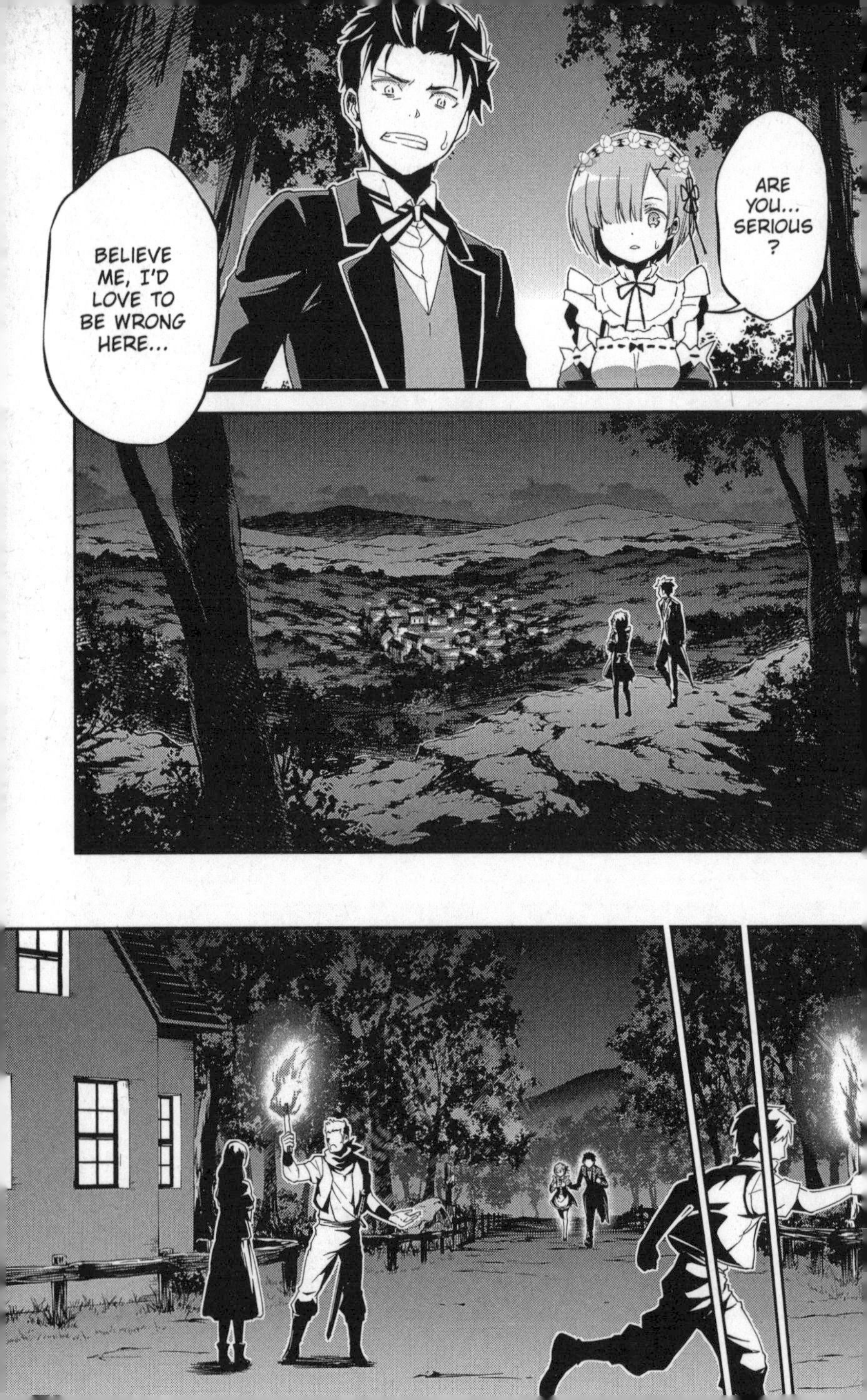
ARE YOU... SERIOUS?
BELIEVE ME, I'D LOVE TO BE WRONG HERE...

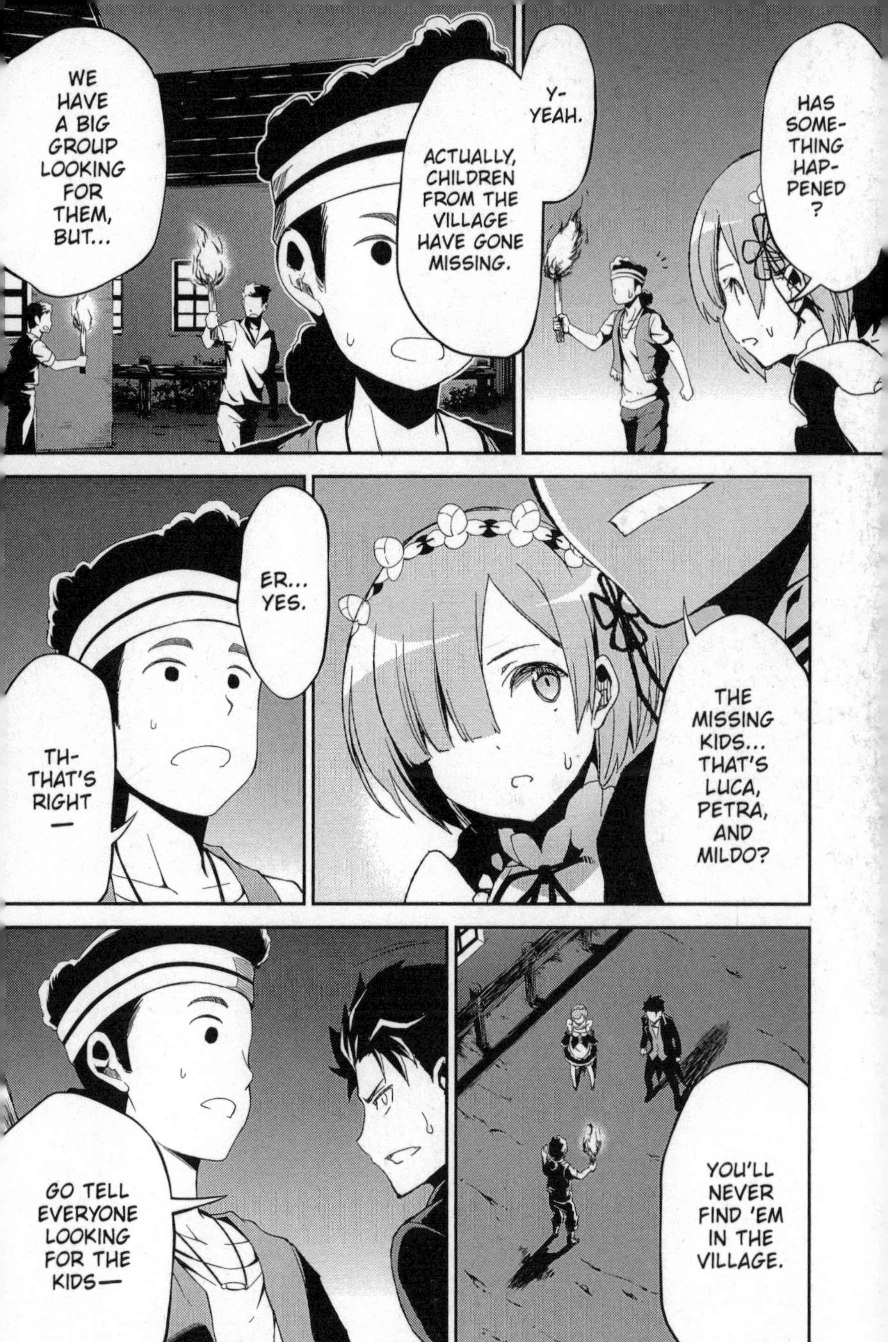
HAS SOME-THING HAP-PENED?
Y- YEAH.
ACTUALLY, CHILDREN FROM THE VILLAGE HAVE GONE MISSING.
WE HAVE A BIG GROUP LOOKING FOR THEM, BUT...
THE MISSING KIDS... THAT'S LUCA, PETRA, AND MILDO?
ER... YES.
TH- THAT'S RIGHT—
YOU'LL NEVER FIND 'EM IN THE VILLAGE.
GO TELL EVERYONE LOOKING FOR THE KIDS—

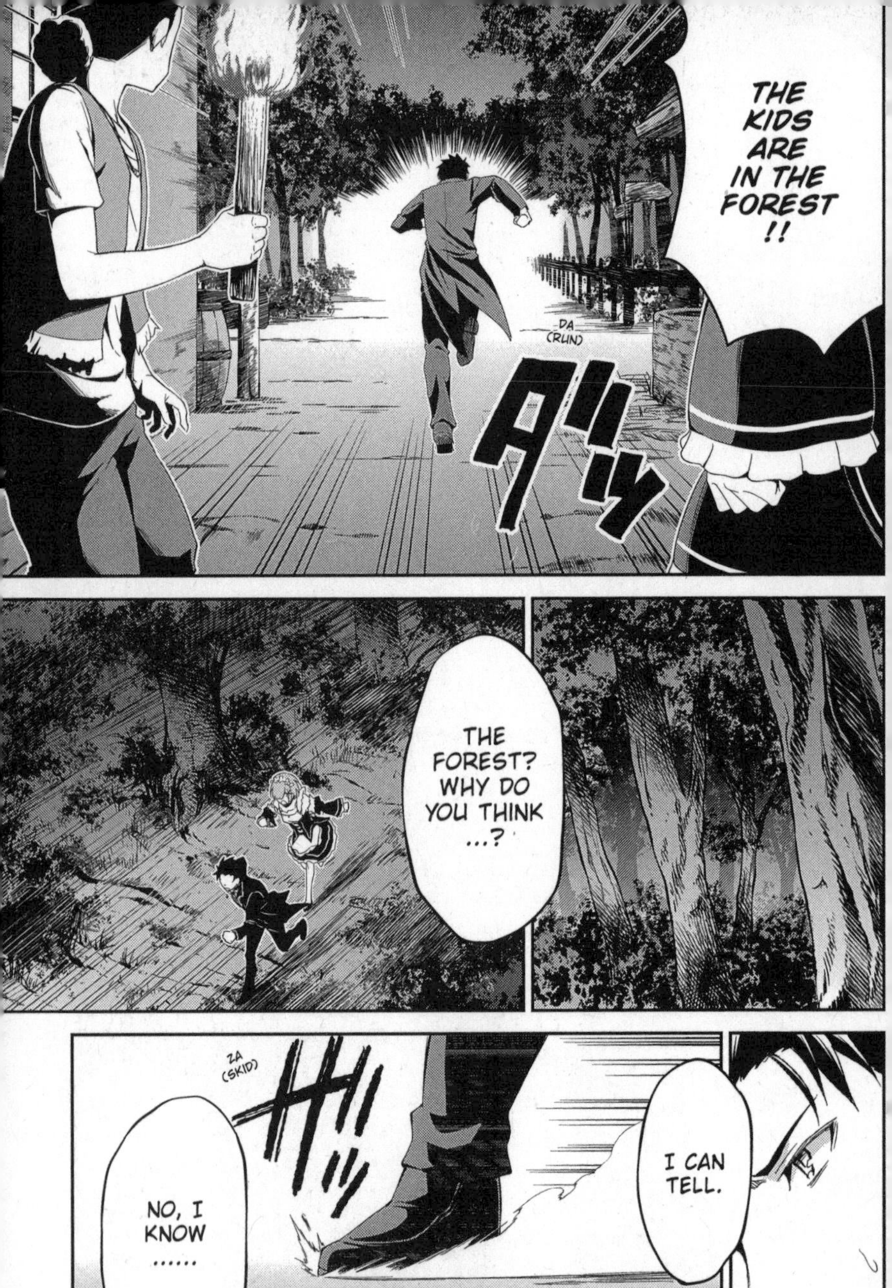
THE KIDS ARE IN THE FOREST !!
DA (RUN)
ダッ
THE FOREST? WHY DO YOU THINK ...?
I CAN TELL.
ZA (SKID)
ザッ
NO, I KNOW ......

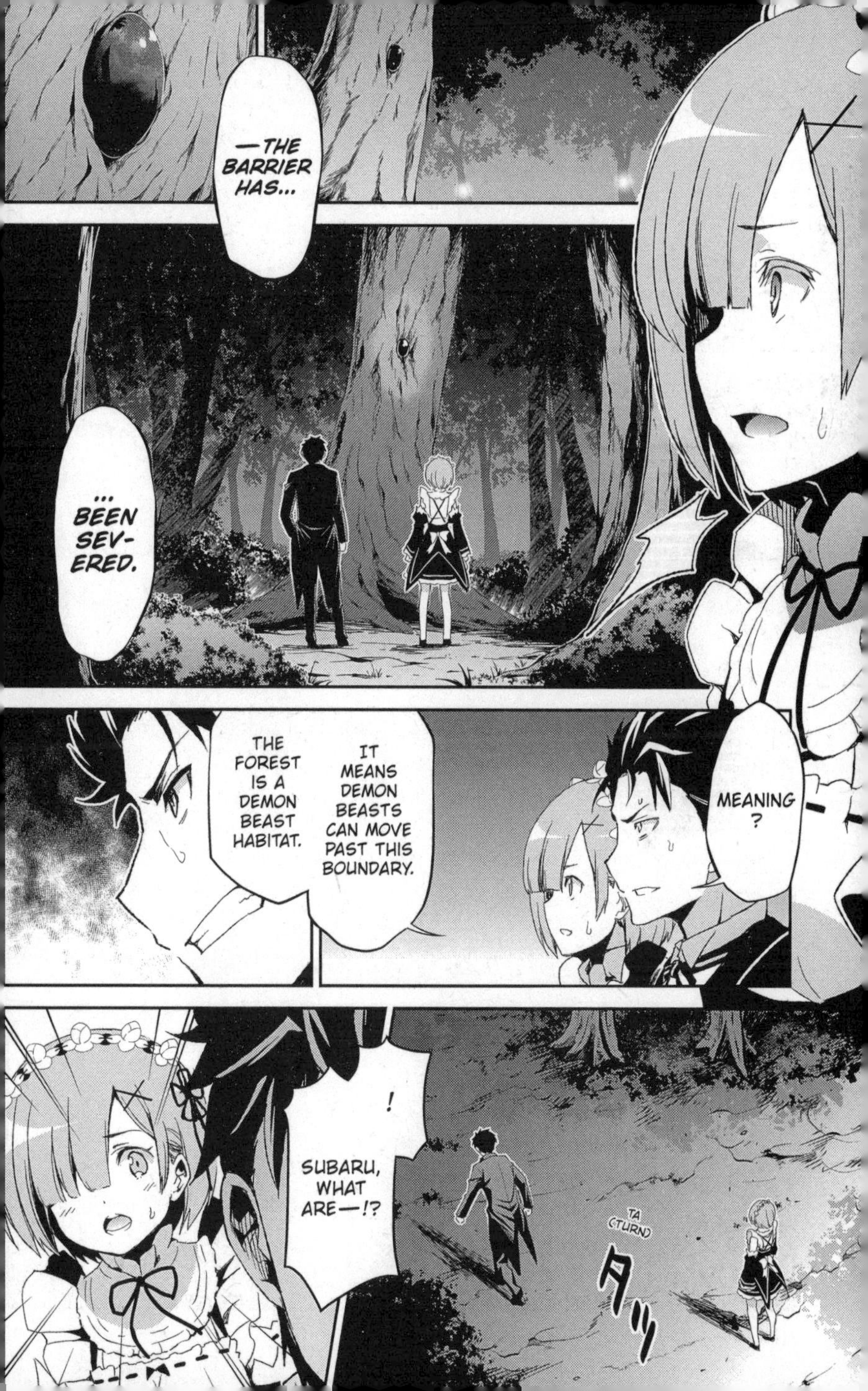
—THE BARRIER HAS...
...BEEN SEV-ERED.
MEANING?
IT MEANS DEMON BEASTS CAN MOVE PAST THIS BOUNDARY.
THE FOREST IS A DEMON BEAST HABITAT.
TA (TURN)
!
SUBARU, WHAT ARE—!?

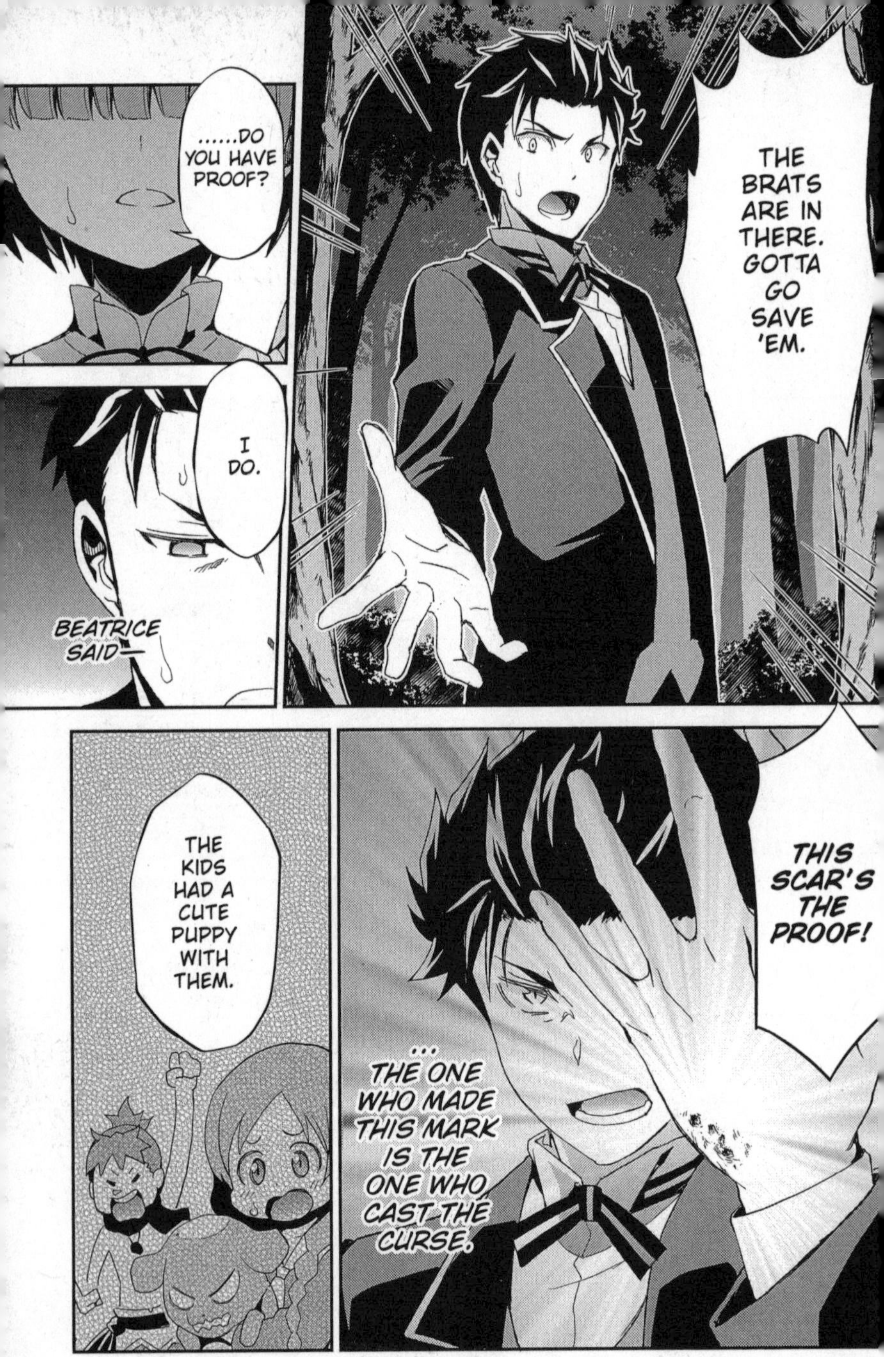
THE BRATS ARE IN THERE. GOTTA GO SAVE 'EM.
......DO YOU HAVE PROOF?
I DO.
BEATRICE SAID—
THIS SCAR'S THE PROOF!
...THE ONE WHO MADE THIS MARK IS THE ONE WHO CAST THE CURSE.
THE KIDS HAD A CUTE PUPPY WITH THEM.

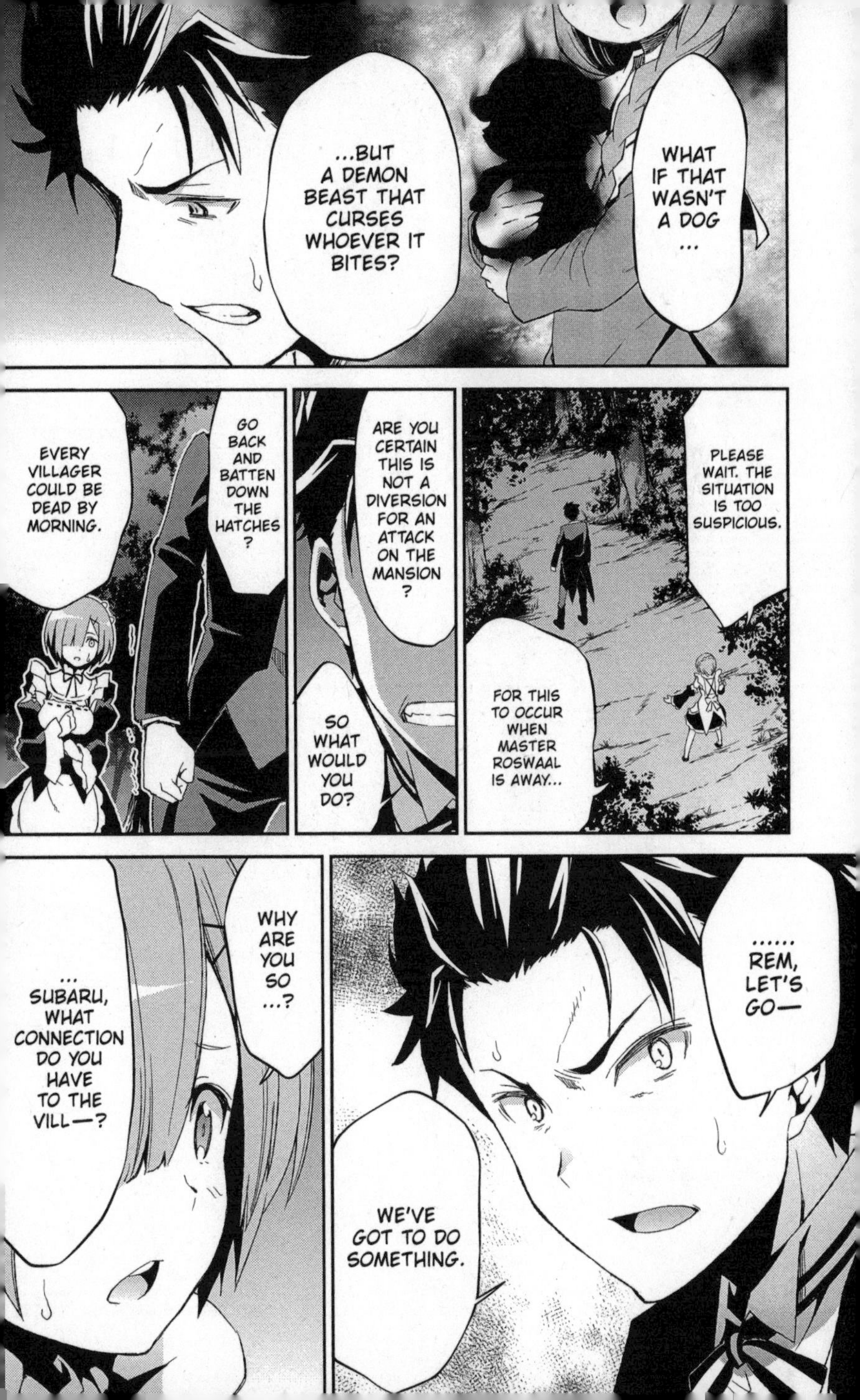
WHAT IF THAT WASN'T A DOG...
...BUT A DEMON BEAST THAT CURSES WHOEVER IT BITES?
PLEASE WAIT. THE SITUATION IS TOO SUSPICIOUS.
FOR THIS TO OCCUR WHEN MASTER ROSWAAL IS AWAY...
ARE YOU CERTAIN THIS IS NOT A DIVERSION FOR AN ATTACK ON THE MANSION?
SO WHAT WOULD YOU DO?
GO BACK AND BATTEN DOWN THE HATCHES?
EVERY VILLAGER COULD BE DEAD BY MORNING.
......REM, LET'S GO—
WE'VE GOT TO DO SOMETHING.
WHY ARE YOU SO...?
...SUBARU, WHAT CONNECTION DO YOU HAVE TO THE VILL—?

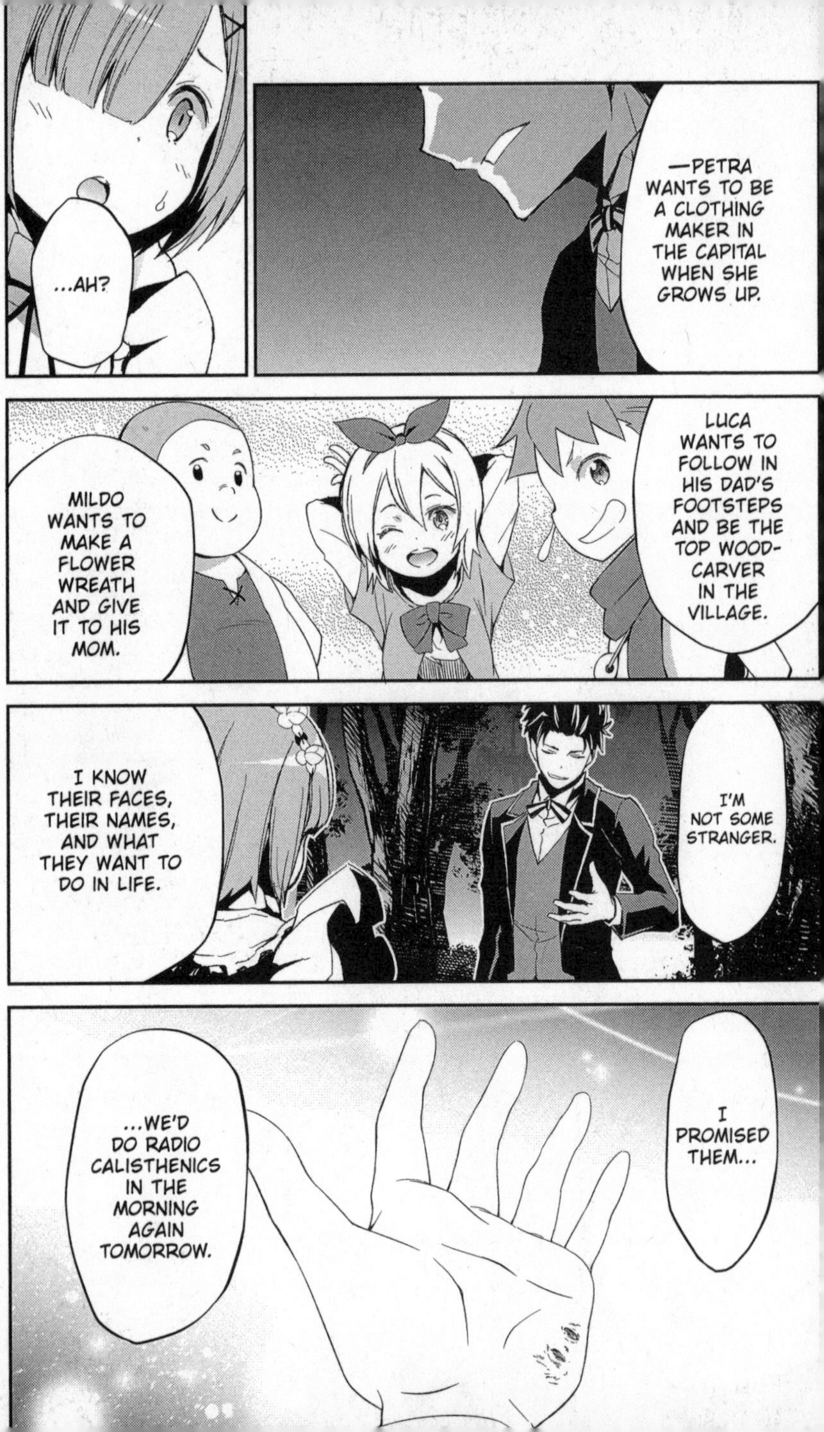
—PETRA WANTS TO BE A CLOTHING MAKER IN THE CAPITAL WHEN SHE GROWS UP.
...AH?
LUCA WANTS TO FOLLOW IN HIS DAD'S FOOTSTEPS AND BE THE TOP WOOD-CARVER IN THE VILLAGE.
MILDO WANTS TO MAKE A FLOWER WREATH AND GIVE IT TO HIS MOM.
I'M NOT SOME STRANGER.
I KNOW THEIR FACES, THEIR NAMES, AND WHAT THEY WANT TO DO IN LIFE.
I PROMISED THEM...
...WE'D DO RADIO CALISTHENICS IN THE MORNING AGAIN TOMORROW.

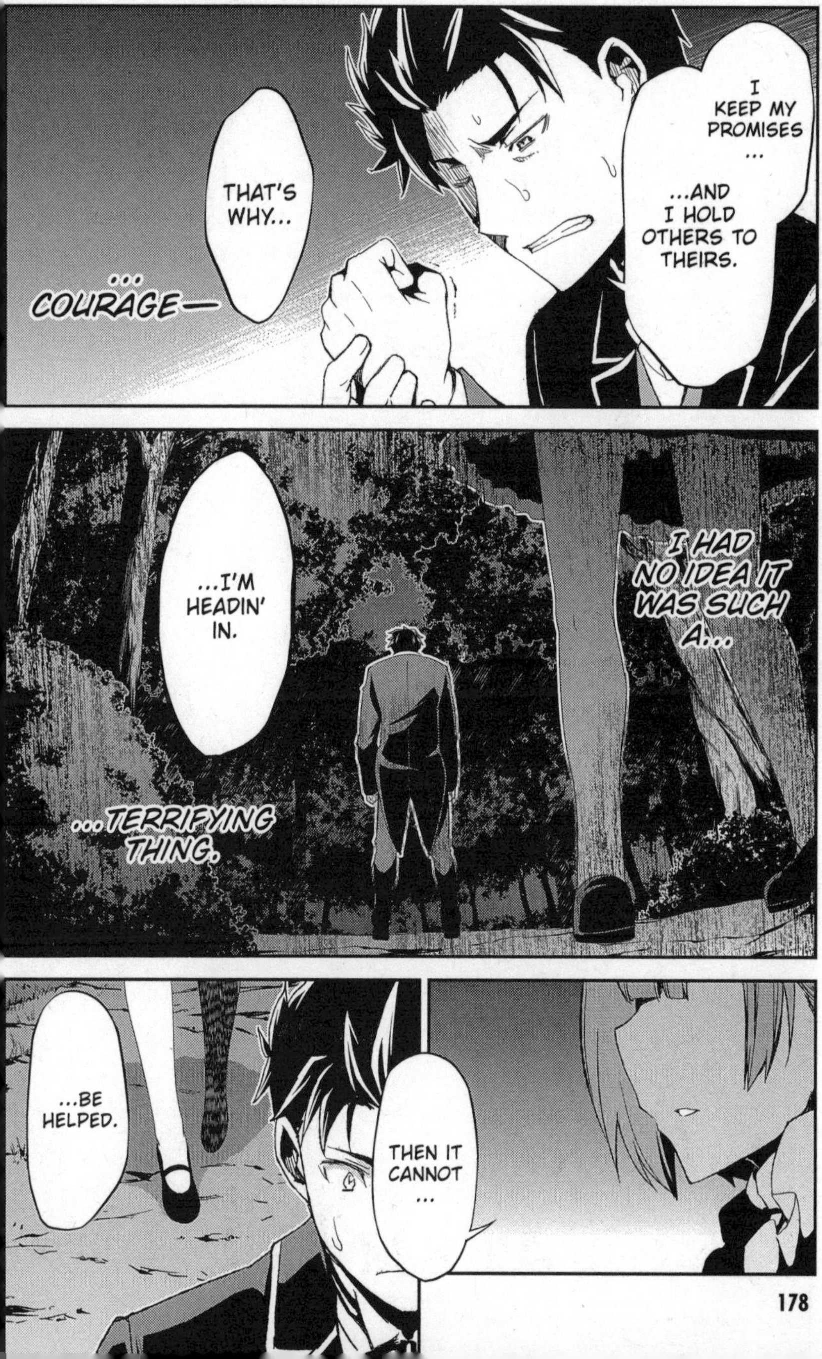
I KEEP MY PROMISES ...
...AND I HOLD OTHERS TO THEIRS.
THAT'S WHY...
...COURAGE—
I HAD NO IDEA IT WAS SUCH A...
...I'M HEADIN' IN.
...TERRIFYING THING.
THEN IT CANNOT ...
...BE HELPED.

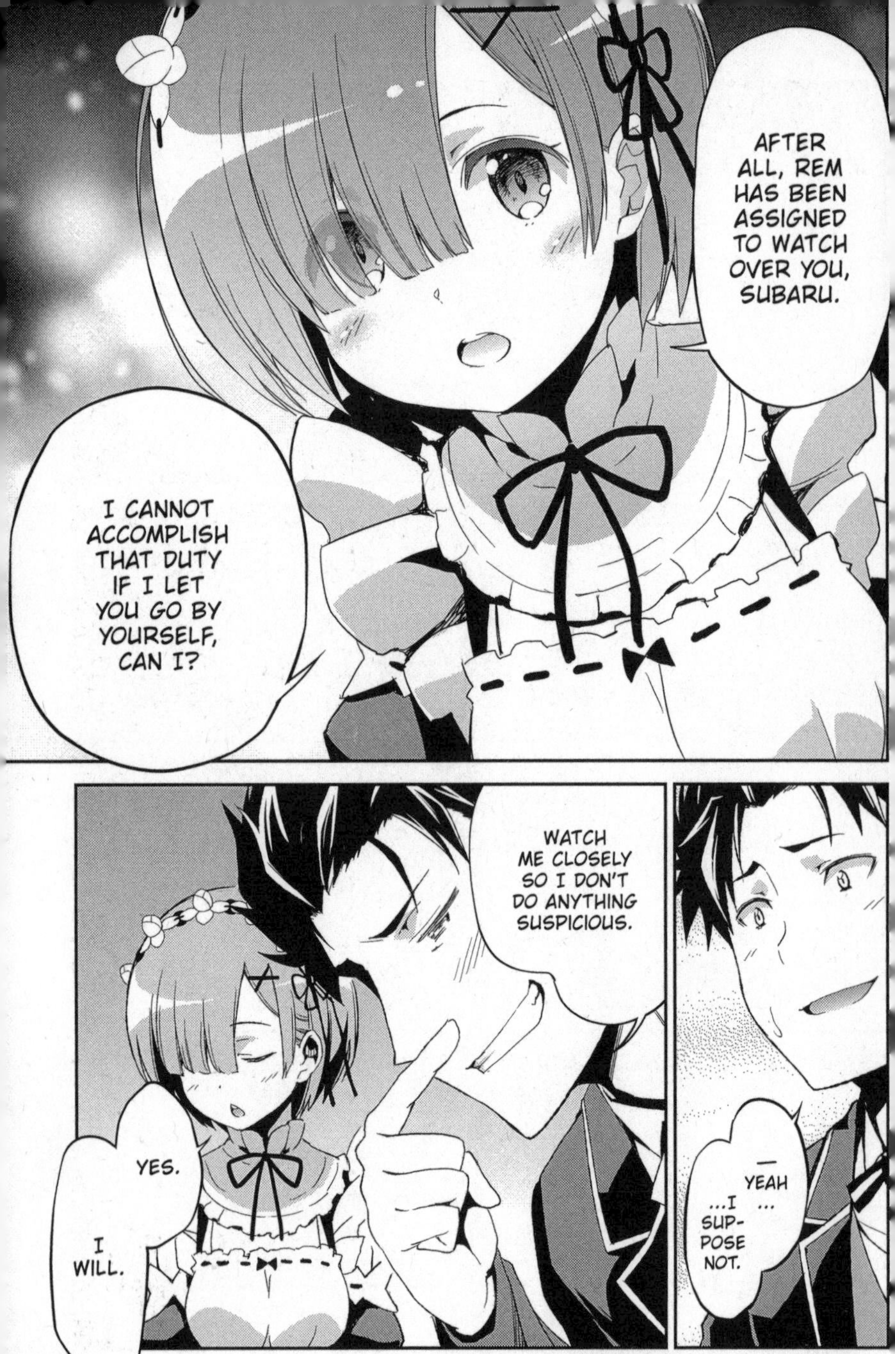
AFTER ALL, REM HAS BEEN ASSIGNED TO WATCH OVER YOU, SUBARU.
I CANNOT ACCOMPLISH THAT DUTY IF I LET YOU GO BY YOURSELF, CAN I?
—YEAH ... ...I SUP-POSE NOT.
WATCH ME CLOSELY SO I DON'T DO ANYTHING SUSPICIOUS.
YES.
I WILL.

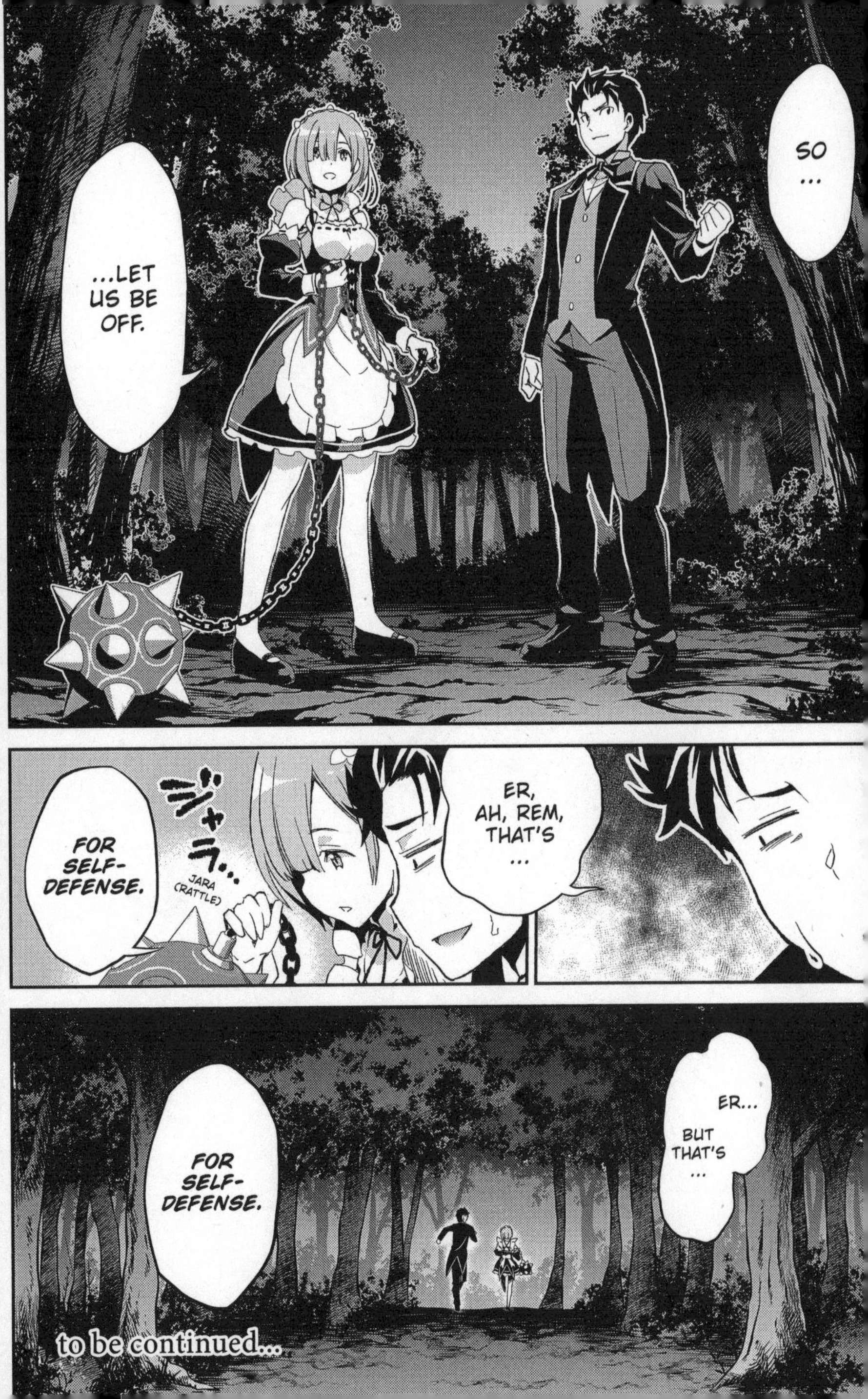
SO ...
...LET US BE OFF.
ER, AH, REM, THAT'S ...
ジャラ…
JARA (RATTLE)
FOR SELF-DEFENSE.
ER...
BUT THAT'S ...
FOR SELF-DEFENSE.
to be continued...

Turn to the end of the book for an original *Re:ZERO* short story from the light novel author, Tappei Nagatsuki!

Supporting Comments from the Character Designer

Congratulations on the sale of Volume 3! Fugetsu-sensei, the characters you draw are all so charming that I always use them for reference! Especially big-foreheaded Beako—I really enjoy how cute she is!

Shinichirou Otsuka

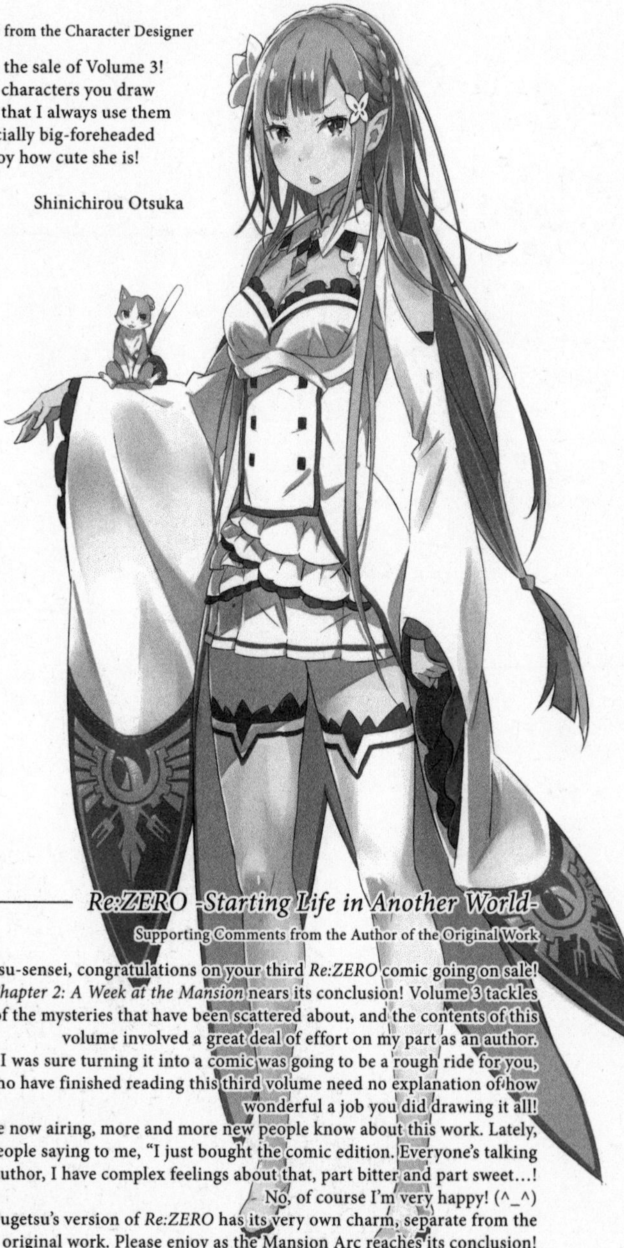

Illustration by
Shinichirou Otsuka
(Character Designer)
First published in:
Re:ZERO -Starting Life in Another World-
Light Novel Volume 1

Re:ZERO -Starting Life in Another World-

Supporting Comments from the Author of the Original Work

Fugetsu-sensei, congratulations on your third *Re:ZERO* comic going on sale! *Re:ZERO Chapter 2: A Week at the Mansion* nears its conclusion! Volume 3 tackles unveiling many of the mysteries that have been scattered about, and the contents of this volume involved a great deal of effort on my part as an author.
Because of that, I was sure turning it into a comic was going to be a rough ride for you, but those who have finished reading this third volume need no explanation of how wonderful a job you did drawing it all!
With the TV anime now airing, more and more new people know about this work. Lately, I have a lot of people saying to me, "I just bought the comic edition. Everyone's talking about it." As the author, I have complex feelings about that, part bitter and part sweet…!
No, of course I'm very happy! (^_^)
Either way, Fugetsu's version of *Re:ZERO* has its very own charm, separate from the anime and the original work. Please enjoy as the Mansion Arc reaches its conclusion!
Thanks again!

Author of the Original Work: Tappei Nagatsuki

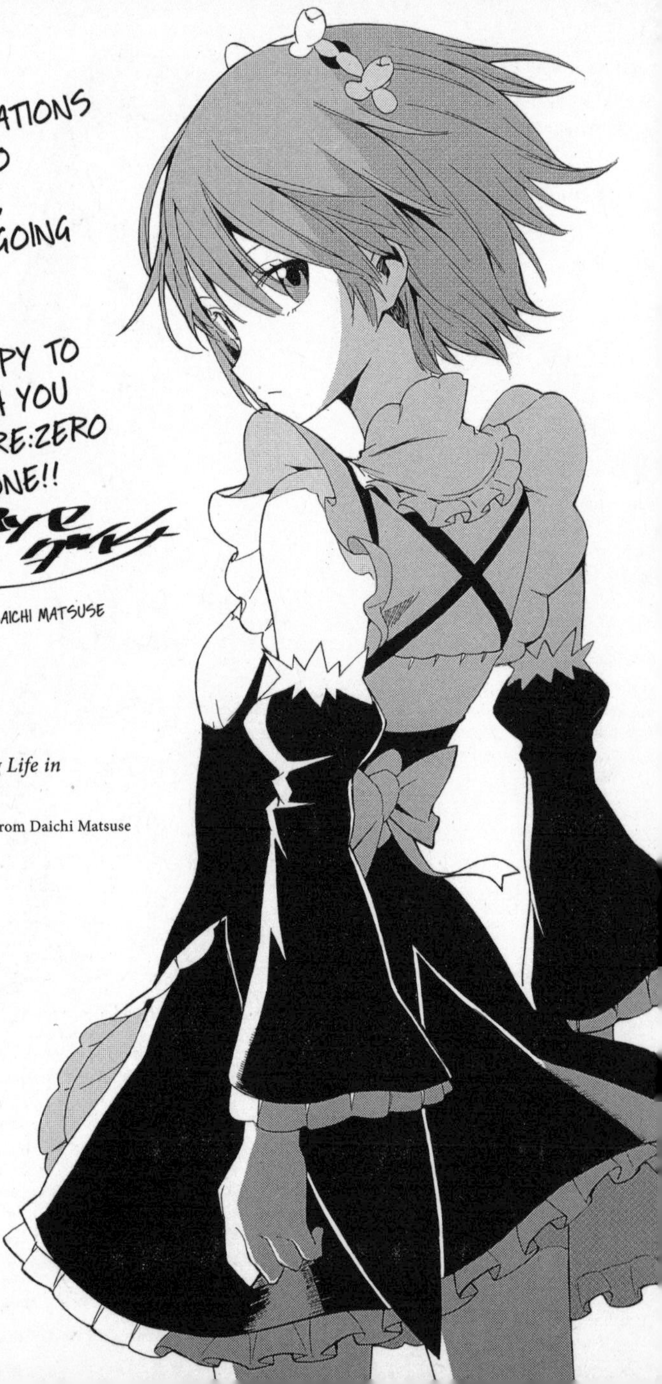
CONGRATULATIONS ON RE:ZERO CHAPTER 2, VOLUME 3 GOING ON SALE!
I'M SO HAPPY TO WORK WITH YOU TO BRING RE:ZERO TO EVERYONE!!
DAICHI MATSUSE

Re:ZERO -Starting Life in Another World-

Supporting Comments from Daichi Matsuse

TV ANIME NOW AIRING!!

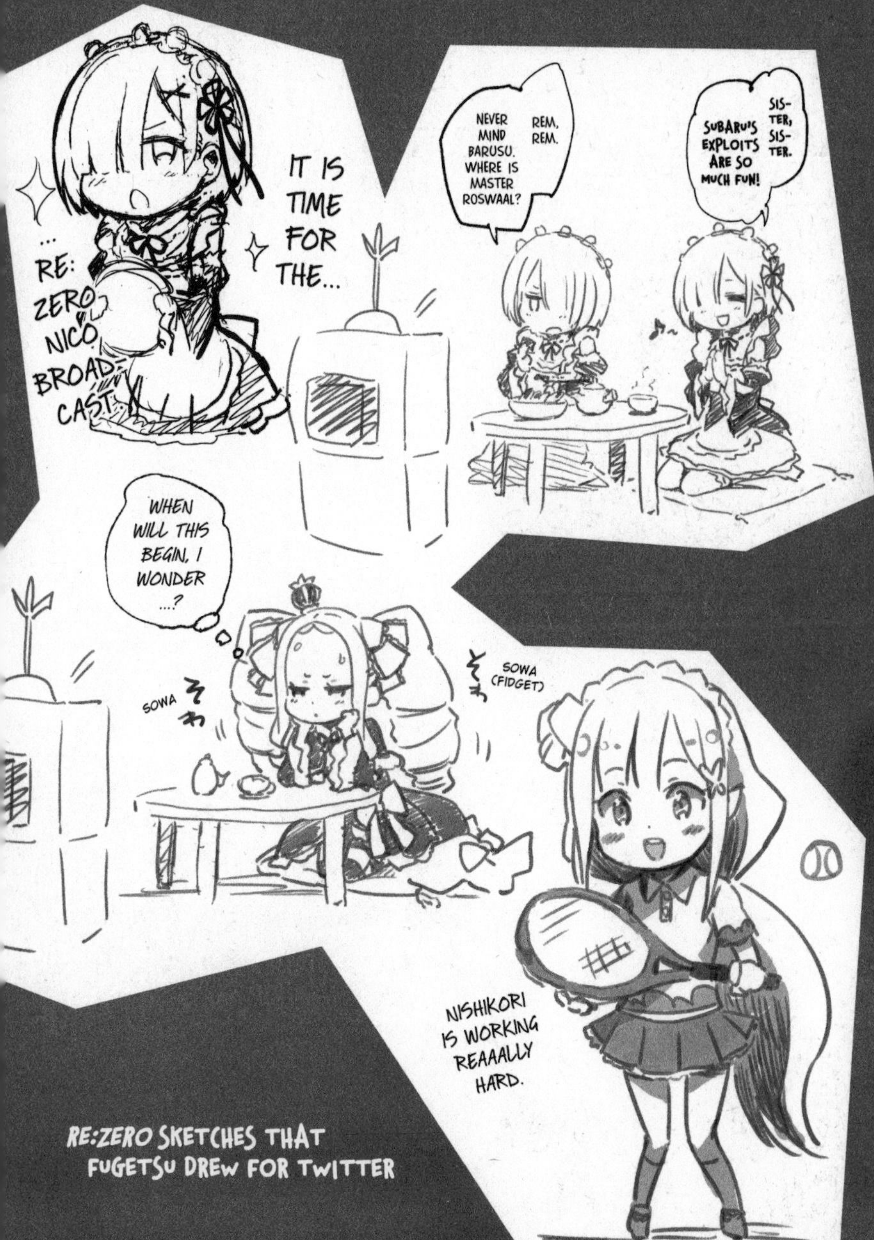
SIS-TER, SIS-TER.
SUBARU'S EXPLOITS ARE SO MUCH FUN!
REM, REM.
NEVER MIND BARUSU. WHERE IS MASTER ROSWAAL?
IT IS TIME FOR THE...
...RE: ZERO NICO BROADCAST
WHEN WILL THIS BEGIN, I WONDER ...?
SOWA (FIDGET)
SOWA
NISHIKORI IS WORKING REAAALLY HARD.

RE:ZERO SKETCHES THAT FUGETSU DREW FOR TWITTER

Re:ZeRo

-Starting Life in Another World-

Chapter 2: A Week at the Mansion

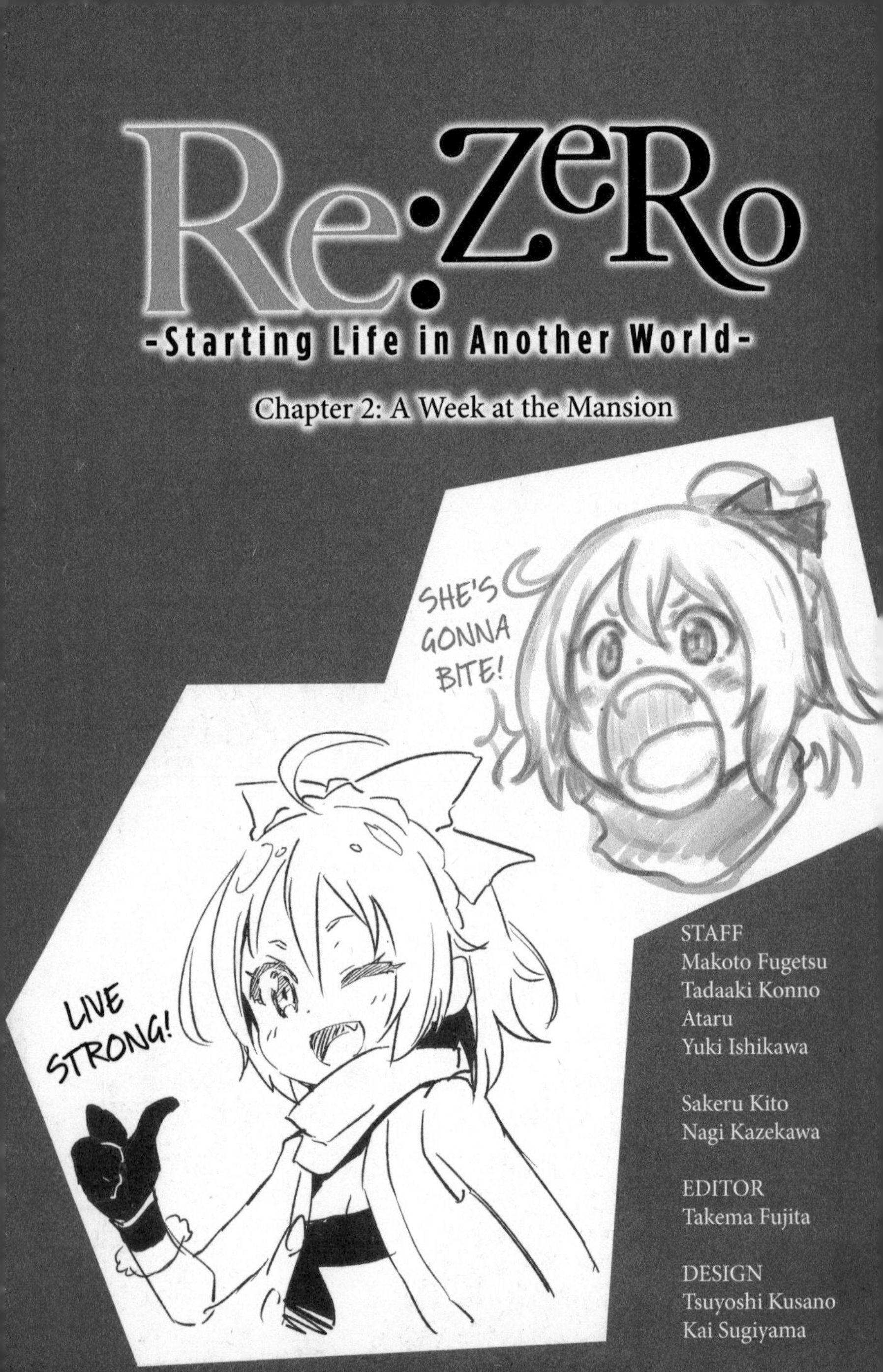
SHE'S GONNA BITE!
LIVE STRONG!

STAFF
Makoto Fugetsu
Tadaaki Konno
Ataru
Yuki Ishikawa

Sakeru Kito
Nagi Kazekawa

EDITOR
Takema Fujita

DESIGN
Tsuyoshi Kusano
Kai Sugiyama

NEXT

Re:ZERO -Starting Life in Another World-

The only ability Subaru Natsuki gets when he's summoned to another world is time travel via his own death. But to save her, he'll die as many times as it takes.

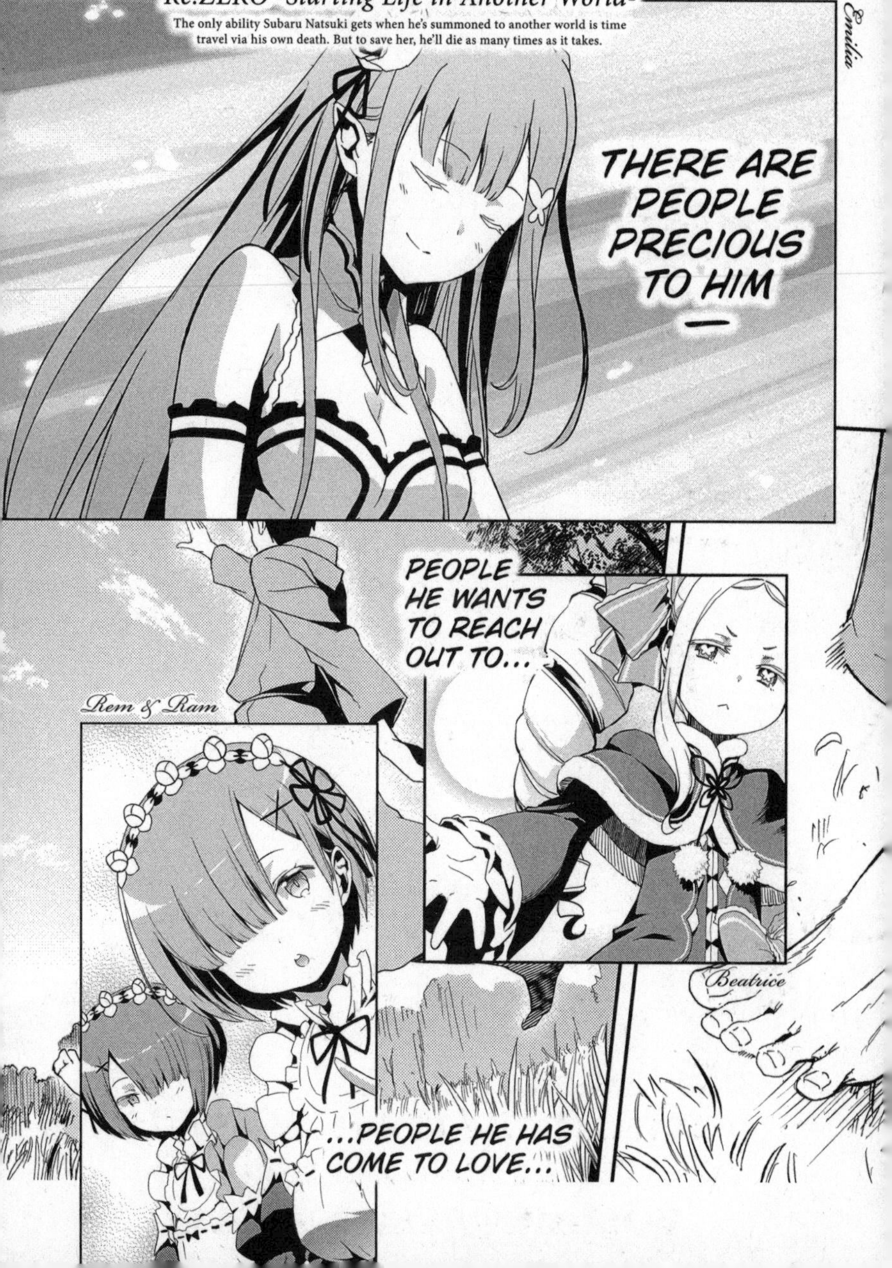
Emilia
THERE ARE PEOPLE PRECIOUS TO HIM —
Beatrice
PEOPLE HE WANTS TO REACH OUT TO...
Rem & Ram
...PEOPLE HE HAS COME TO LOVE...

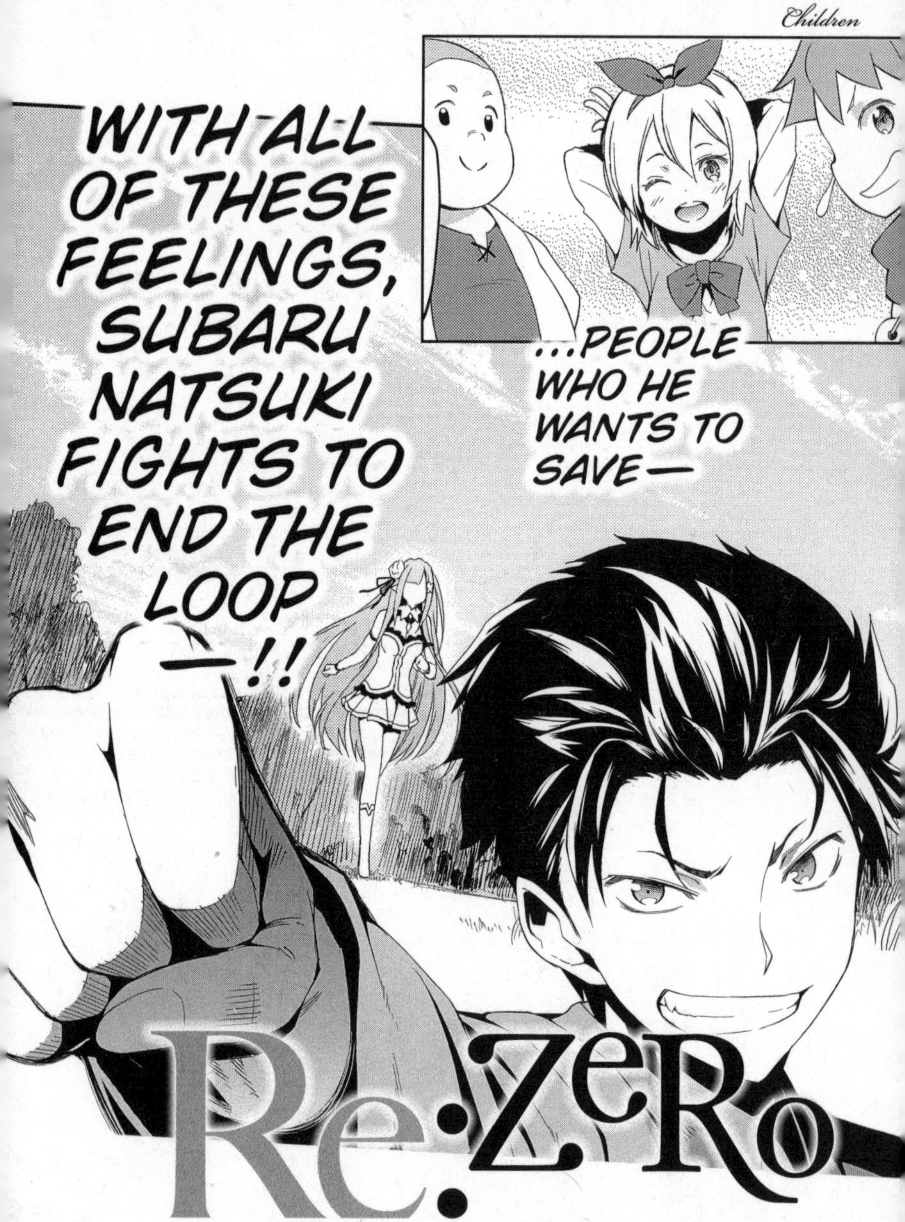
Children
...PEOPLE WHO HE WANTS TO SAVE—
WITH ALL OF THESE FEELINGS, SUBARU NATSUKI FIGHTS TO END THE LOOP—!!
Re:ZeRo
-Starting Life in Another World-

Chapter 2: A Week at the Mansion

VOLUME ④ on sale December 2017

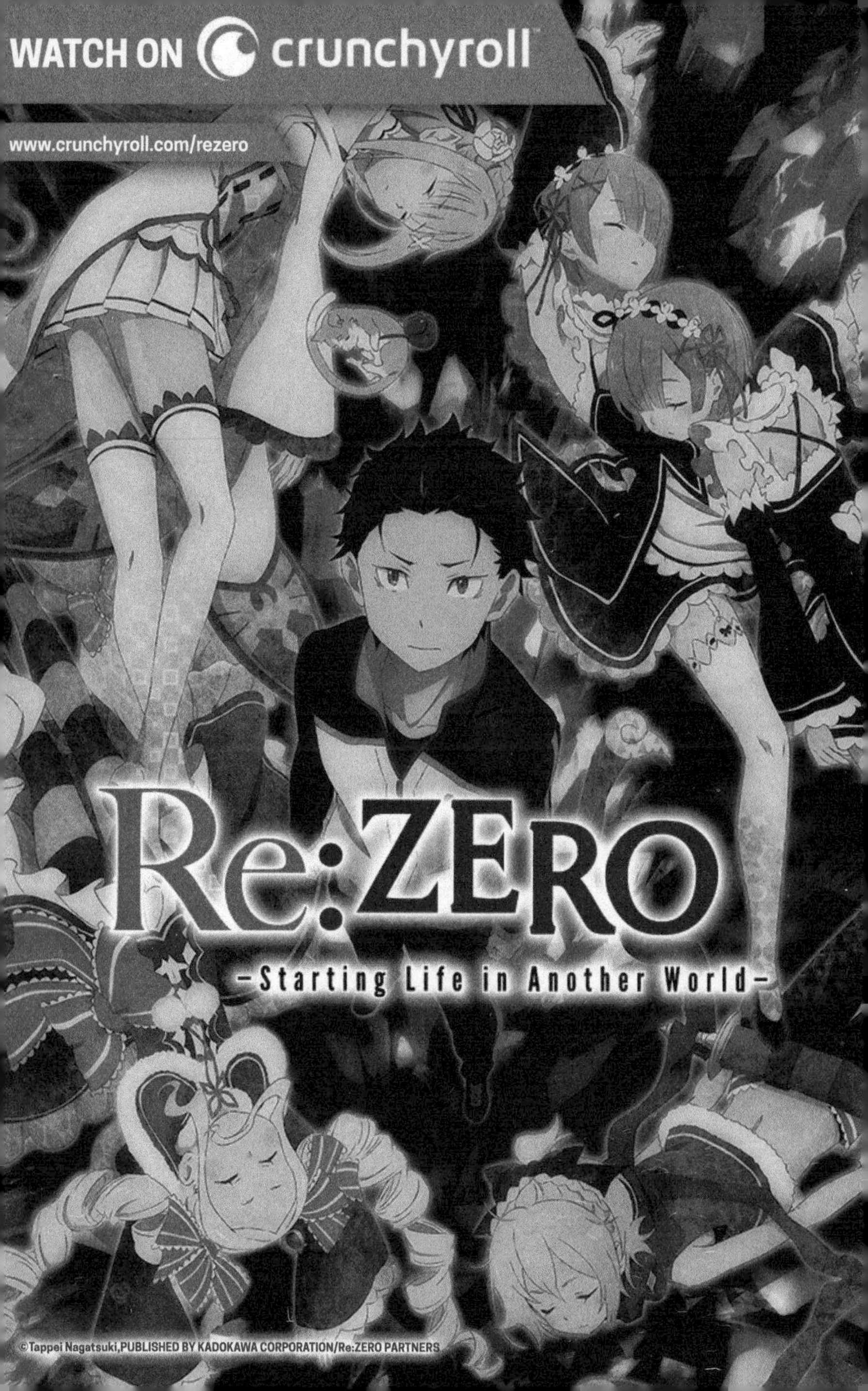

RE:ZERO -STARTING LIFE IN ANOTHER WORLD- ③
Chapter 2: A Week at the Mansion

Art: **Makoto Fugetsu**
Original Story: **Tappei Nagatsuki**
Character Design: **Shinichirou Otsuka**

Translation: ZephyrRZ
Lettering: Bianca Pistillo

RE:ZERO KARA HAJIMERU ISEKAI SEIKATSU DAINISHO YASHIKI NO ISSHUKAN-HEN Vol. 3
© Tappei Nagatsuki 2014
Licensed by KADOKAWA CORPORATION
© 2016 Makoto Fugetsu / SQUARE ENIX CO., LTD.
First published in Japan in 2016 by SQUARE ENIX CO., LTD. English translation rights arranged with SQUARE ENIX CO., LTD. and Yen Press, LLC through TUTTLE-MORI AGENCY, Inc.

English translation © 2017 by SQUARE ENIX CO., LTD.

Yen Press
1290 Avenue of the Americas
New York, NY 10104

Visit us at yenpress.com
facebook.com/yenpress
twitter.com/yenpress
yenpress.tumblr.com
instagram.com/yenpress

First Yen Press Edition: October 2017

Yen Press is an imprint of Yen Press, LLC.
The Yen Press name and logo are trademarks of Yen Press, LLC.

Library of Congress Control Number: 2016936537

ISBNs: 978-0-316-47316-3 (paperback)
       978-0-316-44781-2 (ebook)

10 9 8 7 6 5 4 3 2 1

BVG

Printed in the United States of America